LIBRARY OF NEW TESTAMENT STUDIES

680

formerly the Journal for the Study of the New Testament Supplement series

Editor
Chris Keith

Editorial Board
Dale C. Allison, Lynn H. Cohick, Kylie Crabbe, R. Alan Culpepper, Craig A. Evans, Jennifer Eyl, Robert Fowler, Juan Hernández Jr., John S. Kloppenborg, Michael Labahn, Matthew V. Novenson, Love L. Sechrest, Robert Wall, Catrin H. Williams, Brittany E. Wilson

The Structure of Second Corinthians

Paul's Theology of Ministry

Hiramatsu Kei

LONDON • NEW YORK • OXFORD • NEW DELHI • SYDNEY

T&T CLARK
Bloomsbury Publishing Plc
50 Bedford Square, London, WC1B 3DP, UK
1385 Broadway, New York, NY 10018, USA
29 Earlsfort Terrace, Dublin 2, Ireland

BLOOMSBURY, T&T CLARK and the T&T Clark logo are trademarks of
Bloomsbury Publishing Plc

First published in Great Britain 2023
Paperback edition published in 2025

Copyright © Hiramatsu Kei, 2023

Hiramatsu Kei has asserted his right under the Copyright, Designs and Patents Act, 1988, to be
identified as Author of this work.

For legal purposes the Acknowledgement on p. xiv constitutes an extension of this copyright page.

All rights reserved. No part of this publication may be reproduced or transmitted in any form or by any
means, electronic or mechanical, including photocopying, recording, or any information storage or
retrieval system, without prior permission in writing from the publishers.

Bloomsbury Publishing Plc does not have any control over, or responsibility for, any third-party websites
referred to or in this book. All internet addresses given in this book were correct at the time of going to
press. The author and publisher regret any inconvenience caused if addresses have changed or sites
have ceased to exist, but can accept no responsibility for any such changes.

A catalogue record for this book is available from the British Library.

A catalog record for this book is available from the Library of Congress.

Names: Hiramatsu, Kei, author.
Title: The structure of Second Corinthians : Paul's theology of ministry / Hiramatsu Kei.
Other titles: Structure of 2 Corinthians
Description: London ; New York : T&T Clark, 2023. | Series: Library of New Testament studies,
2513-8790 ; 680 | Includes bibliographical references and index. | Summary: "Employing an inductive
approach, this volume proposes that Paul's second letter to the Corinthians consists of seven major
segments which coherently develop Paul's discourse pertaining to ministry"-- Provided by publisher.
Identifiers: LCCN 2023008749 (print) | LCCN 2023008750 (ebook) | ISBN 9780567708847 (hardback) |
ISBN 9780567708885 (paperback) | ISBN 9780567708854 (pdf) | ISBN 9780567708878 (epub)
Subjects: LCSH: Bible. Corinthians, 2nd–Criticism, interpretation, etc. |
Paul, the Apostle, Saint | Pastoral theology.
Classification: LCC BS2675.52 .H57 2023 (print) | LCC BS2675.52 (ebook) |
DDC 227/.306—dc23/eng/20230405
LC record available at https://lccn.loc.gov/2023008749
LC ebook record available at https://lccn.loc.gov/2023008750

ISBN	HB:	978-0-5677-0884-7
	PB:	978-0-5677-0888-5
	ePDF:	978-0-5677-0885-4
	ePUB:	978-0-5677-0887-8

Series: Library of New Testament Studies, volume 680
ISSN 2513-8790

Typeset by RefineCatch Limited, Bungay, Suffolk

To find out more about our authors and books visit www.bloomsbury.com
and sign up for our newsletters.

Contents

List of Illustrations	xii
Foreword by Chris Tilling	xiii
Acknowledgement	xiv
Abbreviations	xv
Introduction	1

1	Methodological Considerations			3
	1.1	Introduction to Inductive Bible Study		3
		1.1.1	Origin and Development	3
		1.1.2	Definition: Integrative and Inductive Study	5
	1.2	Theoretical Foundations of an Inductive Approach		6
		1.2.1	Compositional Study	6
		1.2.2	Final Form of the Text	7
		1.2.3	Implied Author	8
		1.2.4	Structure and Major Structural Relationships	8
			1.2.4.1 Categories of Major Structural Relationships	9
			1.2.4.2 Rationale for Major Structural Relationships	15
2	Survey of the Literary Structure and the Central Theme of 2 Corinthians			19
	2.1	Literary Structure of 2 Corinthians		19
		2.1.1	Topical Analysis	20
			Evaluation	22
		2.1.2	Epistolary Criticism	22
			Evaluation	24
		2.1.3	Rhetorical Criticism	24
			2.1.3.1 Ben Witherington III	25
			2.1.3.2 Fredrick J. Long	26
			2.1.3.3 Jerry W. McCant	28
			2.1.3.4 J. David Hester Amador	29
			2.1.3.5 Ivar Vegge	31
			2.1.3.6 Evaluation	32

		2.1.4	Literary Criticism	33
			2.1.4.1 Narrative Criticism	33
			2.1.4.2 Analysis Based on Chiastic Structure	34
		2.1.5	Discourse Analysis	36
	2.2	Central Theme of 2 Corinthians		38
		2.2.1	Topical Analysis	39
			2.2.1.1 Apology	39
			2.2.1.2 Suffering and Death	40
			2.2.1.3 Power through Weakness	40
			2.2.1.4 Concord	41
			2.2.1.5 Reconciliation	41
			2.2.1.6 Evaluation	41
		2.2.2	Epistolary Criticism	42
			Evaluation	43
		2.2.3	Rhetorical Criticism	44
			2.2.3.1 Apology	44
			2.2.3.2 Blaming	45
			2.2.3.3 Relationship	46
			2.2.3.4 Reconciliation	47
			2.2.3.5 Evaluation	48
		2.2.4	Literary Analysis	48
			2.2.4.1 Narrative Criticism	48
			2.2.4.2 Analysis Based on Chiastic Structure	49
			2.2.4.3 Evaluation	50
		2.2.5	Discourse Analysis	50
			Evaluation	50
	2.3	Conclusion		51
3	Salutation (1:1–2) and Closing (13:11–13)			53
	3.1	Division of 1:1–2 and 13:11–13		54
	3.2	Major Structural Relationships in Relation to the Letter as a Whole		55
		3.2.1	Preparation/Realization with Inclusio (1:1–2 and 1:3–13:10 with 13:11, 13)	56
		3.2.2	Summarization (13:11–13)	59
	3.3	Conclusion		63
4	Arguments Pertaining to Basis for Ministry: Character of Ministry (1:3–2:13)			65

4.1		Division of 1:3–2:13	65
	4.1.1	1:3–7	66
	4.1.2	1:8–2:11	69
		4.1.2.1 1:8–11	69
		4.1.2.2 1:12–2:11	69
	4.1.3	2:12–13	72
4.2		Major Structural Relationships	72
	4.2.1	In Relation to the Division as a Whole: Particularization and Causation with Substantiation (1:3–7 and 1:8–2:13)	73
		4.2.1.1 Mutuality of Divine Encouragement in Ministry (1:3–7)	73
		4.2.1.2 Mutuality of Ministry through Paul's Experience of Affliction in Asia (1:8–11)	75
		4.2.1.3 Mutuality of Boasting in 1:12–2:11	77
		4.2.1.4 Transitional Travel Narrative (2:12–13)	81
	4.2.2	In Relation to the Letter as a Whole	82
		4.2.2.1 Causation with Particularization (1:3–2:13 and 2:14–13:10)	83
		4.2.2.2 Recurrence of Particularization (1:3–2:13 and 2:14–13:10)	85
		4.2.2.3 Recurrence	85
4.3		Conclusion and Theological Implication	88
5 Arguments Pertaining to Content of Ministry: Thesis Statement (2:14–17)	91
5.1		Division of 2:14–17	91
5.2		Major Structural Relationship in Relation to the Letter as a Whole: Particularization with Contrast (2:14–17 and 3:1–13:10)	93
	5.2.1	God as Ultimate Agent of Ministry	97
		5.2.1.1 Nature of Ministry	98
		5.2.1.2 Content of Ministry: Manifestation of God's Knowledge	101
		5.2.1.3 Summary	103
	5.2.2	Agents of Ministry	103
		5.2.2.1 God's Agents As Χριστοῦ Εὐωδία	104
		5.2.2.2 God's Agents As Ὀσμή	107
		5.2.2.3 Summary	114
	5.2.3	Christ as Intermediate Agent	114
	5.2.4	Counteragents of Ministry	118
5.3		Conclusion	121

6	Arguments Pertaining to Content of Ministry: Proclamation of the Gospel (3:1–7:16)			123
	6.1	Division of 3:1–7:16		123
		6.1.1	3:1–11	126
		6.1.2	3:12–7:3	127
			6.1.2.1 3:12–4:12	128
			6.1.2.2 4:13–5:10	131
			6.1.2.3 5:11–7:3	134
		6.1.3	7:4–16	138
	6.2	Major Structural Relationships in Relation to the Division as a Whole		139
		6.2.1	Causation with Particularization (3:1–11 and 3:12–7:3)	139
		6.2.2	Substantiation (3:1–7:3 and 7:4–16)	144
	6.3	Conclusion		145
7	Arguments Pertaining to Content of Ministry: Response to the Gospel (8:1–9:15)			147
	7.1	Division of 8:1–9:15		147
		7.1.1	8:1–6	149
		7.1.2	8:7–15	151
		7.1.3	8:16–9:5	152
		7.1.4	9:6–15	155
	7.2	Major Structural Relationships		158
		7.2.1	In Relation to Division as a Whole (8:1–9:15)	158
			7.2.1.1 Inclusio (8:1–9:15)	159
			7.2.1.2 Recurrence	159
			7.2.1.3 Comparative Causation (8:1–6 and 8:7–15)	160
			7.2.1.4 Instrumentation (Description of Means; 8:7–15 and 8:16–9:5)	161
			7.2.1.5 Substantiation (8:7–15 and 9:6–15)	161
			7.2.1.6 Summary and Theological Implication	162
		7.2.2	In Relation to Letter as a Whole (3:1–7:16 and 8:1–9:15): Comparative Causation (3:1–7:16 and 8:1–9:15)	162
	7.3	Conclusion and Theological Implication		166
8	Arguments Pertaining to Content of Ministry: Defense of the Gospel (10:1–13:10)			167
	8.1	Division of 10:1–13:10		167
		8:1.1	10:1–12:13	168

			8.1.1.1 10:1–18	171
			8.1.1.2 11:1–12:13	172
		8.1.2	12:14–13:10	174
			8.1.2.1 12:14–21	175
			8.1.2.2 13:1–10	175
	8.2	Major Structural Relationships		176
		8.2.1	In Relation to Division as a Whole	176
			8.2.1.1 Inclusio (10:1–13:10)	176
			8.2.1.2 Instrumentation (Statement of Purpose; 13:10)	176
			8.2.1.3 Causation with Particularization and Contrast (10:1–18 and 11:1–12:13)	177
			8.2.1.4 Causation (10:1–12:13 and 12:14–13:10)	181
		8.2.2	In Relation to the Letter as a Whole	183
			8.2.2.1 Recurrence of Causation (3:1–9:15 and 10:1–13:10)	183
			8.2.2.2 Substantiation with Particularization and Instrumentation (Description of Means; 3:1–9:15 and 10:1–13:10)	184
			8.2.2.3 Generalization with Climax (12:9–10)	187
	8.3	Conclusion and Theological Implication		188
9	Conclusion			193
	9.1	Summary of Argument		193
	9.2	Overview of Division and Major Structural Relationships in Relation to the Letter as a Whole		195
		9.2.1	Division of the Letter	195
		9.2.2	Major Structural Relationships in Relation to the Letter as a Whole	198
			9.2.2.1 Preparation/Realization with Inclusio (1:1–2 and 1:3–13:10 with 13:11, 13) in 3.2.1	198
			9.2.2.2 Summarization (1:3–13:10 and 13:11–13) in 3.2.2	198
			9.2.2.3 Causation with Particularization (1:3–2:13 and 2:14–13:10) in 4.2.2.1	199
			9.2.2.4 Recurrence of Particularization (1:3–2:13 and 2:14–13:10) in 4.2.2.2	199
			9.2.2.5 Recurrence in 4.2.2.3	199
			9.2.2.6 Particularization with Contrast (2:14–17 and 3:1–13:10) in 5.2	200
			9.2.2.7 Comparative Causation (3:1–7:16 and 8:1–9:15) in 7.2.2	200

		9.2.2.8 Recurrence of Causation (3:1–9:15 and 10:1–13:10) in 8.2.2.1	201
		9.2.2.9 Substantiation with Particularization and Instrumentation (Description of Means; 3:1–9:15 and 10:1–13:10) in 8.2.2.2	201
		9.2.2.10 Generalization with Climax (12:9–10) in 8.2.2.3	201
9.3	Overview of Division and Major Structural Relationships of 1:3–2:13 (ch. 4)		202
	9.3.1	Division of 1:3–2:13	202
	9.3.2	Major Structural Relationships in Relation to the Division as a Whole: Particularization and Causation with Substantiation (1:3–7 and 1:8–2:13) in 4.2.1	202
9.4.	Overview of Division and Major Structural Relationships of 3:1–7:16 (ch. 6)		203
	9.4.1	Division of 3:1–7:16	203
	9.4.2	Major Structural Relationships in Relation to the Division as a Whole	203
		9.4.2.1 Causation with Particularization (3:1–11 and 3:12–7:3) in 6.2.1	203
		9.4.2.2 Substantiation (3:1–7:3 and 7:4–16) in 6.2.2	204
9.5	Overview of Division and Major Structural Relationships of 8:1–9:15 (ch. 7)		204
	9.5.1	Division of 8:1–9:15	204
	9.5.2	Major Structural Relationships in Relation to the Division as a Whole	205
		9.5.2.1 Inclusio (8:1–9:15) in 7.2.1.1	205
		9.5.2.2 Recurrence in 7.2.1.2	205
		9.5.2.3 Comparative Causation (8:1–6 and 8:7–15) in 7.2.1.3	205
		9.5.2.4 Instrumentation (Description of Means; 8:7–15 and 8:16–9:5)	205
		9.5.2.5 Substantiation (8:7–15 and 9:6–15)	206
9.6	Overview of Division and Major Structural Relationships of 10:1–13:10 (ch. 8)		206
	9.6.1	Division of 10:1–13:10	206
	9.6.2	Major Structural Relationships in Relation to the Division as a Whole	206
		9.6.2.1 Inclusio (10:1–13:10) in 8.2.1.1	206
		9.6.2.2 Instrumentation (Statement of Purpose; 13:10) in 8.2.1.2	206

		9.6.2.3	Causation with Particularization and Contrast	
			(10:1–18 and 11:1–12:13) in 8.2.1.3	207
		9.6.2.4	Causation (10:1–12:13 and 12:14–13:10) in 8.2.1.4	207
9.7	Theological Implications: Paul's Theology of Ministry and Weakness			207
	9.7.1	Paul's Theology of Ministry		208
	9.7.2	Paul's Theology of Weakness		211
9.8	Further Areas of Research			213

Bibliography	215
Index of Biblical References	229
Subject Index	235

Illustrations

Tables

2.1	Affinities between 1:12–14 and 1:15–2:11	47
3.1	The Elements of Epistolary Closing Present in 2 Cor 13:11–13	55
3.2	Five Structural Elements in 2 Cor 13:11–13	59
4.1	Conjunctive Relations of 1:3–2:13	76
5.1	The Parallel between 2:17 and 4:2, 5	108
5.2	The Parallel between 2:14–17 and 5:18–20	109
5.3	The Parallel between 2:17 and 12:19	110
6.1	Anaphoric and Cataphoric Prenuclear Participial Clauses in 3:12, 4:1, and 4:13	133

Figures

5.1	Christ as Intermediate Agent	93

Foreword

Reading 2 Corinthians is no easy task. What is the shape of Paul's argument? What can account for the major structural developments in the text? Turning to scholarship for answers is a bewildering experience, as there are as many solutions to these questions as there are scholars of 2 Corinthians. Of course, the various partition theories, chronologies of Paul and his letters, and historical-critical reading strategies complicate matters further. What is needed is an integrated approach that doesn't lose sight of the wood for the trees, one that is conversant with the major scholarly issues and can advance a thesis with methodological clarity. Thankfully, into these choppy waters now wades Hiramatsu with a set of elegant and sophisticated proposals to account for the shape of 2 Corinthians as a whole. He is conversant with the insights of topical, epistolary, rhetorical, literary, and discourse analytical findings, but moves beyond them all by employing an inductive and integrated methodology. The result is a compelling account of the major structural relations of the letter as a whole, both in broad sweep and in detail. Hiramatsu's structural analysis and methodology also offer him opportunity to present fresh perspectives on the theology of 2 Corinthians. It is, therefore, a delight that this learned and important work is now available to the wider academic community. Simply put, any future scholarly engagement with 2 Corinthians will need to tackle Hiramatsu's work.

Dr. Chris Tilling, Head of Research and
Senior Lecturer in New Testament Studies,
St Mellitus College

Acknowledgement

First of all, I give thanks to God who manifests the grace and power of Christ in weakness (2 Cor 12:9–10) to which my life is the living testimony. To God be all the glory.

The writing of this monograph could not have come to completion without a host of individuals to whom I owe a debt of gratitude. I am indebted to my doctoral advisor, Dr. David R. Bauer, for his mentorship, encouragement, and friendship throughout my time at Asbury Theological Seminary. I also want to express my gratitude to my examiners, Dr. Fredrick J. Long and Dr. Ruth Anne Reese. There are too many individuals to name, but I express my gratitude to professors, seminary friends, and church friends who enriched my life during my time at Asbury through their teaching, support, and encouragement.

I am grateful to Asbury Theological Seminary, Langham Partnership, and ScholarLeaders International for their scholarship and support for my study. I am also thankful for my former professors and current colleagues at Central Bible College (Tokyo), among whom I particularly want to acknowledge President Miyake Noriyuki and his family.

Thanks to the Takayama family and the Hiramatsu family. Thank you to my grandmother Yamaki Keiko and my brother Hiramatsu Gen for your encouragement and support. I am grateful to my grandfather Yamaki Haruo for his legacy and dedication to theological education and the proclamation of God's Word. I am thankful for my parents Hiramatsu Yoshitsugu and Yuriko. In Japan, where the Christian population is less than 1 percent, one of the most preached passages is 2 Cor 12:9–10, for Christians in Japan often experience marginalization in society and live as the weak in various ways. However, Paul teaches us that Christ's servant is not forced to be weak; he is willing to be weak so that the power and grace of Christ are perfected in weakness. My parents have taught me this truth through their lives.

Finally, I am grateful to my daughters, Hiramatsu Hanaka, Kaho, and Rin for the sacrifices they made to support my study. I am most thankful for my wife, Hiramatsu Saki; you always love me, walk beside me, support me, encourage me, bear burdens with me, serve God and His people with me, and teach me God's love through your sacrifice and care. It is to Saki, Hanaka, Kaho, and Rin that I dedicate this work.

Abbreviations

AB	Anchor Bible
ABD	*Anchor Bible Dictionary*. Edited by David Noel Freedman. 6 vols. New York: Doubleday, 1992
ACNT	Augsburg Commentaries on the New Testament
AJBI	*Annual of the Japanese Biblical Institute*
BECNT	Baker Exegetical Commentary on the New Testament
BETL	Bibliotheca Ephemeridum Theologicarum Lovaniensium
BDF	Blass, Friedrich, Albert Debrunner, and Robert W. Funk. *A Greek Grammar of the New Testament and Other Early Christian Literature.* Chicago: University of Chicago Press, 1961
BDAG	Danker, Frederick W., Walter Bauer, William F. Arndt, and F. Wilbur Gingrich. *Greek-English Lexicon of the New Testament and Other Early Christian Literature*. 3rd ed. Chicago: University of Chicago Press, 2000 (Danker-Bauer-Arndt-Gingrich)
BHT	Beiträge zur historischen Theologie
Bib	*Biblica*
BLS	Bible and Literature Series
BNTC	Black's New Testament Commentaries
BTB	*Biblical Theology Bulletin*
BTS	Biblical Tools and Studies
CBQ	*Catholic Biblical Quarterly*
CTR	*Criswell Theological Review*
DLNT	*Dictionary of the Later New Testament and Its Developments*. Edited by Ralph P. Martin and Peter H. Davids. Downers Grove, IL: InterVarsity Press, 1997
DPL	*Dictionary of Paul and His Letters*. Edited by Gerald F. Hawthorne and Ralph P. Martin. Downers Grove, IL: InterVarsity Press, 1993
DNTB	*Dictionary of New Testament Background*. Edited by Craig A. Evans and Stanley E. Porter. Downers Grove, IL: Inter-Varsity, 2000
ECL	Early Christianity and Its Literature
FF	*Forschungen und Fortschritte*
GBS	Guides to Biblical Scholarship
HNT	Handbuch zum Neuen Testament
IBS	Inductive Bible Study
ICC	International Critical Commentary
Int	*Interpretation*
JAARSup	Journal of the American Academy of Religion Supplements
JBL	*Journal of Biblical Literature*
JSNT	*Journal for the Study of the New Testament*
JSNTSup	Journal for the Study of the New Testament Supplement Series
JSOT	*Journal for the Study of the Old Testament*

KEK	Kritisch-exegetischer Kommentar über das Neue Testament (Meyer-Kommentar)
LEC	Library of Early Christianity
LNTS	The Library of New Testament Studies
LSJ	Henry George, Robert Scott, and Henry Stuart Jones. *A Greek-English Lexicon.* 9th ed. with revised supplement. Oxford: Clarendon, 1996
L&N	Louw, Johannes P., and Eugene A. Nida, eds. *Greek-English Lexicon of the New Testament*: Based on Semantic Domains. 2nd ed. New York: United Bible Societies, 1989
MNTC	*Moffatt New Testament Commentary*
MSR	Major Structural Relationship
NAC	New American Commentary
NCBC	The New Cambridge Bible Commentary
Neot	*Neotestamentica*
NIBCNT	New International Biblical Commentary on the New Testament
NIBCOT	New International Biblical Commentary on the Old Testament
NICNT	New International Commentary on the New Testament
NIDB	*New Interpreter's Dictionary of the Bible.* Edited by Katharine Doob Sakenfeld. 5 vols. Nashville: Abingdon, 2006–09
NIGTC	New International Greek Testament Commentary
NovTSup	Supplements to Novum Testamentum
NTL	New Testament Library
NTS	*New Testament Studies*
RBS	Resources for Biblical Study
ResQ	*Restoration Quarterly*
RHPR	*Revue d'histoire et de philosophie religieuses*
SANT	Studien zum Alten und Neuen Testaments
SBLDS	Society of Biblical Literature Dissertation Series
SBLSPS	SBL Seminar Papers
ScEs	*Science et esprit*
SFL	Systemic Functional Linguistics
SNTSMS	Society for New Testament Studies Monograph Series
SNTW	Studies of the New Testament and Its World
SP	Sacra Pagina
Teol	*Teologia*
TDNT	*Theological Dictionary of the New Testament.* Edited by Gerhard Kittel and Gerhard Friedrich. Translated by Geoffrey W. Bromiley. 10 vols. Grand Rapids: Eerdmans, 1964–76
TF	Theologische Forschung
TNTC	Tyndale New Testament Commentaries
WBC	Word Biblical Commentary
WC	Westminster Commentaries
WGRWSup	Writings from the Greco-Roman World Supplement Series
WUNT	Wissenschaftliche Untersuchungen zum Neuen Testament
ZWT	*Zeitschrift für wissenschaftliche Theologie*
ZNW	*Zeitschrift für die neutestamentliche Wissenschaft und die Kunde der älteren Kirche*

Introduction

As an introduction to the present study, I wish to outline its steps of the procedure and explain the limitation regarding the ways in which I demonstrate and develop arguments.*

Concerning the outline, Chapter 1 discusses methodological considerations for this study, which include an introduction to Inductive Bible Study (IBS) and the theoretical foundations of the inductive approach. Chapter 2 contains a survey of the history of research regarding the literary structure and the primary message of 2 Corinthians. The various methodological approaches will be analyzed in order to indicate a paucity of scholarly consensus as well as the significance and relevance of their insights into an inductive approach. Chapters 3 through 8 examine the segmentation and Major Structural Relationships (MSR) of 2 Corinthians. While the division of the letter and the identification of MSRs mutually inform one another, this study first describes the division of the letter and then explicates the MSRs. Chapter 9 summarizes the findings, draws theological implications of this study, and suggests further areas of research.

Regarding the limitation, the most plausible argument should include a variety of evidence both *for* the proposed thesis and *against* other views, for the former supports the thesis and the latter creates a space for the thesis by refuting other interpretations. However, this study has an emphasis on the presentation of the evidence *for* my interpretation rather than the evidence *against* other interpretations unless crucial and necessary, for two reasons in particular. First, the corpus of this study is large (i.e., the entire letter of 2 Corinthians in the canonical form); thus, the space is limited. Second, refuting other views takes more space than presenting evidence for the thesis, particularly on the subject of this study, because discussion on the literary structure is, whether implicitly or explicitly, virtually present in any exegetical argument. As I will discuss, structural relationships or laws of composition are part of the human cognitive and communicative processes. This does not mean that other interpretations are unhelpful; rather, the wealth of the literature on 2 Corinthians enlightens my discussion. However, for the sake of the presentation of my argument within the limited space, I will focus on the demonstration of the evidence for my argument. Having presented the outline and limitation, I will turn to the first chapter: Methodological Considerations.

---

* All the NT quotations are taken from the NA28 unless otherwise stated.

1

Methodological Considerations

In this chapter, I will first introduce the origin and development of Inductive Bible Study and provide its definition. Then I describe theoretical foundations on the basis of which the present study conducts its analysis.

1.1 Introduction to Inductive Bible Study

1.1.1 Origin and Development

The hermeneutical approach that incorporates in a synthetic fashion the most relevant insights from various methodologies around an emphasis on literary form is often known as Inductive Bible Study (IBS). It has precursors in the history of interpretation, reaching back to the early church, yet in a narrow sense, the origin of the discipline can be traced back to the work of William Rainey Harper and Wilbert Webster White, who insisted on the priority of examining the biblical text in its final form prior to issues behind the final form of the text, including historical-critical questions. The movement initiated by Harper and White was embodied in the curriculum of The Biblical Seminary in New York, founded by White in 1900.[1] Since then, IBS has enjoyed widespread and global dissemination and been taught at a number of theological institutions, including Princeton Theological Seminary, Union Theological Seminary in Virginia, Fuller Theological Seminary, the Associated Mennonite Biblical Seminary, Columbia Theological Seminary, Dallas Theological Seminary, Regent University, Azusa Pacific University, and hundreds of schools outside North America. IBS has influenced the works of several leading biblical scholars, including Brevard Childs,

---

[1] On the work of White and the development of IBS at The Biblical Seminary see Charles R. Eberhardt, *The Bible in the Making of Ministers: The Scriptural Basis of Theological Education: The Lifework of Wilbert Webster White* (New York: Association Press, 1949); Robert A. Traina, "Inductive Bible Study Reexamined in Light of Contemporary Hermeneutics I: Interpreting the Text," in *Interpreting God's Word for Today: An Inquiry into Hermeneutics from a Biblical Theological Perspective*, ed. Wayne McCown and James E. Massey, Wesleyan Theological Perspectives 2 (Anderson, IN: Warner, 1982), 53–83; idem, "Inductive Bible Study Reexamined in Light of Contemporary Hermeneutics II: Applying the Text," in *Interpreting God's Word for Today: An Inquiry into Hermeneutics from a Biblical Theological Perspective*, ed. Wayne McCown and James E. Massey, Wesleyan Theological Perspectives 2 (Anderson, IN: Warner, 1982), 85–109; Maria Freeman, "Study with an Open Mind and Heart: William Rainey Harper's Inductive Method of Teaching the Bible" (PhD diss., The University of Chicago, 2005).

Patrick D. Miller, James Luther Mays, Thomas W. Gillespie, and Donald G. Miller, to name a few.[2] Practitioners of IBS have continued to develop and implement the approach in biblical interpretation on both academic and popular levels, including scholars such as Howard Tillman Kuist and Daniel P. Fuller.[3] Particularly, Asbury Theological Seminary has become the world center of IBS with such scholars as Kenneth Plank Wesche, George Allen Turner,[4] Robert A. Traina, David L. Thompson,[5] David R. Bauer, Joseph R. Dongell, Brian D. Russell, Jim Miller, and Fredrick J. Long. Asbury Theological Seminary has continued to follow the tradition of The Biblical Seminary in New York and train graduate students with IBS. In addition, the school advances the discipline by publishing scholarly articles related to IBS through *The Journal of Inductive Biblical Studies* with Bauer and Long as chief editors.

Specifically, the works of Traina, Bauer, and Long are significant and relevant to both NT studies and the present work. Traina was a graduate of The Biblical Seminary and served on the faculty of that institution almost twenty years before coming to Asbury. In 1952 Traina published his book, *Methodical Bible Study: A New Approach to Hermeneutics*, in which he systematized the inductive method and related IBS to mainstream exegesis and to biblical theology.[6] In 1988 Bauer, a pupil of Traina's, published his dissertation as *The Structure of Matthew's Gospel*, in which he employed IBS categories of structural relations for the study of the literary design in Matthew's

---

[2] David R. Bauer, "Inductive Biblical Study: History, Character, and Prospects in a Global Environment," *The Asbury Journal* 68 (2013): 6–35; David R. Bauer and Robert A. Traina, *Inductive Bible Study: A Comprehensive Guide to the Practice of Hermeneutics* (Grand Rapids: Baker Academics, 2011), 1–2. Also see the overview of the dissemination of IBS in Fredrick J. Long, "Major Structural Relationships: A Survey of Origins, Development, Classifications, and Assessment," *The Journal of Inductive Biblical Studies* 1 (2014): 23–58 at 28.

[3] Howard Tillman Kuist, *These Words Upon Thy Heart: Scripture and the Christian Response* (Richmond, VA: John Knox, 1947); Daniel P. Fuller, *The Inductive Method of Bible Study* (Pasadena, CA: Fuller Theological Seminary, 1955). Also see Patricia Pauline Hunter, "Application of the Inductive Method of Bible Study in the Christian College" (Master Thesis, Fuller Theological Seminary, 1960); Irving L. Jensen, *Independent Bible Study: Using the Analytical Chart and the Inductive Method* (Chicago: Moody Press, 1963); Daniel Ernest Sauerwein, "Inductive Bible Study: A Proposed Program of Study" (DMin diss., Western Conservative Baptist Seminary, 1980); Richard V. Yohn, "Guide to Inductive Bible Study." (DMin diss., Biola University, 1980); Walter L. Liefeld, *New Testament Exposition: From Text to Sermon* (Grand Rapids: Zondervan, 1984); William Henry Jennings, "The Inductive Method of Bible Study: A Uniquely Appropriate Tool for Lay Evangelists" (DMin diss., Columbia Theological Seminary, 1988); Howard G. Hendricks and William Hendricks, *Living by the Book* (Chicago: Moody, 1991); Kay Arthur, *How to Study Your Bible* (Eugene, OR: Harvest House Publishers, 1994); Hans Finzel, *Observe, Interpret, Apply: How to Study the Bible Inductively*, GroupBuilder Resources (Wheaton, IL: Victor, 1994); Mary Creswell Graham, *Inductive Bible Study Explained*, rev. ed. (Graham, Institute of International Studies, 1995); Luke Kyungwhan Pak, "Teaching the Inductive Bible Study Method of Bible Interpretation to Adults: A Comparison of Three Instructional Approaches" (PhD diss., University of North Texas, 1996); Oletta Wald, *The New Joy of Discovery in Bible Study*, rev. ed. (Minneapolis: Augsburg Fortress, 2002); Maria Freeman, "Study with an Open Mind and Heart"; Kevin Bryan Barnes, "A Bible Study about Studying Bible: An Introduction to Inductive Bible Study" (DMin diss., Asbury Theological Seminary, 2018).

[4] George Allen Turner, *Exploring the Bible: Studies in Books of the Bible Using the "Inductive Method" of Approach* (Wilmore, KY: Turner, 1950).

[5] David L. Thompson, *Bible Study That Works*, rev. (Nappanee, IN: Evangel Publishing House, 1994).

[6] Robert A. Traina, *Methodical Bible Study: A New Approach to Hermeneutics* (New York: Ganis & Harris, 1952); Bauer, "Inductive Biblical Study," 8.

Gospel.⁷ In 2011 Traina and Bauer co-wrote *Inductive Bible Study: A Comprehensive Guide to the Practice of Hermeneutics* by giving the most recent and comprehensive exposition of IBS in its more rigorous, academic form.⁸ Furthermore, Long, a pupil of Bauer, continues to synthesize, develop, and explore IBS in relation to other exegetical methodologies in his *In Step with God's Word: Interpreting the New Testament with God's People*.⁹ The present study, therefore, continues the tradition of aforementioned IBS scholars, especially Bauer and Traina, making a foray into the study of 2 Corinthians, specifically the literary structure and its relevance to understanding the theology of the letter.

1.1.2 Definition: Integrative and Inductive Study

Based on critical-realist hermeneutics, Bauer and Traina define IBS as

> a comprehensive, holistic study of the Bible that takes into account every aspect of the existence of the biblical text and that is intentional in allowing the Bible in its final canonical shape to speak to us on its own terms, thus leading to accurate, original, compelling, and profound interpretation and contemporary appropriation.¹⁰

Although no one is free from one's own presuppositions or subjectivity in interpreting the text, critical-realist hermeneutics aim at knowledge that is objective and evidential as much as possible in a way that others can also see it. In other words, IBS employs "the term *inductive* synonymously with *evidential*."¹¹ Thus, it moves from the evidence in and surrounding the text to possible conclusions with an inductive posture "characterized by radical openness to any conclusion required by the biblical evidence."¹²

In practice, this study does not aim to apply a particular methodology as a sole means of analyzing the literary structure of 2 Corinthians and its theological message. Rather, it

---

⁷ David R. Bauer, *The Structure of Matthew's Gospel: A Study in Literary Design*, JSNTSup 31, BLS 15 (Sheffield: Almond Press, 1988).

⁸ Bauer and Traina, *Inductive Bible Study*.

⁹ Fredrick J. Long, *In Step with God's Word: Interpreting the New Testament with God's People*, GlossaHouse Hermeneutics & Translation Series 1 (Wilmore, KY: GlossaHouse, 2017). Also see idem, "Major Structural Relationships" 22–59; idem, "Vital Relations and Major Structural Relationships Heuristic Approaches to Observe and Explore Biblical and Other Discourse," *The Journal of Inductive Biblical Studies* 4 (2017): 92–128. Furthermore, while Long's monograph explores ancient rhetorical tradition, he acknowledges the influence of IBS on his study in the preface (*Ancient Rhetoric and Paul's Apology: The Compositional Unity of 2 Corinthians*, SNTSMS 131 [Cambridge: Cambridge University Press, 2004], xv).

¹⁰ Bauer and Traina, *Inductive Bible Study*, 6. On critical-realist hermeneutics in the biblical interpretation, see N. T. Wright, *The New Testament and the People of God*, vol. 1 of *Christian Origins and The Question of God* (London: SPCK, 1992), 2–143; Ben F. Meyer, *Reality and Illusion in New Testament Scholarship: A Primer in Critical Realist Hermeneutics* (Collegeville, MN: Liturgical Press, 1994).

¹¹ Bauer and Traina, *Inductive Bible Study*, 17.

¹² Ibid., 18.

seeks to employ an approach that integrates all relevant and helpful insights of the NT methodologies into the interpretation of the literary structure and the central message of 2 Corinthians in its final form.[13] While exegesis can be conducted in various forms such as reconstructing historical developments of the letter and exploring Jewish and Roman religious/cultural influences on Paul's discourse, the present study is primarily concerned with the meaning of the text in its final form, particularly the ways in which these various aspects of the passage are related to one another so as to arrive at the aforementioned goal.

1.2 Theoretical Foundations of an Inductive Approach

In order to apply IBS methodology according to its core convictions, this study conducts its analysis based on a few methodological assumptions: compositional study, final form of the text, implied author, and structure and structural relationships.

1.2.1 Compositional Study

First, the present study accepts the compositional unity of 2 Corinthians and considers the literary context to be the primary context for the construal of the text's meaning. Although scholars can differ greatly from one another regarding their approaches to the biblical text, all agree that context is critical for interpretation. Whether they analyze written or oral statements, context is the most important determinant to construe the meaning of any communication.[14] Thus, while some emphasize the context behind the biblical text (e.g., social history) or the context in front of the text (e.g., context of interpreters), this study focuses on literary context in its final form to interpret the text and evaluate scholars' interpretations. Bauer and Traina explain, "The centrality of the final form means that Bible study begins with the text, and all these other realities are pursued in relation to it."[15] In other words, all relevant and significant contexts will be explored in relation to the text in order to understand the meaning of the text, because all the complex historical issues of the letter (e.g., the reconstruction of Paul's opponents and the course of the events between Paul and the Corinthians) are best approached when one understands Paul's train of thought and argument on the basis of the text itself. For this reason, this study does not intend to address all the historical questions, but avoids the danger of engaging in speculative historical reconstructions unless the text requires us to explore some of the historical issues in order to understand the text's message.[16] Bauer and Traina define compositional study as follows:

---

[13] Douglas K. Stuart similarly articulates, "To a considerable degree, the actual task of exegesis involves examining a passage as carefully as possible from as many angles as possible. In practice, this means asking of the text all the questions whose answers might give insight into the text's meaning" ("Exegesis," *ABD* 2: 682–88).

[14] For instance, see the emphasis of context in the description of the principle of scriptural study in Long, *In Step with God's Word*, 40–41.

[15] Bauer and Traina, *Inductive Bible Study*, 54.

[16] Historical background information is indeed helpful for the construal of the text's meaning. However, the intention of this study is to comprehend the sense of the final form of the text, rather than analyze matters behind the text for their own sake.

Thus composition means a putting or placing together and suggests the notion of connectedness or relationship. Words are placed in relation to other words to form sentences; sentences are placed in relation to other sentences to form paragraphs; paragraphs are placed in relation to other paragraphs to form segments; segments are placed in relation to other segments to form sections; sections are placed in relation to other sections to form divisions; and divisions are placed in relation to other divisions to form the book-as-a-whole.[17]

Therefore, this study assumes the composition of 2 Corinthians as a whole to be the basic literary unit and pursues the understanding of individual passages not only in relation to immediate literary context but also in light of their function within the segment, section, division, and eventually the entire book, following Bauer and Traina's definition of compositional study.

1.2.2 Final Form of the Text

Second, the current study takes the final form of 2 Corinthians as a point of departure for its investigation. Bauer and Traina articulate the importance of the final form of the text in biblical interpretation as follows:

The final form is central to the hermeneutical task and thus provides the basis for methodological unity and coherence, because all realities associated with the Bible intersect at the final form of the text. All that lies behind the text is moving toward its final form, and all that lies "in front of the text" (the response of readers and effects upon readers) emerges from encounter with the text. The centrality of the final form means that Bible study begins with the text, and all these other realities are pursued in relation to it.[18]

Indeed, the final form of the NT provides one of the few really solid referential points in reconstructing the history of the early Christianity. While the purpose of this study is not the defense of the unity of 2 Corinthians, the final form of the letter indeed provides a solid foundation for the analysis of the letter. Despite the variety of partition theories,[19] none of the proposed divisions is attested in any manuscript traditions except for 13:13.[20] However, as I will argue in Chapter 3, 13:11–13 is an integral and essential part of Paul's discourse. In addition, one could critique the aforementioned text–critical evidence by arguing that the earliest available manuscripts postdate the redaction processes, yet this type of argument relies on hypotheses rather than

---

[17] Bauer and Traina, *Inductive Bible Study*, 65.
[18] Bauer and Traina, *Inductive Bible Study*, 54.
[19] See my discussion regarding partition theories in Chapter 2.
[20] E.g., Philip W. Comfort considers the possibility that 13:13 was expanded in the textual history (*New Testament Text and Translation Commentary: Commentary on the Variant Readings of the Ancient New Testament Manuscripts and How They Relate to the Major English Translations* [Carol Stream, IL: Tyndale House, 2008], 554–55).

evidence, so it does not undermine the significance of the final form of 2 Corinthians. Therefore, this study begins with the final form of the text and examines all the relevant aspects of the text; it even engages in textual criticism when the text requires it for the construal of its meaning.[21]

1.2.3 Implied Author

Third, as a ramification of the text-centered approach, the present study also assumes the implied author as the basis for the interpretation of 2 Corinthians. Instead of searching for the intent of the historical author of 2 Corinthians, this study seeks to understand the intent of the implied author, who can be constructed with the information derived from the text itself. Moreover, it analyzes the communication between the implied author and the implied reader that the text portrays.[22] However, since the implied author of 2 Corinthians overtly identifies himself as the historical figures Paul and Timothy (1:1), the text invites us to consider any passages of 2 Corinthians in light of what the historical Paul and Timothy thought and did, including the information from other Pauline epistles and the book of Acts as well as relevant social, cultural, and historical information such as knowledge of the OT, which the historical Paul assumed his audience to know in order to understand his message (e.g. 3:1–18).[23]

1.2.4 Structure and Major Structural Relationships

Fourth, in order to demonstrate the literary structure and its relevance to understanding Paul's overarching discourse in 2 Corinthians, this study investigates two major

---

[21] Exegetes usually establish the text through textual criticism and then interpret the text. However, this study, as I will demonstrate in the following chapters, utilizes textual criticism to determine the meaning of the text in its final form. In other words, this study considers textual variants as helpful resources to understand the meaning of the text in its final form.

[22] Since Wayne C. Booth first developed and argued the idea of the implied author and its literary significance (*The Rhetoric of Fiction* [Chicago: University of Chicago Press, 1961]), the concept of the implied author and reader has become one of the methodological hallmarks of narrative criticism. On the history and concept of the implied author in narrative criticism, see Mark Allan Powell, *What Is Narrative Criticism?*, GBS (Minneapolis: Fortress, 1990), 1–21. On the usefulness and significance of the implied author in biblical interpretation, see Bauer and Traina, *Inductive Bible Study*, 42–49.

[23] The history of discussion regarding the critical use of Paul in Acts began with Ferdinand Christian Baur, who contended that Acts does not portray accurate information about Paul (*Paul, the Apostle of Jesus Christ: His Life and Work, His Epistles and His Doctrine: A Contribution to the Critical History of Primitive Christianity*, ed. Eduard Zeller, trans. Allan Menzies, 2 vols [London: Williams and Norgate, 1875–76]). His argument was later countered by William Mitchell Ramsay (*The Bearing of Recent Discovery on the Trustworthiness of the New Testament* [London: Hodder and Stoughton, 1915]). Since then, the debate has been controversial in the NT scholarship. However, a growing number of scholars today advocate that both Acts and Paul's letters are important sources for the information about Paul's life. See the summary of the debate in A. J. Mattill Jr., "The Value of Acts as a Source for the Study of Paul," in *Perspectives on Luke-Acts*, ed. Charles H. Talbert, Association of Baptist Professors of Religion Special Studies Series 5 (Danville, VA: Association of Baptist Professors of Religion, 1978), 76–98; Stanley E. Porter, "The Portrait of Paul in Acts," in *The Blackwell Companion to Paul*, ed. Stephen Westerholm, Blackwell Companions to Religion (Malden, MA: Wiley-Blackwell, 2011), 124–38. See the recent works that contend the reliability of Acts for the study of Paul in Stanley E. Porter, *Paul in Acts*, Library of Pauline Studies (Peabody, MA: Hendrickson, 2001); Craig S. Keener, *Acts: An Exegetical Commentary*, 4 vols (Grand Rapids: Baker Academic, 2012–15) 1:221–57.

components of the literary structure: the division of the letter and the identification of Major Structural Relationships (MSR). An analysis of these two components helps us understand the ways in which the content is communicated in order to understand what is communicated because one cannot separate material (i.e., content) from form (i.e., structure). In other words, "all material content is mediated to us through form,"[24] especially the dimension of the form of literary structure, as I will discuss in the following section.

The division of the letter pertains to the identification of main units and subunits according to the linear arrangement of the materials within the letter. The identification of the MSRs concerns the ways in which materials within and between main units and subunits are related to communicating a message. In fact, MSRs are a central feature of IBS. Bauer and Traina define structural relationships as *"organizational systems* that pertain to the dynamic arrangement of various thoughts and themes throughout the book."[25] This study, therefore, analyzes the MSRs of 2 Corinthians based on the study of Bauer and Traina.

1.2.4.1 Categories of Major Structural Relationships

Employment of MSRs in an analysis of the biblical text has two benefits. First, it aids interpreters to determine identifications of units. Second, it reveals the relationships between and within units. Bauer and Traina provide seventeen major categories of structural relationships:

1. **Recurrence** is the repetition of the same or similar terms, phrases, or other elements, which may involve motifs, concepts, persons, literary forms, or other structural relationships.[26]

---

[24] Bauer and Traina, *Inductive Bible Study*, 125.
[25] Ibid., 94.
[26] Ibid., 95–97; Bauer, *Structure of Matthew's Gospel*, 14. See also Northrop Frye, *Anatomy of Criticism: Four Essays* (Princeton: Princeton University Press, 1957), 77; James Muilenburg, "Form Criticism and Beyond," *JBL* 88 (1969): 16; William Freedman, "The Literary Motif: A Definition and Evaluation," *Novel* 4 (1971): 123; Joanna Dewey, *Markan Public Debate: Literary Technique, Concentric Structure, and Theology in Mark 2:1–36*, SBLDS 48 (Chico, CA: Scholars Press, 1980), 32; Meyer Howard Abrams, *A Glossary of Literary Terms*, 4th ed. (New York: Holt, Rinehart & Winston, 1981), 111; Kenneth R. R. Gros Louis, "Some Methodological Considerations," in *Literary Interpretations of Biblical Narratives*, ed. James Stokes Ackerman and Thayer S. Warshaw, 2 vols (Nashville: Abingdon, 1974), 2:13–24, at 23; R. Alan Culpepper, *Anatomy of the Fourth Gospel: A Study in Literary Design*, FF (Philadelphia: Fortress, 1983), 73, 87, 97, 128; Meir Sternberg, *The Poetics of Biblical Narrative: Ideological Literature and the Drama of Reading* (Bloomington: Indiana University Press, 1985), 365–440; Vernon K. Robbins, *Exploring the Texture of Texts: A Guide to Socio-Rhetorical Interpretation* (Valley Forge, PA: Trinity Press International, 1996), 8–9; James L. Resseguie, *Narrative Criticism of the New Testament: An Introduction* (Grand Rapids: Baker Academic, 2005), 42–54. On examples of analyses of repetition in the biblical text, see Ronald D. Witherup, "Cornelius Over and Over and Over Again: 'Functional Redundancy' in the Acts of the Apostles," *JSNT* 15 (1993): 45–66; Janice Capel Anderson, *Matthew's Narrative Web: Over, and Over, and Over Again*, JSNTSup 91 (Sheffield: JSOT Press, 1994).

2. **Contrast** is the association of opposites or of things whose differences the writer wishes to stress.[27]
3. **Comparison** is the association of like things or of things whose similarities are emphasized by the writer.[28]
4. **Climax** is the movement from the lesser to the greater, toward a high point of culmination.[29]
5. **Particularization** is the movement from general to particular.[30]

---

[27] Bauer and Traina, *Inductive Bible Study*, 97–98; Bauer, *Structure of Matthew's Gospel*, 14. See also Erich Auerbach, *Mimesis: The Representation of Reality in Western Literature*, trans. Willard R. Trask (Garden City, NY: Doubleday, 1957), 23; Gros Louis, "Some Methodological Considerations," 18; Abrams, *Glossary of Literary Terms*, 10; Culpepper, *Anatomy of the Fourth Gospel*, 125. Ancient writers often utilized contrasts in their writings as well (e.g., Maximus of Tyre, *Or.* 26.5–6, cited in Keener, *Acts*, 1:570); see also William W. Batstone, "The Antithesis of Virtue: Sallust's 'Synkrisis' and the Crisis of the Late Republic," *Classical Antiquity* 7 (1988): 1–29.

[28] Bauer and Traina, *Inductive Bible Study*, 98–99; Bauer, *Structure of Matthew's Gospel*, 14. Comparison is observed in various genres of writings: as a form of parallelism in biblical poetry (see Adele Berlin, *The Dynamics of Biblical Parallelism*, rev. and exp. ed. [Grand Rapids: Eerdmans, 2008]); as a rhetorical technique of σύγκρισις in narratives (e.g., Theon, *Progymn.* 2:86–88; Quintilian, *Inst.* 9.2.100–101; *Rhet. Her.* 2.45; cf. Keener, *Acts*, 1:570–71); in letters (e.g., see Christopher F. Evans' treatment on the recurrent and dominant role of σύγκρισις or comparison in Hebrews in *The Theology of Rhetoric: The Epistle to the Hebrews*, Friends of Dr. Williams's Library 42 [London: Dr. William's Trust, 1988]); and poetry (e.g., Aristotle's theory of intimation in *Poet*).

[29] Bauer and Traina, *Inductive Bible Study*, 99–100; Bauer, *Structure of Matthew's Gospel*, 15. See also Muilenburg, *Form Criticism and Beyond*, 10–11; Abrams, *Glossary of Literary Terms*, 10. Scholars frequently acknowledge the existence of climactic structures in biblical narratives; see Paul J. Achtemeier, *Mark*, Proclamation Commentaries (Philadelphia: Fortress, 1975), 88; Harry L. Chronis, "The Torn Veil: Cultus and Christology in Mark 15:37–39," *JBL* 101 (1982): 97–114; Jack Dean Kingsbury, *The Christology of Mark's Gospel* (Philadelphia: Fortress, 1983), 47–155. Moreover, scholars often observe climactic structures in letters. For instance, some recognize 1 Cor 15 to be the climax of the letter; see Karl Barth, *The Resurrection of the Dead*, trans. H. J. Stenning (New York: Fleming H. Revell, 1933); Margaret M. Mitchell, *Paul and the Rhetoric of Reconciliation: An Exegetical Investigation of the Language and Composition of 1 Corinthians* (Louisville: Westminster John Knox, 1993), 287; N. T. Wright, *The Resurrection of the Son of God*, vol. 3 of *Christian Origins and the Question of God* (London: SPCK, 2003), 297; Matthew R. Malcolm, *Paul and the Rhetoric of Reversal in 1 Corinthians: The Impact of Paul's Gospel on His Macro-Rhetoric*, SNTSMS 155 (Cambridge: Cambridge University Press, 2013), 233.

[30] Bauer and Traina identify several forms of particularization: identificational particularization (e.g., Joel 1:1 as a general heading of the material that follows), ideological particularization (e.g., Prov 1:7 and Heb 1:1–4 as a general statement or a thesis statement of the material that follows), historical particularization (e.g., John 1:14 and Psalm 78:2–4 as general descriptions of historical events that are followed by specific descriptions of the details), geographical particularization (e.g., Gen 1–11 as a presentation of a broader geographical area that is followed by the description of a specific location within that broader area), biographical particularization (e.g., Gen 1–11 and John 1:19–12:50 as a presentation of a group of people that is followed by the specific description of a subgroup or an individual person within the group; *Inductive Bible Study*, 100–103; Bauer, *Structure of Matthew's Gospel*, 16). Indeed, scholars often confirm Bauer and Traina's observations, acknowledging similar structures in their commentaries. For instance, Rowland E. Murphy acknowledges that Prov 1:1–7 serves as a motto or preface to the book (*Proverbs*, WBC 22 [Dallas: Word, 1998], 4–6); cf. William L. Lane views Heb 1:1–4 as *exordium* or introduction (*Hebrews 1–8*, WBC 47A [Dallas: Word, 1991], 2. Also see Luke Timothy Johnson, *Hebrews: A Commentary*, NTL [Louisville: Westminster John Knox, 2006], 63).

6. **Generalization** is the movement from particular to general.[31]
7. **Causation** is the movement from cause to effect.[32]
8. **Substantiation** is the movement from effect to cause.[33]

---

[31] Bauer and Traina identify five subcategories of this structural relationship: identificational generalization (e.g., Heb 13:22 as a general description of the preceding material at the end of the book), ideological generalization (e.g., Hos. 14:9 as something similar to a thesis statement at or near the end of the book), historical generalization (e.g., Judg 21:25 as a general description of an event that follows a detailed description of the event), geographical generalization (e.g., Acts 1:8 as a presentation of one geographical area that is followed by the presentation of the larger area of which this smaller area is a part [i.e., Jerusalem in Acts 2–7; Juda and Samaria in Acts 8–12, and the ends of the world in Acts 13–28]), and biographical generalization (e.g., Acts 1:8 as a presentation of one person that is followed by that of a larger group of which the person is a part [i.e., Jews in Acts 2–7; Jews, Samaritans, and God-fearers in Acts 8–12, and Jews, God-fearers, and Gentiles in Acts 13–28]). Again, scholars often confirm Bauer and Traina's observations (*Inductive Bible Study*, 100–103; Bauer, *Structure of Matthew's Gospel*, 16). For instance, Lane describes Heb 13:22 as a concluding blessing or postscript that provides closure to the document as a whole, (*Hebrews 9–13*, WBC 47B [Dallas: Word, 1991], 567). Also see Craig R. Koester, *Hebrews: A New Translation with Introduction and Commentary*, AB 36 (New Haven: Yale University Press, 2001), 581. Likewise, regarding Hos. 14:9, Douglas K. Stuart notes observations similar to Bauer and Traina (*Hosea-Jonah*, WBC 31 [Dallas: Word, 1987], 219–20). Also see William Rainey Harper, *A Critical and Exegetical Commentary on Amos and Hosea*, ICC (New York: Scribner's Sons, 1905), 416–17. In addition, most scholars make observations on Acts 1:8 (e.g., as a preview or outline of the rest of the book) similar to those of Bauer and Traina, especially as to the geographical expansion of the mission; see Robert C. Tannehill, *The Acts of the Apostles*, vol. 2 of *The Narrative Unity of Luke-Acts: A Literary Interpretation*, FF (Philadelphia: Fortress, 1989), 9; Ben Witherington III., *The Acts of the Apostles: A Socio-Rhetorical Commentary* (Grand Rapids: Eerdmans, 1998), 106; Keener, *Acts*, 708.

[32] Bauer and Traina identify three subcategories of causation: historical causation (e.g., the book of Amos is structured according to a repeated, hence recurring, causation between sin and judgment, esp. 1:1–2:16; 3:2, 9–12; 4:1–3; 5:25–27; 8:4–10), logical causation (e.g., Heb 8:1 as a logical conclusion from chs 5–7; Matt 1:17 as an inference from 1:2–16), and hortatory causation (e.g., the book of Ephesians moves from indicatives in chs 1–3 to imperatives in chs 4–6; Bauer and Traina, *Inductive Bible Study*, 105–107; Bauer, *Structure of Matthew's Gospel*, 14–15). Commentators note similar observations with Bauer and Traina. Lane suggests an inferential relationship between Heb 5–7 and 8:1 (*Hebrew 1–8*, 202–5); Donald A. Hagner likewise suggests Matt 1:17 as an inferential conclusion from 1:2–16 (*Matthew 1–13*, WBC 33A [Dallas: Word, 1993], 12). Similarly, Markus Barth observes the movement between indicatives (chs 1–3) and imperatives (chs 4–6) in the book of Ephesians (*Ephesians 1–3: Introduction, Translation, and Commentary on Chapters 1–3*, AB 34 [Garden City, NY: Doubleday, 1974], 53).

[33] Bauer and Traina identify three subcategories of substantiation: historical substantiation (e.g., Jonah 4:1–2 explains the actual reason for Jonah's fleeing at the beginning of the book: Jonah was afraid that the Ninevites would accept his message and that God would not destroy them), logical substantiation (e.g., Rom 1:16–11:36 is structured according to substantiation because 1:18–11:36 provides the cause, reason, or support for the essential claim of 1:16–17), and hortatory substantiation (e.g., the book of Revelation is structured according to substantiation because the great apocalyptic vision of chs 4–22 substantiates or supports the exhortations in the letter to the seven churches in chs 2–3; Bauer and Traina, *Inductive Bible Study*, 107–108; Bauer, *Structure of Matthew's Gospel*, 15). Both substantiation and causation are frequently recognized by scholars. For instance, C. E. B. Cranfield confirms Bauer and Traina's observation, recognizing that Rom 1:18–11:36 elucidates 1:16–17 (*A Critical and Exegetical Commentary on the Epistle to the Romans*, repr. [London: T&T Clark, 2004], 1:103, 2:592). Regarding Bauer and Traina's observation on the relationship between Rev. 2–3 and 4–22, G. K. Beale also suggests a similar relationship, stating that while chs 1–3 express Christ's rule resulting in the glory of God and Christ, chs 4–5 explain the reason of such glorification: Christ's resurrection demonstrates their sovereignty (*The Book of Revelation*, NIGTC [Grand Rapids: Eerdmans, 1999], 151).

9. **Cruciality** is the movement of a radical reversal, a total turning around, or a change of direction of the material because of the pivot passage.[34]
10. **Summarization** is an abridgement or compendium (summing up) either preceding or following a unit of material. While summarization is similar to the general component in particularization or generalization, it is a more deliberate attempt to bring into the statement, in abridged from, the various components of what is being summarized (i.e., a point-by-point recapitulation).[35]
11. **Interrogation** is the employment of a question or a problem followed by its answer or solution.[36]
12. **Preparation/realization** or **introduction** is the inclusion of background or setting for events or ideas. Preparation pertains to the background or introductory material itself, while realization is that for which the preparation is made.[37]

---

[34] Bauer and Traina give examples of this structural relationship from 2 Sam 1–20 and Acts 7:58–28:31. In 2 Sam 1–20, David's sin of adultery with Bathsheba and murder of Uriah in 2 Sam 11–12 serve as the pivot passage that triggers a radical reversal from the presentation of David's unmitigated blessing and prosperity to the presentation of a series of David's disasters in 2 Sam 13–20. In Acts 7:58–28:31, Saul's encounter with the Lord on the road to Damascus in 9:3–19a serves as the pivot passage that brings a radical change from Saul as the great opponent of the gospel and the chief persecutor of the church (7:58–8:3; 9:1–2) to the great proponent of the gospel and the persecuted (9:13b–28:31; *Inductive Bible Study*, 108–10; Bauer, *Structure of Matthew's Gospel*, 15–16). Scholars again confirm Bauer and Traina's findings. For instance, Bill T. Arnold notes a similar movement between 2 Sam 1–10, 11–12, and 13–20 ("Samuel, Books Of," *Dictionary of the Old Testament: Historical Books*, 865–77, esp. at 869). On cruciality, see also Muilenburg, *Form Criticism and Beyond*, 13; Abrams, *Glossary of Literary Terms*, 139; Culpepper, *Anatomy of the Fourth Gospel*, 89; cf. Resseguie, *Narrative Criticism*, 206–208.

[35] Bauer and Traina list Josh 13:1–24:13, Judg 2:6–3:6, 2 Kgs 17:7–23, Esth 9:24–28, and Acts 1:8 as examples of this structural relationship (*Inductive Bible Study*, 110–13; Bauer, *Structure of Matthew's Gospel*, 17). On summarization, see also F. F. Bruce, *The Acts of the Apostles: The Greek Text with Introduction and Commentary*, NICNT (Grand Rapids: Eerdmans, 1952), 39; John Bright, *The Authority of the Old Testament* (Grand Rapids: Baker, 1975), 241; Norman Perrin, "Interpretation of the Gospel of Mark," *Int* 30 (1976): 115–24, at 122; Culpepper, *Anatomy of the Fourth Gospel*, 89.

[36] Bauer and Traina identify two forms of interrogation: a question followed by an answer (e.g., Ps 15 in which the questions raised in 15:1 are answered in the following verses in 15:2–5) and a problem followed by a solution (e.g., the book of Genesis in which the problem of sin leading to curse in chs 1–11 is answered/solved by the covenant leading to blessing in chs 12–50; Bauer and Traina, *Inductive Bible Study*, 113–14; Bauer, *Structure of Matthew's Gospel*, 17–18). Indeed, scholars recognize interrogation in their analyses. For example, Peter C. Craigie notes that Ps 15 is structured according to the worshippers' question (15:1) and the priest's response (15:2–5; *Psalm 1–50*, WBC 19 [Dallas: Word, 1983], 150). Moreover, this type of form is not a modern categorization. One of the well-known literary forms of interrogation in the Greco-Roman world is a diatribe, a form of teaching in which a teacher teaches students truth or knowledge through the means of question and answer; see Stanley Kent Stowers, *The Diatribe and Paul's Letter to the Romans*, SBLDS 57 (Chico, CA: Scholars Press, 1981).

[37] Bauer and Traina list the books of Joshua and Job as some examples of this structure. Joshua 1–2 prepares the reader for the main concern of the book, the conquest of Canaan in Josh 3–24. Job 1–2 provides background or setting for the rest of the book. Moreover, a specific form of preparation/realization is the prediction-fulfillment pattern (e.g., Mark's repeated predictions of Jesus' passion in 8:31, 9:31, and 10:33–34 are fulfilled later in the narrative; the two books of Kings are structured according to a recurrence of preparation/realization: A prediction is made twenty-five times throughout these books that is realized later in the narratives such as 1 Kgs 11:11, 26 and 12:16–24; Bauer and Traina, *Inductive Bible Study*, 114–15; Bauer, *Structure of Matthew's Gospel*, 17). Also see Norman R. Petersen, *Literary Criticism for New Testament Critics*, GBS (Philadelphia: Fortress, 1978), 55–80; Dewey, *Markan Public Debate*, 32; Gérard Genette, *Narrative Discourse: An Essay in Method*, trans. Jane E. Lewin (Ithaca, NY: Cornell University Press, 1980), 75–76; Robert M. Fowler, *Loaves and Fishes: The Function of the Feeding Stories in the Gospel of Mark*, SBLDS 54 (Chico, CA: Scholars Press, 1981), 170; Culpepper, *Anatomy of the Fourth Gospel*, 89.

13. **Instrumentation** is the movement from means to end.[38]
14. **Interchange** is the exchanging or alternation of certain elements in an a-b-a-b arrangement to strengthen contrasts or comparisons.[39]
15. **Inclusio** is the repetition of words or phrases at the beginning and end of a unit, thus creating a bracket effect to establish the main thought or concern of the book or passage.[40]
16. **Chiasm** is the repetition of elements in inverted order: a-b-b'-a'. Sometimes chiasm has a middle element, in which case the order would be a-b-c-b'-a'.[41]
17. **Intercalation** is the insertion of one literary unit in the midst of another literary unit (a-b-a).[42]

---

[38] Bauer and Traina identify two forms of instrumentation: the statement of purpose (e.g., John 20:31 as a purpose statement pertaining to the entire Gospel) and the description of means (e.g., the book of Hebrews is structured according to the recurrence of instrumentation: the book repeatedly emphasizes atonement by means of Christ's sacrificial work; *Inductive Bible Study*, 115; Bauer, *Structure of Matthew's Gospel*, 16–17). Indeed, many commentators agree with Bauer and Traina's observation (e.g., George R. Beasley-Murray, *John*, 2nd ed., WBC 36 [Dallas: Word, 1999], 416). On instrumentation, see also Charles H. Talbert, *Reading Luke: A Literary and Theological Commentary on the Third Gospel* (New York: Crossroad, 1982), 9–10; Culpepper, *Anatomy of the Fourth Gospel*, 201.

[39] Bauer and Traina give examples from the book of Micah and Hebrews. In Micah, declarations of guilt and judgment of Israel (1:2b–2:11; 3:1b–12; 6:1b–7:10) and promises of the restoration of the righteous remnant of Israel (2:12–13; 4:1–5:15; 7:11–20) are alternated in an a-b-a-b pattern. In Hebrews theological argument (1:1–4; 2:14–3:6; 4:1–5:14; 7:1–10:18) and blocks of exhortations (2:1–13; 3:7–19; 6:1–20; 10:19–13:17) are arranged interchangeably (*Inductive Bible Study*, 116–17; Bauer, *Structure of Matthew's Gospel*, 18). Many scholars indeed note a similar observation. For instance, regarding the interchange in the book of Micah, see Gordon J. McConville, "Micah, Book Of," *Dictionary of the Old Testament: Prophets*, 544–54; Elizabeth R. Achtemeier, *Minor Prophets I*, NIBCOT 17 (Peabody, MA: Hendrickson, 1996), 288; Delbert R. Hillers, *Micah*, Hermeneia (Philadelphia: Fortress, 1984), 8.

[40] Bauer and Traina list Ps 8:1 and 8:9 and Matt 19:30 and 20:16 as some examples of *inclusio* (*Inductive Bible Study*, 117–18; Bauer, *Structure of Matthew's Gospel*, 18); see also Bauer's comment on *inclusio* in Matt 1:23 and 28:20 (ibid., 109–28). Also see Charles H. Lohr, "Oral Techniques in the Gospel of Matthew," *CBQ* 23 (1961): 403–35; Muilenburg, *Form Criticism and Beyond*, 9–10; Dewey, *Markan Public Debate*, 31; Richard N. Soulen, *Handbook of Biblical Criticism*, 2nd ed. (Atlanta: John Knox, 1981), 94; David E. Aune, "Inclusio," in *The Westminster Dictionary of New Testament and Early Christian Literature and Rhetoric* (Louisville: Westminster John Knox, 2003), 229; Tremper Longman III., "Inclusio," *Dictionary of the Old Testament: Wisdom, Poetry & Writings*, 323–25; Resseguie, *Narrative Criticism*, 57–58.

[41] Bauer and Traina, *Inductive Bible Study*, 118–21; Bauer, *Structure of Matthew's Gospel*, 18. Also see John W. Welch, *Chiasmus in Antiquity: Structures, Analyses, Exegesis* (Hildesheim: Gerstenberg, 1981); Nils Wilhelm Lund, *Chiasmus in the New Testament: A Study in the Form and Function of Chiastic Structures* (Peabody, MA: Hendrickson, 1992); John Breck, *The Shape of Biblical Language: Chiasmus in the Scriptures and Beyond* (Crestwood, NY: St. Vladimir's Seminary Press, 1994); Aune, "Chiasmus," in W*estminster Dictionary*, 93–96; Craig Arnold Smith, "Criteria for Identifying Chiasm of Design in New Testament Literature: Objective Means of Distinguishing Chiasm of Design from Accidental and False Chiasm" (PhD diss., University of Bristol, 2009).

[42] Bauer and Traina give some examples: Mark's intercalation of 5:25–34 into 5:21–24 and 35–43; 6:14–29 into 6:7–13 and 30–31; 11:15–19 into 11:12–24 and 20–24. Likewise, Gen 38 is inserted into the story of Joseph between ch. 37 and chs 39–50 (*Inductive Bible Study*, 121–22; Bauer, *Structure of Matthew's Gospel*, 18–19). For a detailed examination of the intercalation of Gen 38, see Robert Alter, *The Art of Biblical Narrative* (New York: Basic Books, 1981), 3–10. On Markan intercalations, see Achtemeier, *Mark*, 23–26, 32–33; Fowler, *Loaves and Fishes*, 165; Dewey, *Markan Public Debate*, 34; R. T. France, *The Gospel of Mark*, NIGTC (Grand Rapids: Eerdmans, 2002), 15–20.

Bauer and Traina group MSRs into three major categories: recurrence structure (recurrence), semantic structures (contrast, comparison, climax, particularization, generalization, causation, substantiation, cruciality, summarization, interrogation, preparation/realization, and instrumentation), and rhetorical structures (interchange, *inclusio*, chiasm, and intercalation).[43] Recurrence is employed to indicate emphasis, develop a theme or concept, inviting interpreters to understand individual occurrences in light of the other occurrences or the recurring pattern as a whole.[44] Bauer and Traina further explain regarding semantic and rhetorical structures as follows:

> Semantic structures are characterized by binary or twofold progression employed to indicate sense connection: movement from something to something.[45]

> Rhetorical structures pertain to "the arrangement of material within the text.... Because writers typically employ structural features to communicate meaning ... [they] typically combine a rhetorical relationship with a semantic relationship in order to strengthen (and perhaps develop) that semantic relationship."[46]

Thus, one should note the interrelationship between semantic and rhetorical structures.

Having described categories of structural relationships, several features pertaining to MSRs are worthy of note. First, structural relationships are present on all levels of literature: "They are found not only on the book level but also on the level of the division, section, segment, paragraph, and even sentence."[47] Second, "by their nature some relationships are more general, less precise, or less specific than others."[48] However, one should identify the most specific relationship present in the passage under observation.[49] Third, "a structural relationship may be either explicit or implicit."[50]

---

[43] Bauer and Traina admit, "In a sense, the specific designations 'recurrence,' 'semantic,' and 'rhetorical' are somewhat arbitrary; other terms might be used to differentiate these types of structures" (*Inductive Bible Study*, 95). However, they also note "This terminology does reflect the language used by some practitioners of discourse analysis when describing these types of structural relationships" (ibid.), citing Joseph E. Grimes, *The Thread of Discourse*, Janua Linguarum Series Minor 207 (Hague: Mouton, 1975), 207–10; Eugene A. Nida, *Exploring Semantic Structures*, International Library of General Linguistics 11 (Munich: Fink, 1975), 50–65; John Beekman, John Callow, and Michael Kopesec, *The Semantic Structure of Written Communication*, 5th ed. (Dallas: Summer Institute of Linguistics, 1981), 112–13.

[44] Bauer and Traina, *Inductive Bible Study*, 96–97.

[45] Ibid., 97.

[46] Ibid., 116. For instance, the aforementioned interchange structure in the book of Micah strengthens the contrast between guilt and judgement of Israel and promises of the restoration of the righteous remnant of Israel. Concerning the *inclusio* between Matt 1:23 and 28:20, it seems used in combination with climax: The book is characterized by the presence of Jesus Christ from the beginning in 1:23, which reaches its ultimate climax in the Great Commission in 28:18–20, especially in the promise of continuing presence in 28:20 (ibid., 116–22).

[47] Ibid., 122.

[48] Ibid.

[49] For instance, cruciality often involves recurrence of causation and contrast; however, when one finds a radical reversal caused by a pivot passage, one should identify such movement more precisely as cruciality than recurrence of causation and contrast. See more examples in ibid., 122–23; Bauer, *Structure of Matthew's Gospel*, 19.

[50] Bauer and Traina, *Inductive Bible Study*, 122.

Thus, implicit relationships must be inferred from the sense of the text.[51] Fourth, structural relationships may be simple or complex. Complex structural relationships are present when "one cannot describe the function of a relationship in a book or passage without at the same time talking about another one(s)."[52] Fifth, structural relationships can be either conscious or subconscious and intended or unintended by the author. However, since all material content is communicated by means of form, an analysis of the forms (i.e., the literary structures) helps one understand the content better regardless of the author's intention.[53]

1.2.4.2 Rationale for Major Structural Relationships

One may question why one should employ IBS categories of MSRs to investigate the literary structure of 2 Corinthians, or one could even critique my analysis as merely another attempt to impose those structural categories on the text. These are legitimate concerns that need to be addressed here. Most importantly, structural relationships or laws of composition are part of the human cognitive and communicative processes found in any sort of communication, including literature in various genres, oral communications of any sort, and art in all cultures and time periods.[54] Thus, scholars in various disciplines rightly emphasize the significance of understanding structural relationships or arrangement of materials for their investigation. For instance, the nineteenth-century art instruction of John Ruskin explained the importance of laws of composition in art, which later White and Kuist adopted in their instructions.[55] Ancient orators likewise understood the importance of arrangement in rhetorical speeches.[56] Richard L. Enos describes how Cicero, one of the most influential orators in the Greco-Roman world in the first century BCE, viewed rhetorical arrangement, stating "throughout his career Cicero saw the arrangement as central to the composition, believing that invention is localized, that ideas must be appropriate not only to the situation but also to the proper place within the discourse."[57] Narrative criticism also

---

[51] For instance, Greek conjunction, ἀλλά, often marks contrast and οὖν indicates causation. However, contrast can be present without ἀλλά, and causation can be found without οὖν. Thus, implicit relationships must be inferred from the sense of the text (ibid., 123; Bauer, *Structure of Matthew's Gospel*, 19).

[52] Bauer and Traina, *Inductive Bible Study*, 123 (e.g., recurrence of causation in the book of Amos as described above). See more examples in ibid., 123–24; Bauer, *Structure of Matthew's Gospel*, 19.

[53] Once again, "we can best understand what is said as we carefully analyze how it is said" (Bauer and Traina, *Inductive Bible Study*, 125).

[54] Bauer and Traina, *Inductive Bible Study*, 94; Thompson, *Bible Study That Works*, 41–42; Long, "Major Structural Relationships," 22–59.

[55] Long, "Major Structural Relationships," 27–29; John Ruskin, *The Elements of Drawing in Three Letters to Beginners* (London: Smith, Elder, and Company, 1857); John Ruskin, *The Elements of Drawing and the Elements of Perspective* (New York: Dutton, 1907); Kuist included Ruskin's abridged essay in *These Words Upon They Heart*, 161–81.

[56] Isocrates, *Soph.* 13.16–17; Aristotle, *Rhet.* 5; Quintilian *Inst.* 3.9.1–6. See Long's discussion on rhetorical disposition in *Ancient Rhetoric and Paul's Apology*, 71–96.

[57] Richard L. Enos, "Ciceronian Dispositio as an Architecture for Creativity in Composition: A Note for the Affirmative," *Rhetoric Review* 4 (1985): 109, cited in Long, *Ancient Rhetoric and Paul's Apology*, 71.

stresses rhetorical patterns or structural relations in its analysis.[58] Discourse analysis likewise underscores the significance of structure or patterns of organization as a key element in its analysis.[59]

In fact, one model of analyzing literary structure often overlaps with other approaches. Indeed, scholars have found intersections between IBS and other disciplines. For instance, Vernon K. Robbins, who has established socio-rhetorical interpretation (SRI), admits that interpreters' various construal of the literary structure will lead to highly informative insights. He further acknowledges that a number of strategies of analysis and interpretation in IBS commonly intersect with SRI.[60] Long investigated intersections between IBS categories of MSRs and vital relation within Conceptual Integration Theory.[61] Conceptual integration or blending, which emerged in the 1990s, is a basic cognitive instrument used to construe our realities, and vital relations within this theory serve as the core of meaning-making. Long found a corresponding affinity between vital relations and MSRs.

However, this study attempts to employ IBS categories of MSRs to show its effectiveness for the exegesis, for IBS discusses the ways in which literary structure informs the theological meaning of a biblical text more thoroughly and better than other works; thus, this analytical model has great potential to serve as a better heuristic approach to observe and interpret the biblical text.

I would like to offer three bases for my attempt. First, MSRs are rooted in the history of exegesis. As this study has shown in the descriptions of MSRs, scholars commonly recognize and utilize similar structural relationships in their analysis of the text, although they do not always make explicit use of technical terminologies of MSRs. In addition, when Traina engaged in his development of the structural categories, he drew from Greek and Hebrew grammar to explain paragraphical relations by emphasizing key terms in English, such as "in order that" for purpose clauses, "so" and "then" for result clauses, and "but" for contrast, in order to observe both grammatical and literary relations, yet Traina was aware that literary structure transcends grammatical structure. Bauer further integrated key terms to help identify MSRs.[62] Thus, the identification of structural relationships does not aim to establish a new methodology or to prove the existence of those relationships. Rather, it explicates what exegetes have long engaged in the interpretation of the biblical text. The advantage of developing MSRs based on exegetical tradition is twofold. On the one hand, it prevents IBS from establishing

---

[58] E.g., Resseguie, *Narrative Criticism*, 41–86.
[59] E.g., Cynthia Long Westfall, *A Discourse Analysis of the Letter to the Hebrews: The Relationship Between Form and Meaning*, LNTS 297 (London: T&T Clark, 2005), 22–87.
[60] Vernon K. Robbins, "Sociorhetorical Interpretation (SRI) and Inductive Bible Study (IBS): Outlines of Mark, the Lord's Prayer, and the Son's Prayer in John 17," *The Journal of Inductive Biblical Studies* 1 (2014): 182–222.
[61] Long, "Vital Relations and Major Structural Relationships," 92–128.
[62] Idem, "Major Structural Relationships," 36–38; Traina, *Methodical Bible Study*, 40–55; Bauer and Traina, *Inductive Bible Study*, 94–126. Traina continuously drew his insights from the following works: H. E. Dana and Julius R. Mantey, *A Manual Grammar of the Greek New Testament* (New York: Macmillan, 1927); Wilhelm Gesenius, *Gesenius' Hebrew Grammar*, ed. E. Kautzsch, trans. A. E. Cowley, 2nd ed. (Oxford: Clarendon, 1910). While Traina did not specify which edition of *Gesenius' Hebrew Grammar*, I include the second English edition as his citation based on the availability of the book during the time of Traina.

subjective categories of MSRs. On the other hand, exegetical insights from an analysis of MSRs are directly related to the mainline exegetical tradition. Thus, it serves as a better heuristic approach to help interpreters engage in a dialogue with other scholars.[63]

Second, the scope of MSRs is broader and more comprehensive than other methodologies. As I have described, other methodologies, such as rhetorical and narrative criticism, underscore the importance of the literary structure in their analysis, but the rhetorical disposition is relevant to an analysis of speeches, and rhetorical patterns and structures in narrative criticism are usually applied to narratives.[64] In contrast, an analysis of MSRs is not limited to a certain type of literature but rather found in all kinds of genres and literature. Regarding 2 Corinthians, scholars have long recognized and debated over various types of literary genres of and within the letter, some of which include an analysis of rhetorical species (i.e., judicial, deliberative, and epideictic), epistolary types (e.g., apologetic and commendation), hardship catalogs (4:8–9; 6:3–10; 11:23–28), narrative-like passages (e.g., 1:8–11), and fool's speech (11:1–12:13). A number of scholars have attempted to identify these genres and investigate their literary structure according to their methodology (e.g., ancient rhetorical handbooks and epistolary handbooks). The problem is that scholars do not reach any consensus regarding identifications of those genres within 2 Corinthians. However, since MSRs are universally found in all sorts of communication and genres of literature, they will serve as a better heuristic approach to scrutinize the literary structure regardless of one's identification of specific genres of and within 2 Corinthians.

Third, an analytical model of MSRs in biblical interpretation emerged earlier than other models of literary structure and has been developed and refined by various scholars. As I have previously described, the discipline of IBS traces back to the founding of The Biblical Seminary in New York in 1900, and MSRs go back to John Ruskin's works in the mid-nineteenth century. In a sense, IBS categories of MSRs have influenced and given rise to some methodical approaches of literary structure. Indeed, linguists cited both Traina and Fuller's works in linguistic theoretical works in the 1970s and 1980s.[65] Furthermore, Mark Allan Powell adopted Bauer's categories of compositional relationships in his work of narrative criticism,[66] and James L. Resseguie

---

[63] For instance, Robbins describes some of the similar structural relationships in his SRI (*Exploring the Texture of Texts*, 7–39). However, he does not ground his descriptions of structural relationships in either Greek and Hebrew grammar or history of interpretation. As a result, his categories may be perceived as too subjective.

[64] See more detailed discussion on rhetorical criticism and narrative criticism in the Survey of Literature (Chapter 2).

[65] Long, "Major Structural Relationships," 42; Joseph E. Grimes states, "Daniel P. Fuller's characterization of the recursive relations that link both clauses and the textual units formed from linked clauses has been a major stimulus to this study" (*Thread of Discourse*, 20, see also 7, 107, 208). John Beekman, John C. Callow, and Michael F. Kopesec acknowledge both Traina and Fuller in their bibliography (*Semantic Structure*). Today four major schools of discourse analysis are identified in the field of linguistics: Continental European Discourse Analysis, South African Discourse Analysis, the Summer Institute of Linguistics Discourse Analysis, and Systemic-Functional Linguistics. The North American model of the Summer Institute of Linguistics is concerned with the linguistics and Bible translations, which emerged in the 1960s, and Traina and Fuller's works have influenced their work.

[66] Powell, *What is Narrative Criticism?*, 32–33; cf. Bauer, *Structure of Matthew's Gospel*, 13–20.

cites Bauer's *The Structure of Matthew's Gospel* in his description of the rhetorical pattern of repetition in narrative criticism.[67]

For all these reasons, the employment of MSRs has great promise to serve as a better and effective analytical model to study the literary structure of 2 Corinthians. However, before reapplying these categories to 2 Corinthians, I will survey the history of research into the literary structure and the central theme of the letter.

---

[67] Resseguie, *Narrative Criticism*, 45n11.

2

Survey of the Literary Structure and the Central Theme of 2 Corinthians

Since one's proposal of the literary structure and the central theme of 2 Corinthians is, to some degree, methodologically determined, I will group the survey of the literature according to methodologies. In order to study the literary structure and the primary theme of 2 Corinthians, topical analysis often employs historical–critical methods, epistolary criticism makes use of epistolary features and types, rhetorical criticism stresses the role and function of both modern and ancient rhetoric, literary criticism emphasizes the narrative shapes and substructures of the given passage (narrative criticism) and the literary design of chiasm, and discourse analysis focuses on linguistic aspects.

The purpose of the survey is twofold. First, it justifies the need for the present study by showing a paucity of scholarly consensus on the literary structure and the central theme of the letter. Second, it attempts to show the need for a hermeneutical model that can incorporate findings of different methodologies so as to interpret the meaning of the biblical text. In other words, the survey will indicate the significance and relevance of insights from different methodologies, which an inductive and integrative approach should take into account for the study of the literary structure and the central theme of 2 Corinthians. Because of the limited space, the survey focuses on the works that bear direct insights into the literary structure and the primary message of the letter as a whole, and this study interacts with other relevant works in the following discussions in Chapters 3–8.

2.1 Literary Structure of 2 Corinthians

The survey of literature regarding the literary structure of 2 Corinthians generally reveals a few points. First, despite scholars often identifying similar units (1:1–2; 1:3–11; 1:12–2:13; 2:14–7:4 [and 6:14–7:1]; 7:5–16; 8:1–9:15; 10:1–13:10; and 13:11–13), no consensus regarding the overall structure of the letter has yet been reached. Second, while each methodology can bring unique insights, it cannot serve as a sole means to comprehend the literary structure. Third, the survey shows the significance and relevance of some aspects of the letter that an inductive approach should incorporate and integrate for the study of the literary structure: identification of themes and topics within the text, reconstructions of historical developments and issues, recognition of epistolary and rhetorical structures, awareness of literary design (i.e., chiasm), and attention to linguistic elements.

2.1.1 Topical Analysis

The majority of scholars in the history of interpretation of 2 Corinthians have approached the study of the literary structure according to topics or themes. One representative example is found in the discussion of partition theories. Since Johann S. Semler first proposed a hypothesis in 1776 that 2 Corinthians is composed of several distinct fragments,[1] a variety of partition theories have been suggested.[2] Hans Dieter Betz aptly summarizes the result of partition theories as follows: "Three kinds of observations seem to underlie whatever proposals are found in these works: (1) breaks in the train of thought, (2) discontinuities in reports of events, (3) sudden changes in the tone of the presentation."[3] Thus, these observations help partition theorists understand divisions of materials within the canonical 2 Corinthians by drawing boundaries between discrete topics and themes. Margaret E. Thrall provides a helpful taxonomy of partition hypotheses by categorizing them into three main theories. First, the letter is a compilation of two letters:

I.   Chs 1–9
II. Chs 10–13.

Second, 2 Corinthians is a compilation of three letters:

I.   Chs 1–8
II.   Ch. 9
III. Chs 10–13.

or more letters:

I.   1:1–2:13
II.   2:14–7:4 (and 6:14–7:1)
III. 7:5–16
IV.   Ch. 8
V.   Ch. 9
VI.   Chs 10–13.

---

[1] Johann S. Semler, *Paraphrasis II. Epistolae Ad Corinthios* (Halle: Hemmerde, 1776).
[2] See a summary of origin and development of partition theories and the discussion of the literary unity of the letter in Hans Dieter Betz, *2 Corinthians 8 and 9: A Commentary on Two Administrative Letters of the Apostle Paul*, ed. George W. MacRae, Hermeneia (Philadelphia: Fortress, 1985), 2–36; Margaret E. Thrall, *A Critical and Exegetical Commentary on the Second Epistle of the Corinthians*, 2 vols, ICC (London: T&T Clark, 1994), 1.3–49; Murray J. Harris, *The Second Epistle to the Corinthians*, NIGTC (Grand Rapids: Eerdmans, 2005), 8–51.
[3] Betz, *2 Corinthians 8 and 9*, 26.

Third, 1 Corinthians and 2 Corinthians are an intermixed composition of various fragments, which form multiple letters.[4]

Similarly, those espousing the literary unity of the letter commonly recognize discrete subjects and themes within 1:1–2; 1:3–11; 1:12–2:13; 2:14–7:4 (and 6:14–7:1); 7:5–16; 8:1–9:15; 10:1–13:10; and 13:11–13.[5] For instance, many recognize letter opening and closing (1:1–2, 3–8/3–11; 13:11–13), travel narrative (1:3–2:13; 7:5–16), themes related to apostolic office and ministry (2:14–7:4), a call for open hearts and purification (6:11–7:4), collection (8:1–9:15), and themes related to the defense of apostolic authority (10:1–13:10). Scholars using this approach often adopt an epistolary framework and apply historical–critical methodologies to identify historical issues behind each topic and the composition of the letter.[6]

---

[4] Thrall, *Second Epistle of the Corinthians*, 1:47–49. Thrall includes works of Johannes Weiss and Walter Schmithals in this category. However, I decided to omit their analyses of the literary structure due to two facts. First, their identification of units overlaps with some of those espousing three or more letters in 2 Corinthians. Second, as Weiss and Schmithal's proposals changed over the years, their influence on the following scholarship is limited compared to other scholars (see Harris, *Second Epistle to the Corinthians*, 8–10).

[5] Examples of works include Albert Klöpper, *Kommentar über das zweite Sendschreiben des Apostel Paulus an die Gemeinde Zu Korinth* (Berlin: Reimer, 1874); Adolf Hilgenfeld, *Historisch-Kritische Einleitung in Das Neue Testament* (Leipzig: Fues, 1875); Heinrich J. Holtzmann, "Das gegenseitige Verhältniss der beiden Korintherbriefe," *ZWT* 22 (1879): 455–92; C. F. Georg Heinrici, *Das zweite Sendschreiben Des Apostel Paulus an die Korinthier* (Berlin: Hertz, 1887); James Denney, *The Second Epistle to the Corinthians*, The Expositor's Bible (New York: Armstrong and Son, 1894); J. H. Bernard, "The Second Epistle to the Corinthians," in *The Expositor's Greek Testament*, ed. W. Robertson Nicoll, 7 vols (London: Hodder and Stoughton, 1903), 3:1–119; Philipp Bachmann, *Der zweite Brief des Paulus an die Korinther*, ed. Theodor Zahn, Kommentar zum Neuen Testament 8 (Leipzig: Deichert, 1909); Allan Menzies, *The Second Epistle of the Apostle Paul to the Corinthians: Introduction, Text, English Translation and Notes* (London: Macmillan, 1912); Adolf von Schlatter, *Paulus, der Bote Jesu: Eine Deutung seiner Briefe an die Korinther* (Stuttgart: Calwer, 1934); Ernest Bernard Allo, ed., *Saint Paul: Seconde Épître Aux Corinthiens* (Paris: Gabalda, 1937); Hans Lietzmann, *An die Korinther I–II*, HNT 9 (Tübingen: Mohr Siebeck, 1949); R. V. G. Tasker, *Second Epistle of Paul to the Corinthians: An Introduction and Commentary*, TNTC 8 (Grand Rapids: Eerdmans, 1958); Philip E. Hughes, *Paul's Second Epistle to the Corinthians*, NICNT (Grand Rapids: Eerdmans, 1962); W. H. Bates, "The Integrity of II Corinthians," *NTS* 12 (1965): 56–69; Niels Hyldahl, "Die Frage nach der literarischen Einheit des Zweiten Korintherbriefes," *ZNW* 64 (1973): 289–306; Frances M. Young and David F. Ford, *Meaning and Truth in 2 Corinthians* (Grand Rapids: Eerdmans, 1988); Frederick W. Danker, *II Corinthians*, ACNT (Minneapolis: Augsburg, 1989); Ben Witherington III., *Conflict and Community in Corinth: A Socio-Rhetorical Commentary on 1 and 2 Corinthians* (Grand Rapids: Eerdmans, 1995); Simon J. Kistemaker, *Exposition of the Second Epistle to the Corinthians*, New Testament Commentary (Grand Rapids: Baker, 1997); Paul W. Barnett, *The Second Epistle to the Corinthians*, NICNT (Grand Rapids: Eerdmans, 1997); James M. Scott, *2 Corinthians*, NIBCNT (Peabody, MA: Hendrickson, 1998); Jan Lambrecht, *Second Corinthians*, ed. Daniel J. Harrington, SP 8 (Collegeville, MN: Liturgical Press, 1999); David E. Garland, *2 Corinthians*, NAC 29 (Nashville: Broadman & Holman, 1999); Jerry W. McCant, *2 Corinthians*, Readings: A New Biblical Commentary (Sheffield: Sheffield Academic, 1999); Scott J. Hafemann, *2 Corinthians*, The NIV Application Commentary (Grand Rapids: Zondervan, 2000); Long, *Ancient Rhetoric and Paul's Apology*; Harris, *Second Epistle to the Corinthians*; Craig S. Keener, *1–2 Corinthians*, NCBC (Cambridge: Cambridge University Press, 2005); George H. Guthrie, *2 Corinthians*, BECNT (Grand Rapids: Baker Academic, 2015).

While partition theorists attribute these topics to historical settings and developments behind the letter, others provide counterarguments for the unity of the letter "based on deductions from (1) the underlying structure of Paul's thought, (2) reconstruction of the course of events, (3) Paul's psychological state at the time of composition" (Betz, *2 Corinthians 8 and 9*, 26).

[6] Also see discussions in epistolary criticism below.

Evaluation

The significance and relevance of insights through topical analysis to the study of the literary structure are twofold. First, its careful attention to topics and themes in each division and segment is commended. Whether one attributes them to a partition theory or literary unity, scholars frequently note similar topics in each division and segment. This study agrees with some of their observations. Second, it highlights the relevance of historical information. Topical analysis often reconstructs background information behind themes and topics. While the scholarly debates concerning the literary structure often concentrate on the issues pertaining to the unity of the letter, topical analysis aptly emphasizes the relevance of historical information in understanding the literary structure.

While this study appreciates various insights from topical analysis, a few weaknesses of this approach should be noted. First, a scarcity of agreements regarding historical issues requires interpreters to handle the information with caution. While the significance of the sociohistorical milieu from which the letter emerged is undeniable, scholarly reconstructions of historical issues continue to be the most debated and challenging discussions in the study of 2 Corinthians. For instance, endless proposals regarding identifications of Paul's opponents illustrate this point.[7] In addition, Betz raises a legitimate concern regarding the debates of partition theories, stating "None of these arguments operates at the level of the text itself, but on hypothetical constructions lying beneath the text."[8] As a result, ceaseless proposals over historical issues call for another methodology. For this reason, this study proposes that all the complex historical issues are best approached when we understand Paul's discourse in its literary context prior to examining its historical context.

Second, topical analysis often overlooks the significance of the material arrangement of Paul's discourse in understanding his theology. Except for some scholars who argue for an overarching theme of the letter using the historical–critical approach, as discussed later, the topical analysis often concentrates on historical issues behind each topic and theme rather than the ways in which the material arrangement informs the theology of 2 Corinthians. While historical information at times provides data to study the theology of the letter, the same difficulty of the historical reconstruction as discussed above calls for another methodology. Therefore, this study argues for the significance and relevance of the literary structure to the study of the theology of 2 Corinthians.

2.1.2 Epistolary Criticism

Epistolary criticism situates 2 Corinthians in the practice of ancient Greco–Roman letter-writing and provides interpreters with insights into the epistolary framework of

---

[7] At least more than twenty proposals have been made. See a summary of proposals in Victor Paul Furnish, *II Corinthians*, AB 32A (Garden City, NY: Doubleday, 1984), 48–54; Harris, *Second Epistle to the Corinthians*, 79–80.

[8] Betz, *2 Corinthians 8 and 9*, 26.

the letter. Many interpreters assume that 2 Corinthians consists of letter opening, letter body, and letter closing. Those espousing the unity of the letter often recognize 1:1–2, 1:1–8, or 1:1–11 to be the letter opening and 13:11–13 to be the letter closing.[9] Others who espouse the existence of separate letters within 2 Corinthians still assume an epistolary framework.[10] In addition, epistolary criticism recognizes common epistolary features such as thanksgiving formula and disclosure formula.

While most scholars adopt an epistolary framework in their analysis of the literary structure, Linda L. Belleville and Mark A. Seifrid propose that Paul's unique adaptation of epistolary structure departs from standard Greco-Roman epistolary conventions. In her monograph, Belleville first contends the overall structure of chs 1–7 as follows:

I.   Letter Opening (1:1–2)
II. Introductory Eulogy (1:3–7)
III. Body Opening (1:8–11)
IV. Body Middle (1:12–7:2)
V.   Body Closing (7:3–16).[11]

She later proposes in her commentary the structure of the entire letter as follows:

I.   Letter Opening (1:1–2)
II. Introductory Eulogy (1:3–7)
III. Body Opening (1:8–11)
IV. Body Middle (1:12–13:9)
V.   Body Closing (13:10–11)
VI. Letter Closing (13:12–14).[12]

---

[9] E.g., Keener, *1–2 Corinthians*, 156–58, 246–47; Ralph P. Martin, *2 Corinthians*, 2nd ed., WBC 40 (Grand Rapids: Zondervan Academic, 2014), 134, 690–91; Guthrie, *2 Corinthians*, 53–61, 649–55.

[10] For instance, Furnish, who espouses two separate letters (i.e., chs 1–9 and chs 10–13), understands 1:1–11 to be letter opening and 1:12–9:15 to be letter body of chs 1–9 and 10:1–13:10 to be letter body and 13:11–13[14] to be letter closing of chs 10–13 (*II Corinthians*). Also see some works related to epistolary criticism in the study of 2 Corinthians, Stanley N. Olson, "Confidence Expressions in Paul: Epistolary Conventions and the Purpose of 2 Corinthians" (PhD diss., Yale University, 1976); John T. Fitzgerald, "Paul, the Ancient Epistolary Theorists, and 2 Corinthians 10–13: The Purpose and Literary Genre of a Pauline Letter," in *Greeks, Romans, and Christians: Essays in Honor of Abraham J. Malherbe*, ed. Abraham J. Malherbe et al. (Minneapolis: Fortress, 1990), 190–200; Belleville, *Reflections of Glory: Paul's Polemical Use of the Moses-Doxa Tradition in 2 Corinthians 3.1–18*, JSNTSup 52 (Sheffield: JSOT Press, 1991); Margaret M. Mitchell, "New Testament Envoys in the Context of Greco-Roman Diplomatic and Epistolary Conventions: The Example of Timothy and Titus," *JBL* 111 (1992): 641–62; K. Yamada, "Epistolary Theoretical and Rhetorical Analyses of 2 Cor 1–9," *AJBI* 24 (1998): 83–116; Lee Ann Johnson, "The Epistolary Apostle: Paul's Response to the Challenge of the Corinthian Congregation" (PhD diss., University of St. Michael's College, 2002); Fredrick J. Long, *Ancient Rhetoric and Paul's Apology*; Ivar Vegge, *2 Corinthians – A Letter About Reconciliation: A Psychagogical, Epistolographical, and Rhetorical Analysis*, WUNT 2/239 (Tübingen: Mohr Siebeck, 2008).

[11] Belleville, *Reflections of Glory*, 104–69.

[12] Idem, *2 Corinthians*, The IVP New Testament Commentary (Downers Grove, IL: InterVarsity Press, 1996), 21–22.

Similarly, Seifrid offers that the structure of the letter is as follows:

I.   The Opening of the Letter (1:1–2:17)
II. The Body of the Letter (3:1–7:16)
III. The Closing of the Letter (8:1–13:14).[13]

Seifrid explains, "The closings of Paul's letters are marked by a shift from the theme of the body to a reference to Paul's next contact with the church, either through representatives or by a visit of his own."[14] While many recognize the presence of letter opening and closing, Belleville and Seifrid observe the closing section of the letter to be more expansive: Seifrid identifies 8:1–13:14 to be the closing of the letter; Belleville recognizes the existence of two body-closing sections in 7:3–16 and 13:10–11.[15]

Evaluation

Epistolary criticism provides historical evidence to the study of the literary structure, especially regarding the letter's opening and closing based on an analysis of extant ancient Greco–Roman letters. In addition, its recognition of epistolary features, such as confidence formula, disclosure formula, and thanksgiving formula, helps interpreters identify boundaries between some small units.[16] However, epistolary criticism raises a couple of concerns as well.

First, while recognition of epistolary conventions is significant in the study of the literary structure, the epistolary structure provides only a broad understanding of the literary structure of 2 Corinthians (i.e., letter opening, letter body, and letter closing). Thus, its insights into understanding the details of the literary structure, especially regarding the content of the letter body, are limited. Second, more specifically, Belleville and Seifrid's proposals suffer from the lack of historical evidence. While there may be possibilities of Paul's unique adaptation of the Greco–Roman conventions of letter writing, their identification of 7:3–16 and 13:10–11 as body closings (Belleville) or chs 8–13 as letter closing (Seifrid) goes beyond the historical evidence that epistolary criticism can offer. Thus, their proposals remain only possibilities and require further studies. Therefore, the limitation of epistolary criticism calls for an integrative approach to the study of the literary structure.

2.1.3 Rhetorical Criticism

Rhetorical criticism approaches the letter with a concern for the larger social context of communication between the rhetor and audience.[17] Scholars using this approach

---

[13] Mark A. Seifrid, *The Second Letter to the Corinthians*, The Pillar New Testament Commentary (Grand Rapids: Eerdmans, 2014), v–viii.
[14] Ibid., 314.
[15] Belleville, *Reflections of Glory*, 169; idem, *2 Corinthians*, 21.
[16] On confidence formula, see Olson, "Confidence Expressions in Paul"; Vegge, *2 Corinthians*.
[17] Rhetorical criticism is connected to and sometimes discussed under the discipline of literary analysis. See the relation between rhetorical and literary criticism in Margaret M. Mitchell, "Rhetorical and New Literary Criticism," in *The Oxford Handbook of Biblical Studies*, ed. J. W. Rogerson and Judith Lieu (Oxford: Oxford University Press, 2006), 615–33.

analyze the ways in which the rhetor's techniques function to persuade the audience to accept the purpose of the speech. Thus, rhetorical approaches attempt to read the text of 2 Corinthians alongside the ancient rhetorical handbooks, ancient speech exemplars, and modern rhetoric, thus identifying rhetorical features and structures in light of them.[18]

While most scholars have applied the rhetorical approach to a portion of 2 Corinthians, some scholars espousing a compositional unity have proposed the literary structures of the entire letter based on their rhetorical analysis.

2.1.3.1 Ben Witherington III

Ben Witherington III identifies the letter as an example of ancient forensic or judicial rhetoric and analyzes the structure as follows:

I. Epistolary Prescript (1:1–2)
II. Epistolary Thanksgiving and *Exordium* (1:3–7)
III. *Narratio* (1:8–2:16)
IV. *Propositio* (2:17)
V. *Probatio* (*refutatio*) (3:1–13:4)
    A. Argument I (3:1–6:13)
        1. Division 1 (3:1–18)
        2. Division 2 (4:1–5:10)
        3. Division 3 (5:11–6:2)
        4. Division 4 (6:3–13)
    B. Argument II: Digression (6:14–7:1)
    C. Argument III (7:2–16)
    D. Argument IV (8:1–9:15)
    E. Argument V (10:1–13:4)
        1. Division 1 (10:1–18)
        2. Division 2 (11:1–12:10)
        3. Division 3 (12:11–13:4)
VI. *Peroratio* (13:5–10)
VII. Closing Epistolary Greetings and Remarks (13:11–13).[19]

---

[18] See overviews of rhetorical criticism in G. Walter Hansen, "Rhetorical Criticism," *DPL*, 822–26; Dennis L. Stamps, "Rhetoric," *DNTB*, 953–59. For further information see Kennedy, *New Testament Interpretation Through Rhetorical Criticism*; Burton L. Mack, *Rhetoric and the New Testament*, GBS (Minneapolis: Fortress, 1989); Stanley E. Porter, ed., *Handbook of Classical Rhetoric in the Hellenistic Period, 330 B.C.–A.D. 400* (Leiden: Brill, 1997); Carl Joachim Classen, *Rhetorical Criticism of the New Testament* (Boston: Brill, 2002); Duane F. Watson, *The Rhetoric of the New Testament: A Bibliographic Survey*, Tools for Biblical Study 8 (Blandford Forum, UK: Deo, 2006); Stanley E. Porter and Dennis L. Stamps, eds., *Rhetorical Criticism and the Bible*, JSNTSup 195 (London: Sheffield Academic, 2002); Ben Witherington III, *New Testament Rhetoric: An Introductory Guide to the Art of Persuasion in and of the New Testament* (Eugene, OR: Cascade, 2009); Stanley E. Porter, ed., *Paul and Ancient Rhetoric: Theory and Practice in the Hellenistic Context* (New York: Cambridge University Press, 2016).
[19] Witherington, *Conflict and Community in Corinth*, viii–ix.

The strength of Witherington's analysis of the literary structure is that while he recognizes distinct topics within each division and segment, he attempts to show organic connections between these topics by grouping them together under each rhetorical structure (i.e., *exordium, narratio, propositio, probatio,* and *peroratio*). This study agrees with some of the observations as discussed in detail in chs 3–8.

However, this study disagrees with some of his analyses. For instance, contrary to the majority of scholars, Witherington does not view 2:14 as marking the beginning of a new unit; instead, he identifies 1:8–2:16 as *narratio*. However, as Thrall argues, 2:14 clearly marks a new beginning of a section as an introductory thanksgiving, and Witherington indeed admits the transition by citing and commenting on her work.[20] It would be more plausible to argue 1:8–2:13 as *narratio* and 2:14–17 as *propositio*; yet, he identifies 2:17 as *propositio*, which necessitates the preceding material (1:8–2:16) to be identified as *narratio* according to the convention of the ancient rhetoric (i.e., *propositio* usually follows *narratio*; e.g., Quintilian, *Inst.* 4.2.), though 2:14–16 is clearly a part of the thanksgiving. Thus, this study contends that 2:14 is the beginning of a new section, viewing 2:14–17 as the thesis statement of the letter.

2.1.3.2 Fredrick J. Long

Fredrick J. Long further advances Witherington's study by arguing that 2 Corinthians is a rhetorically unified apology that draws on the Greco-Roman forensic tradition including the Greco-Roman rhetorical handbooks, speech exemplars, letters, and educational exercises. He identifies the structure of the letter as follows:

I. Epistolary opening (1:1–2)
II. *Prooemium* (1:3–7)
III. *Narratio* (1:8–16; 2:12–13; 7:2–16)
IV. *Divisio* and *partitio* (1:17–24)
V. *Probatio* (2:1–9:15)
    A. (2:1–11)
    B. (2:14–3:18)
    C. (4:1–5:10)
    D. (5:11–7:1)
    E. (8:1–9:15)
VI. *Refutatio* (10:1–11:15)
VII. Self-adulation (11:16–12:10)
VIII. *Peroratio* (12:11–13:10)
IX. Epistolary closing (13:11–13).[21]

---

[20] Margaret E. Thrall, "A Second Thanksgiving Period in II Corinthians," *JSNT* 16 (1982): 101–24; Witherington, *Conflict and Community in Corinth*, 365.

[21] Long, *Ancient Rhetoric*, 143–45, 165; Long also recently published an article to show correlations of the literary structure of 2 Corinthians between IBS and rhetorical analysis ("2 Corinthians," in *Discourse Analysis of the New Testament Writings*, ed. Todd A. Scacewater [Dallas: Fontes, 2020], 261–95). For the details and evaluation of his identification of the structure of 2 Corinthians, see my discussion in chs 3–8.

While I commend Long's well-documented evidence that makes a plausible connection between 2 Corinthians and ancient rhetorical tradition, I will offer some disagreements with his analysis. Long identifies 1:17–24 as *divisio* and *partitio* (i.e., thesis with several heads), for the passage reflects several distinctive features of *partitio* observed in the ancient rhetorical tradition:

1. It follows *narratio*;
2. it is frequently dialectically formulated;
3. it sometimes contains rhetorical questions;
4. it can include several argument heads;
5. these heads usually outline the *probatio* in the same order;
6. the *partitio* in actual speeches is subtle.[22]

Thus, according to these features, he attempts to demonstrate the ways in which Paul's argument in 1:17–24 follows the ancient rhetorical tradition.[23] However, I identify 2:14–17 as the thesis statement of the letter. While Long notes how 2:14–17 breaks the principle of the *partitio* (e.g., 2:14–17 does not outline the *probatio* in the same order), concluding 2:14–17 as a general statement for the argument in 2:14–3:18, he does not mention the similarities between 1:17–24 and 2:14–17, which suggests the plausibility of 2:14–17 being the thesis statement. Both come after a narrative (1:8–16; 2:12–13) and contain a rhetorical question (1:17; 2:16b). Furthermore, 2:14–17 includes argument heads, and I will argue in detail in Chapter 5 that 2:14–17 outlines the major theme regarding the agents in ministry developed in 3:1–13:10 in a clearer fashion than 1:17–24 does. However, Long does not think that the explicit argument heads in 2:14–17 serve as evidence for these verses to be the thesis statement because the ancient speech exemplars show subtleness regarding corresponding key terms and themes between the *partitio* and *probation*.[24] However, Long himself admits, "In theory *partitio* heads should be explicit – but in actual speeches this is the exception rather than the rule."[25] In other words, ancient rhetorical theory indeed prefers to have explicit argument heads in *partitio*; the paucity of examples that reflect the theory should not invalidate the instruction. Therefore, I argue that the ancient rhetorical theory actually supports the identification of 2:14–17 as the thesis statement of the letter. Even if one denies such a claim, it is hard to ignore that the literary context reveals the significant interconnections between the thesis statement in 2:14–17 and the rest of the letter in 3:1–13:10, as I will demonstrate in Chapter 5.

Most importantly, in addition to the insights from rhetorical criticism, other pieces of evidence from multifarious methodologies, such as topical analysis and epistolary criticism, suggest 2:14–17 as the thesis statement (see Chapter 5).[26] Therefore, while I

---

[22] Ibid., 85–89; 157.
[23] Ibid., 157–62.
[24] Ibid., 86, 157.
[25] Ibid., 85.
[26] For instance, Long himself recognizes that the processional theme in 2:14–17 is repeatedly found in chs 3–7. See his work, "'The God of This Age' (2 Cor 4:4) and Paul's Empire-Resisting Gospel," in *The First Urban Churches*, ed. James R. Harrison and Laurence L. Welborn, vol. 2 of WGRWSup 7 (Atlanta: SBL Press, 2016), 219–69.

appreciate Long's emphasis on the rhetorical disposition and I will incorporate the historical evidence into my analysis, this study will argue that the inductive and integrative approach is more advantageous in scrutinizing the literary structure of 2 Corinthians.

2.1.3.3 Jerry W. McCant

Third, Jerry W. McCant contends that 2 Corinthians is a parodic defense. He postulates that the letter was written in the form of judicial rhetoric, but it functioned like epideictic rhetoric because parody subverts the expectations of judicial rhetoric. Thus, he identifies the structure as follows:

I. Parodic Defense of Behavior (chs 1–7)
    A. Epistolary Greeting (1:1–2)
    B. A Congratulatory Benediction (1:3–7)
    C. An Emotional Appeal (1:8–11)
    D. Paul's Side of the Story (1:12–2:17)
    E. Letters of Commendation (3:1–6:13)
    F. A Digression for Shame (6:14–7:1)
    G. Report and Summation (7:2–16)
II. Parody of Benefaction (chs 8–9)
    A. An Exemplum (8:1–5)
    B. An Appeal to Corinth (8:6–15)
    C. A Letter of Commendation (8:16–24)
    D. A Challenge to Honor (9:1–5)
    E. A Theology of Benevolence (9:6–15)
III. A Parodic Defense of Authority (chs 10–13)
    A. "Defense" of Apostolic Authority (10:1–18)
    B. The Foolishness of Boasting (11:1–12:18)
    C. Paul's Final Word to Corinth (12:19–13:13).[27]

While McCant rightly recognizes some divisions (e.g., chs 8–9 and 10–13), his analysis of the literary structure does not best represent the sense of the literary context. For instance, he identifies 6:14–7:1 as a digression. However, the passage is integral to and congruous with both his immediate and larger discourse in the letter.[28] Moreover, the inclusion of 12:14–18 into 11:1–12:13 does not do justice to the flow of the literary context: Paul clearly begins a new topic regarding his third visit to the Corinthians in 12:14.[29]

---

[27] McCant, *2 Corinthians*, 7.
[28] See my discussion in 6.2.1.
[29] See my discussion in 8.1.1.

2.1.3.4 J. David Hester Amador

Fourth, J. David Hester Amador analyzes the letter according to a rhetorical theory of dynamic argumentation based on the work of Chaïm Perelman and Lucie Olbrechts-Tyteca.[30] He identifies the structure as follows:

I. Introductory Unit (1:1–14)
   A. Letter Opening (1:1–2)
   B. Argument developing the *topos* of "affliction," with disclosure formula in 1:8–11 (1:3–11)
   C. Letter *causa* or *propositio* concerning "boasting," "sincerity" and "frankness" (1:12–14)
II. Unit 1: Plans for Corinth and Achaia as They Relate to the Past (1:15–2:13)
   A. *Narratio* concerning the rhetor's trip to Macedonia (1:15–16)
   B. Justification through dissociation of human from divine standards (1:17–22)
   C. Previous visit "with grief" and decision, based on "confidence," to write "that I might know the results of your testing, whether you are obedient in everything" (1:23–2:11)
   D. *Narratio* (2:12–13)
III. Unit 2: Purpose of the Ministry as Related to the Present (2:14–7:4)
   A. Recap and variation of causa ("sincerity" in *causa*; 2:14–17)
   B. *Topos* of "confidence" through Christ to God in a new covenant proclaiming Jesus Christ as Lord (3:1–4:6)
   C. Dissociation of earthly weakness, with *topoi* of "confidence," "building up" (5:1) related to "affliction" through the promise of salvation (4:7–6:10)
   D. Peroration and extension of object of "sincerity" and "boasting" in "affliction" elaborated through an argument for separation based on the notion of righteousness in which the believer participates (6:11–7:4)
IV. Unit 3: Plans for Corinth and Achaia for the Future (7:5–9:15)
   A. *Narratio* (from 2:12–13) (7:5)
   B. Letter reception, with themes of "affliction," "proof," "boasting" and "confidence" (7:6–16)
   C. *Narratio* (from 7:5) (8:1–2)
   D. Argument from sharing and reciprocity (8:3–24)
   E. *Narratio* (from 8:2) (9:1)
   F. Argument from abundance and return (9:2–24)[31]

---

[30] Chaïm Perelman and Lucie Olbrechts-Tyteca drew upon both ancient rhetoric in the tradition of Aristotle's *Rhetoric* and modern social psychology and logic. See Chaïm Perelman and Lucie Olbrechts-Tyteca, *La Nouvelle Rhétorique: Traité de l'Argumentation* (Paris: Presses universitaires de France, 1958); idem, *The New Rhetoric: A Treatise on Argumentation*, trans. John Wilkinson and Purcell Weaver (Notre Dame: University of Notre Dame Press, 1969).
[31] Amador misquotes the range of the passage. See my comment below.

V. Unit 4: Apostolic Apologia (10:1–13:4)
   A. Boasting no longer in "you," but in "me" and "my authority" (10:1–18)
   B. Fool's speech (11:1–12:13)
   C. Apostolic parousia (12:14–13:4)
VI. Concluding Remarks (13:5–13)
   A. Closing appeal (13:5–9)
   B. Appeal to authority based on "building up" (13:10)
   C. Final appeals and salutations (13:11–13).[32]

The significance of Amador's work pertains to his careful attention to *narratio* references, which he argues "provide a narrative framework that ties together the various argumentative situations encountered throughout the greater argument" in chs 1–9.[33] Thus, he identifies the literary structure, especially that of chs 1–9, according to the narrative references.

However, some concerns arise from his analysis, which makes readers wonder if his analysis is more forced than fair to the literary context. First, he could have clarified what counts as *narratio*. He identifies narrative references in 1:8–9, 15–16, 2:12–13; 7:5–7; 8:1–2, 6, 16–19; 9:3, 5; 11:8–9; and 12:18,[34] explaining that verbs in these passages are in the aorist tense with a few exceptions.[35] However, this does not explain why he excludes some passages such as 2:1 and 2:3 from the *narratio*. Moreover, he identifies 9:1 as *narratio*, elucidating that 9:1 functions as a *paralepsis* figure drawing from the *narratio* in 8:1–2.[36] He does not, nevertheless, provide explanations to make a case for his analysis. Again, further explanations regarding the criteria of *narratio* would help readers understand his arguments better. Second, some recurring citation errors in his works are confusing to readers. For instance, he indicates 9:2–24 to be one of the units

---

[32] J. David Hester Amador, "The Unity of 2 Corinthians: A Test Case for a Re-Discovered and Re-Invented Rhetoric," *Neot* 33 (1999): 411–32; idem, "Revisiting 2 Corinthians: Rhetoric and the Case for Unity," *NTS* 46 (2000): 92–111; idem, "Re-Reading 2 Corinthians: A Rhetorical Approach," in *Rhetorical Argumentation in Biblical Texts: Essays from the Lund 2000 Conference*, ed. Anders Eriksson, Thomas H. Olbricht, and Walter G. Übelacker, Emory Studies in Early Christianity 8 (Harrisburg, PA: Trinity, 2002), 276–95.

[33] Amador, "Revisiting 2 Corinthians," 98.

[34] These passages describe the circumstances of Paul's travel intentions and experiences from Troas to Macedonia to Corinth.

[35] Ibid., 98. The exceptions include the verbs in perfect tenses (1:8–9; 2:13; 7:5); the verb in imperfect tense (1:15); the verb in the present tense (8:1). Regarding verb tenses, scholars such as Stanley E. Porter (*Verbal Aspect in the Greek of the New Testament: With Reference to Tense and Mood*, Studies in Biblical Greek 1 [New York: Lang, 1989]; idem, *Idioms of the Greek New Testament*, 2nd ed. [Sheffield: JSOT Press, 1999]) and Constantine R. Campbell (*Verbal Aspect and Non-Indicative Verbs: Further Soundings in the Greek of the New Testament*, Studies in Biblical Greek 15 [New York: Lang, 2008]) argue that authors' choice of a verb's tense-form conveys a particular perspective; thus, tense-forms do not communicate the time of action (cf. Daniel B. Wallace, *Greek Grammar Beyond the Basics: An Exegetical Syntax of the New Testament* [Grand Rapids: Zondervan, 1996], 494–512). However, as some indicate (e.g., Benjamin L. Merkle, "The Abused Aspect: Neglecting the Influence of a Verb's Lexical Meaning on Tense-Form Choice," *BBR* 26 [2016]: 57–74), both the traditional view and verbal aspect theory have strengths and weaknesses; thus, the consensus has not been reached among grammarians. This study tends toward the view that verbal tenses in indicative mood reflect time of action, supporting the traditional view.

[36] Ibid., 107, 110.

when ch. 9 consists of only 15 verses.[37] He identifies 13:10–14 as concluding remarks at the beginning of the 1999 article when the Greek text of 2 Corinthians ends with 13:13; furthermore, he later identifies 13:5–13 to be the conclusion in the same article. Neither his identification of the unit nor citation of the passage is consistent.[38]

2.1.3.5 Ivar Vegge

Fifth, Ivar Vegge analyzes the letter in light of the Hellenistic rhetorical, psychagogical, and epistolary tradition.[39] He emphasizes the epideictic nature of the letter, which does not follow the standard forensic rhetoric. He offers an outline of the letter as follows:

I. Letter Opening (1:1–11)
   A. Address (1:1–2)
   B. Thanksgiving (1:3–11)
II. Letter Body (1:12–13:10)
   A. Thesis Statement for the Letter (1:12–14)
   B. Apology and Appeals for Reconciliation (1:15–7:16)
     1. Apology concerning travel plans & the tearful letter (1:15–2:4)
     2. Attempt to foster reconciliation by restoring the offender (2:5–11)
     3. Travel narrative (2:12–13)
     4. Apology for Paul's ministry & appeals for reconciliation (2:14–7:4)
     5. Travel narrative continued (7:5)
     6. Idealized description of reconciliation functioning as an implicit appeal for full reconciliation (7:5–16)
   C. Appeal to Complete the Collection and for Full Reconciliation (2 Cor 8–9)
   D. A New "Tearful Letter" (2 Cor 10:1–13:10)
     1. Gentleness and harshness as alternative ways of coming to Corinth (10:1–11)
     2. A comparison (*synkrisis*) of Paul and the opponents (10:12–18)
     3. The "fool's speech" (11:1–12:18)
     4. Not an apology but a letter for the Corinthians' "edification" (12:19–21)
     5. Last warnings before coming (13:1–10).
III. Letter Closing (13:11–14).[40]

The significance of Vegge's work is that he does not view each division and segment as a separate entity; rather, he recognizes their interconnections in the letter regarding the theme of reconciliation. In other words, Vegge understands the importance and relevance of the literary structure for the theology of the letter. While this study agrees with some of his identification of the division of the letter, some disagreements must

---

[37] Ibid., 110.
[38] Idem, "The Unity of 2 Corinthians," 414, 416. Also, he makes some changes in his works: while he identifies 9:1–2 as *paralepsis* in both of his 1999 article and 2000 article, he identifies 9:2 as *narratio* in the 1999 article and 9:1 as *narratio* in the 2000 article.
[39] Vegge, *2 Corinthians*.
[40] Ibid., 374–75.

be noted.⁴¹ For instance, Vegge analyzes 1:3-11 as an introductory thanksgiving.⁴² He argues that the word, εὐχαριστέω, in 1:11 is a positive indication that 1:8-11 belongs to the thanksgiving in 1:3-7, although he admits a division between 1:3-7 and 8-11.⁴³ However, a disclosure formula and the Greek conjunction γάρ in 1:8 indicate that 1:8-11 introduces another topic that substantiates the description of God's character in 1:3-7.⁴⁴ Furthermore, Vegge overlooks the fact that 2:14-17 introduces many themes that are developed in 3:1-13:10, although he acknowledges that 2:14-17 does introduce some of the main themes in 3:1-6:10.⁴⁵

2.1.3.6 Evaluation

Rhetorical criticism provides important observations to the study of the literary structure of 2 Corinthians. First, it highlights potential influences from which Paul developed his arrangement of discourse materials based on its species (judicial, deliberative, and epideictic), rhetorical features, and argumentative strategies. Second, it offers historical evidence that situates the study of the literary structure in the ancient Greco-Roman rhetorical tradition and practice.

However, rhetorical criticism also involves some challenges. First, scholars using rhetorical analysis disagree with one another regarding the identification of the structure. As shown previously, scholars who espouse a compositional unity of the letter neither agree on major divisions of the letter nor share a common understanding of significant rhetorical elements. For instance, Witherington identifies 2:17 to be the *propositio* of the letter, whereas Long understands 1:17-24 to be the *divisio* and *partitio* that outline the entire *probatio* in 2:1-9:15, and Amador and Vegge construe 1:12-14 to be a proposition of the letter. Moreover, one's understanding of rhetorical structure depends on a prior understanding of the unity of the letter.⁴⁶

---

⁴¹ Note that agreement with the identification of the division of the letter must be differentiated from the agreement with the ways in which each division and segment are related to one another (i.e., MSRs). For instance, Vegge and I agree with the recognition of chs 8-9 to be a distinct literary unit; however, I do not view the relationships between chs 8-9 and 1-7 in terms of the theme of reconciliation, as Vegge argues. See more discussions on the evaluation of Vegge's work in 2.2.3.4.
⁴² Vegge, *2 Corinthians*, 150-53.
⁴³ Ibid.
⁴⁴ See more discussions in ch. 4.
⁴⁵ Vagge, *2 Corinthians*, 1.
⁴⁶ For instance, George A. Kennedy, who was a classicist and the first one to provide a methodology to use the Greco-Roman rhetoric for the analysis of the NT texts, understands chs 1-7, 8-9, and 10-13 to be different letters (*New Testament Interpretation Through Rhetorical Criticism* [Chapel Hill: University of North Carolina Press, 1984], 86-96), and Hans Dieter Betz, whose commentaries sparked a new trend in commentary writing with rhetorical analysis, construed 2 Cor 8-9 an independent letter (*2 Corinthians 8 and 9*). Also see Hans-Michael Wünsch, *Der paulinische Brief 2 Kor 1-9 als ommunikative Handlung: Eine rhetorisch-iteraturwissenschaftliche Untersuchung*, Theologie 4 (Munster: LIT, 1996); K. Yamada, "Epistolary Theoretical and Rhetorical Analyses," 83-116; Brian K. Peterson, *Eloquence and the Proclamation of the Gospel in Corinth*, SBLDS 163 (Atlanta: Scholars Press, 1998); J. Paul Sampley, "Paul, His Opponents in 2 Corinthians 10-13, and the Rhetorical Handbooks," in *The Social World of Formative Christianity and Judaism: Essays in Tribute to Howard Clark Kee*, ed. Jacob Neusner et al. (Philadelphia: Fortress, 1988), 162-77; Duane F. Watson, "Paul's Boasting in 2 Corinthians 10-13 as Defense of His Honor: A Socio-Rhetorical Analysis," in *Rhetorical Argumentation in Biblical Texts: Essays from the Lund 2000 Conference*, ed. Anders

Second, some methodological assumptions with which rhetorical criticism operates have invited ongoing scholarly debates until today. They include the extent of Paul's use of rhetoric, the presence of both deliberative (chs 8–9) and forensic speeches (especially chs 10–13) within 2 Corinthians, the lack of information about Paul's rhetorical training in the NT, and the discord between epistolary and rhetorical handbooks.[47]

Third, while the flexibility of rhetoric allows an exegete to fit different pieces of rhetorical elements into a coherent rhetorical argument,[48] the potential danger of imposing rhetorical structures on the biblical text always exists.[49] Thus, incorporating insights from other methodologies is advantageous for a better rendering of the structure.

2.1.4 Literary Criticism

Literary criticism is concerned with the final form of the text as a literary object. Thus, it focuses on the literary character of the text as presented in its final form rather than historical questions. Within literary criticism, narrative criticism and chiastic analysis are particularly relevant to the study of the literary structure of 2 Corinthians.

2.1.4.1 Narrative Criticism

Narrative criticism is an exegetical method that attends to literary qualities of biblical narratives.[50] As the term narrative criticism itself implies, the methodology is generally applied to narratives, yet some scholars have applied it to Pauline letters.[51] However, since narrative readings have been applied to a portion of the letter but not the entire

---

Eriksson, Thomas H. Olbricht, and Walter G. Übelacker (Harrisburg, PA: Trinity Press International, 2002), 260–75; Charles A. Wanamaker, "'By the Power of God': Rhetoric and Ideology in 2 Corinthians 10–13," in *Fabrics of Discourse: Essays in Honor of Vernon K. Robbins*, ed. David B. Gowler, L. Gregory Bloomquist, and Duane F. Watson (Harrisburg, PA: Trinity Press International, 2003), 194–221.

[47] E.g., Ryan S. Schellenberg's recent monograph that offers critiques against scholarly assumptions of Paul's rhetorical education (*Rethinking Paul's Rhetorical Education: Comparative Rhetoric and 2 Corinthians 10–13*, ECL 10 [Atlanta: Society of Biblical Literature, 2013]).

[48] See Witherington, *Conflict and Community in Corinth*, 77; Long, *Ancient Rhetoric and Paul's Apology*, 24–28.

[49] G. Walter Hansen rightly describes, "If such analysis leads to a preoccupation with form over substance, then rhetorical criticism may be an obstacle to understanding the meaning of Paul's letters" ("Rhetorical Criticism," *DPL*, 822–26).

[50] See overviews of narrative criticism in Powell, *What Is Narrative Criticism?*; Resseguie, *Narrative Criticism*.

[51] Richard B. Hays is one of the very first scholars who applied the narrative reading to a Pauline letter and aptly demonstrated the narrative substructure of Galatians (*The Faith of Jesus Christ: An Investigation of the Narrative Substructure of Galatians 3:1-4:11*, SBLDS 56 [Chico, CA: Scholars Press, 1983]). See other works of narrative criticism on Pauline epistles, Norman R. Petersen, *Rediscovering Paul: Philemon and the Sociology of Paul's Narrative World* (Philadelphia: Fortress, 1985); Corneliu Constantineanu, *The Social Significance of Reconciliation in Paul's Theology: Narrative Readings in Romans*, LNTS 421 (London: T&T Clark, 2010); cf. Ben Witherington III, *Paul's Narrative Thought World: The Tapestry of Tragedy and Triumph* (Louisville: Westminster John Knox, 1994).

letter, their insights are mostly relevant to subunits of the literary structure.[52] Thus, their works are dealt with in Chapters 3–8.

One significant insight of narrative criticism is its emphasis on the literary qualities of the NT. Attentive observations of key aspects of the text, such as reader, rhetoric, setting, point of view, plot, and characterization, help one identify main units and subunits of the given passages and observe the ways in which materials are related.[53]

One fundamental weakness of narrative criticism regarding the study of the literary structure pertains to its application to the letters. While some parts of 2 Corinthians are more narrative-like (e.g., 1:8–11) than other parts, applying narrative readings to a text that is not fundamentally a narrative requires tweaking of some aspects of the narrative criticism. In order to accomplish their goal, scholars generally reconstruct a narrative world implied from the text and apply some aspects of narrative criticism to this reconstructed world. However, their "narrative" is a scholarly reconstruction, and one should not equate the text with their reconstructed narrative. While narrative readings can be useful to learn a substructure of a given passage, their insights into the understanding of the literary structure are limited.

2.1.4.2 Analysis Based on Chiastic Structure

Others present the literary structure of 2 Corinthians based on a chiastic structure. Chiasm or chiasmus is the repetition of the same elements in inverted order such as a-b-b'-a' or a-b-c-b'-a', resembling the Greek letter X.[54] While many provide analyses of chiastic structures for a portion of the letter,[55] Giuseppe Segalla outlines the entire letter according to a chiasm in order to defend the unity of the letter as follows:

A. *Prologo* (1:1–11): 1, 2–3.7/13, 11–13
    B. *Apologia della gloria di Paolo* (1, 12–7, 16):

---

[52] Some of the works on 2 Corinthians include Paul Brooks Duff, "2 Corinthians 1–7: Sidestepping the Division Hypothesis Dilemma," *BTB* 24 (1994): 16–26; Kar Yong Lim, *"The Sufferings of Christ Are Abundant in Us" (2 Corinthians 1:5): A Narrative-Dynamics Investigation of Paul's Sufferings in 2 Corinthians*, LNTS 399 (London: T&T Clark, 2009); Ma. Marilous S. Ibita, "The Unity of Paul's Narrative World in 2 Corinthians 1–7: N. Petersen's Narrative-Critical Approach and the Coherence of 2 Corinthians," in *Theologizing in the Corinthian Conflict: Studies in the Exegesis and Theology of 2 Corinthians*, ed. Reimund Bieringer et al., BTS 16 (Leuven: Peeters, 2013), 17–42; Mason Lee, "'Now Is the Acceptable Time; Now Is the Day of Salvation': Reading 2 Corinthians 5:11–6:2 in Light of Its Narrative Structure," *ResQ* 56 (2014): 1–13.
[53] See Powell, *What is Narrative Criticism?*, 23–84; Resseguie, *Narrative Criticism*, 41–240.
[54] David R. Bauer, "Chiasm," *NIDB* 1:587–88; the description of chiasm in 1.2.4.1. See also Welch, *Chiasmus in Antiquity*; Lund, *Chiasmus in the New Testament*; Breck, *Shape of Biblical Language*.
[55] See Craig L. Blomberg, "The Structure of 2 Corinthians 1–7," *CTR* 4 (1989): 3–20; Max-Alain Chevallier, "L' Argumentation de Paul Dans 2 Corinthiens 10 à 13," *RHPR* 70 (1990): 3–15; David E. Garland, *2 Corinthians*, 422–23; Guy Bonneau, "À La Vie, à La Mort: Le Conflit à Corinthe et Ses Enjeux Théologiques En 2 Co 2,14-7,4," *ScEs* 51 (1999): 351–66; cf. Philippe Rolland, "La Structure Littéraire de La Deuxième Épître Aux Corinthiens," *Bib* 71 (1990): 73–84. Also see the following works, which provide analyses of chiastic structures throughout 2 Corinthians: Jan Lambrecht, *Second Corinthians*; Fredrick J. Long, *2 Corinthians: A Handbook on the Greek Text*, Baylor Handbook on the Greek New Testament (Waco, TX: Baylor University Press, 2015).

a. Apologia di Paolo e Tito (1, 12–2, 13)
      b. Apologia polemica del ministero di Paolo (2, 14–4, 6)
         c. Escatologia presente e futura (4, 7–5, 10)
      b'. Apologia critica del ministero di Paolo (5, 11–7, 3)
   a'. Apologia di Paolo e Tito (7, 4–16)
   C. La grazia della colletta (8, 1–9, 15):
      a. La colletta: una grazia, una *diakonia*, un sopperire alla "indigenza dei santi" (8, 1–15)
         b. Missione di Tito e dei fratelli (8, 16–24)
         b'. Missione dei "fratelli" all' Acaia (9, 1–5)
      a'. La colletta: una grazia, una *diakonia*, e un sopperire alla "indigenza dei santi" (9, 6–15)
B'. L'apologia dell'autorità apostolica di Paolo (10, 1–13, 10):
   a. L'autorità di Paolo, difesa "per l'edificazione della comunità" (10, 1–11)
      b. Apologia del ministero di Paolo contro gli "intrusi" (10, 12–18)
         c. Il discorso da stolto (11, 1–12, 10):
            polemico contro i "superapostoli" (11, 1–21a)
            apologetico in favore del "ministro di Cristo" (11, 21b–12, 10)
      b'. Apologia dell'apostolo nei confronti della communità di Corinto (12, 11–18).
   a'. L'autorità di Paolo, esercitata nei moniti conclusivi, "per la edificazione" (12, 19–13, 10).
A'. Conclusione con saluti ed auguri, che si richiamano al prologo (13, 11–13 e 1, 2–3.7).[56]

Literary analysis, according to a chiastic structure, brings a couple of significant observations to the study of the literary structure. First, it shows the significance of thematic connections. A careful analysis of corresponding elements in a chiastic structure can signal boundaries of discourse units. Second, it pays attention to linguistic elements of the literary structure, such as verbal and formal correspondences.

The weakness of the chiastic analysis is twofold. First, identifications of some elements seem rather forced. For instance, Segalla's recognition of corresponding elements is sometimes based on themes (e.g., B and B') and sometimes on linguistic elements (e.g., a and a'); it is not consistent. Second, related to the first critique, an analysis according to a chiastic structure often lacks objective criteria for discerning chiasm and its elements. Craig Arnold Smith seems right that a survey of the history of scholarship on chiasm reveals insufficient theoretical foundation.[57]

---

[56] Giuseppe Segalla, "Struttura Letteraria e Unità Della 2 Corinzi," *Teol* 13 (1988): 189–218, especially at 217–18.
[57] Therefore, Smith, in his work, "Criteria for Identifying Chiasm," surveys the history of scholarship on chiasm and attempts to establish objective criteria to identify chiasm for biblical exegesis as follows: (1) Coherence with other structures; (2) Significant correspondences; (3) Discernable symmetry; (4) Discernable Function; and (5) Authorial Affinity.

2.1.5 Discourse Analysis

Some approach the literary structure by giving special attention to the linguistic aspects of the text; this approach is often called discourse analysis. It concerns the language used in a written discourse (text-linguistics) as a tool to analyze human communications. Thus, it investigates the form, function, and organization of all the parts and the letter as a whole.[58] While different schools of discourse analysis exist today, Christopher D. Land applies Systemic Functional Linguistics (SFL) to the study of 2 Corinthians.[59] SFL emphasizes texts as the locus of linguistic meaning and studies the ways in which texts function in human culture. Thus, Land states, "According to SFL, *a text is an instance of language that realizes an instance of human culture (i.e., a situation).*"[60] SFL presupposes that a certain situation is encoded in a text and can be recognized by applying some institutionalized situation types.[61] Thus, Land carefully pays attention to the linguistic features of 2 Corinthians and proposes its literary structure as follows:

I. A Ministry Update (1:3–2:13)
II. Some Advice on Responding to Critics (2:14–5:21)
III. Yet Another Warning about Problematic Social Relations (2 Cor 6–7)
IV. Remarks Concerning the Bearers of the Letter and Their Mission (2 Cor 8–9)
V. One Last Warning (10:1–13:10).[62]

While fruition of applications of linguistics to the NT studies is still in the process of maturing, discourse analysis has brought a few significant insights into the study of the literary structure of 2 Corinthians. First, its careful investigation of the language, such as analyzing conjunction relations and use of personal references, provides sound evidence of material shifts of Paul's discourse in 2 Corinthians that contributes to the identification of the literary structure. Insofar as the sociohistorical situation and rhetorical exigency can be one explanation to how Paul arranges his discourse materials in the letter, discourse analysis can provide linguistic evidence to the literary structure

---

[58] See brief overviews of discourse analysis in George H. Guthrie, "Discourse Analysis," in *Interpreting the New Testament: Essays on Methods and Issues*, ed. David Alan Black and David S. Dockery (Nashville: Broadman & Holman, 2001), 253–71; Steven E. Runge, "Discourse Analysis," *The Lexham Bible Dictionary*, as found in the Logos Bible Software; Duane F. Watson, "Structuralism and Discourse Analysis," *DLNT*, 1129–35. Also see works that apply discourse analysis to the NT studies in Ralph Bruce Terry, *A Discourse Analysis of First Corinthians*, Summer Institute of Linguistics and the University of Texas at Arlington Publications in Linguistics 120 (Dallas: Summer Institute of Linguistics; University of Texas at Arlington, 1995); Jeffrey T. Reed, *A Discourse Analysis of Philippians: Method and Rhetoric in the Debate Over Literary Integrity*, JSNTSup 136 (Sheffield: Sheffield Academic, 1997); Westfall, *A Discourse Analysis of the Letter to the Hebrews*; Mark Edward Taylor, *A Text-Linguistic Investigation into the Discourse Structure of James*, LNTS 311 (London: T&T Clark, 2006); William C. Varner, *The Book of James: A New Perspective: A Linguistic Commentary Applying Discourse Analysis* (Woodlands, TX: Kress Biblical Resources, 2010); Long, *2 Corinthians*.
[59] Christopher D. Land, *The Integrity of 2 Corinthians and Paul's Aggravating Absence* (Sheffield: Sheffield Phoenix, 2015).
[60] Ibid., 50 (italics are original).
[61] Ibid., 3.
[62] Ibid., v–vi, 82–237.

of Paul's argument. Second, Land's work is commendable for its attempt to establish a methodological framework for the previous study of the linguistic aspect of the letter.

While this study agrees with some of Land's identifications of the literary structure of the letter, I will note some disagreements. For instance, I disagree with his identification of chs 6–7 as a literary unit. Land argues that a concentration of exhortations (6:1, 13, 14, 17 [3x]; 7:1, 2) suggests 6:1 as a major transition from the previous literary unit.[63] Nevertheless, such demarcation is unnecessary; rather, one can see 5:20–7:3 as consequent exhortations from 5:11–19, since Paul already begins to employ an imperative (καταλλάγητε τῷ θεῷ) to exhort the Corinthians in 5:20.

Another example is that Land identifies 4:16–5:11a and 5:11b–21 to be distinct units because he believes 5:11b as a beginning of what he calls "meta-commentaries" where "Paul explicitly comments on what he is doing or how he regards his relations with his Corinthian addressees."[64] The segment is specifically important for Land's analysis because he believes that meta-commentaries in 3:1–3 and 5:11b–21 reveal Paul's understanding of the context of the situation pertaining to the criticism against Paul and Timothy's leadership.[65] Noting the repetition of φανερόω in 5:10, 11a, and 11b, Land concludes that the connection between 5:10 and 5:11a is more significant, while φανερόω in 5:11a and 5:11b is a typical Pauline transitioning device.[66] However, his analysis results in other linguistic issues needing explanation. If 5:11a belongs to 4:16–5:11a, an inferential conjunction οὖν in 5:11a signals a concluding statement of the segment. However, Paul's indicative statement, ἀνθρώπους πείθομεν, in 5:11a does not fit into the immediately preceding context in 4:16–5:10. Moreover, 5:9–10 seems to conclude the discussion in 4:16–5:10 with another inferential conjunction διό. If he insists on the demarcation between 4:16–5:11a and 5:11b–21, Land should have explained more as to why there are two concluding comments and how 5:11a fits into Paul's discourse in 4:16–5:10.

In addition, one may posit methodological concerns pertaining to discourse analysis. First, SFL defines contexts based on an analysis of socio-semiotic constructs and emphasizes the text as the locus of meaning.[67] However, it is impossible to separate Paul's discourse from historical information in interpretation, especially when the text requires such information. For instance, the text itself overtly identifies the author as a historical person, Paul (1:1). Therefore, one should consider the text's meaning based on what the historical Paul did and said.[68] Thus, linguistic insights should be evaluated in light of historical studies required by the literary context and incorporated into an exegesis since their insights are not exclusive to one another.

---

[63] Ibid., 171–72.
[64] Ibid., 67.
[65] Ibid., 133–37.
[66] Ibid., 133.
[67] Ibid., 51.
[68] E.g., see some general works that describe Paul's biography: Ben Witherington III., *The Paul Quest: The Renewed Search for the Jew of Tarsus* (Downers Grove, IL: InterVarsity Press, 1998); Douglas A. Campbell, *Paul: An Apostle's Journey* (Grand Rapids: Eerdmans, 2018); N. T. Wright, *Paul: A Biography* (San Francisco: HarperOne, 2018).

Second, Land's attention to certain linguistic elements is not comprehensive. Some semantic structures are explicitly indicated by linguistic keys such as conjunctions (e.g., for, because, as, and, therefore), yet his work can benefit from investigating other MSRs because MSRs, especially some of the implicit ones, transcend grammatical structures. Therefore, relying on linguistic analysis as a sole means is not sufficient to identify the literary structure; one needs to make observations beyond the linguistic connections.[69]

Third, discourse analysts are significantly disadvantaged with the lack of systematic descriptions of the biblical Greek. For instance, discourse grammarians generally agree that one of the most common and significant Greek conjunctions, γάρ, can function to provide supporting information. However, the degree of distance γάρ can support (e.g., whether it functions to provide supporting information only for an immediately preceding sentence or for the main statement of a paragraph) seems unresolved and waits for further investigation. Therefore, these weaknesses call for a need for an integrative approach that can evaluate and incorporate the insights of discourse analysis into an interpretation.

2.2 Central Theme of 2 Corinthians

Regarding the study of the central theme of the letter, the survey of the literature reveals a few considerations. First, it finds a number of proposals in the history of interpretation: apology (Bornkamm; Kistemaker; Guthrie; Witherington; Long), suffering and death (Harvey; Hafemann; Lim), antithesis of power and weakness (Savage), concord (Scott), reconciliation (Hubbard; Vegge), apologetic commendation (Belleville), relationship between Paul and the Corinthians (Amador), blaming (McCant), cross and resurrection (Segalla), and leadership (Land). However, scholarship lacks agreement on the primary message of the letter. Second, the multifarious proposals arise from the application of various methodological emphases, though related, on certain aspects of the text of 2 Corinthians. Topical analysis often employs historical–critical methods; epistolary criticism makes use of epistolary features and types; rhetorical criticism stresses the role and function of both modern and ancient rhetoric; literary criticism emphasizes the narrative shapes and substructures of the given passage (narrative criticism) and the literary design of chiasm; and discourse analysis focuses on linguistic aspects. Third, the survey indicates the importance and relevance of some aspects of the letter, which an inductive approach should take into account for the study of the central theme of the letter: consideration of redactional process (Bornkamm), Paul's biography (Harvey), sociocultural influence (Savage), Paul's historical relationship with the Corinthian church (Guthrie; Hafemann; Hubbard; Kistemaker; Scott), epistolary type (Belleville; Long), rhetorical exigency and species of rhetoric (Witherington; Long; McCant; Vegge), rhetorical disposition

---

[69] As we will discuss in Chapters 3–8, this does not mean that interpreters should choose one or the other; in fact, linguistic markedness and the presence of MSRs often converge to mark such relationships.

(Witherington; Long; Amador), narrative substructure (Lim), implications of literary design (i.e., chiasm), and attention to cohesive linguistic ties between segments (Land).

2.2.1 Topical Analysis

As described previously, the topical analysis generally focuses on the sociohistorical circumstances from which 2 Corinthians emerged. Scholars taking this approach often relate their findings of historical issues to discrete topics and themes found in each division and segment. This diachronic approach is not generally interested in the ways in which topics and themes in each unit are related to one another to form an overarching message in the letter as a whole, yet some scholars propose a central message of the letter based on their topical analysis.

2.2.1.1 Apology

First, some scholars propose that Paul's apology is the primary message of the letter. Based on an analysis of the redactional process, Günther Bornkamm considers 2:14–7:4, the great apology of the apostolic office, to be the earliest and most important part of the whole correspondence.[70] Then, the redactor added the letter of reconciliation (1:1–2:13 and 7:5–16), the letter regarding collections (ch. 8 and ch. 9), and the letter of tribulation (chs 10–13) to 2:14–7:4. Thus, recognition of the earliest part of the letter (2:14–7:4) suggests that Paul's apology of the apostolic office is the core message of the canonical 2 Corinthians. Bornkamm's careful attention to distinct topics in the letter is commendable. Nevertheless, his analysis suffers from a lack of explanation regarding the ways in which the text supports his conclusion. As previously pointed out, reconstructions of the redactional processes and partition theories are speculative. While I admit that a certain degree of speculation is inevitable in the historical-critical study, lack of evidence from the literary context is crucial to doubt his proposal.

Simon J. Kistemaker argues, according to his content analysis, that the general content of the letter pertains to Paul's vindication of being an apostle to the Gentiles, though he later admits that there is no unifying theme in the letter.[71] Likewise, George H. Guthrie contends that the relational tension between Paul and the Corinthian church urged Paul to commend his ministry to them as one of integrity. Thus, Paul proclaims the nature of his authentic ministry in 2:14–7:14 and prepares the Corinthians in chs 8–13 for Paul's impending visit.[72]

On the one hand, the theme of apology is indeed one of the most prominent themes in the letter; however, on the other hand, neither Guthrie nor Kistemaker explicates or

---

[70] Günther Bornkamm, "The History of the Origin of the So-Called Second Letter to the Corinthians," *NTS* 8 (1962): 258–64; Günther Bornkamm, *Geschichte und Glaube*, 2 vols (Munich: Kaiser, 1971).
[71] Kistemaker, *II Corinthians*, 3–29; also see Frank J. Matera, *II Corinthians: A Commentary*, NTL (Louisville: Westminster John Knox, 2003), 3–9.
[72] Guthrie, *2 Corinthians*, 46–51.

demonstrates in their commentaries how the thesis is supported by the literary context.[73]

2.2.1.2 Suffering and Death

Second, A. E. Harvey finds suffering and death to be the central theme of the letter. Reconstructing Paul's biography, he contends that Paul's near-death experience and suffering in Asia (1:8–10) between the composition of 1 and 2 Corinthians is the interpretive key to understanding 2 Corinthians.[74] According to Harvey, the affliction in Asia caused Paul not only to despair of his life but also to lose his apostolic credibility, inviting criticism from the Corinthians. Thus, Harvey attempts to show the ways in which Paul responds to charges against him in the letter. Harvey aims to demonstrate his case by diachronically showing connections between various passages and his reconstructions of consequences of that event in the form of running commentary. While Harvey's creative interpretive imagination is commendable, his analysis at some places goes beyond the evidence that the literary context can offer; he does not describe how his analysis of the historical situation is supported by the literary context.

Scott J. Hafemann likewise contends that the central theme pertains to "the relationship between suffering and the power of the Spirit in Paul's apostolic experience."[75] Thus, Paul's suffering becomes a means to manifest God's knowledge in the cross of Christ and the power of Spirit. I agree that suffering is one of the major themes of the letter. Nevertheless, Hafemann does not explain the ways in which his thesis is supported by the literary context of the letter as a whole.

2.2.1.3 Power through Weakness

Third, Timothy B. Savage argues that the theme of power through weakness is the core of Paul's teaching in 2 Corinthians.[76] Savage first investigates and reconstructs the Hellenistic cultural influence on Corinthians' criticism against Paul, which can be summarized as egocentrism, such as self-exalting, self-boasting, and exploiting others. Then, he demonstrates the ways in which Paul responds to their culturally conditioned evaluations toward him by insisting upon a Christ-centered perspective. Thus, Savage

---

[73] Harris also argues the unified character of 2 Corinthians as an *apologia*, though he does not insist that this character is the only main theme of the letter. He indeed contends that preparation for Paul's imminent visit is another single and coordinating purpose in the letter. Thus, Harris argues that Paul's experience of death and God's comfort (1:3–11), explanation of Paul's conduct as a traveling pastor against the accusations (1:12–2:13; 7:5–16), description of nature of the apostolic ministry (2:14–6:13; 7:2–4) and insistence of separation from all idolatrous associations (6:14–7:1), completion of the collection (8:1–9:15), defense of his apostolic authority (10:1–12:13), and emphasis on self-examination, repentance, and mending (12:14–13:10) prepare the Corinthians for Paul's impending visit by seeking to remove present or potential obstacles that could prevent the visit (*Second Epistle to the Corinthians*, 42–54). See my critique on his argument in my note in 8.2.2.2.

[74] A. E. Harvey, *Renewal Through Suffering: A Study of 2 Corinthians*, SNTW (Edinburgh: T&T Clark, 1996).

[75] Hafemann, *2 Corinthians*, 34.

[76] Timothy B. Savage, *Power Through Weakness: Paul's Understanding of the Christian Ministry in 2 Corinthians*, SNTSMS 86 (Cambridge: Cambridge University Press, 1996).

contends that while Paul expresses these two opposing worldviews in a number of paradoxes in the letter, the heart of what it means to Paul to be a minister of Christ is best found in his paradoxical teaching: "When I am weak, then I am strong" (12:10), because for Paul, weakness is an affirmation of apostolic office as well as a locus in which divine power is manifested.[77]

Savage rightly observes the importance of the idea of power through weakness in Paul's discourse. However, while Savage explicates key passages that reflect Paul's counterarguments against culturally infused egocentrism of the Corinthians, he does not demonstrate how the proposed theme of the paradox is related to the rest of the text. His exposition concentrates on selective passages, particularly 4:7–18; thus, he does not adequately support the theme of power through weakness as the central message of the letter.

2.2.1.4 Concord

Fourth, James M. Scott claims that the letter as a whole can be described as an appeal for concord or harmony, based on 13:11.[78] The theme is supported by Paul's emphasis on various aspects of the mutuality between himself and the Corinthians (e.g., 1:1–2, 3–11, 14, 18–22, 24; 2:2; 3:18; 4:12, 14; 6:11–13; 7:2; 8:1, 16–17; 9:11; 12:14–15; 13:11) as well as his use of familial language (e.g., brothers in Christ and sons of the Father). While his thesis is appealing, Scott does not expound his thesis or demonstrate the evidence in his commentary. Thus, his thesis remains unconvincing until he shows the ways in which the literary context supports such an idea.

2.2.1.5 Reconciliation

Fifth, Moyer V. Hubbard proposes that reconciliation and restoration are the overarching purposes of 2 Corinthians.[79] Based on Paul's prayer for the Corinthians in 13:9, Hubbard understands that the Corinthians must restore relationships among themselves, with God, and with Paul so that the letter will prepare them for Paul's impending visit. Hubbard is not the only one who insists the theme of reconciliation as the main focus of the letter.[80] In addition, he does not provide evidence to prove his thesis from the literary context other than the evidence already described; thus, it remains inconclusive.

2.2.1.6 Evaluation

Topical analysis has brought a couple of significant insights to the study of the central message of 2 Corinthians. First, it highlights the importance of historical issues in

---

[77] Savage assumes that chs 1–9 and 10–13 represent separate letters. However, these two letters contemplate the same situation.
[78] Scott, *2 Corinthians*, 5.
[79] Moyer V. Hubbard, *2 Corinthians*, Teach the Text Commentary (Grand Rapids: Baker Books, 2017), 3–4.
[80] See 2.2.3.4.

understanding the overarching message of the letter. Scholars commonly recognize similar themes and topics in the letter, but they stress different overall themes based on their reconstruction of historical issues or analysis of thematic connections.

Second, related to the first point, topical analysis, according to the historical critical studies, has drawn upon relevant interpretive considerations in the study of the primary message of the letter. Redactional process (Bornkamm), Paul's biography (Harvey), sociocultural influence (Savage), and Paul's historical relationship with the Corinthian church (Guthrie; Hafemann; Hubbard; Kistemaker; Scott) are all relevant aspects of the investigation into the central message of the letter.

However, topical analysis is faced with some challenges. First, scholarly reconstructions of the historical development of the letter can be notoriously speculative (Bornkamm). Second, many commentators (Guthrie; Hafemann; Hubbard; Kistemaker; Scott), due to the nature and space of commentaries, do not demonstrate the ways in which the proposed thesis is related to the details of the text. Third, historical studies sometimes seem to impose scholarly reconstructions of historical issues on the text; thus, they lack the evidence from the literary context (Harvey; Savage). Fourth, while this study affirms many of the observations topical analysis makes, especially thematic connections on the basis of their careful attention to the text, their conclusions must be synthesized. As shown, various proposals of the central message of the letter arise from scholars' emphasis on different aspects of historical issues, and some of their observations at the textual level are strong. However, these conclusions are not mutually exclusive to one another, and this study proposes that Paul's discourse of ministry encompasses many of the proposed primary messages of the letter.

2.2.2 Epistolary Criticism

Epistolary criticism, especially regarding its identification of letter types (e.g., private, official, and literary), can suggest an overarching message of 2 Corinthians.[81] While many study Pauline letters as private or personal letters,[82] some scholars propose different identifications of the letter type(s) based on epistolary handbooks of Pseudo-Demetrius and Pseudo-Libanius. For instance, Hans Dieter Betz proposes that 2 Cor 10–13 is an apologetic letter,[83] while John T. Fitzgerald identifies 2 Cor 10–13 as an excellent example of a mixed letter type.[84] Linda L. Belleville contends that the

---

[81] See following works for epistolary criticism of the NT: David E. Aune, *The New Testament in Its Literary Environment*, LEC 8 (Philadelphia: Westminster, 1987); M. Luther Stirewalt, *Studies in Ancient Greek Epistolography*, RBS 27 (Atlanta: Scholars Press, 1993); Hans-Josef Klauck, *Ancient Letters and the New Testament: A Guide to Context and Exegesis*, trans. Daniel P. Bailey (Waco, TX: Baylor University Press, 2006); Jeffrey A. D. Weima, *Paul the Ancient Letter Writer: An Introduction to Epistolary Analysis* (Grand Rapids: Baker Academic, 2016).

[82] For instance, John L. White, *Light from Ancient Letters*, FF (Philadelphia: Fortress, 1986), especially 136–39.

[83] Hans Dieter Betz, *Der Apostel Paulus Und Die Sokratische Tradition: Eine Exegetische Untersuchung Zu Seiner Apologie 2 Korinther 10–13*, BHT 45 (Tübingen: Mohr, 1972), 40.

[84] Fitzgerald, "Paul, the Ancient Epistolary Theorist," 190–200.

epistolary features and language of 1:8–7:16 can best be explained in light of the Hellenistic letter of recommendation and thus concludes 2 Cor 1–7 as a letter of apologetic commendation.[85]

Particularly noteworthy contributions come from the works of Hans Windisch and Fredrick J. Long. Windisch identified that 2 Corinthians represents different types of letters,[86] yet Long argues that Paul constructed an official apologetic letter by drawing on ancient forensic practice so as to respond to specific charges against him.[87] Long's work is particularly important regarding the overarching theme of the letter. His identification of the letter type as an official apologetic letter and its rhetorically unified characteristic suggest that the primary theme of 2 Corinthians is Paul's apology.[88]

Evaluation

One significant contribution of epistolary criticism to the study of the central message of 2 Corinthians is its historically informed identification of the letter type(s). Its analysis of letter types reveals the disposition of the letter as a key to understanding Paul's overall discourse by situating 2 Corinthians in the milieu of the practice of Greco-Roman letter writings. Particularly, Long's work is commendable because of his demonstration of similarities between rhetorically informed ancient apologetic letters and 2 Corinthians.

However, epistolary criticism is faced with some challenges. First, the categories of letter types are primarily informed by historical studies of the pseudonymous epistolary handbooks (i.e., Pseudo-Demetrius' *Epistolary Types* and Pseudo-Libanius' *Epistolary Styles*), sporadic discussions found in the ancient rhetorical handbooks (e.g., Demetrius, Cicero, Quintilian, Then, Philostratus of Lemnos, Gregory of Nazianzus, and Julius Victor), the ancient educational curriculum (e.g., inferences from Dionysius of Alexander and Apollonius Dyscolus and Bolgna Papyrus, PBon 5 as an example of a student's exercise with an epistolary theory manual), and the thousands of extant Greco-Roman letters. However, difficulties with the available sources for the study of ancient letter writings not only call into question the reliability of its conclusions but also require further evaluation of its studies. Some of the difficulties of the sources include uncertainties of the authorship and date of the epistolary handbooks (Pseudo-Demetrius and Pseudo-Libanius), discords between the epistolary handbooks and actual practices of extant letter writings, lack of systematic treatment of letter writings by rhetoricians, uncertainties of the relationship between rhetorical and epistolary practice, and absence of extant epistolary manuals in the educational curriculum.[89]

---

[85] Belleville, *Reflections of Glory*. Although she deals with only chs 1–7 in her monograph, she later acknowledges in her commentary the existence of two body-closing sections in the letter (7:3–16; chs 10–13). Thus, if chs 10–13 serves as a body-closing, the theme of apologetic commendation (chs 1–7) is the central theme of the letter (*2 Corinthians*, 21).

[86] Hans Windisch, *Der Zweite Korintherbrief*, KEK 6 (Göttingen: Vandenhoeck & Ruprecht, 1924), 8–9.

[87] Long, *Ancient Rhetoric and Paul's Apology*, especially 97–116.

[88] Cf. Benjamin G. White, *Pain and Paradox in 2 Corinthians*, WUNT 2/555 (Tübingen: Mohr Siebeck, 2021), especially 1–7, in which he rejects this theme based on the immediate literary context 2:1–7; 7:5–16 along with other passages such as 12:19.

[89] See a brief overview of the sources of epistolary criticism in Jeffrey A. D. Weima, "Epistolary Theory," *DNTB* 327–30.

Second, disagreements among the scholars over the identification of letter types call for a further investigation. For instance, while Long's work demonstrates affinities between ancient epistolary and rhetorical practice and 2 Corinthians, the letter also exhibits possibilities of other letter types recognized by the epistolary handbooks, such as a counteraccusation (e.g., 10:2, 7, 12, 15; cf. Ps.-Libanius, *Epistolary Styles*, 22 [Malherbe]) and ironic letter (11:23–12:10; cf. Ps.-Demetrius, *Epistolary Types*, 20 [Malherbe]).[90]

2.2.3 Rhetorical Criticism

Some scholars using rhetorical criticism also suggest the overarching message of the letter based on their analysis of rhetorical exigency, species of rhetoric, and rhetorical disposition.

2.2.3.1 Apology

First, identifying 2 Corinthians as an example of ancient forensic or judicial rhetoric, Witherington contends that Paul's argument is "a form of *apologia*—a defense of Paul's apostleship."[91] He argues that exigencies of the needs for reconciliation between Paul and his converts urged him to respond to the charge against his apostleship.[92] Thus, the primary contention to which Paul responds in his discourse is summarized in 2:17, as Witherington recognizes it to be *propositio* of the letter: Paul is not an apostle.[93] In order to achieve his defense, Witherington argues that Paul employs a rhetorical strategy known as *insinuatio*, which "alludes to the major issue that is under dispute in the early stages of the rhetorical discourse, reserving the real discussion of the major bone of contention for the end of the discourse, where it is attacked, using much *pathos*, in a more direct fashion."[94] Thus, Paul consistently alludes to the false apostles in chs 1–9 and moves to attack them directly in chs 10–13, which explains the difference in tone between chs 1–9 and 10–13.[95]

Second, Long advances Witherington's study and argues that 2 Corinthians is an official apologetic letter drawing from the ancient forensic tradition. In contrast to Witherington, Long contends that Paul's defense is not about his apostleship in general; instead, Paul is offering a real defense to the Corinthians specifically regarding his "manner of preaching, ministry practice, and itinerant intentions."[96] While Witherington

---

[90] Fitzgerald, "Paul, the Ancient Epistolary Theorists," 190–200.
[91] Witherington, *Conflict and Community in Corinth*, 336.
[92] Witherington attributes obstacles to the reconciliation to the issues pertaining to the practice of Corinthian Christians participating in temple feasts (6:14–7:1), Paul's inconsistency of travel plans (1:15–17.; chs 7–8; 12:14; 13:1–2, 14), and his refusal to accept patronage relationships with the Corinthians (chs 7–8) (*Conflict and Community in Corinth*, 339–43).
[93] Ibid., 371.
[94] Ibid., 429.
[95] Witherington numerates following verses: Ch.1; 2:17; 3:1; 3:7; 4:2; 5:12; 6:3; 6:4–10; 7:2 in which he explains such allusions (ibid., 429–31).
[96] Long attributes the rhetorical exigency to his inconsistency on his denial of worldly rhetoric yet forceful use of rhetoric in First Corinthians; his failure to visit the Corinthians when he said he would; and his financial inconsistency to receive fiscal support from the Macedonians but deny it from the Corinthians (*Ancient Rhetoric and Paul's Apology*, 7, 115–42).

develops the central message based on his identification of *propositio* in 2:17, Long insists that the central theme of the letter is an apology based on the Greek word ἀπολογέομαι in 12:19 and argues that its scope extends beyond chs 10–13 and encompasses the entire letter.[97]

The strength of the proposals from Witherington and Long is their recognition of significance and relevance of the literary structure (i.e., rhetorical disposition) for understanding the text's meaning. Also, they rightly observe that apology is a prominent theme in the letter, especially chs 10–13. However, the flow of the text may not support the evidence identifying 8:1–9:15 as *probatio*. Witherington argues, and Long agrees, that the deliberative argument was meant to improve Paul's integrity before the Corinthians; therefore, it serves Paul's larger forensic purposes.[98] However, one needs to read between the lines in order to find such an intention based on one's understanding of rhetorical exigency. Instead of viewing chs 8–9 as a part of *apologia*, the flow of the literary context indicates that Paul's discourse in chs 8–9 is a consequent exhortation based on the arguments Paul expounds in 3:1–7:16 (i.e., a movement from indicatives to imperatives).[99] Therefore, it moves from proclamation (chs 3–7) to exhortation (chs 8–9).

Moreover, while understanding the letter as an apology based on the word ἀπολογέομαι in 12:19 in the *peroratio* may correspond to a typical forensic discourse,[100] the literary context does not seem to support such a claim. Indeed, Paul seems to deny that he has been defending himself by saying, κατέναντι θεοῦ ἐν Χριστῷ λαλοῦμεν, in the same verse. The phrase is not a clarification of ἀπολογέομαι: While the Corinthians may have perceived his proclamation as his apology, Paul emphasizes that he is not defending himself but proclaiming God's word. This becomes clear when one understands 12:19 in light of the thesis statement of the letter, especially in 2:17. In 12:19, the verb, λαλέω, lacks the direct object; however, Paul employs the verbatim expression, κατέναντι θεοῦ ἐν Χριστῷ λαλοῦμεν, in 2:17 in which he clarifies τὸν λόγον τοῦ θεοῦ as the object of the verb implied from the immediately preceding sentence. Therefore, in 12:19, Paul is not speaking about himself but about God's word. In other words, Paul's apology does not encompass the entire letter, but Paul's proclamation of the word does, in which the theme of apology/defense is a major aspect.[101]

2.2.3.2 Blaming

McCant postulates that Paul's goal of the letter is not self-defense but "reorientation of Corinthian criteria for apostleship and the gospel."[102] Thus, it is an apologetic forensic

---

[97] Ibid., 118–19.
[98] Witherington, *Conflict and Community in Corinth*, 411–12; Long, *Ancient Rhetoric and Paul's Apology*, 177.
[99] See my argument in 7.2.2.
[100] Long, *Ancient Rhetoric and Paul's Apology*, 117–18.
[101] See more discussions in 5.2.2.2 and 8.2.2.2.
[102] McCant, *2 Corinthians*, 13.

parody.[103] Based on Paul's desire to build up and not to tear down the church (10:8; 13:10), McCant applies the rhetorical practice of parodic speech to the letter. He argues that because Paul is an apostle of Jesus Christ by the will of God (1:1), he neither needs to defend himself nor feels threatened by the Corinthian appraisal. Rather, his pastoral concern permeates the letter.[104] Thus, he wrote the letter in the form of judicial rhetoric, and his use of parody subverts the judicial functions of the letter and makes the letter "function more like an epideictic (i.e., 'blaming') speech."[105]

The significance of McCant's work pertains to the question he raises regarding the ways in which the study of the letter is often conducted. He insists that Paul's opponents did not exist since the identification of such a group is frequently based on the problematic practice of mirror-reading.[106] His work suggests the danger of the speculative nature of reconstruction of the situation behind the letter in the study of 2 Corinthians. McCant conducts his analysis with caution; however, when it comes to his identification of the entire letter being parodic, his argument is based upon inadequate evidence. While I agree with the existence of some parodic elements in the fool's speech in chs 11–12, McCant does not convincingly demonstrate the ways in which the literary context supports his reading of the entire letter to be parodic.

2.2.3.3 Relationship

J. David Hester Amador reconstructs distinct argumentative situations that Paul must address in 2 Corinthians and explains Paul's rhetorical and argumentative strategies as evidence for the unity of the letter. He contends that while each rhetorical unit deals with distinctive circumstances, 1:12–14 serves as *causa* or *propositio* of the letter in which Paul emphasizes "frankness" and "sincerity." Thus, Paul addresses the various relationships between himself and the Corinthians throughout the letter.[107]

Amador rightly observes Paul's insistence of the sincerity of his ministry in his discourse to be one of the prominent themes in the letter (cf. 2:17). However, his recognition of 1:12–14 as *causa* or *propositio* faces a challenge. A careful reading of the text indicates that 1:12–14 is more closely related to 1:15–2:11 than to the entire letter. In 1:12–14, Paul declares two facts, and he defends these in 1:15–2:11 (see Table 2.1).

Therefore, 1:12–14 functions as a part of the discussion in 1:12–2:11 but not as *causa* or *propositio* of the letter, which suggests that the theme of relationship is not the central focus of the letter.

---

[103] Ibid., 19.
[104] Ibid., 18.
[105] Ibid., 16.
[106] Ibid., 17–18, 26.
[107] Amador, "Unity of 2 Corinthians," 411–32; idem, "Revisiting 2 Corinthians," 92–111; idem, "Re-Reading 2 Corinthians," 276–95). For instance, he argues that an argumentative situation behind 1:23–2:11 and 2:5–13 pertains to the ethos of someone in the community, whereas the situation behind chs 10–13 has to do with Paul's ethos.

Table 2.1 Affinities between 1:12–14 and 1:15–2:11

Topic	1:12–14	1:15–2:11
Conduct	Paul and his fellow workers have conducted themselves in this world (1:12).	Paul defends his conduct regarding his change of plan (1:23–2:2).
Letter	They wrote a letter to the Corinthians (1:13).	Paul defends his previous letter (2:3–11).

2.2.3.4 Reconciliation

Ivar Vegge argues that the central thesis of 2 Corinthians pertains to reconciliation between Paul and the Corinthians. He insists that 7:5–16 most visibly reflects such tension. Moreover, the main idea coheres with the thesis statement of the letter in 1:12–14.[108] Instead of identifying the letter as an example of forensic or judicial rhetoric, Vegge emphasizes the epideictic element in the letter and argues that 7:5–16 functions as idealized praise. He contends that flexibility of rhetorical practice allows such an epideictic rhetorical feature (i.e., idealized praise) to function as an exhortation in the letter, although exhortation is sometimes not considered a primary function of epideictic rhetoric. However, the hortative use of idealized praise is seen in the Hellenic rhetorical theory and speeches, psychagogy among moral philosophers, and epistolography.[109] In order to achieve this aim, Vegge develops two arguments. First, Paul's expressions of confidence (1:13b–14, [15]; 2:3b; 5:11; 7:4, [14], 16; 8:5, 7, 22b, 24; 9:1–2; 10:15b; 13:5) function as a rhetorical amplification, which seeks to create a sense of obligation to follow the exhortation of reconciliation.[110] Second, Paul's harsh criticism and threats of punishment serve as devices for the correction and reconciliation in chs 10–13.[111]

Vegge's work is another example that understands the interconnections between the literary structure and theology of the letter. He identifies the most prominent passage that reflects the idea of reconciliation (i.e., 7:5–16) and attempts to situate his findings in both the socio-rhetorical circumstance and the literary context. However, his analysis does not provide sufficient evidence from the literary context to make his case. For instance, Vegge attempts to relate the expression of hope in the thesis statement of the letter in 1:12–14 to that of confidence.[112] While he is right to point to Paul's emphasis on mutual boasting in that passage, the Greek words ἐλπίζω (1:13), καύχησις (1:12) and καύχημα (1:14) do not consistently appear throughout the letter: ἐλπίζω appears only in 1:10, 13; 5:11; 8:5; and 13:6; καυχαομαι and its cognate words do not appear in 3:1–5:10. Thus, Vegge focuses on key passages that he considers important to his thesis

---

[108] Vegge, *2 Corinthians*, 34–37, 106, 376.
[109] Ibid., 53–70.
[110] Ibid., 141–252.
[111] Ibid., 253–359.
[112] Ibid., 169–76.

but does not demonstrate the ways in which each division and segment in the letter relate to one another. Simply put, one wonders why Vegge does not explain the relationship between the apology for Paul's apostolic ministry (2:14–5:10) and an appeal for reconciliation (5:11–7:4) when the former serves as the basis of the latter.

Moreover, regarding the relationship between the thesis statement (1:12–14) and the idealized praise (7:5–16), Vegge does not sufficiently explain why Paul refrains from explicitly expressing the main theme as reconciliation in his thesis statement.

2.2.3.5 Evaluation

Rhetorical criticism regarding the central theme of the letter indicates a couple of important observations. First, it shows the relevance of the rhetorical exigency and sociohistorical situation of the letter. Since the exigency determines the purpose of a rhetorical speech or writing, the primary message or persuasive goal depends on one's reconstruction of Paul's *stasis* as a rhetor or writer. Second, it underscores the importance of rhetorical disposition. Related to the issue of rhetorical exigency, one's identification of rhetorical disposition or structure affects his or her interpretation of the principal message of the letter. Particularly, one's recognition of *divisio, partitio, causa,* or *propositio* plays an important role in discerning the central message of the letter.

As I have already discussed the weaknesses of rhetorical criticism regarding the literary structure, the same challenges are applied to the relationships between the principal message of the letter and rhetorical criticism. Disagreements on rhetorical exigency, species, and disposition of the letter among scholars, methodological assumptions, and flexibility of rhetorical practice call for an inductive approach that can incorporate insights from rhetorical criticism and evaluate them in light of other methodological insights, particularly that of the literary context.

2.2.4 Literary Analysis

The traditional methodology of higher criticism, such as source, form, and redaction criticism, paved a way to a new criticism that emphasizes the literary character of the biblical text and finds the key to meaning in the form and structure of the writing. Within this literary criticism, narrative criticism and analysis based on chiastic structures are applied to 2 Corinthians to propose a central message of the letter.

2.2.4.1 Narrative Criticism

While narrative readings are usually applied to a portion of the letter and thus not able to argue for an overarching theme of the letter, Kar Yong Lim investigated the description of Paul's suffering throughout the letter and argued, "Paul's understanding of his suffering is grounded in the story of Jesus."[113] Thus, Lim concluded, "The frequent

---

[113] Lim, *"Sufferings of Christ,"* 197.

repetitions about Paul's suffering strongly suggest that this theme not only plays a crucial role in Paul's thought but also is fundamental to his argument in 2 Corinthians."[114]

Lim's application of narrative reading of the letter helps one see the potential source on the basis of which Paul understands his suffering and the ways in which he develops it as one of the major themes of the letter. However, apart from the concern I have raised (i.e., analyses on the reconstructed narratives), one weakness of Lim's work lies in the fact that he does not demonstrate how the description of Paul's suffering (1:3–11; 2:14–16; 4:7–12; 6:1–10; 11:23–12:10) relates to the rest of his discourse. For instance, Lim does not explain how the theme of suffering is fundamental in Paul's discourse of the collection (2 Cor 8–9).[115] Moreover, while I agree with the notion of suffering as one of the key themes, one can trace other prominent and pervasive themes throughout the letter (e.g., credentials for ministry, God's knowledge, sacrificial image, and proclamation of the gospel).[116]

2.2.4.2 Analysis Based on Chiastic Structure

Since chiastic structures more or less identify corresponding topics (e.g., A and A′), it is possible to include this discussion within the category of topical analysis. However, a concentric arrangement of materials often structurally implies the central message. Thus, it is discussed in a separate section.

As discussed, Segalla outlines the entire letter according to a chiastic structure and suggests that the *kerygma* of cross and resurrection (13:4; cf. 8:9) is the guiding idea that organizes 2 Cor 1–7, 8–9, and 10–13 (see Segalla's chiastic analysis in 2.1.4.2). He further concludes that a dialectic of suffering-sadness and comfort-joy in chs 1–7 and 8–9, and that of weakness and power in chs 10–13, are the central theme of the letter.[117]

Although Segalla's analysis observes important themes in the letter, his proposal regarding the principal message of the letter suffers from a lack of explanations. In addition to the weaknesses I have already raised (i.e., arbitrary identification of corresponding elements and lack of objective criteria), Segalla does not explain the ways in which the macro-chiastic outline relates to the central theme. Moreover, since many consider the center of the chiasm to be the climax with the greatest theological significance,[118] Segalla's analysis implies that 2 Cor 8–9 (item C) is the central significance in the letter. However, he neither demonstrates nor explains how the theological core and the proposed themes of the letter (i.e., the antithesis of suffering and comfort and of weakness and power) are expressed in 2 Cor 8–9.

---

[114] Ibid., 1.
[115] Lim later published an article in which he shows that Paul's understanding of generosity is rooted in Jesus's story ("Generosity from Pauline Perspective: Insights from Paul's Letters to the Corinthians," *Evangelical Review of Theology* 37 [2013]: 20–33). However, the question still remains concerning the ways in which the narrative substructure of Jesus' story in Paul's discourse is related to the rest of the discursive materials in 2 Corinthians.
[116] See my discussion in ch 5.
[117] Segalla, "Struttura Letteraria e Unità Della 2 Corinzi," 217.
[118] For instance, see Blomberg, "Structure of 2 Corinthians 1-7," 3–20; Lund, *Chiasmus in the New Testament*, 40–41.

2.2.4.3 Evaluation

Literary criticism brings a few significant insights into the study of the principal message of the letter. First, the emphases of narrative criticism on the final form of the text and the notion of the implied author (and the implied reader) are significant regarding the investigation of the principal message of the letter.[119] Instead of focusing on the information behind the text and authorial intention, it focuses on the construal of the meaning and theology of the given text.

Second, an analysis of the macro-chiastic structure of the letter shows the relevance and significance of the literary design for the study of the central message of the letter. If the text is indeed structured according to a certain literary design in both micro and macro levels, the connection between the content of the message and the ways in which the content is expressed needs to be taken into account. For this reason, analysis of the MSRs, which includes chiasm, in 2 Corinthians will offer more fruitful insights into both the literary design and its function for understanding Paul's discourse.

Third, since the insights from narrative criticism and the literary design of chiasm lack the evidence from the literary context, especially regarding the ways in which each division, section, and segment supports the proposed themes, IBS can both incorporate and evaluate their analyses in light of the attentive reading of the flow of Paul's discourse through the study of its form.

2.2.5 Discourse Analysis

Discourse analysis aims to understand organizations of material by analyzing cohesive ties of discourse materials. Defending the unity of 2 Corinthians, Land proposes that 2 Corinthians consists of a single and coherent context of the situation in which Paul and Timothy enact church leadership in relation to their converts in Corinth. Namely, his leadership within the sphere of the church serves as an overarching theme of the letter.[120] In order to argue his thesis, Land attempts to demonstrate the ways in which linguistic elements, such as conjunctive relations and semantic domains, support the theme of leadership as a prominent theme in each unit (1:3–2:13; 2:14–5:21; chs 6–7; chs 8–9; 10:1–13:10), and then reconstructs a situation Paul is attempting to address in the letter.

Evaluation

In addition to the strengths previously indicated, this discipline brings a couple of significant insights into a construal of the primary message of 2 Corinthians. First, discourse analysis rightly emphasizes the importance of cohesive ties within the text. Rather than treating each segment as an independent and unrelated topic, it seeks to show the ways in which each segment is linguistically related to form a consistent and coherent message of the letter. Second, related to the first point, it underscores the

---

[119] Also see methodological consideration (ch. 1).
[120] Land, *Integrity of 2 Corinthians*, 82–281.

relevance of the literary structure to the understanding of the central message of 2 Corinthians. Land successfully demonstrates that one's construal of segmentation plays a significant role in understanding Paul's message. Particularly, his careful attention to conjunctive relations is helpful to know how sentences and paragraphs are related to form a larger message in Paul's discourse.

While I commend many insights that Land offers, I question whether some of Land's readings of the text are fair to the flow of the literary context. For instance, in order to maintain his thesis, Land attempts to demonstrate the ways in which 1:3–2:13 supports the theme of leadership. He claims that 1:3–7 is the primary statement in 1:3–2:13, which expresses Paul's gratitude, and that the rest of the materials (1:8–2:13) support the assertion in 1:3–7. Specifically, he insists that 1:3–2:13 concerns Paul and Timothy giving a ministry update.[121] While I agree that 1:3–7 is a general statement of the division, my reading of the text of 1:3–7 disagrees with Land's conclusion. The focus of 1:3–7 pertains to God's activity but not Paul's gratitude. Linguistically speaking, God is the main focus of the Greek sentences in 1:3–5; Paul proclaims God's character.[122] Then, Paul draws implications of God's character regarding the relationship between Paul and Corinthians in 1:6–7. Thus, 1:3–2:13 is not an update from Paul and Timothy pertaining to their leadership but about God's character, which characterizes the rest of the letter.[123] If so, this suggests some difficulties in maintaining Land's thesis.

2.3 Conclusion

The survey of the literature regarding the literary structure and the central theme of 2 Corinthians has demonstrated a paucity of both scholarly consensus and methodology that incorporates various insights into an interpretation. In addition, it has suggested relevant issues and interpretive determinants for an inductive and integrative approach to the subject. However, not all interpretive determinants are equally significant and relevant, as this study reveals their strengths and weaknesses.

Therefore, the following is a summary of the relevant issues that must be addressed in any investigation of the literary structure and the principal message of 2 Corinthians:

1. The existence of discrete topical units within the letter and historical issues behind them;
2. The relevance of epistolary types, features, and structure;
3. The significance of rhetorical species and its dispositions;
4. The function of narrative substructures within some passages;
5. The existence of literary designs and their function;

---

[121] Ibid., 82–112.
[122] Greek sentence in 1:3 begins as Εὐλογητὸς ὁ θεός. Land seems to understand Paul and Timothy to be the focus because they are the ones who give thanks, whereas I argue God as the focus because of the copular sentence structure: ὁ θεὸς is the subject of the sentence and Εὐλογητὸς is the predicate adjective. Thus, semantically speaking, God is the subject and focus of 1:3–5.
[123] See further discussion in 4.2.

6. The relevance of linguistically cohesive ties in Paul's discourse;
7. The interrelationships between units (1:1–2; 1:3–11; 1:12–2:13; 2:14–7:4 [and 6:14–7:1]; 7:5–16; 8:1–9:15; 10:1–13:10; 13:11–13) and their relevance to the understanding of the central theme of the letter.

Having presented the history of interpretation and the significant issues for the present study, I shall turn to the investigation of the literary structure and the central message of 2 Corinthians.

3

Salutation (1:1–2) and Closing (13:11–13)

In Chapter 1, I have described the origin and development of IBS and provided theoretical foundations for the present study. In Chapter 2, I have demonstrated the need for this study by showing (1) a paucity of scholarly consensus regarding the literary structure and overarching theme of the letter, and (2) the need for a hermeneutical model that incorporates various insights into the interpretation. At the end of the chapter, I also identified the relevant issues for the study of the literary structure and principal message of 2 Corinthians. I now turn to analyze the literary structure of 2 Corinthians.

In the following chapters, 3 through 8, I will present (1) identifications of main units and subunits of each division, and (2) the MSRs in relation both to the division as a whole and the letter as a whole. The main units and subunits are frequently marked by (1) shifts of emphasis within the book, division, section, segment, paragraph, and even sentence, and (2) the implications from the MSRs.[1] Thus, identification of main units and subunits and the MSRs are indivisible components of the literary structure. While my presentation begins with the demarcation of units and moves to the MSRs, readers should keep in mind that those two elements mutually inform one another. In addition, this study focuses on the MSRs as opposed to minor structural relationships. Since structural relationships are part of the human cognitive and communicative processes, one can observe structural relationships in all levels in Paul's discourse (i.e., book, division, section, segment, paragraph, and sentence). However, the present study especially focuses on the MSRs, which control all or at least more than half of the material under observation. In other words, while one can analyze structural relationships on a sentence or paragraph level, this study focuses on the MSRs that control the bulk of the letter (i.e., the MSRs in relation to the book as a whole) and that of the division (i.e., the MSRs in relation to division as a whole).[2] In addition, one must note that the study of the literary structure is not an end in itself, for it is meant to help

---

[1] Bauer and Traina, *Inductive Bible Study*, 88–94.
[2] The focus on the MSRs is not meant to undermine the value of minor structural relationships in interpretations. In fact, sometimes, implications of minor structural relationships can inform the identification of MSRs. However, in order to understand Paul's overall discourse of the letter, one should not become bogged down in detail, failing to see the wood for the trees. Instead, one should focus on the MSRs to comprehend Paul's thrust of the argument in the entire letter. Also see Bauer and Traina, *Inductive Bible Study*, 94–95.

exegetes understand the theological message of the letter. However, due to the limited space, I will focus on the identification of the division and MSRs of the letter, but in the last chapter (Chapter 9), I will draw theological implications from this study.

In this chapter, my concern is to discuss the literary structure of the salutation (1:1–2) and the closing (13:11–13) of the letter. I will explain each division as an independent literary unit and expound two MSRs in relation to the letter as a whole. The salutation prepares readers for Paul's discourse on ministry to be developed in 1:3–13:10, and the closing concludes the letter by revisiting the significant aspects of his arguments regarding ministry developed in 1:3–13:10.

3.1 Division of 1:1–2 and 13:11–13

Paul begins the letter with the salutation in 1:1–2, which functions as an independent literary unit. Two observations support this claim. First, the flow of the literary context indicates the existence of a material shift between salutation (1:1–2) and blessing (1:3–7).[3] Second, 1:1–2 follows a standard epistolary opening.[4] Today, scholars agree that Paul's letters correspond to the form of the Hellenistic letters and that a standard epistolary salutation includes sender, recipient, and greeting formula.[5] Second Corinthians follows this convention, identifying Paul and Timothy as the sender (1:1), naming the church in Corinth and all the saints in the region of Achaia as the recipients (1:1), and expressing greeting of grace and peace (1:2).

Likewise, I maintain that 13:11–13 is an independent literary unit, functioning as the closing of the letter, based on three observations. First, the Greek adjective λοιπός is adverbially used here to signal a transition from the previous passage.[6] Second, the vocative use of ἀδελφός seems to mark the presence of a unit boundary.[7] Third, 13:11–13 closely corresponds to the epistolary formulas Paul often employs to signal the closing of the letter. Jeffrey A. D. Weima enumerates five standard epistolary conventions that frequently signal the closings in Paul's letters:

1. The peace benediction,
2. The hortatory section,
3. The greetings,

---

[3] On blessing/thanksgiving in 1:3–7, see discussion in 4.1.1 and 4.2.1.
[4] Virtually, all scholars agree to view 1:1–2 as an independent literary unit. However, scholars take different positions regarding the actual beginning of Paul's discourse (1:3, 1:8 or 1:11). See my discussion in 4.1.
[5] See Weima, *Paul the Ancient Letter Writer*, 12.
[6] BDAG, s.v. "λοιπός" (3b).
[7] Stephen H. Levinsohn argues that a vocative can be evidence for a unit boundary, though he admits that the presence of a vocative does not automatically indicate it (*Discourse Features of New Testament Greek: A Coursebook on the Information Structure of New Testament Greek*, 2nd ed. [Dallas: SIL International, 2000], 278). See also Long, *2 Corinthians*, 19–20, 258. Also, Weima describes vocative form of address marking a shift in Paul's argument (*Paul the Ancient Letter Writer*, 104–105).

Table 3.1 The Elements of Epistolary Closing Present in 2 Cor 13:11–13

Element	Text[8]
The Peace Benediction	ὁ θεὸς τῆς ἀγάπης καὶ εἰρήνης ἔσται μεθ' ὑμῶν
The Hortatory Section	Λοιπόν, ἀδελφοί, χαίρετε, καταρτίζεσθε, παρακαλεῖσθε, τὸ αὐτὸ φρονεῖτε, εἰρηνεύετε
The Greetings	Ἀσπάσασθε ἀλλήλους ἐν ἁγίῳ φιλήματι. Ἀσπάζονται ὑμᾶς οἱ ἅγιοι πάντες.
The Grace Benediction	Ἡ χάρις τοῦ κυρίου Ἰησοῦ Χριστοῦ καὶ ἡ ἀγάπη τοῦ θεοῦ καὶ ἡ κοινωνία τοῦ ἁγίου πνεύματος μετὰ πάντων ὑμῶν.[9]

4. The autograph,
5. The grace benediction.[10]

Second Corinthians includes all elements except (4) (see Table 3.1). Therefore, I maintain that 1:1–2 and 13:11–13, respectively, function as an independent literary unit.

3.2 Major Structural Relationships in Relation to the Letter as a Whole

Because of the brevity of the salutation and closing, I will focus on the MSRs of these two divisions in relation to the letter as a whole. The salutation (1:1–2) is structured according to preparation/realization with *nclusion* (1:1–2 and 13:10, 11, 13), and the closing (13:11–13) is structured according to summarization. Regarding the lack of scholarly attention to the relevance and significance of the salutation and closing of the letter in interpretation, Weima legitimately expresses his concern:

> In secular letters the primary function of the letter opening is to establish or enhance personal contact with the letter recipient. Many biblical commentators downplay the importance that this reconnecting function has in Paul's letter openings and view this first major unit of the letter (along with the letter closing) as being entirely conventional in nature, in contrast to the thanksgiving and body sections of the letter, which are judged to be more important since here the apostle takes up the specific issues that he wishes to address.[11]

---

[8] All Greek texts are from NA[28] unless otherwise noted.
[9] See more discussions in Weima, *Paul the Ancient Letter Writer*, 165–204.
[10] Weima, *Paul the Ancient Letter Writer*, 12. According to Weima, the peace benediction begins the letter closing, whereas the grace benediction signals the end of the letter (ibid., 166, 200). Also, David E. Aune similarly lists five Pauline epistolary conventions: (1) peace wish, (2) request for prayer, (3) secondary greetings, (4) holy kiss, and (5) autographed greeting (*New Testament in Its Literary Environment*, 186–87).
[11] Weima, *Paul the Ancient Letter Writer*, 11; see also Robert W. Funk, *Language, Hermeneutic, and Word of God: The Problem of Language in the New Testament and Contemporary Theology* (New York: Harper & Row, 1966), 270; Belleville, *Reflection of Glory*, 106–108; Seifrid, *Second Letter to the Corinthians*, 1–11.

Indeed, in the study of 2 Corinthians, many scholars overlook the significance of the letter opening and closing in relation to the content of the letter.[12] However, the analysis of the MSRs with the insights from epistolary criticism reveals the ways in which the opening and the closing are related to Paul's discourse pertaining to ministry in 1:3–13:10.

3.2.1 Preparation/Realization with *Inclusio* (1:1–2 and 1:3–13:10 with 13:11, 13)

I propose that 1:1–2 and 1:3–13:10 are structured according to preparation/realization with *nclusion*.[13] The salutation in 1:1–2 prepares readers by providing a threefold background for Paul's discourse regarding ministry in 1:3–13:10: writers, recipients, and greeting. This MSR indicates that Paul establishes himself as an apostle, God's human agent, who will develop the arguments pertaining to the ministry of χάρις in 2 Corinthians to address the issues that emerged from the specific situations of the Corinthian church. However, it also suggests that he wishes to develop a theological discourse that has significance and relevance to other Christian communities.

To begin, Paul establishes himself as an apostle (i.e., God's human agent) and then develops his discourse in 1:3–13:10. In 1:1 Paul identifies the senders of the letter as Paul and Timothy. Moreover, Paul overtly identifies himself as an apostle with an appositional phrase, ἀπόστολος Χριστοῦ Ἰησοῦ διὰ θελήματος θεοῦ. This epithet is significant for Paul's discourse because he uses it to establish his apostolic status in three ways.[14] First, Paul purposefully employs the title ἀπόστολος. While the title

---

[12] For instance, partition theorists often assume that various letters, which form the canonical form of 2 Corinthians, are not related to one another for an overarching message of the letter. Thus, they are not interested in the ways in which the opening and closing are connected to the remainder of the letter. Besides, many regard 13:11–13 as an appendix or addition to one of the letters (see Betz, *2 Corinthians 8 and 9*, 1–36). Scholars using rhetorical criticism recognize the letter opening and closing. Nevertheless, some do not comment on the ways in which 1:1–2 and 13:11–13 are related to their rhetorical analysis (Long, *Ancient Rhetoric and Paul's Apology*, 143–44; Amador, *The Unity of 2 Corinthians*, 414; idem, *Revisiting 2 Corinthians*, 110). Others try to make connections between the opening and closing with the overarching theme of the letter. Witherington argues that Paul's defense already begins in 1:1–2 and continues until 13:11–13, attempting to establish *ēthos* in 1:1–2 and *pathos* in 13:11–13 (*Conflict and Community in Corinth*, 353–35, 474–75). McCant insists that the closing contributes to Paul's parody to reinforce his blaming and help the reorientation of the Corinthians (*2 Corinthians*, 168–72). Vegge maintains that the closing highlights the principal theme of the letter: reconciliation (Vegge, *2 Corinthians*, 365–70). While they are right about the significance of the opening and closing of the letter, this study disagrees with the primary theme they attempt to connect with the opening and closing. The same goes for literary criticism and discourse analysis. Neither does Lim include 1:1–2 and 13:11–13 in his narrative analysis (*"The Sufferings of Christ,"* 27), nor does Land do so in his discourse analysis (*The Integrity of 2 Corinthians*, 82). Segalla, in his analysis of the macro-chiasm of the letter, sees the corresponding elements between the opening and the closing; however, his analysis lacks both the explanation regarding the ways in which 1:1–2 and 13:11–13 are related to the remainder of the book and the criteria to determine the chiastic structure (see 2.1.4.2 and 2.2.4.2).

[13] Long also identifies the MSR of 1:1–2 as preparation/realization, though he employs the term, "introduction" ("2 Corinthians," 261–95 at 271–75).

[14] See a summary of the origin and scholarly debates regarding apostle and apostleship in the NT in Paul W. Barnett, "Apostle," *DPL*, 45–51.

ἀπόστολος appears in the openings of other Pauline letters (Rom 1:1; 1 Cor 1:1; Gal 1:1; Eph 1:1; Col 1:1; 1 Tim 1:1; 2 Tim 1:1; Titus 1:1), he refrains from using the title in some letters (Phil 1:1; 1 Thess 1:1; 2 Thess 1:1; Phlm 1:1) and combines it with other titles in other letters (Rom 1:1; Titus 1:1), depending on the audience and their circumstances.[15] He consciously describes himself as an apostle in 2 Corinthians.

Second, Paul stresses Christ as the sender of the apostle: The genitival phrase Χριστοῦ Ἰησοῦ functions as a subjective genitive to denote the sender of the apostle—Christ Jesus. In other words, while ἀπόστολος, a noun form of ἀποστέλλω, underscores Paul's status as an apostle, the genitival phrase clarifies the agency of ἀποστέλλω,[16]

Third, Paul underscores God as the cause of his apostleship. The prepositional phrase διὰ θελήματος θεοῦ (cf. 8:5) conveys a causal sense, indicating that God willed Paul to be an apostle.[17] Therefore, Paul prepares his audience not merely by identifying himself and Timothy as the senders of the letter, but also by clarifying his status as an apostle. Furthermore, we already begin to see Paul's emphasis and portrayal of God as the ultimate agent, Christ as the intermediate agent, and Paul as the human agent in the salutation, which he explicates in the remainder of the letter (see full discussion in 4.2.1.1, 4.2.2.2, and 5.2).

Moreover, the identification of the recipient of the letter suggests the nature of Paul's discourse pertaining to ministry in 1:3–13:10. In 1:1 Paul indicates that the intended recipients of the letter are (1) the church in Corinth, and (2) all the saints in all Achaia. This identification suggests two facts. On the one hand, the specific identification of the recipient implies that his discourse in 1:3–13:10 is intended to address *ad hoc* situations in the Corinthian church. Paul's discussion in 1:3–13:10 reflects some of the issues needed to address in this letter. For instance, Paul develops his arguments pertaining to the ways in which God's servants proclaim the gospel (3:1–7:16) as a part of his response to those who corrupt the gospel (2:17; 4:2; cf. 11:4) and question his ministerial qualification and integrity (3:1; 4:2; 5:12; 7:2). Paul expounds the arguments pertaining to the response to the gospel (8:1–9:15) because the Corinthians have not completed the collection for the saints (8:11; 9:5).[18] Paul develops the discussion pertaining to the defense of the gospel (10:1–13:10) because some members in the Corinthian church denounce his status as a servant of Christ (10:7; 11:21); thus, the gospel he proclaims is at stake. On the other hand, the identification of the general recipient shows Paul's intention of a wider circulation of

---

[15] For instance, Joseph H. Hellerman contends regarding the letter opening of Philippians (1:1) that Paul purposefully calls himself δοῦλος instead of ἀπόστολος because he was writing the letter to counter the Roman cultural preoccupation of honor associated with titles (*Reconstructing Honor in Roman Philippi: Carmen Christi as Cursus Pudorum*, SNTSMS 132 [New York: Cambridge University Press, 2005], 116–21). Also, Weima argues regarding the opening in Rom 1:1-6 that Paul has intentionally expanded his sender formula, over against the typical form, to his unknown readers in Rome because he needs to present to them both himself as an apostle and the gospel that should be accepted (*Paul in the Ancient Letter Writer*, 14–19).

[16] Louw and Nida explain that difference between ἀπόστολος and ἄγγελος is that the former focuses on who is sent, while the latter highlights the message (L&N, s.v. "ἀπόστολος"). This is true in 2 Corinthians; when ἄγγελος is used in 12:7, Paul does not highlight the agency of Satan but the message that a thorn in the flesh/a messenger of Satan brings to keep him humble.

[17] BDAG, s.v. "διά" (A3d).

[18] On the designation of Paul's discourse in 8:1–9:15, see my discussions in Chapter 7.

the letter. Particularly, the repetition of inclusive scope with the adjectives πᾶς and ὅλος is significant, for it emphasizes that Paul both/either develops theological discourse beyond the *ad hoc* circumstances of the Corinthian church and/or assumes the relevance of his responses to other believers.[19] Thus, the identification of the recipients reveals that Paul's argument pertaining to ministry in 1:3–13:10 addresses the specific issues of the Corinthian church and its relationship with Paul as an apostle, yet it also reflects his desire to develop his theology in the letter.[20]

In addition, in 1:2 Paul introduces the major theme of his discourse to be developed in 1:3–13:10: the ministry of χάρις. He expresses the greeting of χάρις and εἰρήνη, which frames the entire letter as *nclusion* (1:2; 13:11, 13). This is Paul's standard way of beginning and closing his letters,[21] which parallels the Hellenistic and Jewish opening greeting, χαίρειν and שלום.[22] However, the word χάρις has special significance to Paul's discourse in 2 Corinthians.[23] Indeed, χάρις and its cognates describe Paul's ministry in 2 Corinthians.[24] Paul employs χάρις to depict the demeanor of his conduct (1:12). He calls his visit χάρις (1:15). He characterizes the thesis statement of his discourse with χάρις (2:14). He employs χάρις to refer to the ministry of proclamation (4:15; 6:1) and service to the poor (8:1, 4, 6, 7, 9, 19; 9:8, 14, 15). He describes the essence of his status as a servant of Christ with χάρις at the pinnacle of his defense (12:9). Moreover, he employs cognates of χάρις in the letter in relation to the ministry. He employs χάρισμα to describe God's deliverance from the affliction in his ministry (1:11), εὐχαριστέω and εὐχαριστία to express the outcome and purpose of ministry (1:11; 4:15; 9:11, 12), χαρά and χαίρω to depict the result and appropriate response to the ministry of χάρις (1:24; 2:3 [twice]; 6:10; 7:4, 7, 9, 13, 16; 8:2; 13:9, 11),[25] and χαρίζομαι to explain the proper response to the offender of the community (2:7, 10³; cf. 12:13) as the way to protect both Paul and the Corinthians from Satan's scheme (2:11). Therefore, Paul's greeting of χάρις and εἰρήνη is not merely modifications of the Greek and Jewish customary greeting. Rather, he purposefully substitutes χαίρειν with χάρις (cf. Acts 15:23; 23:26; Jas 1:1) and frames the entire letter with χάρις in order to underscore the essence of ministry that connects his various discourse in the letter.[26]

---

[19] Also see Harris, *Second Epistle to the Corinthians*, 115.
[20] In fact, this observation is reinforced by the fact that Paul generalizes the audience of his discourse in 13:11–13. In 13:11 Paul generalizes the audience of the letter by addressing them as brethren (ἀδελφοί). Moreover, in the grace benediction in 13:13, Paul adds an adjective, πᾶς, to the personal pronoun (πάντων ὑμῶν) to indicate the generalization of the recipient of the benediction. These identifications of the general audience signify the relevance of his theology of ministry to other Christian communities.
[21] Rom 1:7; 16:20; 1 Cor 1:3; 16:24; Gal 1:3–5; 6:18; Eph 1:2; 6:24; Phil 1:2; 4:23; Col 1:2; 4:18; 1 Thess 1:1; 5:28; 2 Thess 1:2; 3:18; 1 Tim 1:2; 6:21; 2 Tim 1:2; 4:22; Titus 1:4; 3:15; Phlm 3, 25.
[22] Weima, *Paul the Ancient Letter Writer*, 42.
[23] The *inclusio* with χάρις is unique to Paul's letters. Revelation is the only other book in the NT that employs χάρις to frame the content (Rev. 1:4; 22:21); other NT authors sometimes begin their letter with χάρις (1 Pet 1:2; 2 Pet 1:2; 2 John 3) or conclude it with χάρις (Heb 13:25). On the significance of εἰρήνη, see my discussions under summarization (13:11–13).
[24] Χάρις and its cognates are found in 1:2, 11, 12, 15, 24; 2:3, 7, 10, 14; 4:15; 6:1, 10; 7:4, 7, 9, 13, 16; 8:1, 2, 4, 6, 7, 9, 16, 19; 9:8, 11, 12, 14, 15; 12:9, 13; 13:9, 11, 13.
[25] See more discussions on χαρά and χαίρω in 3.2.2.
[26] See also Weima, *Paul in the Ancient Letter Writer*, 12; Harris, *Second Epistle to the Corinthians*, 135.

Therefore, the MSR of preparation/realization with *nclusion* prepares readers for Paul's discourse in 1:3–13:10 in three ways. First, Paul is going to develop a discourse as an apostle, emphasizing that God is the ultimate agent, Christ is the intermediate agent, and Paul is God's human agent. Second, his discourse is both a response to specific circumstances of the Corinthian church and a relevant message to the broader audience. Third, the ministry of χάρις describes the essence of Paul's theology of ministry.

3.2.2 Summarization (13:11–13)

I propose that 13:11–13 is structured according to summarization.[27] The MSR shows that Paul closes the letter by recapitulating major elements of his argument pertaining to ministry in 1:3–13:10. Structurally speaking, 13:11–13 consists of five elements: introduction, exhortations, peace benediction, greetings, and grace benediction (see Table 3.2). Each element revisits essential topics developed in Paul's argument regarding ministry in 1:3–13:10.

Table 3.2 Five Structural Elements in 2 Cor 13:11–13

Element	Text
Introduction	Λοιπόν, ἀδελφοί,
Exhortations	(1) χαίρετε,
	(2) καταρτίζεσθε,
	(3) παρακαλεῖσθε,
	(4) τὸ αὐτὸ φρονεῖτε,
	(5) εἰρηνεύετε,
Peace Benediction	καὶ ὁ θεὸς τῆς ἀγάπης καὶ εἰρήνης ἔσται μεθ' ὑμῶν.
Greetings	(1) Ἀσπάσασθε ἀλλήλους ἐν ἁγίῳ φιλήματι.
	(2) Ἀσπάζονται ὑμᾶς οἱ ἅγιοι πάντες.
Grace Benediction	Ἡ χάρις τοῦ κυρίου Ἰησοῦ Χριστοῦ καὶ ἡ ἀγάπη τοῦ θεοῦ καὶ ἡ κοινωνία τοῦ ἁγίου πνεύματος μετὰ πάντων ὑμῶν.[28]

---

[27] One should note that summarization differs from generalization in essence. While summarization usually involves "a point-by-point recapitulation" (Bauer and Traina, *Inductive Bible Study*, 110), generalization involves a general description (ibid., 103). In the case of 2 Cor 13:11–13, summarization is more fitting because in the closing, Paul revisits the major elements of his argument in 1:3–13:10 through thematic and lexical connections in a more deliberate fashion. However, these two MSRs may, at times, overlap, as Bauer and Traina explain, "Summarization is thus similar to the general component in generalization or particularization.... But a general statement is usually less precise, vaguer, with fewer details, while summarization is a more deliberate attempt to bring into the statement, in abridged form, the various components of what is being summarized (ibid., 110)." In fact, the closing of 2 Corinthians involves some components that represent generalization. See my notes above on the recipients of the letter (3.2.1) regarding how Paul also generalizes the audience in 13:11–13.

[28] Weima, *Paul the Ancient Letter Writer*, 165–204.

Regarding the introduction, Paul employs the words λοιπός and ἀδελφός to prepare his audience for the following material in 13:11b-13. Then, Paul succinctly gives five exhortations. Each admonition makes lexical and thematic connections to recapitulate the essence of Paul's discourse in 1:3-13:10. First, Paul exhorts the Corinthians to respond to the ministry of χάρις by rejoicing (χαίρετε). The exhortation is not only appropriate but also significant to conclude his discourse.[29] As already indicated above, Paul employs χάρις and its cognates to describe his ministry; thus, χαίρω and χαρά are closely related to the ministry of χάρις. Indeed, χάρις and χαρά frequently have overlaps in their semantic domain; they are interchangeably employed in poetry.[30] However, in the context of 2 Corinthians, χαίρω and χαρά are more precisely used to express the result and appropriate response to the ministry characterized by χάρις. Paul's visit was to bring the Corinthians joy (χαρά) but not pain (1:24); the purpose of Paul's ministry through the previous letter was that the Corinthians would make him rejoice (χαρά and χαίρω in 2:3); Paul is sorrowful but rejoices (χαίρω) in his ministry (6:10); Paul rejoices because of the Corinthians' appropriate response to his ministry through the letter (χαρά in 7:4; χαίρω in 7:7, 9); Paul rejoices (χαίρω) because of the Corinthians' ministry to Titus (7:13, 16); Macedonians' joy (χαρά) overflowed in their affliction because of God's grace (8:1-2); and Paul rejoices (χαίρω) when the Corinthians are strong in faith as his ministry intends to build them up (13:9-10).[31] Therefore, Paul exhorts the Corinthians to rejoice because joy is the proper response to the ministry of χάρις.

Second, Paul connects the word καταρτίζω with 9:5 and 13:9 to revisit his discussion pertaining to the ministry of the collection (8:1-9:15) and Paul's impending visit (12:14-13:10). First, Paul connects καταρτίζω to the immediately preceding context in 12:14-13:10, especially 13:9. In 12:14-13:10 Paul prepares the Corinthians for his impending visit,[32] in which Paul employs κατάρτισις, the noun form of καταρτίζω in 13:9, to convey his prayer for the Corinthians' maturity, and in 13:11 he again employs καταρτίζω to highlight what he has just said.[33] Second, Paul may also refer to his discussion pertaining to the collection with καταρτίζω. In 9:5 by employing the word

---

[29] While some understand χαίρετε to mean "farewell" (e.g., Alfred Plummer, *A Critical and Exegetical Commentary on the Second Epistle of St. Paul to the Corinthians*, ICC [Edinburgh: T&T Clark, 1915], 380), the word should be understood as "rejoice" because Paul seems intentional to employ χαίρετε instead of ἔρρωσθε as we see in Acts 15:29.

[30] BDAG, s.v. "χάρις."

[31] This relationship between χάρις and χαρά are also seen in the works of literature outside the NT. For instance, the Apostolic Fathers understood the direct connections between those terms: *Martyrdom of Polycarp* employs χάρις and χαρά to describe Polycarp's demeanor (12.1); Polycarp understands that joy is the result of salvation by grace (*Pol. Phil.* 1.3). Sirach 1:12-13 expresses that fear of the Lord results in χαρά and χάρις. Also, 3 Macc 5:14 articulates that grace results in joy. Likewise, Philo's writing shows the same idea in *Alleg. Interp.* 3.81 that the unwillingness of the Ammonites and Moabites to give food results in the cessation of God's grace and assembly.

[32] See 8.1.2 and 8.2.1.4.

[33] Scholars debate regarding (1) whether the sense of the word should be construed as restoration (e.g., C. K. Barrett, *A Commentary on the Second Epistle to the Corinthians*, BNTC [London: Black, 1973], 341-42; Furnish, *II Corinthians*, 581; Martin, *2 Corinthians*, 709) or perfection/completion (e.g., Plummer, *Second Epistle to St. Paul to the Corinthians*, 380) and (2) whether the voice of the word should be parsed as passive (e.g., Furnish, *II Corinthians*, 581) or middle (e.g., Martin, *2 Corinthians*, 709). Nevertheless, they agree that καταρτίζω should be understood in relation to the noun form of καταρτίζω, κατάρτισις in 13:9.

προκαταρτίζω (πρό + καταρτίζω), he explains that he encouraged the brothers to go to the Corinthians and prepare their contribution in advance. These two lexical connections suggest that the second exhortation in 13:11 may be translated as "prepare yourself" or "be prepared," reminding the Corinthians to participate in the ministry to the saints (8:1–9:15) and to prepare themselves for his impending visit (12:14–13:10),[34] both of which are to be accomplished before Paul's next visit to the Corinthians.

Third, Paul employs παρακαλέω to revisit the character of ministry. Paul begins the content of the letter by describing God's character, especially that of encouragement in 1:3–7, which serves as one major theme of the letter.[35] With the third exhortation, Paul reminds the Corinthians of the character of the ministry.[36]

Fourth, Paul connects the fourth exhortation, τὸ αὐτὸ φρονεῖτε, with the defense of his status as a servant of Christ in 10:1–12:13. The literal translation of τὸ αὐτὸ φρονεῖτε is "think or judge the same." Paul has to urge them regarding this exhortation because the Corinthians do not think or judge the same way Paul does: The Corinthians do not think that Paul is a servant of Christ (10:7), but Paul insists that he is (11:23); Paul does not think that super-apostles are servants of Christ (11:13, 15), but the Corinthians think that they are (11:23).[37] Thus, he must defend his status in 10:1–12:13 so that they would "think or judge the same" on this matter. Therefore, with the four exhortations, Paul is reminding the Corinthians that they must accept Paul as a servant of Christ according to his defense (esp. 11:1–12:13).[38]

---

[34] This does not deny the presence of other possibilities of semantic meaning and parsing of the voice; one does not have to exclusively choose either/or. I believe that the ambiguity, particularly of its voice, may have been intended to convey broader meanings.

[35] See further discussion in 4.2.2.1–2.

[36] The word, παρακαλεῖσθε in 13:11, can be parsed as middle or passive voice; thus, it can be translated as "encourage one another" or "be encouraged." Some scholars do not consider the possibility of middle voice because Paul elsewhere expresses such idea by employing a reciprocal pronoun (i.e., παρακαλεῖτε ἀλλήλους in 1 Thess 4:18; 5:11; e.g., Harris, *The Second Epistle to the Corinthians*, 933). However, this does not eliminate the possibility of the middle voice because the literary context in 1:3–7 clarifies that encouragement has both a vertical and horizontal dimension: One is encouraged by God (vertical) so that s/he can encourage others (horizontal). Therefore, Paul may have intended to employ the middle/passive form of παρακαλέω to convey both dimensions in a pithy fashion in the hortatory section, where five exhortations are succinctly and rhythmically expressed with asyndeton.

[37] The exhortation also has an overtone to address the existence of fractions among the Corinthians in 12:20 (cf. 1 Cor 1:10), for the strife often occurs due to people not "thinking or judging the same." See BDAG, s.v. "φρονέω"; Garland, *2 Corinthians*, 552; Thrall, *Second Epistle of the Corinthians*, 2:907; Harris, *Second Epistle to the Corinthians*, 933–34; Martin, *2 Corinthians*, 709–10; Guthrie, *2 Corinthians*, 651.

[38] Noteworthy is the correlation between the word φρονέω in 13:11 and its cognates in 11:1–12:13. While Paul urges the Corinthians to "think or judge the same" emplying φρονέω in 13:11, the Corinthians think that they indeed have sound judgement in 11:19: ἡδέως γὰρ ἀνέχεσθε τῶν ἀφρόνων φρόνιμοι ὄντες. Thus, Paul sarcastically accuses them of their misjudgment employing φρόνιμος and ἄφρων, the cognates of φρονέω. Moreover, Paul repeatedly and ironically describes his fool's speech with antonymous cognates of φρονέω: ἀφροσύνη (11:1, 7, 21), ἄφρων (11:16[2]; 12:6, 11), φρόνιμος (11:19), and παραφρονέω (11:23). Paul intends the contrast between φρονέω (13:11; and its cognate, φρόνιμος in 11:19) and its antonymous cognates in order to pursue the Corinthians to "think or judge the same" way Paul does regarding his status. Describing one of those terms, ἀφροσύνη, Harris explains, "ἀφροσύνη refers to an act of deliberate folly in pursuing a particular course of action in order to achieve commendable ends, and therefore is neither ignorant stupidity nor crass foolhardiness" (*Second Epistle to the Corinthians*, 733). This is exactly what Paul is doing in his skillful employment of these words.

Fifth, in addition to framing the entire letter with εἰρηνεύω and εἰρήνη (*inclusio* in 3.2.1), the literary context of the letter suggests that Paul exhorts the Corinthians to live in peace in three ways (cf. 5:11–6:2; 7:2; 12:20). He urges them to live in peace with one another despite the factions (12:20). Furthermore, the Corinthians are to live in peace with God because of his reconciling work (5:11–7:3). Paul, as a servant of God's reconciling work (5:18) and ambassador for Christ (5:20), urges them to be reconciled to God (5:20–6:10), and the consequence is to live in peace with the One who reconciled them to himself.[39] Paul also urges the Corinthians to be reconciled to God's servants (6:11–7:3); thus, they are also to live in peace with Paul and his fellow workers. In other words, the ramification of God's reconciling work involves the restoration and peace between not only God and the Corinthians but also between his servants and the Corinthians.

Moreover, the presence of τῆς ἀγάπης is unique to 2 Corinthians; it is found neither in the NT nor the OT.[40] However, the Greek verb ἀγαπάω and its cognates (ἀγάπη and ἀγαπητός) capture one of the main emphases of Paul's discourse in the letter: Love is the basis of Paul's ministry. Paul proclaims and defends the gospel because he loves the Corinthians (2:4; 7:1; 11:11; 12:15, 19) and because the love of Christ urged him to proclaim the ministry of reconciliation (5:14). He encourages them to participate in the ministry to the saints through the collection because the fiscal contribution is the expression of love (8:7, 8, 24) and because God loves a cheerful giver (9:7). Thus, he urges the Corinthians to reaffirm the same love for the one who offended the community in the expression of forgiveness and encouragement (2:8).[41] Therefore, the peace benediction revisits a critical theme of love in Paul's discourse pertaining to ministry.

Concerning the greeting, Paul revisits his emphasis on love and peace and his exhortation pertaining to the collection. Paul expresses two types of greeting: the second-person and the third-person greeting.[42] These greetings continue to describe the emphasis and content of Paul's discourse in 1:3–13:10. First, the command to greet one another with a holy kiss continues to challenge the Corinthians to live in the reality

---

[39] Indeed, the ideas of reconciliation (καταλλάσσω) and peace (εἰρήνη) are closely related. In the NT, we find in Stephen's speech in Acts 7:26 that συναλλάσσω, a cognate of καταλλάσσω, is used with εἰρήνη in the context where Moses tried to reconcile the fighting men in peace (συνήλλασσεν αὐτοὺς εἰς εἰρήνην). Also, the author of Second Maccabees employed both terms in close proximity in prayer (1:4–5). Eusebius equates God's work of καταλλάσσω with εἰρήνη (*Praep. ev.* 1.1.8; *Comm. Isa.* 1.54). Moreover, ancient historians understand the relationship between reconciliation and peace in a way similar to Paul in 2 Corinthians. Diodorus Siculus indicates that peace is the result of reconciliation (*Bib. his.* 22.8.4). Dio Cassius expresses the same idea (*Hist. rom.* 44.25.3–4).

[40] Plummer, *Second Epistles*, 381; Furnish, *II Corinthians*, 582.

[41] In terms of the logical connection between the five exhortations and the peace benediction, the benediction can be either an apodosis of conditional imperatives or a basis for the exhortations. Grammatically speaking, on the one hand, an imperative + καί + future indicative construction can be used to form a conditional imperative: the imperative as protasis and the future indicative as apodosis (Wallace, *Greek Grammar Beyond the Basics*, 489–92). Therefore, the presence of God's peace and love forms a result or fulfillment of the exhortations. However, on the other hand, the literary context suggests that the love of Christ and God (5:4; 9:7) functions as a basis for Paul's ministry. Thus, one might not have to choose one or the other; instead, both possibilities are present.

[42] The second-person greeting is the sender asking the recipient of the letter to greet someone else on his or her behalf. The third-person greeting is the sender greeting the recipient of the letter on someone's behalf. See Weima, *Paul the Ancient Letter Writer*, 182–93.

of the peace and love of God (13:11).⁴³ The practice of exchanging kisses was widespread in the ancient world.⁴⁴ However, Weima argues that the addition of ἅγιος to the practice of kiss greeting signifies "not merely friendship and love, but more specifically reconciliation and peace."⁴⁵ Second, on the one hand, the third-person greeting serves as a reminder that the Corinthian church belongs to the larger body of Christ,⁴⁶ yet, more specifically, it seems reminding the Corinthians of the exhortation to participate in the collection in chs 8–9 because Paul repeatedly refers to the recipient of the collection as the saints (8:4; 9:1, 12).⁴⁷ Therefore, Paul continues to exhort the Corinthians to live in God's love, to live in peace in greeting with one another with a holy kiss, and to remember other believers and their need.

Finally, the grace benediction also recapitulates the crucial themes of Paul's discourse: χάρις, ἀγάπη, and κοινωνία. I have already discussed the ways in which the themes of grace and love are related to Paul's arguments pertaining to ministry. Here he adds one more theme—κοινωνία—to that of grace and love. Particularly, κοινωνία is an important theme in 1:3–2:13, 6:14–7:1, and 8:1–9:15. In 1:3–2:13, Paul characterizes his ministry with the theme of mutuality, especially that of encouragement. He and the Corinthians are participants/sharers (κοινωνός) in suffering and encouragement (1:7). In 6:14–7:1, Paul urges the Corinthians to partner with believers.⁴⁸ In 8:1–9:15, Paul encourages the Corinthians' participation (κοινωνία) in the ministry to the saints (8:4; 9:13; cf. 8:23).⁴⁹ Therefore, the MSR of summarization (1:3–13:10 and 13:11–13) reveals that while Paul follows the conventional letter closing, he selects key terms and themes to recapitulate major elements of his discourse regarding ministry.

3.3 Conclusion

In this chapter, I have identified 1:1–2 and 13:11–13 as independent literary units and expounded two MSRs: preparation/realization with *inclusio* in the salutation (1:1–2 and 1:3–13:10 with 13:11, 13) and summarization in the closing (13:11–13). The preparation/realization with *inclusio* has shown the ways in which the threefold

---

⁴³ Ibid., 187–93.
⁴⁴ Gustav Stählin, "φιλέω," *TDNT* 9:118–46.
⁴⁵ Weima, *Paul the Ancient Letter Writer*, 188. Also see Rom 16:16; 1 Cor 16:20; 1 Thess 5:26; 1 Pet 5:14.
⁴⁶ Ibid., 193.
⁴⁷ If, as Ralph J. Korner argues, Paul's use of the term, οἱ ἅγιοι, refers to Christ-followers associated and loyal to the apostles in Jerusalem, while that of ἐκκλησία refers to Christ-followers associated with Paul and his gentile mission (*The Origin and Meaning of Ekklēsia in the Early Jesus Movement*, Ancient Judaism and Early Christianity 98 [Leiden; Boston: Brill, 2017], especially 150–263; idem, "Paul's Corinthian Ekklēsia: A Non-Misogynistic, Sacred 'Location' for Jewish Manumission Ethics?" (presentation, Power and Authority Working Group at Annual Meeting of the Pacific Northwest Region of the Society of Biblical Literature, Virtual Meeting, May 13–14, 2022), it reinforces my observation because the collection is for the church in Jerusalem (Rom 15:26).
⁴⁸ See full discussion in 6.2.1.
⁴⁹ Scholars often call the blessing in 13:13 "the trinitarian blessing." On the trinitarian formula and its origin in 2 Cor 13:11, see Thrall, *Second Epistle of the Corinthians*, 2: 914–21; Harris, *Second Epistle to the Corinthians*, 936–40.

background prepares his audience for Paul's discourse regarding ministry in 1:3–13:10. Paul writes the letter as an apostle, who is God's human agent sent by Christ (the intermediate agent) and willed by God (the ultimate agent), and develops his discourse in both addressing specific circumstances of the Corinthian church and expounding his theology of ministry that is relevant to other Christian communities. In addition, Paul frames the entire letter with the notion of χάρις and εἰρήνη, which characterizes his ministry.

I have also argued that summarization in the closing (13:11–13) recapitulates the essential aspects of Paul's discourse in 1:3–13:10. Paul gives five brief exhortations to the Corinthians. Paul exhorts them to rejoice because χαίρω and χαρά are suitable responses to the ministry of χάρις. He urges them to be prepared/prepare themselves for the ministry to the saints (chs 8–9) and his impending visit (12:14–13:10). He admonishes them to be encouraged/encourage one another because God's encouragement characterizes Paul's ministry (1:3–2:13). He exhorts them to think/judge the same because they misjudge Paul as not being the servant of Christ (10:1–12:13). He reminds them to live in peace despite the dissensions among themselves (12:20) and as the consequence of reconciliation with God and with his servants (5:11–7:3). After the exhortation, Paul gives the peace benediction to remind them of love as the foundation of his ministry (2:4, 8; 5:4; 7:1; 8:7, 8, 24; 9:7; 11:11; 12:15, 19). Then, he proceeds to the greetings in which he highlights remembering the larger body of Christ and particularly the ministry of the collection to the saints (8:4; 9:1, 12). Finally, Paul concludes the closing with the grace benediction to recapture the essence of his argument: grace, love, and, specifically, sharing/partnership in the ministry (1:7; 6:14–7:1; 8:1–9:15). Having studied the literary structure of 1:1–2 and 13:11–13, I will now turn to the analysis of 1:3–2:13.

4

Arguments Pertaining to Basis for Ministry: Character of Ministry (1:3–2:13)

In Chapter 3, I identified the divisions of 1:1–2 and 13:11–13 and demonstrated that the MSRs of the salutation (1:1–2) and the closing (13:11–13) show the ways in which each division is related to Paul's discourse of ministry in 1:3–13:10. In this chapter, I turn to what many scholars consider the first major division of the letter. My task is (1) to identify main units and subunits according to the linear arrangement of the materials within the letter, and (2) to explain the MSRs in relation both to the division as a whole and the letter as a whole. The purpose of this task is to show Paul's coherent discourse regarding the theme of mutuality throughout 1:3–2:13, which serves as a basis for the rest of his arguments and introduces some major themes to be developed in 2:14–13:10.

4.1 Division of 1:3–2:13

Regarding the division of 1:3–2:13, I propose its main units and subunits as follows:

A. General Statement: Mutuality of Suffering and Encouragement (1:3–7)
   1. Description of God's Character and Mutuality of Suffering and Encouragement (1:3–5)
   2. Mutuality of Suffering and Encouragement in Relationship between God's Agents and the Corinthians (1:6–7)
B. Examples and Reasons for Mutuality of Suffering and Encouragement: Mutuality of Ministry and Boasting (1:8–2:11)
   1. Mutuality of Encouragement and Ministry (1:8–11)
      a) God's Deliverance from Affliction as a Testimony of Divine Encouragement in Suffering (1:8–10)
      b) Mutuality of Ministry: the Corinthians' Cooperation in Ministry (1:11)
   2. Mutuality of Boasting (1:12–2:11)
      a) Mutuality of Boasting: Integrity of Paul's Conduct as His Boasting (1:12–14)
      b) Mutuality of Joy in Paul's Defense of Change of Travel Plan (1:15–2:2)
      c) Mutuality of Joy, Love, Sorrow, and Forgiveness in Paul's Defense of Previous Letter (2:3–11)
C. Transitional Travel Narrative (2:12–13)

Scholars continue to debate regarding the identification of the first major division of the letter. Some scholars identify 1:1–2:13 as a literary unit, but others disagree with it (see 2.1). In this chapter, I contend that 1:3–2:13 is a major division of the letter. One must address at least two issues in order to demonstrate the segmentation of the letter: Where it begins and ends. Thus, I will first demonstrate the beginning and ending of the division and then explain the identification of main units and subunits within the division.

Regarding the beginning, virtually no scholars disagree that 1:3 starts a new literary unit, since they recognize a shift of literary form from the salutation/epistolary opening (1:1–2) to thanksgiving/blessing (1:3–7 or 1:3–11). However, some scholars differ on the identification of the ending of the division. I agree with many scholars that 2:13 marks the ending of the division because it is signaled by a shift of content and literary form. Namely, readers encounter not only a disruption of the content but also a change of the literary form from a travel narrative (2:12–13) to thanksgiving (2:14–17); thus, most scholars, including partition theorists, recognize the presence of the abrupt transition.[1] With the identification of 1:3–2:13 as a major division, I shall turn to discuss the main units of the division: 1:3–7, 1:8–2:11, and 2:12–13.

4.1.1 1:3–7

Regarding the first main unit (1:3–7), scholars differ with one another on the identification of the ending of the so-called introductory thanksgiving or blessing.[2] Some think that the blessing ends in 1:7,[3] and others maintain that it continues to 1:11.[4] However, insights from topical, epistolary, rhetorical, and linguistic analysis suggest that 1:3–7 and 1:8–11 should be treated each as an independent literary unit.

---

[1] Because of the break between 2:13 and 2:14, many partition theorists, such as Johannes Weiss, Rudolf Bultmann, Walter Schmithals, Dieter Georgi, Günther Bornkamm, Willi Marxsen, Philipp Vielhauer, Alfred Suhl, and Hans M. Schenke and Karl M. Fischer, postulate that 1:1–2:13 and 7:5–16 or 1:1–2:13 and 7:5–8:24 belong to the same letter, often called "Letter of Reconciliation" (see the summary of partition theorists in Thrall, *Second Epistle of the Corinthians*, 1:47–49). Others who maintain the unity of the letter also acknowledge the discontinuity between 2:13 and 2:14 as well as the continuity between 2:13 and 7:5; thus, some consider 2:14–7:4 the major digression since it was a common phenomenon in the ancient writings, such as in the work of Homer (e.g., Hughes, *Paul's Second Epistle to the Corinthians*, 76; Harris, *Second Epistles to the Corinthians*, 240–41; Keener, *1–2 Corinthians*, 163–64).

[2] Scholars argue that the blessing follows the form of a traditional Jewish *berakah*. On the introductory Berakah in 2 Corinthians, see Peter T. O'Brien, *Introductory Thanksgivings in the Letters of Paul*, NovTSup 49 (Leiden: Brill, 1977), 233–58; also, Keener, *1–2 Corinthians*, 157, citing Ps 72:18; Tob 13:1; 3 Macc 7:23; 1 En. 63:2; m. Ber. passim; Laura D. Alary, "Good Grief: Paul as Sufferer and Consoler in 2 Corinthians 1:3–7: A Comparative Investigation" (PhD diss., University of St. Michael's College, 2003).

[3] E.g., Belleville, *Reflections of Glory*, 108–14; Witherington, *Conflict and Community in Corinth*, 356–59; Garland, *2 Corinthians*, 52–70; McCant, *2 Corinthians*, 29–30; Martin, *2 Corinthians*, 139–46; Seifrid, *Second Letter to the Corinthians*, 11–30; Land, *Integrity of 2 Corinthians*, 83–86; cf. Long, *Ancient Rhetoric and Paul's Apology*, 145–51.

[4] E.g., Plummer, *Second Epistles*, 6–22; Barrett, *Second Epistle to the Corinthians*, 56–68; O'Brien, *Introductory Thanksgivings*, 235–36; Furnish, *II Corinthians*, 108–25; Thrall, *Second Epistle of the Corinthians*, 1:98–127; Scott, *2 Corinthians*, 23–33; Matera, *II Corinthians*, 33–44; Vegge, *2 Corinthians*, 150–53; Lim, "The Sufferings of Christ," 40–43.

First, a shift of topic occurs between 1:3–7 and 1:8–11. Many scholars espousing 1:3–11 as an introductory thanksgiving or blessing base their argument on (1) their observation of a coherent theme of suffering and comfort between 1:3–7 and 1:8–11, and/or (2) the presence of γάρ in 1:8, indicating the close connection with 1:3–7.[5] Indeed, I agree that a strong continuity regarding the theme of suffering exists between these units. However, 1:8–11 also exhibits a shift of topic from the theme of suffering (1:8–10) to the Corinthians' cooperation in ministry (1:11).[6] Moreover, the appeal to the conjunction γάρ connecting 1:3–7 and 1:8–11 is not sufficient. While interpreters take γάρ in 1:8 as a positive indication of the connection between 1:3–7 and 1:8–11, their appeal is not based on the grammatical function of the conjunction but on the theme of suffering and comfort. In other words, if the grammatical function of γάρ connects 1:3–7 and 1:8–11, the same conjunction in 1:12 should be construed as evidence that 1:12–14 is a part of the introductory thanksgiving or blessing. However, interpreters do not consider γάρ in 1:12 to be functioning in that way.[7] Their appeal to the function of γάρ in 1:8 is not consistent.

Second, a shift of a literary form exists between 1:3–7 and 1:8–11: While 1:3–7 is a form of blessing, 1:8–11 is a narrative. Other Pauline letters do not attest to an inclusion of a narrative as a part of introductory thanksgiving or blessing. In fact, scholars using a rhetorical analysis identify 1:8 as the beginning of *narratio*, for they recognize the change of the literary form, signaling the boundary of the segmentation.[8] In addition, this shift of a literary form serves as the evidence against the argument that εὐλογητός in 1:3 and εὐχαριστέω in 1:11 frame 1:3–11 as an introductory thanksgiving.[9] Specifically speaking, 1:3–7 is a form of blessing but not that of thanksgiving: Paul chose to express blessing instead of thanksgiving.[10] Thus, framing 1:3–11 with reference to thanksgiving seems coincidental because we do not find any other Pauline letters framing thanksgiving with εὐχαριστέω. Moreover, 1:3–7 and 1:8–11 belong to different literary forms; Paul typically does not combine introductory thanksgiving and blessing.

---

[5] E.g., Plummer, *Second Epistles*, 15; Barrett, *Second Epistle to the Corinthians*, 81; O'Brien, *Introductory Thanksgivings*, 235; Furnish, *II Corinthians*, 121–22; Lambrecht, *Second Corinthians*, 22; Lim, "The Sufferings of Christ," 40–43l.

[6] See further discussion in 4.2.1.

[7] Thus, scholars try to provide explanations on γάρ in 1:12 in relation to the immediately preceding literary context. For instance, Plummer argues that γάρ shows the connection with the preceding material regarding thanksgiving and hope (*Second Epistle*, 23; cf. Thrall, *Second Epistle of the Corinthians*, 1:129). Furnish and Garland translate γάρ as "now" by understanding it as functioning like the conjunction δέ (Furnish, *II Corinthians*, 126; Garland, *2 Corinthians*, 93. Also see Vagge, *2 Corinthians*, 170).

[8] Although scholars disagree where the *narratio* of 2 Corinthian ends, they agree that 1:8 is the beginning of *narratio*. See Kennedy, *Rhetorical Criticism*, 87; Witherington, *Conflict and Community in Corinth*, 360–61; Long, *Ancient Rhetoric and Paul's Apology*, 151–56.

[9] O'Brien, *Introductory Thanksgiving*, 235–36; Vegge, *2 Corinthians*, 150–52.

[10] O'Brien notes the difference between thanksgiving and blessing as follows: "Of far greater significance is the fact ... that although either the εὐχαριστέω- or εὐλογητός- formulas could have been used of thanksgiving or praise to God for blessings *either* to others *or* for oneself, Paul, in the introductions of his letters, uses εὐχαριστέω consistently of Fürdank for God's work in the lives of the addresses, and εὐλογητός for blessings in which he himself participated" (*Introductory Thanksgiving*, 239). This is exactly what we find in 2 Cor 1:3–7, for Paul proceeds to describe his testimony of God's deliverance from the affliction in Asia in 1:8–11.

Third, the epistolary convention of disclosure formula in 1:8 (Οὐ γὰρ θέλομεν ὑμᾶς ἀγνοεῖν) indicates a major transition between 1:7 and 1:8. Scholars employing epistolary criticism understand that the presence of disclosure formula in 1:8 marks the boundary of the division. Weima explains, "The primary function of the disclosure formula is transitional: to signal a major (or less often a minor) shift either in the subject matter or in a stage of Paul's argumentation."[11] This general function of a disclosure formula fits well into the literary context of 2 Cor 1:8, as described above.

Fourth, the vocative expression ἀδελφοί in 1:8 appears to mark the presence of a unit boundary.[12] Weima explains the function of the vocative form of address, stating, "In addition to its grammatical function as a form of address, the vocative also has a literary function: as a transition marker indicating either a major or minor shift in Paul's argument."[13] Although the presence of the vocative itself may not be taken as affirmative evidence, it is an additional confirmation that a new literary unit begins in 1:8, especially given the convergence of evidence regarding the existence of the shifts of emphases between 1:7 and 1:8 as previously described. Therefore, while I admit the transitional nature of 1:8–11, I conclude that 1:3–7 and 1:8–11 should be respectively treated as an independent unit. Thus, 1:3–7 is the first main unit within 1:3–2:13, and 1:8–11 belongs to the second main unit, 1:8–2:11.

The division of 1:3–7 consists of two subunits: 1:3–5 and 1:6–7. The boundary of the subunits is marked by two observations. First, Paul moves from a general description of mutuality among God, Christ, and Paul and his fellow workers (1:3–5) to a particular description of the same theme (1:6–7). In addition, the former (1:3–5) causes the latter (1:6–7); Paul begins to apply the description of mutuality of suffering and encouragement (1:3–5) to the relationship between Paul and his fellow workers and the Corinthians by directly addressing them in 1:6–7. Second, the presence of the conjunction δέ suggests the beginning of a new subunit. Levinsohn explains, "The basic function of δέ is the same in narrative and nonnarrative text. In both it is used to mark new developments, in the sense that the information it introduces builds on what has gone before and makes a distinct contribution to the argument."[14] Thus, 1:3–7 comprises two subunits: 1:3–5 and 1:6–7.

---

[11] Weima, *Paul the Ancient Letter Writer*, 95. Also see Jack T. Sanders, "The Transition from Opening Epistolary Thanksgiving to Body in the Letters of the Pauline Corpus," *JBL* 81 (1962): 348–62; John L. White, "Introductory Formulae in the Body of the Pauline Letter," *JBL* 90 (1971): 91–97; Belleville, *Reflections of Glory*, 115–19; Stanley E. Porter and Andrew W. Pitts, "The Disclosure Formula in the Epistolary Papyri and in the New Testament: Development, Form, Function, and Syntax," in *The Language of the New Testament: Context, History, and Development*, ed. Stanley E. Porter and Andrew W. Pitts, Linguistic Biblical Studies 6 (Leiden: Brill, 2013), 421–38.

[12] See my discussion on vocative in 3.2.2.

[13] Weima, *Paul the Ancient Letter Writer*, 104.

[14] Levinsohn, *Discourse Features*, 112–18 at 112. Levinsohn attempts to address the issue that scholars often treat the most common conjunctions in the NT, δέ and καί, as indistinguishable terms. However, in his inductive analysis of the conjunctions, he concludes that each conjunction has a distinct discourse function in both narrative and non-narrative texts in the Bible (see ibid., 71–131); See also Long, *2 Corinthians*, 9–10. However, it is wrong to assume that δέ always signifies a unit boundary, though it does in many cases (e.g., δέ in 1:6 marks a unit boundary between 1:3–5 and 1:6–7; δέ in 1:13b signals a boundary unit between 1:12–13a and 1:13b–14 as subunits within 1:12–14). For instance, δέ in 1:12 does not mark the beginning of a subunit; rather, it marks a further development of Paul's statement regarding his conduct.

4.1.2 1:8–2:11

Having identified the division of 1:3–7 as the first main unit of 1:3–2:13, I will turn to the second main unit—1:8–2:11. As already demonstrated, evidence suggests that 1:8 begins a new literary unit that ends in 2:11.[15] The second main unit comprises two subunits: 1:8–11 and 1:12–2:11.

4.1.2.1 1:8–11

Regarding the first subunit (1:8–11) of 1:8–2:11, I demarcate it into 1:8–10 and 1:11. Grammatically speaking, 1:11 continues the sentence that begins in 1:9 with the participle form of συνυπουργέω. However, a shift of topic takes place between 1:8–10 and 1:11, which signals a division. Namely, Paul switches a topic from God's deliverance (1:8–10) to the Corinthians' cooperation in ministry (1:11).[16]

4.1.2.2 1:12–2:11

Regarding the second subunit of 1:8–2:11, some scholars maintain that 1:12–2:13 is a major literary unit of the letter,[17] but others disagree with the segmentation.[18] However, I claim that 1:12–2:11 is the second subunit of 1:8–2:13.[19] While I admit the possibility of the inclusion of 2:12–13 into 1:12–2:11, I treat 2:12–13 separately, for it functions as a transitional and bridging section between 1:12–2:11 and 2:14–7:16.[20] Three observations suggest 1:12 as the beginning of a new literary unit: a shift of topic, a shift of literary form, and the discourse feature of a demonstrative pronoun (αὕτη) in 1:12.

First, a shift of topic exists between 1:8–11 and 1:12–2:11. Paul develops mutuality of divine encouragement in suffering and cooperation of ministry in 1:8–11 and proceeds to expound that of boasting, particularly in 1:12–14.[21]

Second, while some scholars using rhetorical criticism consider that *narratio* continues beyond 1:8–11, leading to disagreements among the rhetorical critics,[22] a shift of literary form from a narrative (1:8–11) to a defense (1:12–2:11) suggests that

---

[15] Regarding the ending, see my discussion on 2:12–13 in 4.1.3.
[16] See more discussion in 4.2.1.2.
[17] E.g., Furnish, *II Corinthians*, 126–72; Thrall, *Second Epistle of the Corinthians*, 1:128–87; Barnett, *Second Epistle to the Corinthians*, 91–137; Scott, *2 Corinthians*, 34–58; Lambrecht, *Second Corinthians*, 25–36; Harris, *Second Epistle to the Corinthians*, 182–240; Guthrie, *2 Corinthians*, 91–149.
[18] E.g., Plummer, *Second Epistle*, 23–75; Barrett, *Second Epistle to the Corinthians*, 68–95; Belleville, *Reflections of Glory*, 120; Witherington, *Conflict and Community in Corinth*, 360–70; McCant, *2 Corinthians*, 32–36; Matera, *II Corinthians*, 46–65; Long, *Ancient Rhetoric and Paul's Apology*, 151–77; Vegge, *2 Corinthians*, 374–75; Martin, *2 Corinthians*, 153–80; Seifrid, *Second Letter to the Corinthians*, 45–95.
[19] See also Hafemann, *2 Corinthians*, 79–104.
[20] See further discussion in 4.2.1.4.
[21] See my discussion in 4.2.1 regarding the ways in which Paul develops his claim in 1:3–7 in the following material in 1:8–2:13 and the ways in which γάρ in 1:8 and 1:12 functions.
[22] Kennedy understands 1:8–2:13 as *narratio* (*Rhetorical Criticism*, 87); Witherington maintains 1:8–2:16 as *narratio* (*Conflict and Community in Corinth*, 360–70); Long argues that 1:8–16, 2:12–13, and 7:2–16 are *narratio* (*Ancient Rhetoric and Paul's Apology*, 151–57).

1:12 begins a new literary unit.[23] Furthermore, Paul's use of verb tenses supports the shift, most prominently in 1:12-14 as the introduction of 1:12-2:11. A narration typically reports events leading up to the occasion of the writing, so Paul naturally describes the event in 1:8-11, mainly with past-tense verbs.[24] However, he switches to present-tense verbs in 1:12-14.[25] Thus, it makes more sense to construe the material in 1:12-2:11 as a discursive text, especially that of defense regarding his conduct, rather than a narration.

Third, the discourse function of a demonstrative pronoun αὕτη in 1:12 suggests the unit boundary between 1:8-11 and 1:12-2:11, for it functions as a forward-pointing reference.[26] Runge explains that forward-pointing references point forward to a target, stating, "Expressions like these are a way of slowing down the flow of the discourse before something surprising or important is about to be disclosed."[27] In the case of 1:12, the demonstrative pronoun αὕτη points both to a noun phrase, τὸ μαρτύριον τῆς συνειδήσεως ἡμῶν, and an epexegetical clause introduced by ὅτι. Since pronouns usually point back to something already mentioned, the forward-pointing reference marked by αὕτη in 1:12 suggests the presence of discontinuity between 1:8-11 and 1:12-2:11. For these reasons, I conclude that 1:12 begins a new literary unit.

Thus, I now proceed to discuss 1:12-14 as a subunit within 1:12-2:11.[28] One major factor of this claim is the coherent theme of boasting in 1:12-14. Paul boasts about the integrity of his conduct, especially toward the Corinthians (1:12-13a) and hopes for the Corinthians' full comprehension of such boasting (1:13b-14). The theme of boasting continues throughout 1:12-14, but it does not extend beyond 1:14; the words καύχησις, καύχημα, and their cognates do not reappear until 5:12.[29] In fact, one may argue that 1:12-14 is structured according to an *inclusio*, which frames 1:12-14 with the word καύχησις (1:12) and καύχημα (1:14).[30] Thus, agreeing with many scholars, I maintain 1:12-14 as a literary unit within 1:12-2:11.

---

[23] The terms καύχησις (1:12) and καύχημα (1:14) appear first time in the letter. Boasting is one significant characteristic of the apologetic speech in the forensic discourse (Witherington, *Conflict and Community in Corinth*, 432-41; Also see Long, *Ancient Rhetoric and Paul's Apology*, 71-96). Thus, Paul shifts from a narrative to a defense in 1:12-2:11.

[24] The Greek verbs βαρέω (1:8) and ῥύομαι (1:10) are in aorist indicative form, while ἔχω (1:9) and ἐλπίζω (1:10) are in perfect indicative forms. On the relationship between verb tenses and the action of time, see my footnote in 2.1.3.4.

[25] Paul employs aorist indicative verbs in 1:12 (ἀναστρέφω) and 1:14 (ἐπιγινώσκω; see the table of verb tense in 2 Cor 1:8-16 in Long, *Ancient Rhetoric and Paul's Apology*, 153). However, the presence of the two past-tense indicative verbs does not indicate 1:12-14 to be a part of *narratio* for two reasons. First, the use of present-tense indicative verbs (εἰμί in 1:12 and 14; γράφω, ἀναγινώσκω, ἐπιγινώσκω, and ἐλπίζω in 1:13) is more prominent than past-tense indicatives in 1:12-14. Second, Paul often appeals to the past experience in his defense (e.g., 2 Cor 11:23-9). So, it is not surprising that Paul appeals to his behaviors in the past to emphasize his boasting in 1:12-14.

[26] On discourse function of γάρ in 1:12, see my discussion in 4.2.1.2.

[27] Runge, *Discourse Grammar*, 62; See also Long, *2 Corinthians*, 20, 25.

[28] Many scholars view 1:12-14 as a unit. E.g., Plummer, *Second Epistle*, 23; Furnish, *II Corinthians*, 126-27; Thrall, *Second Epistle of the Corinthians*, 1:129-135; Lambrecht, *Second Corinthians*, 33-34; Barnett, *Second Epistle to the Corinthians*, 92-98; Garland, *2 Corinthians*, 83-94; Amador, *Revisiting 2 Corinthians*, 111; Hafemann, *2 Corinthians*, 81; Matera, *II Corinthians*, 46-50; Harris, *Second Epistle to the Corinthians*, 182-13; Vegge, *2 Corinthians*, 374-75; Martin, *2 Corinthians*, 154.

[29] This does not mean that 1:12-14 is unrelated to the material in 1:15-2:11; see my discussion in 4.2.1.

[30] See also Martin, *2 Corinthians*, 154.

Regarding 1:15–2:2, scholars contend for various views on the ending of the material.³¹ However, I maintain 1:15–2:2 as a literary unit based on a topical unity regarding Paul's defense of the change of the travel plan.³² The unit comprises three subunits: description of Paul's intended travel plan (1:15–17), theological ground for the change (1:18–22),³³ and the purpose behind this change (1:23–2:2),³⁴ in which Paul consistently develops his defense. In 1:15–17, Paul first describes his intended plan to visit the Corinthian church twice (1:15–16) to emphasize his integrity and sincerity (1:17). In 1:18–22, he expounds on the theological reason behind the change of his travel plan. While many construe 1:18/19–22 as an excursus or digression,³⁵ Paul strategically establishes the foundation for his defense, underscoring that the faithful God is the ultimate cause of the change of the plan. Then, in 1:23–2:2, he reveals the purpose of the change of the plan: to spare the Corinthians (1:23) and to avoid sorrow (2:1). This topical unity is further supported by Paul's repetitive employment of travel-related verbs, such as ἔρχομαι and προπέμπω in 1:15–2:2 (ἔρχομαι in 1:15, 16, 23, and 2:1; διέρχομαι in 1:16; προπέμπω in 1:16). These verbs do not show up until Paul comes back to the transitional travel narrative in 2:12–13, except for 2:3.³⁶

Regarding 2:3–11, as mentioned, only a few scholars view it as a literary unit.³⁷ However, I maintain 2:3–11 as a unit based on (1) a thematic unity regarding Paul's defense of the previous letter and (2) the discourse function of the expression τοῦτο αὐτό in 2:3.³⁸ First, Paul shifts from the defense of the travel plan to that of the previous letter by beginning to employ the verb γράφω (2:3, 4, 9). Paul repeatedly reminds the

---

³¹ E.g., some scholars maintain 1:15–22 as a unit (Garland, *2 Corinthians*, 94–108; Lambrecht, *Second Corinthians*, 33; Hafemann, *2 Corinthians*, 83–86; Matera, *II Corinthians*, 50–57; Harris, *Second Epistle to the Corinthians*, 190–211; Martin, *2 Corinthians*, 157–66; Seifrid, *Second Letter to the Corinthians*, 54–69; Guthrie, *2 Corinthians*, 101–118). Some view that the unit continues to 1:24 (Thrall, *Second Epistle of the Corinthians*, 128–68). Others further extend it to 2:4 (Plummer, *Second Epistle*, 29–52; Vegge, *2 Corinthians*, 374) or 2:11 (Barnett, *Second Epistle to the Corinthians*, 98–132).
³² So Furnish, *II Corinthians*, 132–53.
³³ In 1:18, the conjunction δέ signals a new subunit within 1:15–2:2 since it marks a new development within Paul's discourse.
³⁴ Some construe the oath formula in 1:23 as a marker of a new literary unit (e.g., Matera, *II Corinthians*, 51). I agree that the formula and the conjunction δέ mark a new development in Paul's discourse. However, in light of the strong continuity in 1:15–2:2 regarding the defense of the travel plan, it is better to construe 1:23 signaling a subunit within 1:15–2:2.
³⁵ Barrett, *Second Epistle to the Corinthians*, 76; Furnish, *II Corinthians*, 76; Barnett, *Second Epistle to the Corinthians*, 98–99; Lambrecht, *Second Corinthians*, 35; Matera, *II Corinthians*, 54–55; Keener, *1–2 Corinthians*, 160.
³⁶ We do find ἔρχομαι in 2:3; however, the presence of the word in 2:3 cannot be taken as strong evidence to claim that Paul continues to defend his travel plan, extending it to 2:4. Two plausible reasons indicate that 2:3 belongs to another literary unit. First, Paul shifts from his defense of the travel plan to that of his previous letter in 2:3 (see the discussion in 2:3–11 below). Second, ἔρχομαι in 2:3 functions as a temporal adverbial participle in a purpose ἵνα clause; thus, Paul does not employ the verb to describe his travel plan but rather to emphasize the purpose of the previous letter.
³⁷ E.g., Furnish, *II Corinthians*, 153–68.
³⁸ One may question the discourse function of καί in 2:3 and δέ in 2:5. While καί denotes a close association with the preceding (see further discussion in 5.1), the καί in 2:3 signals the association regarding Paul's defense of conduct. Namely, Paul begins the section with a general statement in 1:12–14 and connects his twofold defense regarding the change of the travel plan (1:15–2:2) and the previous letter (2:3–11) with the conjunction καί. Also, δέ in 2:5 signals a new development within 2:3–11.

Corinthians that the defense he develops in 2:3–11 pertains to his previous letter. Second, Paul begins the unit with a forward-pointing reference, τοῦτο, with intensive use of the pronoun αὐτό, which points forward to a target introduced by ἵνα in 2:3.[39] The expression seems to mark a section break, for such devices create a discontinuity with the preceding material.

The unit consists of two subunits: introduction (2:3–4) and the defense of the previous letter (2:5–11).[40] In 2:3–4, Paul expresses the purpose and mode of his writing as an introduction of his defense, and in 2:5–11, he moves to develop a defense regarding the content he wrote in the previous letter; namely, regarding forgiveness of the offender in the community.

4.1.3 2:12–13

Finally, I contend that 2:12–13 is the third main unit within 1:3–2:13. While scholars often include 2:12–13 in 1:12–2:13,[41] I decided to treat 2:12–13 as an independent literary unit for four reasons: a shift of topic, a shift of literary form, style of writing, and discourse function of δέ in 2:12. First, one immediately recognizes that Paul moves from the defense of his conduct (1:12–2:11) to a travel narrative to Troas and Macedonia (2:12–13). Second, the topical transition is further signaled by the change of the literary form from a discursive text (1:12–2:11) to a narration (2:12–13). Third, related to the second point, the change of the literary form is further evinced by the observation of Paul's style of writing. While Paul persistently addresses the Corinthians in the second person in 1:12–2:11 (1:12, 13, 14 [twice], 15, 16 [three times], 18, 19, 21, 23, 24 [twice]; 2:1, 2, 3 [twice], 4 [twice], 5, 7, 8, 9, 10), he does not address them at all in 2:12–13. Fourth, the conjunction δέ in 2:12 seems to signal the beginning of a new subunit, for it frequently marks a new development of Paul's discourse.[42] For these reasons, 2:12–13 should be treated as an independent literary unit.

In this section, I have demonstrated the segmentation of 1:3–2:13. I will now turn to the second half of the investigation of the literary structure: the identification of the MSRs.

4.2 Major Structural Relationships

While the division of 1:3–2:13 pertains to the identification of its main units and subunits, the identification of the MSRs explains the ways in which materials within

---

[39] Long, *2 Corinthians*, 44. On forward-pointing references, see my discussion on a demonstrative pronoun αὕτη in 1:12 above.
[40] Two factors signal a unit boundary between 2:3–4 and 2:5–11: a shift from introduction to the content and the conjunction δέ in 2:5. One can analyze that 2:3–4 and 2:5–11 are structured according to preparation/realization or generalization. The introduction in 2:3–4 prepares readers for the content to be revealed in 2:5–11. Besides, this shift of emphasis from 2:3–4 to 2:5–11 is further supported by the conjunction δέ, marking a new development within the unit (see my note above).
[41] On scholars who espouse 1:12–2:13 as the main unit, see my note on 1:12–2:11 in 4.1.2.2.
[42] Long, *2 Corinthians*, 53.

and between main units and subunits are related. In 1:3–2:13, I identify the MSR of particularization and causation with substantiation in relation to the division as a whole and the MSRs of causation with particularization, recurrence of particularization, and recurrence in relation to the letter as a whole. The MSR in relation to the division as a whole shows that the primary message of Paul's arguments in 1:3–2:13 pertains to the theme of mutuality. The MSRs in relation to the letter as a whole reveal that Paul establishes a basis in 1:3–2:13 for his following discourse in 2:14–13:10. In addition, he introduces the themes regarding mutuality, encouragement and suffering, and agents in ministry to be further developed in his discourse in 2:14–13:10. Recurrence regarding the themes of service/work, boasting, grace, love, and Christ also shows the emphasis on these notions in Paul's discourse in the letter.

4.2.1 In Relation to the Division as a Whole: Particularization and Causation with Substantiation (1:3–7 and 1:8–2:13)

Regarding the MSR in relation to the division as a whole, I propose that 1:3–2:13 is structured according to particularization and causation with substantiation (1:3–7 and 1:8–2:13).[43] The theme regarding mutuality of suffering and encouragement in 1:3–7 serves as a general statement (particularization) as well as a theological basis (causation) for the material that follows in 1:8–2:13. At the same time, Paul's discussion in 1:8–2:13 reinforces the statement made in 1:3–7 (substantiation), for he provides examples and reasons for his claim in 1:8–2:13. Many recognize that an overarching theme of 1:12–2:13 pertains to Paul's defense.[44] Others, especially partition theorists, such as Weiss, Schmithals, Bornkamm, Georgi, Suhl, Marxsen, and Schenke and Fischer, consider 1:1–2:13 and 7:5–16 the letter of reconciliation.[45] However, an analysis of the MSR indicates that the central theme of 1:3–2:13 pertains to the mutual character of ministry based on three observations: epistolary formula of thanksgiving, thematic unity, and conjunctive relations according to the discourse function of γάρ (1:8, 12; cf. δέ in 2:12).[46]

4.2.1.1 Mutuality of Divine Encouragement in Ministry (1:3–7)

To begin, I argue that the blessing in 1:3–7 outlines the theme to be developed in 1:8–2:11. Although the nature of Paul's use of blessing and thanksgiving is distinguished (i.e.,

---

[43] More precisely, 1:3–2:13 is structured according to ideological particularization with logical causation. Ideological particularization, according to Bauer and Traina, "involves a general statement that the writer spells out or unpacks or develops in the material that follows" (*Inductive Bible Study*, 100). Also, Bauer and Traina define, "Logical causation occurs when one statement logically causes, or leads to, another statement, when a writer draws an inference from what he has just said. Because *A* is so, therefore you ought to do *B*" (ibid., 106).
[44] E.g., Thrall, *Second Epistle of the Corinthians*, 1:128–87; Barnett, *Second Epistle to the Corinthians*, 91–137; Harris, *Second Epistle to the Corinthians*, 182–240; Guthrie, *2 Corinthians*, 91–149.
[45] See the summary of partition theorists in Betz, *2 Corinthians 8 and 9*, 2–36; Thrall, *Second Epistle of the Corinthians*, 1:47–49.
[46] John T. Fitzgerald argues that the theme of mutuality runs through chs 1–9 (*Cracks in an Earthen Vessel: An Examination of the Catalogues of Hardships in the Corinthian Correspondence*, SBLDS 99 [Atlanta: Scholars Press, 1988], 150).

εὐχαριστέω for God's work in the lives of the recipients of the letter and εὐλογητός for blessings in which he participated),[47] the functions of thanksgiving and blessing overlap, as O'Brien describes, "The use of εὐχαριστέω does not necessarily exclude the idea of praise (be it public or private), while the appearance of the εὐλογητός-formula does not rule out any thought of personal gratitude, as the present context of 2 Cor 1:3ff. makes plain."[48] If so, the blessing in 1:3–7 functions to set the theme to be developed, as O'Brien summarizes the function of the introductory thanksgiving as follows:

> Paul's introductory thanksgivings have a varied function: epistolary, didactic and paraenetic, and they provide evidence of his pastoral and/or apostolic concern for the addressees. In some cases one purpose may predominate while others recede into the background. But whatever the particular thrust of any passage, it is clear that Paul's introductory thanksgivings were not meaningless devices. Instead, they were integral parts of their letters, setting the tone and themes of what was to follow.[49]

In the case of 2 Corinthians, Paul introduces the theme of mutuality in 1:3–7 and continues to expound and substantiate it in 1:8–2:11.

In 1:3–5, Paul explains the mutuality of divine encouragement in vertical and horizontal dimensions.[50] On the one hand, he proclaims that divine encouragement comes from God (1:4; vertical) through Christ as its mediator (διὰ τοῦ Χριστοῦ; 1:5), because Christ shares suffering with his servants (vertical; 1:5).[51] On the other hand, divine encouragement is not intended to remain with the recipients; it is to overflow into others (horizontal). Therefore, Paul expounds the purpose of divine encouragement with an infinitive clause that divine encouragement enables the recipients to become agents to the afflicted (1:4b). Thus, God is the ultimate agent and source of encouragement (vertical) through the mediator Christ, who shares suffering with his servants (vertical) so that they can also be agents of divine suffering and encouragement to others (horizontal).[52]

---

[47] See my comments in 4.1.1; O'Brien, *Introductory Thanksgivings*, 239.
[48] Ibid., 239.
[49] Ibid., 263; Weima also argues, "the thanksgiving has a foreshadowing function: it looks ahead to the main topics that will be taken up in the body of the letter" (*Paul the Ancient Letter Writer*, 59).
[50] Regarding the term παρακαλέω, lexicons list a wide range of the semantic meanings (e.g., to ask, to comfort, to encourage, and to implore; see BDAG, s.v. "παρακαλέω"; Otto Schmitz, "παρακαλέω, παράκλησις," *TDNT* 5:773–99). While many interpreters prefer to translate παρακαλέω as "to comfort" in English (e.g., RSV; NIV; Barrett, *Second Epistle to the Corinthians*, 56–57), I translate the word as "to encourage" for it conveys a better sense in English. As many scholars comment, Paul's use of παρακαλέω in 2 Corinthians communicates more than a sense of consolation, solace, or sympathy. Rather, παρακαλέω communicates "a consolatory strengthening in the face of adversity that affords spiritual refreshment" in the sense of the Latin *confortare* (Harris, *Second Epistle to the Corinthians*, 143; Also see Furnish, *II Corinthians*, 109; Martin, *2 Corinthians*, 142–43; cf. Thrall, *Second Epistle to the Corinthians*, 1:103).
[51] Paul employs a causal conjunction ὅτι and a comparative clausal construction καθώς + οὕτως to substantiate God's character of encouragement.
[52] Also see my discussion in 3.2.1 and 5.2 regarding the ways in which Paul portrays himself as God's human agent, Christ as the intermediate agent, and God as the ultimate agent in the salutation (1:1–2).

In 1:6–7, Paul then proceeds to describe the ways in which the mutuality of divine suffering and encouragement is embodied in the relationship between Paul and his coworkers and the Corinthians. Paul repeatedly emphasizes the mutual character of suffering and encouragement between him and his coworkers and the Corinthians and summarizes that they are sharers/partners of suffering and encouragement: ὡς κοινωνοί ἐστε τῶν παθημάτων, οὕτως καὶ τῆς παρακλήσεως (1:7b).

Therefore, Paul first describes divine suffering and encouragement in the vertical and horizontal dimensions (1:3–5) and applies the mutuality to the relationship between him and his coworkers and the Corinthians (1:6–7). Moreover, the mutual character of ministry is not limited to suffering and encouragement. Paul continues to develop the theme in 1:8–2:13 (particularization): Paul and his coworkers and the Corinthians share ministry (1:11), boasting (1:14), joy (1:24; 2:3), love (2:4, 8), sorrow (2:5), and forgiveness (2:7, 10; particularization). At the same time, his claim in 1:3–7 implicitly serves as a theological foundation for Paul's discussion pertaining to the mutual character of ministry in 1:8–2:13; because God is the ultimate agent, Christ is the mediator, and Paul and his fellow workers are God's agents in ministry, *therefore*, Paul continues to depict his ministry in 1:8–2:13 on that basis (causation). In addition, the descriptions of mutuality in the relationship between God's agents and the Corinthians in 1:8–2:13 provide reasons and examples for his claim in 1:3–7 (substantiation; see Table 4.1 below).

4.2.1.2 Mutuality of Ministry through Paul's Experience of Affliction in Asia (1:8–11)

Having introduced a theme of mutuality in the general statement in 1:3–7, Paul expounds and substantiates it in 1:8–11. As explained, the debate regarding the relationship between 1:3–7 and 1:8–11 hinges on one's understanding of Paul's description of the affliction in Asia (1:8–11) in relation to the immediate literary context. The difficulty of the discussion pertains to the fact that 1:8–11 functions somewhat as a bridging or transitional unit between 1:3–7 and 1:12–2:11.[53] However, the discourse function of the conjunction γάρ in 1:8 and a topical transition from divine encouragement (1:8–10) to the Corinthians' cooperation of ministry (1:11) suggest that Paul continues to develop the theme of mutuality in 1:8–11.[54]

Paul begins 1:8–11 with the conjunction γάρ. The discourse function of γάρ marks that the material in 1:8–11 provides supports for the content described in 1:3–7

---

[53] E.g., O'Brien, *Introductory Thanksgivings*, 235; Barnett, *Second Epistle to the Corinthians*, 81; Land, *Integrity of 2 Corinthians*, 86.

[54] Land, in his discourse analysis of 2 Corinthians, also argues that an analysis of the interpersonal moves (i.e., enactment of social exchanges) and conjunctive relations in 1:2–2:13 reveals that 1:8–2:13 support and develop the idea (i.e., interpersonal core) presented in 1:3–7 (*Integrity of 2 Corinthians*, 82–112).

Table 4.1 Conjunctive Relations of 1:3–2:13

General Statement (1:3–7)
γάρ in 1:8 introduces supporting material 1 for 1:3–7 (1:8–11)
γάρ in 1:12 introduces supporting material 2 for 1:3–7 (1:12–2:11)
δέ in 2:12 introduces transitional travel narrative (2:12–13)

(substantiation; see Table 4.1). Discourse grammarians explain that γάρ strengthens or provides supports for the preceding material.[55]

In this way, 1:8–11 is related to the discussion in 1:3–7 in two ways. First, Paul's testimony of God's deliverance from his affliction in Asia (1:8–10) provides further support for the notion of divine encouragement in 1:3–7. Second, the Corinthians' cooperation in ministry (1:11) also strengthens the theme of mutuality in 1:3–7. Paul begins the first section (1:8–10) by testifying to God's deliverance from his affliction in Asia. His testimony provides a proof and example of the ways in which the vertical dimension of divine encouragement embodied in a particular circumstance of Paul's ministry in Asia.[56] Then, he expresses the hope of future deliverance by the same God who delivered Paul and his coworkers from the affliction in Asia. However, in 1:11, Paul strategically shifts the topic, highlighting the Corinthians as co-participants in his ministry in four ways.

First, the genitive absolute construction introduces and underscores the Corinthians' role in God's future deliverance. Levinsohn explains the function of the genitive absolute constructions as "switch-reference" because "a construction that indicates switch reference provides a natural way of highlighting the introduction to an existing scene of participants who perform significant actions that change the direction of the

---

[55] See Levinsohn, *Discourse Features*, 69; Runge, *Discourse Grammar*, 54; Fredrick J. Long, *Koine Greek Grammar: A Beginning-Intermediate Greek Exegetical and Pragmatic Handbook* (Wilmore, KY: GlossaHouse, 2015), 157; cf. Porter, *Idioms of the Greek New Testament*, 207–208; Wallace, *Greek Grammar*, 673. Andrew R. Rillera recently argues, "γάρ is often used in the NT as a transition particle that provides no inferential basis for what preceded. It simply signals that people are beginning to speak" ("Paul's Philonic Opponent: Unveiling the One Who Calls Himself a Jew in Romans 2:17" [PhD diss., Duke University, 2021], 136) and applies this to γάρ in Rom 1:18. However, his argument does not refute my analysis in 2 Corinthians for three reasons. First, Rillera's examples for the proposed function of γάρ come from non-Pauline text in the NT (2 Pet 3:5; John 7:41; Matt 15:27); thus, I wonder if the proposed reading can be applied to Paul's writings, which have distinct language style and sophistication. Second, discourse grammarians contend that the function of γάρ strengthens or provides supports, which can be expressed in various ways; its function does not always have to be inferential or causal as Rillera argues. Third, although there are times, as Rillera argues, when γάρ provides no inferential basis for immediately preceeding context, I argue that the function of γάρ can at times provide supporting information for a larger discourse but not for an immediately preceding sentence, as I demonstrate conjunctive relations of 1:3–2:13 in Table 4.1 below. It seems to me that γάρ in Rom 1:18 does not provide support for Rom 1:17; rather, γάρ Rom 1:17 and 1:18 respectively provide supporting information for Rom 1:14–16, just as γάρ in 2 Cor 1:8 and 1:12 support the general statement in 2 Cor 1:3–7.

[56] This becomes especially explicit when Paul interpreted the purpose of the severe affliction in Asia with a ἵνα clause in 1:9b–10a. Just as the divine encouragement in affliction comes from God through Christ (1:3–5), the deliverance of God's servants directly came from God.

story, etc."⁵⁷ Thus, Paul switches the focus of the passage from God's deliverance in his ministry (the vertical relationship between Paul and God) to cooperation in ministry (the horizontal relationship between Paul and the Corinthians). Second, Paul stresses the Corinthians' participation in ministry with the word συνυπουργέω (*hapax legomenon*). The word is a combination of σύν and ὑπουργέω. The basic meaning of ὑπουργέω is "to be helpful," "to assist," or "to render service."⁵⁸ By adding the prefix σύν to ὑπουργέω, Paul stresses the Corinthians' "togetherness" in his ministry through their prayers. Third, Paul employs an additive καί to stress that the Corinthians are participants in his ministry and emphasizes their cooperation in his ministry.⁵⁹ Fourth, Paul underscores the role of the Corinthians in ministry by emphasizing that thanksgiving is not just a result of God's gracious gift of deliverance (χάρισμα) but also an outcome of the Corinthians' ministry of prayers for him and his coworkers.⁶⁰ Therefore, Belleville appropriately summarizes that the central theme of 1:8–11 pertains to reciprocity in order "to establish right at the start a basis for mutuality between the Corinthians and himself, and to show the impact that his mutuality has on the church universal."⁶¹ In this way, Paul highlights the Corinthians' participation in ministry since both Paul and the Corinthians share ministry by playing different roles.

4.2.1.3 Mutuality of Boasting in 1:12–2:11

Having explained the mutuality of encouragement and suffering (1:3–7) and ministry (1:11), Paul further expounds and substantiates the theme of mutuality in 1:12–2:11. While many scholars recognize 1:12 as the beginning of a new unit, they do not give

---

⁵⁷ Levinsohn, *Discourse Features*, 182; see also Long, *2 Corinthians*, 23; idem, *Koine Greek Grammar*, 386–91.
⁵⁸ BDAG, s.v. "ὑπουργέω"; LSJ, s.v. "ὑπουργέω."
⁵⁹ BDAG, s.v. "καί." Also see Wallace, *Greek Grammar Beyond the Basics*, 670–1; Runge, *Discourse Grammar*, 337–48; Long, *2 Corinthians*, 8.
⁶⁰ The word χάρισμα appears only in 1:11 in the letter. Scholars argue whether χάρισμα refers to Paul's vocation as an apostle (Johann E. Osiander, *Commentar über den zweiten Brief Pauli an die Korinthier* [Stuttgart: Besser, 1858], 43) or to the collection (Long, *Ancient Rhetoric and Paul's Apology*, 143; idem, *2 Corinthians*, 24). However, as most scholars note, the immediate literary context suggests that χάρισμα refers to God's deliverance from the affliction (e.g., Plummer, *Second Epistle*, 21; Harris, *Second Epistle to the Corinthians*, 160; Guthrie, *2 Corinthians*, 86).

Also, scholars continue to struggle to understand and translate this notoriously difficult ἵνα clause in 1:11b. One of the difficulties pertains to the translation of ἐκ πολλῶν προσώπων. In the context of 2 Corinthians, πρόσωπον is employed in multivalent meanings (2:10; 3:7, 13, 18; 4:6; 5:12; 8:24; 10:1, 7; 11:20). Interpreters understand this prepositional phrase in 1:11 to be (1) "from many mouths" which give thanksgiving in light of the literal translation of πρόσωπον, "face" (Plummer, *Second Epistles*, 21–22); (2) "from many persons/people" (Windisch, *Zweite Korintherbrief*, 50; Furnish, *II Corinthians*, 115); or "by the agency of many figures" in light of the image of drama (1 Cor 4:9) in which many people play different parts (Thrall, *Second Epistle of the Corinthians*, 1:123–26). I think that these options are related to one another to construe the sense of the text. I translate the clause as follows: so that many would give thanks (to God) on our behalf for the gracious gift of deliverance given to us by many people (who cooperate with us in prayer). The prepositional phrase ἐκ πολλῶν προσώπων should be understood in relation to the immediately preceding sentence: συνυπουργούντων καὶ ὑμῶν ὑπὲρ ἡμῶν τῇ δεήσει. Thus, Paul seems to understand ἐκ πολλῶν προσώπων as a source of God's gracious gift of deliverance.
⁶¹ Belleville, *Reflections of Glory*, 119.

adequate attention to the interconnection of the materials between 1:3-7, 1:8-11, and 1:12-2:11.[62] However, the conjunctive relation and Paul's emphasis on mutuality in his defense indicate a coherent topical connection throughout 1:3-2:11.

Concerning the conjunctive relation, 1:12-2:11 begins with the conjunction γάρ in the same way Paul starts his testimony in 1:8-11. It introduces supporting materials for the theme of mutuality described in 1:3-7 (substantiation; see Table 4.1).[63]

Regarding 1:12-14, many scholars concur that 1:12-14 is a literary subunit within the main unit they identify. However, they disagree with one another regarding the ways in which 1:12-14 is related to the rest of the context.[64] Nonetheless, I claim that 1:12-14 serves as a general statement for 1:12-2:11. In 1:12-14, Paul raises two major concerns against which he will develop his defense in 1:12-2:11: his conduct (1:12) and his previous letter (1:13). Paul stresses the integrity and sincerity of his conduct as his boasting, especially toward the Corinthians (1:12).[65] He substantiates this claim by appealing to the fact that his writing is not different from what he writes to the Corinthians (1:13).[66] Thus, in the material that follows, he defends (1) his conduct toward the Corinthians, particularly regarding the change of his travel plan (1:15-22), and (2) the previous letter (2:3-11).[67]

Moreover, in his defense, Paul consistently develops the theme of mutuality. In 1:12-14, Paul reminds the Corinthians that they did understand mutual boasting, though their comprehension is limited (1:14). He thus expresses that his ultimate and eschatological desire is the Corinthians' full comprehension of the reality that Paul and

---

[62] See my note in 4.1.2.2.
[63] On the discourse function of γάρ, see my discussion in 4.2.1.2.
[64] E.g., some scholars using rhetorical criticism understand 1:12-14 as *propositio* or *causa* of the letter (Amador, *Revisiting 2 Corinthians*, 111; Vegge, *2 Corinthians*, 374-75). Likewise, some consider 1:12-14 as the theme statement of the letter (Garland, *2 Corinthians*, 83-94; Matera, *II Corinthians*, 46-50) or chs 1-7 (Fitzgerald, *Cracks in an Earthen Vessel*, 149). Others identify 1:12-14 to be a transitional section (Plummer, *Second Epistle*, 23; Lambrecht, *Second Corinthians*, 33-34; Hafemann, *2 Corinthians*, 81; Martin, *2 Corinthians*, 154); the introduction of the letter body (Furnish, *II Corinthians*, 126-27); or the introduction of self-defense in 1:12-2:13 (Thrall, *Second Epistle of the Corinthians*, 1:129-35; Barnett, *Second Epistle to the Corinthians*, 92-98; Harris, *Second Epistle to the Corinthians*, 182-83).
[65] The syntax of the sentence highlights his integrity of conduct in two manners. First, a forward-pointing reference underscores his conduct. In 1:12 the demonstrative pronoun αὕτη functions as a forward-pointing reference whose target was marked by ὅτι to highlight the content of boasting (see my discussion on forward-pointing references in 4.1.2.2). Second, the list of prepositional phrases that modify the verb ἀναστρέφω (ἐν ἁπλότητι καὶ εἰλικρινείᾳ τοῦ θεοῦ; καὶ οὐκ ἐν σοφίᾳ σαρκικῇ; ἀλλ᾽ ἐν χάριτι θεοῦ) highlights his integrity of conduct. Paul first explains the manner of his conduct with the prepositional phrase, ἐν ἁπλότητι καὶ εἰλικρινείᾳ τοῦ θεοῦ. Then, he expounds its meaning with οὐκ ... ἀλλὰ construction (on this construction and its function, see Levinsohn, *Discourse Features*, 92-100; Long, *2 Corinthians*, 17-18). Thus, the lengthy prepositional phrases stress the manner of Paul's conduct.
[66] The conjunction γάρ in 1:13 substantiates the immediately preceding context in 1:12. The present tense of γράφω in 1:13 can refer to his current writing (i.e., 2 Corinthians). However, the present tense can be gnomic present; thus, the verb can refer to his writing in general, including all his earlier letters to the Corinthians (see Harris, *Second Epistle to the Corinthians*, 186-87). In either way, Paul underscores that his message does not have a hidden meaning; rather, it could be comprehended simply by reading.
[67] Also note that Paul equates καύχησις with τὸ μαρτύριον τῆς συνειδήσεως in an appositional position. Paul's boasting is profoundly connected to the idea of conscience.

his coworkers and the Corinthians are sharers of boasting in the day of the Lord Jesus (1:14b). Therefore, in the material that follows (1:15–2:11), Paul expounds what it means to be sharers of boasting, especially regarding mutuality of joy (1:24; 2:3), sorrow (2:5), love (2:4, 8), and forgiveness (2:7, 10).

Having clarified that Paul's boasting is about his integrity of conduct toward the Corinthians, he now moves to the content of the defense regarding the change of the travel plan and the previous letter in 1:15–2:11.[68] Regarding 1:15–2:2, Paul defends his conduct in three ways. First, he insists that the change of his travel plan was not due to his vacillation or self-interest (1:17). Second, he attributes the ultimate reason for the change to God: God, who is always faithful, is the cause of the change (1:18–22). Third, Paul explains the purpose of the change: to spare the Corinthians (1:23) and to avoid sorrow (2:1). Furthermore, while developing his defense, Paul also emphasizes the mutuality of joy as an underpinning reason for the defense. Paul changed the plan because he and the Corinthians should be coworkers of joy: συνεργοί ἐσμεν τῆς χαρᾶς ὑμῶν (1:24). In fact, while Paul states two purposes of the change (i.e., to spare the Corinthians [1:23] and to avoid sorrow [2:1]), they are distilled into the mutuality of joy for two reasons. First, after stating the first purpose of the change of the travel plan (1:23), Paul explicates what "sparing" means: not because he is authoritative to lord it over the Corinthians' faith but because Paul wanted to come to Corinth as a coworker of joy (1:24). Second, he, therefore, restates the first purpose of the change of the plan in 2:1–2 that he decided not to come to the Corinthians in sorrow because he and the Corinthians were to share joy but not sorrow. Thus, the flow of Paul's discussion indicates that this mutuality of joy centers on his explanation of the purpose of the travel change in 1:18–22.

Having defended his conduct toward the Corinthians (i.e., the change of the travel plan), Paul now defends the previous letter he wrote to the Corinthians (2:3–11) in which he emphasizes the mutuality of joy (2:3), love (2:4, 8), sorrow (2:5), and forgiveness (2:7, 10). On the one hand, Paul defends the previous letter in explaining three purposes of his writing: to avoid sorrow in his visit (2:3–4), to inform the Corinthians of his love (2:4), and to test the Corinthians' obedience regarding the forgiveness of the one who caused sorrow to the Corinthian community (2:5–11).

On the other hand, he consistently develops the theme of mutuality in this section. First, Paul shares joy with the Corinthians (2:3). As I have already described above, joy and avoidance of sorrow are closely associated: he and the Corinthians should share joy but not sorrow (2:1–2). Thus, Paul underscores that the purpose of the previous letter was to avoid sorrow (2:3).

Second, Paul emphasizes the mutuality of love (2:4, 8). In 2:4, Paul explains the mode of writing as affliction and anguish; he was sorrowful when he wrote the previous letter. However, he does not expect the Corinthians to bear such sorrow; instead, he wants to inform them of his love (2:4). Moreover, Paul urges the Corinthians to affirm

---

[68] The prepositional phrase, Καὶ ταύτῃ τῇ πεποιθήσει, connects 1:12–14 with 1:15–2:11. Paul's πεποίθησις with a demonstrative pronoun refers back to the boasting Paul and the Corinthians share in 1:12–14.

love for the offender (2:8) because just as Paul shares love with the Corinthians (2:4), the Corinthians are also to share the love with the offender (2:8).

Third, Paul describes the mutuality of sorrow (2:5). Despite his desire to be a sharer of joy and love with the Corinthians, Paul must also describe the reality of sorrow that both he and the Corinthian community share. Just as Paul and the Corinthians share joy, they also share sorrow. Pain caused to an individual (in this case, Paul) affects the rest of the community of which she or he is a part. Thus, mutuality of joy and sorrow is two sides of the same coin. In other words, mutuality of sorrow is the reason Paul emphasizes mutuality of joy so that they can avoid sorrow (2:5; cf. 2:7).

Fourth, Paul stresses the mutuality of forgiveness (2:7, 10). While the literary context suggests that Paul understands forgiveness as an expression of encouragement and love (2:7–8; cf. 1:3–7),[69] he underlines its mutual character. On the one hand, forgiveness involves two parties: The ones who forgive and the one who is forgiven. However, on the other hand, the text also shows that Paul's emphasis is not only on the relationship between the forgivers and the forgiven (2:5–8) but also the relationship among the forgivers: between Paul and the Corinthians (2:10). Thus, Paul explains that he and the Corinthians share the same verdict of forgiveness regarding the offender and that he indeed forgave the offender for the sake of the Corinthians in the presence of Christ. In other words, Paul has forgiven the offender on behalf of the Corinthians as the representative of Christ or under Christ's approval.[70]

In sum, Paul develops his defense regarding the change of the travel plan (1:15–2:2) and the previous letter (2:3–11). More specifically, Paul underscores that the purpose of the change of his travel plan was to spare the Corinthians (1:23) and avoid sorrow in his visit (2:1–2). Likewise, he describes that the purpose of the previous letter was to avoid sorrow in his visit (2:3), to inform the Corinthians of his love (2:4), and to test their obedience regarding forgiveness to the one who caused sorrow (2:9).[71] However, I have also demonstrated that behind his defense, Paul expands the notion of mutuality as the underpinning theme of the section. In other words, Paul changed his travel plan to spare the Corinthians (1:23) and to avoid sorrow (2:1–2), because Paul and the Corinthians should be coworkers of joy (1:24) but not of sorrow (2:1–2). Paul wrote the previous letter to avoid sorrow in his visit because they should be sharers of joy (2:3). Paul wrote a letter to inform the Corinthians of his love (2:4) because they should also share the same love by affirming love for the offender (2:8), despite the sorrow the offender brought on Paul and the Corinthians (2:5). Paul also wrote the letter to test their obedience regarding forgiveness of the offender (2:9) because Paul has already forgiven the offender so that they would also share the same forgiveness (2:10). Therefore, Paul coherently explicates the theme of the mutuality throughout 1:3–2:11.

---

[69] In 1:3–7 Paul describes both vertical and horizontal dimensions of divine encouragement. Here Paul emphasizes encouragement among the Corinthians (horizontal) because the Corinthians should forgive and encourage (παρακαλέω) the offender (2:7) and Paul, as an agent of divine encouragement, urges (παρακαλέω) them to affirm love for such a person (2:8).

[70] Harris, *Second Epistle to the Corinthians*, 232–33; "πρόσωπον," *TDNT* 6:777; BDAG, s.v. "πρόσωπον."

[71] As Paul insists the consistency of the message in his writing (1:13–14), the purposes of the change of the travel plan and the previous letter are also consistent.

4.2.1.4 Transitional Travel Narrative (2:12-13)

Although the travel narrative to Troas and Macedonia in 2:12-13 does not appear to be directly related to the theme of mutuality per se, it plays an important function as transitional and bridging verses: 2:12-13 functions to connect both the preceding (1:12-2:11) and following (2:14-7:16) literary context.

Regarding the preceding literary context, the travel narrative is related to Paul's defense (1:12-2:11) in two ways.[72] First, the description of Paul's travel to Troas and Macedonia supplements Paul's defense of the change of the travel plan. He has already defended his conduct by explaining his intended travel plan (1:15-17), the theological reason (1:18-22), and the purpose of the change (1:23-2:2), and 2:12-13 adds information regarding his travel.[73] Second, 2:12-13 substantiates his defense of the previous letter (2:3-11), especially highlighting the love he shares with the Corinthians (2:4, 8). Thrall explains the function of the narrative as proof of Paul's concern for the Corinthians, stating, "He was so anxious about them that he abandoned a promising opportunity for evangelism, the sooner to meet with Titus and hear news of them."[74] Thus, 2:12-13 provides further evidence of his care and love for the Corinthians.

Regarding the following literary context, 2:12-13 (1) prepares for the thesis statement of the letter (2:14-17), and (2) grounds his arguments (2:14-7:3) in the history of his ministry to the Corinthians. First, Paul prepares his audience for the thesis statement in 2:14-17 through the travel narrative. Despite an abrupt transition from his defense (1:12-2:11) to a narrative (2:12-13), the practice of ancient rhetoric and writing helps us understand how Paul transitions his discourse. Ancient rhetorical tradition often outlines a narrative or narratives (*narratio*) before the thesis statement of the letter (e.g., *propositio*, *divisio*, and *partitio*).[75] While I do not concur that Paul strictly follows a macro-rhetorical outline in his writing,[76] I admit the influence of

---

[72] It is possible to make a connection between 1:8-11 and 2:12-13. Dieter Georgi and Harris comment that 2:12-13 continues Paul's affliction narrative introduced in 1:8 (Dieter Georgi, *Die Geschichte der Kollekte des Paulus Für Jerusalem*, TF 38 [Hamburg-Bergstedt: Reich, 1965], 190n51; Harris, *Second Epistle to the Corinthians*, 235. Also see Plummer, *Second Epistle*, 64; Barnett, *Second Epistle to the Corinthians*, 132-33). However, the text is not explicit about the connection. Moreover, as Furnish explains, it is more fitting to read 2:12-13 in the context of 1:12-2:11, especially 1:15-2:2 in which Paul predominantly employs the first-person singular form (Furnish, *II Corinthians*, 170).
[73] See also Barrett, *Second Epistle to the Corinthians*, 93-95; Furnish, *II Corinthians*, 170.
[74] Thrall, *Second Epistle of the Corinthians*, 1:182. See also Scott, *2 Corinthians*, 51-52; Garland, *2 Corinthians*, 132; Matera, *II Corinthians*, 64; Seifrid, *Second Letter to the Corinthians*, 80.
[75] I do not agree that the entire section of 1:3-2:13 is *narratio* (see my discussion in 4.1.2.2). However, one should note that in the ancient rhetorical practices, a narration or *narratio* can be distributed in different sections (e.g., 1:8-11 and 2:12-13). Frank W. Hughes explains, "Although ancient rhetorical handbooks customarily provided for a separate section of *narratio* between the *exordium* and the *probatio*, rhetorical theories also allowed the more-or-less standard pattern to be altered in favor of omitting the *narratio* or in favor of inserting pieces of *narratio* within other parts of the oration" ("The Rhetoric of Reconciliation: 2 Corinthians 1.1-2.13 and 7.5-8.24," in *Persuasive Artistry: Studies in New Testament Rhetoric in Honor of George A. Kennedy*, ed. Duane F. Watson, JSNTSup 50 [Sheffield: Sheffield Academic, 1991], 246-61 at 252; see also Witherington, *Conflict and Community in Corinth*, 407, citing Quintilian, *Inst*. 4.2.5, 79; *Rhet. Alex*. 1438b.15-25); Long, *Ancient Rhetoric and Paul's Apology*, 151-57. On *propositio* after *narratio*, see Witherington, *Conflict and Community in Corinth*, 371-74, citing Quintilian, *Inst*. 4.4.3-8. On *divisio* and *partitio* after *narratio*, see Long, *Ancient Rhetoric and Paul's Apology*, 157-62.
[76] See my evaluation on rhetorical criticism in 2.1.3.6.

ancient rhetoric in his communication. Furthermore, the inclusion of narratives was common among ancient writings. Keener explains, "Introductory narratives summarizing the events leading up to the matter under discussion were common, including in defense speeches and deliberative speeches as well as other genres."[77] In the case of 2 Corinthians, Paul's move to revisit his travel narrative in 2:12–13 signals his audience for the most significant statement of the letter in 2:14–17.

Second, 2:12–13 and 7:4–16 frame his discourse in 2:14–7:3.[78] As many scholars note, 7:4/5 resumes the narrative Paul left off at 2:13; thus, some consider 2:14–7:4 a major digression.[79] However, this narrative framing shows Paul's skillful crafting, in which he grounds his argument (2:14–7:3) in the history of his ministry to the Corinthians and his relationship with them, because his discourse is not an empty theory but has a foundation in what he does and did as God's servant.[80] Furthermore, another reason Paul emphasizes his arguments (2:14–7:3) with this framing is that the thesis statement in 2:14–17 and the discourse regarding the proclamation of the gospel in 3:1–7:3 are fundamental in order to understand the rest of his arguments in 8:1–13:10. As I will explicate more in the following chapters, the thesis statement (2:14–17) introduces major themes for the rest of the letter (see Chapter 5). Moreover, Paul develops his discourse regarding the collection as a consequent exhortation (8:1–9:15) of his discussion in 3:1–7:3 (see 7.2.2). Likewise, his defense of the gospel (10:1–13:10) reinforces his message in 3:1–9:15 (see 8.2.2.2). Therefore, the transitional travel narrative in 2:12–13 reveals Paul's brilliant skill as a communicator to make both a bridge between the preceding (1:12–2:11) and following (2:14–7:16) literary context and a transition to the thesis statement of his discourse (2:14–17).

Having identified the MSR of particularization with causation in 1:3–2:13 that reveals Paul's coherent message of mutuality, I will turn to the analysis of the MSRs in relation to the letter as a whole.

4.2.2 In Relation to the Letter as a Whole

Regarding the relationships between 1:3–2:13 and the rest of the letter, many scholars neither consider the ways in which 1:3–2:13 relates to the remainder of the letter nor adequately explain such relationships.[81] Therefore, my task in this section is to

---

[77] Craig S. Keener, *Galatians: A Commentary* (Grand Rapids: Baker Academic, 2018), 74–75, citing Cicero, *Quintc.* 3.11–9.33; idem, *De or.* 2.335; Aristotle, *Rhet.* 3.16.11; Quintilian, *Inst.* 3.8.8–10, 3.8.36, 66; *Rhet. Her.* 3.5.9; see also Witherington, *Conflict and Community in Corinth*, 360–70; Long, *Ancient Rhetoric and Paul's Apology*, 151–57.

[78] Many scholars consider 7:5 as the beginning of the narrative. See my discussion regarding the division of 7:4–16 in 6.1.2.3 and 6.1.4.

[79] E.g., Harris, *Second Epistle to the Corinthians*, 240–521.

[80] See further discussion in 6.2.2.

[81] For instance, partition theorists often consider 1:1–2:13 and 7:5–16 forming the letter of reconciliation (see my note in 4.2.1). In topical analyses, some, especially those espousing some forms of the unity of the letter, attempt to explain continuities between 1:1–2:13 and 2:14–17 regarding lexical and thematic connections (see the overview of the debates in Thrall, *Second Epistle of the Corinthians*, 1:22–25), but others simply acknowledge 2:14–7:4 as a digression (e.g., Plummer, *Second Epistle*, 61; Harris, *Second Epistle to the Corinthians*, 240–41); thus, they are reluctant to explicate the relationships between 1:1–2:13 and 2:14–7:4. In discourse analysis, Land claims that the

demonstrate the interconnections between 1:3–2:13 and 2:14–13:10 by expounding the MSRs. Therefore, I propose that 1:3–2:13 and 2:14–13:10 are structured according to three MSRs: causation with particularization, recurrence of particularization, and recurrence.

4.2.2.1 Causation with Particularization (1:3–2:13 and 2:14–13:10)

I posit that 1:3–2:13 and 2:14–13:10 are structured according to causation with particularization.[82] On the one hand, Paul's discourse moves from basis (1:3–2:13) to content (2:14–13:10; causation). This causational movement is not as explicit as the hortatory causation in 3:1–9:15, in which Paul moves from indicatives (3:1–7:16) to imperatives (8:1–9:15; see my discussion in 7.2.2). However, in 1:3–2:13, Paul establishes a basis for his discourse in 2:14–13:10 by reporting events (i.e., his affliction in Asia [1:8–11]; his travels [1:15–2:2; 2:12–13]; his previous letter to the Corinthians [2:3–2:11]) that led to the writing of 2 Corinthians in 1:3–2:13. Thus, Paul's discourse in 2:14–13:10 is grounded in the history of Paul's ministry and his relationship with the Corinthians (1:3–2:13). Particularly, his understanding of mutual character of ministry in 1:3–2:13 serves as a basis for his discourse in 2:14–13:10. Because Paul recognizes his ministry and his relationship with the Corinthians in light of mutuality (1:3–2:13), his discourse in 2:14–13:10 also reflects the theme of mutuality.[83]

On the other hand, Paul's discourse in 1:3–2:13 and 2:14–13:10 is structured according to particularization regarding the themes of mutuality, encouragement and suffering, and agents in ministry. First, Paul expounds the theme of mutual character of ministry in 1:3–2:13 and continues to develop the notion in his discourse in 2:14–13:10 in two levels. In general, just as Paul describes that he and the Corinthians share suffering and encouragement (1:3–7), ministry (1:11), boasting (1:14), joy (1:24; 2:3), love (2:4, 8), sorrow (2:5), and forgiveness (2:7, 10), he develops the theme of mutuality by urging the Corinthians to be reconciled to God and Paul and his fellow workers

---

discussion in 2:14–5:21 is foreshadowed in 1:3–2:13, particularly regarding the theme of leadership (*Integrity of 2 Corinthians*, 113–14). However, these scholars do not pay adequate attention to the ways in which 1:3–2:13 is related to the entire letter. Concerning this issue, rhetorical criticism should be commended for understanding the significance of *narratio*, preparing the audience by narrating events or stating the facts of the case under debate. However, as I have already raised some questions above, scholars neither agree with one another on their identifications of *narratio* in 1:3–2:13, nor do they sufficiently address the issue that their identifications of *narratio* consist of not only narratives but also discursive texts (see 4.1.2.2).

[82] Long identifies 1:17–24 and the rest of the letter as structured according to recurrence of problem-solution, arguing "Paul's failure to visit as he had promised and the consequentially poor evaluation of his ministry as discussed in 1:15–17 is a PROBLEM to which Paul offers SOLUTIONS in the remainder of the letter. Then, in 2:16b Paul raises another facet of the problem, 'Who is sufficient for these things ...?'" ("2 Corinthians," 261–95 at 275). However, it is more appropriate to identify the relationship between chs 1–2 and the rest of the book as causation. The context of the problem discussed in 1:15–17 pertains to the defense against his travel plan in the past. Thus, Paul defends his integrity in the past, and then he moves to argue the ongoing problem in 2:16b, moving his discussion from the past to present. In other words, his integrity in the past serves as a basis for his argument in the present. See further discussion in 4.2.2.1.

[83] See also my discussion on the MSR of substantiation (3:1–7:3 and 7:4–6) in 6.2.2.

(5:20–7:3) so that the Corinthians can share the ministry of the collection with them (8:1–9:15). Specifically, the idea of partnership is significant. In 1:7, Paul emphasizes that he and his coworkers and the Corinthians are partners (κοινωνός) of suffering and encouragement and continues to explicate the theme of partnership, which becomes especially clear in 6:14–7:1 and chs 8–9. In 6:14–7:1, Paul accuses the Corinthians of partnership (κοινωνία) with unbelievers and urges the Corinthians to dissociate from them (6:14). The basis behind this exhortation is that believers must be sharers and partners with other believers in ministry, but not with unbelievers. Furthermore, this understanding becomes clearer in Paul's argument in chs 8–9, in which he encourages the Corinthians to participate in the ministry of the collection to the saints. Paul tells the Corinthians about the Macedonians' willingness to participate (κοινωνία) in the ministry to the saints (8:4); he calls Titus his partner (κοινωνός; 8:23); he calls the Corinthians' fiscal contribution κοινωνία (9:13). The underpinning idea behind the exhortation of the collection is that believers are partners and sharers with one another, including Titus (chs 8–9) but not with unbelievers (6:14), just as Paul emphasizes in 1:7.

Second, Paul introduces the notion of encouragement and suffering in 1:3–11 and develops it in 2:14–13:10 in two ways: as the recipient and agent of divine encouragement. As the recipient of divine encouragement, Paul was encouraged (παρακαλέω) by God (7:4, 6) in all affliction (7:4, 5), especially encouraged (παρακαλέω) by the coming of Titus (7:6), who was encouraged (παρακαλέω) by the Corinthians (7:7). Namely, Paul was encouraged (παρακαλέω) by the report that the Corinthians repented and properly responded to Paul's previous letter (7:13). Moreover, at the pinnacle of his defense in 12:7–10, Paul implores (παρακαλέω) the Lord to remove his thorn in the flesh to be the recipient of divine healing/deliverance (12:8–9),[84] and he receives the divine encouragement by the Lord in his suffering: Ἀρκεῖ σοι ἡ χάρις μου, ἡ γὰρ δύναμις ἐν ἀσθενείᾳ τελεῖται.

As God's agent, Paul encourages (παρακαλέω) the Corinthians to accept the gospel of reconciliation (5:20) and encourages them not to receive God's grace in vain (6:1), for which he suffers (6:3–10). Moreover, he shows the Corinthians the encouragement (παράκλησις) of the Macedonians that they are willing to participate in the ministry to the saints (8:4) despite their affliction (8:2). Thus, he encourages (παρακαλέω) Titus and other workers to be agents of the ministry to the saints (8:6, 17; 9:5). Paul, as the servant of Christ who suffers more than anyone (11:23b–30), also urges (παρακαλέω)

---

[84] I must note the significance of Paul's employment of παρακαλέω in 12:8. This is the only time Paul directly prays to Christ rather than God the Father (Windisch, *Zweite Korintherbrief*, 388; Jean Héring, *The Second Epistle of Saint Paul to the Corinthians* [London: Epworth, 1967], 93). At the beginning of the letter, Paul clarifies that Christ is the agent of divine encouragement (1:5). So, Paul seems to be appealing to the One who mediates divine healing/deliverance as a form of divine encouragement (cf. 1:8–11). Moreover, when the word παρακαλέω is used in the Gospel narratives, 17 times out of 25 are addressed to Christ, especially for pleas for healing (e.g., Matt 8:5; Mark 5:23; Luke 8:41). Thus, Paul seems intentional to make his address to Christ as the mediator of God's healing as a form of divine encouragement so that he himself can be an agent of such encouragement. If Paul's thorn in the flesh is partly related to the Corinthians' accusation of his physical weakness (10:10), their charge against him may pertain to the seemingly contradictory reality that Paul does not receive the healing, but acts as an agent of divine encouragement for the Corinthians.

the Corinthians not to force him to exercise his authority over them (10:1–2; cf. 10:10; 13:1–10). In this way, Paul develops the theme of divine encouragement and suffering throughout the remainder of the letter in 2:14–13:10.[85] In addition to the lexical connection, Paul also characterizes his proclamation of the gospel with encouragement and suffering in 3:1–7:3. Having described the qualification and description of the ministry of the new covenant (3:1–11), Paul begins to proclaim the gospel in 3:12–7:3 (see Chapter 6). Notably, he characterizes his responses to the new covenant with παρρησία (3:12), ἐγκακέω (4:1, 16), and θαρρέω (5:6, 8), stressing that he and his fellow workers are not discouraged despite the challenges and afflictions (4:13–5:10). Furthermore, the antithesis of encouragement and suffering (1:3–7) is substantiated not only by the immediately following context regarding the testimony of his affliction in Asia, in which he highlights God's mighty deliverance from the burden of affliction Paul could not bear with his strength (1:8–11), but also by the theme of divine paradox (2:14; 4:6–7, 10–12, 17; 8:1–2, 9; 12:9–10; 13:4; see Chapter 5).

Third, Paul introduces the notion of agents in ministry in 1:3–7 and further develops it in 2:14–13:10 (see 4.2.2.2). Therefore, in 1:3–2:13, Paul establishes a ground for his discourse in 2:14–13:10 and also introduces the themes of mutuality, encouragement in suffering, and agents in ministry, which are further developed in his discourse in 2:14–13:10.

4.2.2.2 Recurrence of Particularization (1:3–2:13 and 2:14–13:10)

Moreover, I contend that 1:3–2:13 and 2:14–13:10 are organized according to recurrence of particularization (1:3–2:13 and 2:14–13:10), for Paul's discourse in both 1:3–2:13 and 2:14–13:10 moves from a general statement (1:3–7; 2:14–17) to particulars (1:8–2:13; 3:1–13:10), especially regarding the notion of agents in ministry. As I have already discussed, in 1:3–2:13, Paul begins the division with a general statement in which he highlights God as the ultimate agent, Christ as the mediator, and Paul and his fellow workers as God's agents of divine encouragement (1:3–7).[86] He continues to develop the general statement, especially regarding the mutual character of ministry, in 1:8–2:13. Likewise, Paul begins his discourse in 2:14–13:10 with a thesis statement in 2:14–17, in which he underscores God as the ultimate agent, Christ as the intermediate agent, Paul and his coworkers as God's agents, and false apostles as counteragents, and fully develops the notion of agency in 3:1–13:10 (see Chapter 5).

4.2.2.3 Recurrence

Furthermore, the MSR of recurrence regarding the themes of service/work, boasting, grace/joy/forgiveness/thanksgiving, love, and Christ reveals Paul's major emphases in the letter. As I have demonstrated, Paul develops the theme of mutuality in 1:3–2:13, especially regarding suffering and encouragement (1:3–7), partnership (1:7),

---

[85] Also see Long, *2 Corinthians*, 5–6.
[86] See also my discussion (3.2.1) regarding the same theme in 1:1–2.

cooperation in ministry (1:11), boasting (1:12-14), joy (1:23; 2:3), sorrow (2:5), love (2:4, 8), and forgiveness (2:7, 10). While Paul particularly expounds the themes regarding the roles of God, Christ, and God's agents, divine encouragement, and partnership in 2:14-13:10, the rest of the themes also hold the significance as recurrence structures. These themes include the following keywords: service/work (συνυπουργέω; διακονέω; διάκονος; διακονία; δοῦλος; καταδουλόω; ἐνεργέω; συνεργός; κατεργάζομαι; συνεργέω; ἐργάζομαι; ἔργον; ἐργάτης), boasting (καύχησις; καύχημα; καυχάομαι), grace/joy/forgiveness/thanksgiving (χάρις; χαρά; εὐχαριστέω; εὐχαριστία), and love (ἀγάπη; ἀγαπάω). These lexical and thematic connections consistently appear in the rest of Paul's discourse pertaining to ministry (2:14-13:10).

First, the recurring notion of service (διακονία) and work (ἔργον) is the most prominent theme in the letter. In 1:11, Paul highlights the Corinthians' cooperation in his ministry with the word συνυπουργέω.[87] The idea behind 1:11 pertains to service (διακονία) and work (ἔργον) in ministry. Indeed, Paul again underscores the mutuality of service in 1:24, making sure that he and the Corinthians are coworkers (συνεργός). Paul continues to emphasize the theme of service and work in ministry in 2:14-13:10 through the recurrence structure.

In 3:1-7:16, Paul employs διακονία (3:7, 8, 9 [twice]; 4:1; 5:18; 6:3, 4), its cognates (διακονέω in 3:3 and διάκονος in 3:6), and the cognates of ἔργον—πανουργία (4:2), ἐνεργέω (4:12), κατεργάζομαι (4:17; 5:5; 7:10, 11), συνεργέω (6:1), and ἐργάζομα (7:10)—to describe major components of his arguments pertaining to the proclamation of the gospel. Paul insists that the Corinthians themselves are a letter of commendation from Christ, which is ministered (διακονέω) by Paul and his fellow workers (3:3), and God qualifies them to be servants (διάκονος) of the new covenant (3:6), whose ministry (διακονία) reflects the surpassing glory in contrast to that of the old covenant (3:7, 8, 9). Because God's servants have this glorious ministry (διακονία; 4:1), they do not walk in deceptive work/craftiness (πανουργία), but carry the death of Jesus so that death works (ἐνεργέω) in them but life works in the Corinthians (4:12). Moreover, they are not discouraged by affliction, because their sufferings produce (κατεργάζομαι) glory (4:17) and because God prepared (κατεργάζομαι) them for this ministry (5:5). Therefore, they are entrusted with the ministry (διακονία) of reconciliation (5:18; 6:3), coworking (συνεργέω) with God (6:1), and commending themselves as servants (διάκονος) of God in all afflictions (6:4). Moreover, Paul reinforces this message by explicating the outcomes of the proclamation of the gospel (7:4-16), in which he justifies his ministry to the Corinthians through the previous letter, because godly sorrow produces (κατεργάζομαι) repentance that leads to salvation (7:10, 11), whereas the worldly sorrow produces (κατεργάζομαι) death (7:10).

In 8:1-9:15, Paul employs διακονία (8:4; 9:1, 12, 13) and its cognate διακονέω (8:19, 20), and ἔργον (9:8) and its cognates (συνεργός in 8:23 and κατεργάζομαι in 9:12), to describe the crucial elements of his arguments pertaining to response to the gospel. Paul encourages the Corinthians to participate in and complete the ministry of the

---

[87] The word denotes to "cooperate with," "join in helping," or "join in serving." See BDAG, s.v. "συνυπουργέω"; L&N, s.v. "συνυπουργέω"; LSJ, s.v. "συνυπουργέω."

fiscal support to the saints, and he calls this service διακονία throughout the division (8:4; 9:1, 12, 13; cf. διακονέω in 8:19, 20; cf. λειτουργία in 9:12). Moreover, when Paul introduces workers of the offering (8:16–16–9:5), he describes Titus as a fellow worker (συνεργός) of this ministry (8:23) and explains that God makes grace abound for good work (ἔργον ἀγαθόν; 9:8) so that this διακονία will produce (κατεργάζομαι) thanksgiving to God (9:12).

In 10:1–13:10, Paul employs διακονία (11:8) and its cognate διάκονος (11:15 [twice], 23), and ἔργον (10:11; 11:15) and its cognates (πανουργία in 11:3; ἐργάτης in 11:13; κατεργάζομαι in 12:12; πανοῦργος in 12:16), to explain key elements in his arguments pertaining to the defense of the gospel. When Paul is charged with his inconsistency and weakness of his presence and speech (10:1–2, 10a), he insists that he is strong in both word and deed (ἔργον) when present (10:10b). Thus, he begins his boasting as his response to the accusation in 11:1–12:13. He feels godly jealousy over the Corinthians (11:2) because they are led astray by the deceptive work (πανουργία) of false apostles (11:3) and because they misunderstand Paul's financial independence in ministry (διακονία; 11:8). Thus, Paul counter-accuses the false apostles as deceitful workers (ἐργάται δόλιοι; 11:13) and Satan's servants (διάκονος; 11:15 [twice]), who will be judged according to their deeds (ἔργον) at the end (11:15). Although the Corinthians consider Paul to be deceitful (πανοῦργος; 12:12), Paul must insist that the false apostles are not true servants of Christ (διάκονος), but Paul is (11:23), having even performed (κατεργάζομαι) signs, wonders, and miracles among the Corinthians (12:12).

Second, the theme of boasting describes Paul's discourse in 2 Corinthians. Paul underlines that Paul and the Corinthians are sharers of boasting (1:12–14). As I have demonstrated, this boasting pertains to his defense of conduct toward the Corinthians and the previous letter, so the theme of boasting continues to describe Paul's discourse in 2:14–13:10.

In 3:1–7:16, Paul employs καύχημα (5:12), καυχάομαι (5:12; 7:14), and καύχησις (7:4, 14) to describe his argument. Unlike those boasting (καυχάομαι) in external matters, Paul does not commend himself. Instead, he proclaims the gospel in order to give the Corinthians an opportunity to be sharers of boasting (καύχημα; 5:12). Likewise, Paul expresses his boasting (καύχησις in 7:4 and 14; καυχάομαι in 7:14) when the Corinthians responded well to the gospel proclaimed through his previous letter (7:4).

Similarly, in 8:1–9:15, Paul stresses that the Corinthians' participation and completion of the collection for the saints is the proof of Paul's boasting (καύχησις; 8:24). Having confidence in the Corinthians' involvement, he boasts (καυχάομαι) about them to the Macedonians (9:2) and sends emissaries of the collection to make sure that his boasting (καύχημα) will not be emptied (9:3).

While the theme of boasting sporadically appears in 3:1–9:15, Paul brings it to the fore in his arguments in 10:1–13:10, particularly regarding the defense of his status as a servant of Christ (10:1–12:13). In response to the criticisms against Paul, he develops his defense through the means of boasting. Fundamentally, Paul boasts (καυχάομαι) about the authority God gave him (10:8); thus, he boasts (καυχάομαι) in the Lord (10:17 [twice]). He does not boast (καυχάομαι) about himself by taking credit for others' work (10:13, 15, 16), and he will continue to hold on to the boasting (καύχησις) about his fiscal independence in his ministry (11:10) so that he can eliminate the boasting (καυχάομαι) of the false apostles (11:12). However, since the Corinthians forced him to engage in an empty boasting competition (12:11), and many boast (καυχάομαι) according to the flesh (11:18), Paul must boast (καυχάομαι) like a fool (11:16, 18; 12:1, 5, 6; cf. καύχησις in 11:17) about his heritage (11:22–23), suffering (11:23–29), and vision and revelation (12:1–5a), yet the kernel of his boasting is found in his weakness. More than anything else he boasts (καυχάομαι) in his weakness (11:30; 12:5b, 9) because he has been shown that his weakness is a locus of God's grace and power (12:9).

Third, grace (χάρις) and its cognates (χαίρω; χαρά; εὐχαριστέω; εὐχαριστία; χαρίζομαι) also characterize Paul's discourse pertaining to ministry. As I have already discussed in Chapter 3, χάρις and its cognates describe Paul's ministry in 2 Corinthians.[88]

Fourth, the theme of love serves as a foundation for Paul's discourse in 3:1–13:10. In 1:3–2:13, Paul expresses his love for the Corinthians (2:4) and urges them to affirm love for the offender (2:8). In 3:1–13:10, Paul continues to describe his ministry with love as its foundation.[89] Therefore, tracing lexical and thematic connections itself helps one see the contour of his arguments throughout the letter, for the theme of service and work, boasting, grace, and love characterize Paul's discourse in the letter.

Finally, Paul repeatedly refers to Χριστός (1:1, 2, 3, 5, 19, 21; 2:10, 12, 14, 15, 17; 3:3, 4, 14; 4:4, 5, 6; 5:10, 14, 16, 17, 18, 19, 20; 6:15; 8:9, 23; 9:13; 10:1, 5, 7, 14; 11:2, 3, 10, 13, 23; 12:2, 9, 10, 19; 13:3, 5, 13), Ἰησοῦς (1:1, 2, 3, 14, 19; 4:5, 6, 10, 11, 14; 8:9; 11:4, 31; 13:5, 13), and κύριος (1:2, 3, 14; 2:12; 3:16, 17, 18; 4:5, 14; 5:6, 8, 11; 6:17, 18; 8:5, 9, 19, 21; 10:8, 17, 18; 11:17, 31; 12:1, 8; 13:10, 13) in his discourse throughout the letter (see a full discussion in 5.2.3).

4.3 Conclusion and Theological Implication

In this chapter, I analyzed the literary structure of 1:3–2:13 by identifying its segmentation and demonstrating the MSRs of 1:3–2:13 in relation to both the division and the letter as a whole. First, I have demonstrated the MSR of particularization and causation with substantiation (1:3–7 and 1:8–2:13) in relation to the division as a whole. The MSR shows that Paul introduces the theme of mutuality in 1:3–7 as a general statement as well as a basis and develops it by providing examples and reasons in 1:8–2:13. Then, I have expounded three MSRs in relation to the letter as a whole. The MSR of causation with particularization (1:3–2:13 and 2:14–13:10) shows that the theme of mutuality in 1:3–2:13 serves as a basis for Paul's discourse in 2:14–13:10. At the same time, Paul introduces the major themes regarding mutuality, encouragement and suffering, and agents in ministry in 1:3–2:13, and continues to develop them in 2:14–13:10. The MSR of recurrence of particularization (1:3–2:13 and 2:14–13:10) denotes that Paul introduces general statements regarding agents in ministry in 1:3–7

---

[88] See my comments on the greeting in the opening (1:1–2) and the first exhortation in the closing (13:11–13) in Chapter 3.
[89] See also my comments on the peace benediction in 13:11 (3.2.2).

and 2:14–17 and develops the theme in 1:8–2:13 and 3:1–13:10. Recurrence structure underscores Paul's emphasis on the themes of service and work, boasting, grace, love, and Christ.

Having summarized the findings, I will draw an implication regarding the designation of Paul's discourse in 1:3–2:13. I call his discourse "Arguments Pertaining to Basis for Ministry," for the MSRs of causation with particularization (1:3–2:13 and 2:14–13:10) and recurrence of particularization (1:3–2:13 and 2:14–13:10) indicate that his discussion in 1:3–2:13 establishes theological bases regarding the themes of mutuality, encouragement, and agents in ministry for the rest of Paul's discourse in 2:14–13:10. Moreover, I designate his argument as "Character of Ministry," for the MRS of particularization and causation with substantiation (1:3–7 and 1:8–2:13) points to the central theme of the division regarding the mutual character of ministry. Having argued the literary structure of 1:3–2:13, I will turn to the study of 2:14–17.

5

Arguments Pertaining to Content of Ministry: Thesis Statement (2:14–17)

In Chapter 4, I have identified the segmentation of 1:3–2:13 and demonstrated that the MSRs of the division indicate (1) Paul's coherent argument regarding the character of ministry in 1:3–2:13 and (2) the ways in which Paul's discourse in 1:3–2:13 establishes bases for and introduces major themes to be developed in his argument in 2:14–13:10. In this chapter, I will argue that attentive scrutiny of the literary structure of 2:14–17 reveals that the division serves as the thesis statement of the letter, providing an overview of Paul's discourse in 3:1–13:10. In order to substantiate the aforementioned conclusion, I will first explicate that 2:14–17 is a major division of the letter and then demonstrate that 2:14–17 and 3:1–13:10 are structured according to particularization with contrast. The identification of particularization with contrast is especially significant and beneficial for interpretation of 2 Corinthians, for one is to understand the particulars of Paul's discourse (3:1–13:10) in light of the thesis statement (2:14–17) as well as to interpret the thesis statement (2:14–17) in light of the particulars of his discourse (3:1–13:10).

5.1 Division of 2:14–17

Regarding the unit boundaries, it does not impose difficulty on exegetes to discern 2:14 as the beginning of the literary unit. A majority of scholars recognize an abrupt break between 2:13 and 2:14, noting a shift of topic as well as of literary form.[1] Indeed, any alert readers recognize a shift from a travel narrative (2:12–13) to a form of thanksgiving (2:14–17). Moreover, the presence of the conjunction δέ in 2:14 further signals a unit boundary by marking a new development in Paul's discourse.[2]

However, some scholars disagree with the ending of the unit. Some consider 2:16a the ending, and others claim that it extends to 2:17.[3] In this study, I argue that 2:14–17

---

[1] See overview of scholarly arguments concerning the continuity between 2:13 and 2:14 in Thrall, "A Second Thanksgiving," 101–11. Also see my discussion in 4.1.
[2] See the discourse function of δέ in my discussion in 4.2.1.
[3] E.g., Scott J. Hafemann (*Suffering and the Spirit: An Exegetical Study of II Cor 2:14-3:3 Within the Context of the Corinthian Correspondence*, WUNT 2/19 [Tübingen: Mohr Siebeck, 1986] and Lim ("*Sufferings of Christ*," 64–65) argue that 2:14–16a is a literary unit, whereas Thrall (*Second Epistle of the Corinthians*, 1:190–217) and Barnett (*Second Epistle to the Corinthians*, 145–59) view 2:14–17 as a unit.

is a literary unit. While interpreters debate over the transition of Paul's argument from 2:14–16a to 2:16b,[4] a careful reading of the text indicates at least two observations: grammatical discontinuity between 2:16a and 2:16b (i.e., 2:14–16a forming a sentence) and a shift of literary form (i.e., from thanksgiving to a question). However, conjunctive relations and a thematic unity suggest that the thanksgiving extends to 2:17.

First, the discourse function of the conjunction καί in 2:16b suggests continuity with the preceding material rather than a discontinuity. Grammatically speaking, 2:14–16a constitutes a single sentence. Thus, understandably, some scholars identify 2:16b as the beginning of a new literary unit. However, the presence of καί suggests a close association with the preceding material. Levinsohn explains the discourse function of conjunctive καί as follows: "In non-narrative text, it [καί] constrains the material it introduces to be processed as being added to and associated with previous material.... In contrast with δέ, the material it [καί] introduces does *not* represent a new development with respect to the context."[5] But how is Paul's question in 2:16b associated with or added to his discourse in 2:14–16a? This brings us to the second point: thematic unity.

Second, despite a shift of literary form, a strong thematic continuity regarding agents of ministry signals that 2:14–16a and 2:16b–17 belong to the same literary unit. In 2:14–17 Paul's argument highlights four agents in ministry: God, God's agents, Christ, and counteragents. To begin, Paul portrays God as the ultimate agent of ministry. In 2:14, Paul not only highlights God as the recipient of thanksgiving (Τῷ δὲ θεῷ χάρις), but also emphasizes his actions as the ultimate agent of the ministry by elaborating them with two attributive participle clauses: θριαμβεύοντι ἡμᾶς ἐν τῷ Χριστῷ and τὴν ὀσμὴν τῆς γνώσεως αὐτοῦ φανεροῦντι δι' ἡμῶν ἐν παντὶ τόπῳ. The focus of the verse centers on God and his actions.

Moreover, Paul expounds his fellow workers and him as God's human agents in ministry. In 2:14, he has already indicated the instrumentality of God's agents by the phrase δι' ἡμῶν. In 2:15–16a he further substantiates the claim with the causal conjunction ὅτι, explicating the functions of God's agents with metaphors of sacral incense: They are a fragrance of Christ and an aroma (of Christ). Moreover, 2:17 clarifies that the dissemination of God's knowledge pertains to the speech of God's agents.

In addition, Paul depicts Christ as the intermediate agent of ministry. In 2:14, Christ is the means of God's triumphal procession (ἐν τῷ Χριστῷ). Moreover, Christ is not only an instrument of God's activity but also that of the activities of God's agents. In 2:15–16, the fusion between Christ and God's agents (Χριστοῦ) enables them to become a fragrance to God and an aroma of God's knowledge to others. In 2:17, Christ characterizes (ἐν Χριστῷ) their proclamation of God's word in contrast to those who peddle God's word (see Figure 5.1 and 5.2.3).

Finally, Paul depicts counteragents through a contrast. In 2:17, Paul highlights the contrast between God's agents and counteragents. Counteragents peddle God's word

---

[4] See the history of interpretation on 2:16b in Hafemann, *Suffering and the Spirit*, 42–43.
[5] Levinsohn, *Discourse Features*, 124 (italics are original). Also see Runge, *Discourse Grammar*, 23–27.

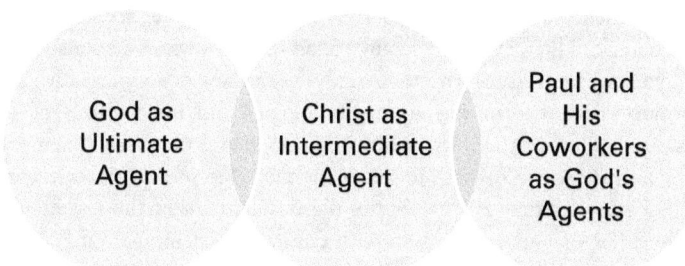

Figure 5.1 Christ as Intermediate Agent.

(2:17a), but God's agents speak God's word in the sight of God as persons of sincerity as well as persons from God (2:17b).

Therefore, in 2:14–17, Paul identifies four agents in ministry: God as the ultimate agent, Paul and his coworkers as God's agents, Christ as the intermediate agent, and peddlers of God's word as counteragents of ministry. This thematic continuity regarding the agents of ministry suggests that 2:14–17 constitutes a literary unit. Having discussed the segmentation of 2:14–17, we will now turn to the MSR.[6]

5.2 Major Structural Relationship in Relation to the Letter as a Whole: Particularization with Contrast (2:14–17 and 3:1–13:10)

Because of the brevity of 2:14–17, I will focus on the MSR of 2:14–17 in relation to the letter as a whole: Second Corintians 2:14–17 and 3:1–13:10 are structured according to particularization with contrast.[7] Namely, 2:14–17 is a thesis statement of the letter, introducing the major topic regarding agents in ministry, that involves a contrast between God's agents and counteragents, which Paul fully develops in the material that follows in 3:1–13:10 (particularization). As discussed in the survey of the literature in Chapter 2, scholars have proposed various identifications of a thesis statement or

---

[6] In relation to the notion of agents, one also finds the contingency of agents in the proclamation of the gospel of Christ in 1:18–22 (cf. 4:4, 6): God, Christ, agents (Paul, Silvanus, and Timothy), and the Spirit, which Long identifies 1:17–24 as *Divisio* and *Partitio* (*Ancient Rhetoric and Paul's Apology*, 157–62). Thus, one observes a continuity between 1:17–24 and 2:14–17 regarding the theme of agents in ministry. However, I identify 2:14–17 as the thesis of the letter, for Paul's discussions regarding his ministry and relationship with the Corinthians in the past (1:3–2:13) serves a basis for the following discussion (2:14–13:10). In other words, Paul shows that just as God, Christ, and agents were organically involved in Paul's and his fellow workers' ministry of the proclamation in the past (1:3–2:13), they continue to play essential roles in the proclamation of God's word (2:14–13:10).

[7] More precisely, 2:14–17 and 3:1–13:10 are structured according to ideological particularization. On the definition of this type of particularization, see my comment on the MSR of particularization with causation in 4.2.1. Long also identifies 2:14–17 as a general statement for the following arguments, though he refuses to identify 2:14–17 as the rhetorical *propositio* (i.e., thesis statement of the letter; "2 Corinthians," 261–95 at 278–79). However, it is more fitting to identify 2:14–17 as the thesis statement of the letter (see my evaluation on his identification in 2.1.3.2).

thesis-like statement that suggests the central theme of the letter according to topical, epistolary, rhetorical, literary, and discourse analyses. However, I have also repeatedly indicated two consistent issues with their analyses: the lack of an integrative approach to incorporate insights from various methodologies and insufficiency of scholars' demonstrations regarding the ways in which Paul develops the thesis statement in the rest of the letter. Therefore, my task in this section is (1) to present the convergence of evidence that suggests that 2:14–17 is the thesis statement of the letter, and (2) to explicate the MSR of particularization with contrast by demonstrating the ways in which Paul develops the thesis statement in the rest of his arguments in 3:1–13:10.

Concerning the literary function of 2:14–17, at least three pieces of evidence suggest that 2:14–17 is the thesis statement of the letter: insights from rhetorical criticism, epistolary criticism, and topical analysis. First, rhetorical criticism brings two insights. One insight is that the travel narrative in 2:12–13 prepares Paul's audience for the thesis statement. As already discussed, ancient writers, including rhetoricians, frequently summarize the events before they introduce a thesis of the writing and speech.[8] What we find in 2:12–13 and 2:14–17 fits into the conventional practice of ancient writing and speech. In addition, Paul's use of metaphors in 2:14–17 may indicate that the passage is the thesis statement of the letter.[9] Wayne C. Booth argues, based on the tradition of ancient rhetorical handbooks, that authors/rhetors employ metaphors with rhetorical motivations, which include desires (1) to make speech active and energetic, (2) to be succinct, (3) to heighten or diminish appropriately, (4) to accommodate one's audience, and (5) to build the speaker's *ethos*.[10] Ted Cohen claims that the use of metaphors provides the author with an opportunity to cultivate intimacy with the audience.[11] Building on Booth and Cohen's study, Stephen B. Heiny demonstrates such case in Paul's use of three metaphors in 2:14–4:16: εὐωδία, ἐπιστολή, and φωτισμός.[12] While his analysis extends beyond 2:14–17, Heiny particularly notes the significance of Paul's metaphor in 2:14–17 to establish his *ethos*.[13] In fact, one finds Paul's discussion in 2:14–17 filled with metaphors: triumphal procession (θριαμβεύω in 2:14), sacral incense (ὀσμή in 2:14, 16; εὐωδία in 2:15), and huckster (καπηλεύω in 2:17). Although Heiny does not identify 2:14–17 as the thesis statement of the letter, it makes much more sense that Paul's use of metaphors in 2:14–17 reflects his desire not

---

[8] See my discussion regarding the ways in which introductory narratives prepare audience for the thesis statement in 4.2.1.4.

[9] Rhetorical criticism often calls the thesis of the speech *propositio* (e.g., Witherington, *Conflict and Community in Corinth*, 371-74); however, Long argues, "If the thesis contains several heads, then it is called a *partitio*" (*Ancient Rhetoric and Paul's Apology*, 157). Though my study does not aim to analyze the letter according to the ancient rhetorical tradition, my identification of the thesis statement has some similarities with the rhetorical category of *partitio*.

[10] Wayne C. Booth, "Metaphor as Rhetoric: The Problem of Evaluation," in *On Metaphor*, ed. Sheldon Sacks (Chicago: University of Chicago Press, 1978), 47-70, especially at 54-56.

[11] Ted Cohen, "Metaphor and the Cultivation of Intimacy," in *On Metaphor*, ed. Sheldon Sacks (Chicago: University of Chicago Press, 1978), 1-10.

[12] Stephen B. Heiny, "2 Corinthians 2:14–4:6: The Motive for Metaphor," in *Society of Biblical Literature 1987 Seminar Papers*, SBLSPS 26 (Atlanta: Society of Biblical Literature, 1987), 1-22. Also see Paul Brooks Duff, "Metaphor, Motif, and Meaning: The Rhetorical Strategy Behind the Image 'Led in Triumph' in 2 Corinthians 2:14," *CBQ* 53 (1991): 79-92.

[13] Heiny, "2 Corinthians 2:14–4:6," 20-21.

merely to establish his *ethos* but also to make his statement active, vivid, energetic, and economical according to rhetorical motivations, especially when considering the function of 2:14–17 as the thesis statement of the letter.

Second, the presence of the epistolary formula of thanksgiving shows that 2:14–17 is the thesis statement of the letter. In her article, "A Second Thanksgiving Period in II Corinthians," Thrall convincingly made a case that 2:14–17 serves as a second introductory thanksgiving based on three observations. To begin, building upon Paul Schubert's study of Pauline thanksgiving,[14] she found some general similarities between Pauline thanksgivings and the structure of 2 Cor 2:14–15. Moreover, she found an eschatological overtone (εἰς θάνατον and εἰς ζωήν) similar to other Pauline thanksgivings (e.g., 1 Cor 1:8; Phil 1:11). In addition, she observes the presence of πᾶς and its compounds in both 2 Cor 2:14 and other Pauline thanksgivings (Rom 1:8, 10; 1 Cor 1:4–5; 2 Cor 1:3–4; Phil 1:3–4; 1 Thess 1:2).[15] If so, 2:14–17 most likely outlines main themes that will be developed in the material that follows, especially when taking the function of introductory thanksgiving into consideration. As I have already discussed the function of 1:3–7 in Chapter 4, introductory thanksgivings or blessings frequently set the tone and themes to be developed.[16] This epistolary function is true in the thanksgiving in 2 Cor 2:14–17. However, one may object to her conclusion since the other thanksgiving in 1:3–11 employs εὐχαριστέω (1:11) instead of Χάρις (although this study identifies 1:3–7 as the introductory blessing instead of 1:3–11 as the thanksgiving). Thrall addresses this concern by explaining that εὐχαριστέω and Χάρις have the same function based on the studies of Schubert and O'Brien. Schubert argues that a papyrus letter from the third century BCE attests the use of χάρις in its introduction, and O'Brien also notes χάρις functions such as an introductory thanksgiving by appealing to the similar use of the term in 1 Tim 1:12.[17] Besides, I would add that Paul's employment of χάρις in the thesis statement (2:14) has a theological significance in light of his arguments in its literary context. Paul intentionally employs χάρις to describe God's activities in 2:14–17, sketching out the divine reality in which the ministry is conducted.[18]

Third, Paul develops the themes introduced in 2:14–17 in the following material in 3:1–13:10. The flow of argument indicates that Paul underscores four agents and their activities in ministry: God as ultimate agent (2:14), Christ as intermediate agent (2:14, 15, 17), Paul and his coworkers as human agents (2:15–17), and peddlers of God's word as counteragents (2:17). Paul continues to develop these themes in the following material in 3:1–13:10. Some scholars have already postulated that 2:14–17 is the thesis statement of 2:14–7:4.[19] However, no scholars have demonstrated that 2:14–17 is the

---

[14] Paul Schubert, *Form and Function of the Pauline Thanksgivings* (Berlin: Töpelmann, 1939).
[15] Thrall, "A Second Thanksgiving Period," 115–16.
[16] See my comments and notes in 4.2.1.1.
[17] Thrall, "A Second Thanksgiving Period," 113–14; Schubert, *Form and Function*, 159–160; O'Brien, *Introductory Thanksgivings*, 236n19.
[18] See further discussion in 5.2.1.
[19] E.g., Jean-François Collange, *Enigmes de La Deuxième Épître de Paul aux Corinthiens: Etudes Exégétique de 2 Cor 2,14–7,4*, SNTSMS 18 (Cambridge University Press, 1972); Thrall, *The Second Epistle of the Corinthians*, 1:188; James I. H. McDonald, "Paul and the Preaching Ministry: A Reconsideration of 2 Cor 2:14–17 in Its Context," *JSNT* 17 (1983): 35–50; Seifrid, *The Second Letter to the Corinthians*, 84.

thesis for the entire letter.[20] Therefore, this study argues that Paul introduces the major topic regarding the agents in ministry in 2:14–17 and thematically and lexically develops it in 3:1–13:10.

Regarding my second task in this section, to understand the ways in which Paul develops the major themes in the following material, we must first scrutinize the thrust of Paul's argument in 2:14–17. To begin, Paul underlines God's activity in two ways in 2:14. First, God receives χάρις. The word order, Τῷ δὲ θεῷ χάρις, in 2:14 indicates Paul's emphasis on God as the focus of the sentence. While other thanksgivings in the letter express χάρις before God (Χάρις δὲ τῷ θεῷ in 8:16; χάρις τῷ θεῷ in 9:15), he emphasizes God who receives χάρις in 2:14.[21] Second, Paul continues to describe God's activities in ministry by two attributive participial clauses with verbs, θριαμβεύω and φανερόω, in present-tense forms.[22] God (1) always leads us in triumph in Christ and (2) manifests the aroma of his knowledge through us in every place. In doing so, Paul highlights God's activities: He receives χάρις and acts. In other words, Paul characterizes God's divine activities with χάρις because of what he does.

In addition, Paul discusses the ways in which God's agents are involved in divine activities: God involves them in triumph (θριαμβεύοντι ἡμᾶς) and manifests his knowledge through them (δι' ἡμῶν). Paul later clarifies that God's agents refer to the servants of the new covenant (3:6), servants of God (6:4), servant of Christ (11:23; cf. 11:15), and slave for Christ (4:5).[23] Thus, he substantiates the notion of God's agents and their activities, beginning with a causal ὅτι in 2:15, to describe their roles in ministry. He first employs the images of incense (εὐωδία and ὀσμή) in 2:15–16 and then contrasts God's agents with peddlers of God's word in 2:17. Therefore, (1) God's agents are a fragrance (εὐωδία) of Christ to God (2:15); (2) they are aroma (ὀσμή) to people (2:16); and (3) they speak God's word in Christ in the sight of God (2:17).

Moreover, Paul also highlights Christ's intermediary roles in 2:14–17.[24] Christ is instrumental in God's triumph (ἐν τῷ Χριστῷ; 2:14). A union of God's agents and Christ takes place; thus, their life and service become the fragrance of Christ (Χριστοῦ εὐωδία; 2:15) to God and aroma (ὀσμή) to others. Christ is the cause, source, and/or standard of their proclamation of God's word (ἐν Χριστῷ; 2:17).[25]

---

[20] Except Amadar, who identifies 2:14–17 as *causa*, and Witherington, who identifies 2:17 as *propositio*; see my critique against their analysis in 2.1.3.

[21] On emphasis through word orders and information structure, see Runge, *Discourse Grammar*, 192–93, 269–86.

[22] The present tenses indicate God's ongoing activity in ministry.

[23] Paul's heavy emphasis on the notion of service (διακονία) and work (ἔργον) throughout the letter (see recurrence in 4.2.2.3) supports that God's agents are servants of slave of God/Christ. However, it is also possible to posit that God's agents refer to apostles not in the technical sense (i.e., apostles sent by Christ), but in a broader sense, for three reasons. First, Paul begins the letter as an apostle (1:1). Second, Paul calls the workers of the collection apostles (8:23; cf. Phil 2:25) and calls Timothy and Silvanus apostles of Christ elsewhere (1 Thess 2:6). Third, Paul contrasts himself with super-apostles (11:5; 12:11) and false apostles (11:16) who disguise themselves as apostles of Christ (11:13), and he relates his defense of his status as a servant of Christ (11:21b–12:10) to the sign of apostle (12:12).

[24] My definition of Christ's "intermediary" or "intermediate agency" is much broader than grammatical categories. See my discussion below in 5.2.3.

[25] Lim also notes the importance of Christ in Paul's argument in 2:14–16a and insists on the presence of the narrative substructure of Jesus in 2:14–16a ("*Suffering of Christ*," 64–96).

Finally, Paul highlights another group of people who act as counteragents in ministry. They are peddlers of God's word (2:17), whom Paul later calls false apostles (11:13). Furthermore, Paul's portrayal of contrast between God's servants and counteragents indicates that they lack qualifications: They are neither persons of sincerity nor persons from God (2:17).

Therefore, the thesis statement in 2:14–17 revolves around four agents in ministry: (1) God as the ultimate agent who executes his ministry through his agents, (2) God's agents who speak God's word and whose ministry is directed both to God and people, (3) Christ as the intermediate agent in God's ministry, and (4) counteragents who peddle God's word and lack integrity in their ministry. Having explained the main thrust of the discussion in 2:14–17, I will turn to show the ways in which Paul develops the theme of those agents and their activities in the material that follows in 3:1–13:10.

5.2.1 God as Ultimate Agent of Ministry

Paul describes God's two major activities in 2:14: God's triumph and the dissemination of his knowledge. Paul continues to expound these themes throughout the material that follows in 3:1–13:10. Exegesis of God's triumphal metaphor in 2:14 has been one of the most controversial passages in 2 Corinthians. Unfortunately, no scholars have "triumphed" over a scholarly consensus with their interpretations. The debate concentrates on the historical contexts of the metaphor and Paul's role in the imagery. In doing so, interpreters frequently trace the Jewish and/or Hellenistic influences on Paul's discourse to study the enigmatic expression of God's triumph in 2:14.[26] However, scholars sometimes overlook the most pertinent context: the literary context of 2 Corinthians. Indeed, the literary context provides interpreters with another way to construe 2:14 in light of Paul's larger discourse in the letter. Namely, 2:14 describes the nature and content of God's ministry. Before investigating the material in 3:1–13:10, three preliminary observations should be noted.

First, the grammar in 2:14 shows a close interconnection between the metaphors of God's triumph and manifestation of his knowledge. Paul explains God's activities with two attributive participial clauses with verbs, θριαμβεύω and φανερόω, in present-tense forms. Thus, the parallel structure of these clauses suggests that these two divine activities are closely related.

Second, a chiastic structure in 2:14 further bolsters the interconnection of the divine activities. Long analyzes 2:14 as follows:

Τῷ δὲ θεῷ χάρις
   [A.] τῷ πάντοτε
      [B.] θριαμβεύοντι ἡμᾶς

---

[26] On possible Greco-Roman and Jewish traditions behind 2:14–17, see Roger David Aus, *Imagery of Triumph and Rebellion in 2 Corinthians 2:14–17 and Elsewhere in the Epistle: An Example of the Combination of Greco-Roman and Judaic Traditions in the Apostle Paul*, Studies in Judaism (Lanham, MD: University Press of America, 2005); Christoph Heilig, *Paul's Triumph: Reassessing 2 Corinthians 2:14 in Its Literary and Historical Context*, BTS 27 (Leuven: Peeters, 2017).

[C.] ἐν τῷ Χριστῷ
[D.] καὶ
[C'.] τὴν ὀσμὴν τῆς γνώσεως αὐτοῦ
[B'.] φανεροῦντι δι' ἡμῶν
[A'.] ἐν παντὶ τόπῳ.[27]

Although his analysis is not strictly lexical, one can observe corresponding elements in it. A and A' express the inclusive scope of God's activities regarding the occasion (always) and locus (every place). C and C' refer to the same entity: The literary context reveals that God's knowledge (2:14) is the gospel of Christ (4:4). Moreover, while verbs in B and B' do not share lexical similarities, both activities involve God's agents (ἡμᾶς and δι' ἡμῶν). If so, one may deduce that θριαμβεύω and φανερόω refer to the same reality but different aspects of God's activity.

Third, having observed a close link between the two divine activities, one must ask how these two statements are related. Observations of Paul's use of χάρις elsewhere in the letter may provide categories for them. In Chapter 3, I showed that χάρις and its cognates characterize Paul's ministry in 2 Corinthians. Χάρις describes the content (1:15; 4:15; 6:1; 8:1, 4, 6, 7, 19; 9:8, 14, 15) and manner or nature of the ministry (1:12; 8:1, 9; 12:9). Thus, it is no coincidence that Paul employs χάρις to characterize God's activities in the thesis statement. Rather, with the term χάρις, Paul purposefully describes the nature and content of God's activities in 2:14. Namely, the metaphor of God's triumph portrays the nature of God's activity, and the metaphor of aroma that manifests God's knowledge depicts the content of God's activity. With these preliminary observations, I shall now turn to examine thematic and lexical connections between 2:14–17 and 3:1–13:10 regarding God's activities in the ministry.

5.2.1.1 Nature of Ministry

As previously mentioned, one perplexity in the interpretation of God's triumphal metaphor in 2:14 pertains to the construal of the role of Paul and his coworkers, for analyses of syntax and literary context point to different pictures of their role in the imagery. Syntactically speaking, when the word θριαμβεύω functions as a transitive verb, taking an accusative personal object, it conveys the sense of leading the person as a captive or a conquered enemy in the triumphal procession.[28] In 2:14, θριαμβεύω takes a personal pronoun (ἡμᾶς) as an accusative object. Thus, the grammar suggests that Paul portrays himself and his fellow workers as the conquered captives in God's triumphal procession.[29]

---

[27] Long, *2 Corinthians*, 59.
[28] Cilliers Breytenbach studied the use of the θριαμβεύω in *corpus hellenisticum* and demonstrated that the intransitive usage of the term has the sense of "to celebrate a prior victory by means of a triumph," while the transitive usage carries the meaning of "to lead as a conquered enemy in a victory parade" ("Paul's Proclamation and God's 'Thriambos': (Notes on 2 Corinthians 2:14–16b)," *Neot* 24 (1990): 257–71 at 260, 261. See also Heilig, *Paul's Triumph*; Hafemann, *Suffering and the Spirit*, 22–39.
[29] Many recent interpreters support this reading. See BDAG, s.v. "θριαμβεύω" (1a); Thrall, *Second Epistle of the Corinthians*, 1:194–95; Witherington, *Conflict and Community in Corinth*, 367–78; Garland, *2 Corinthians*, 142–43; Harris, *Second Epistle to the Corinthians*, 243; Seifrid, *Second Letter to the Corinthians*, 84–85; Guthrie, *2 Corinthians*, 160.

However, the following literary context in 2:14b-17 portrays another picture: They are active participants in God's triumphal ministry, in which God manifests his knowledge through them. The picture becomes more complex when one considers the military image in 10:3-6 (cf. 6:7), in which Paul appears to depict himself and his fellow workers as soldiers. Thus, Aus claims, "Paul in 2 Cor 2:14 can describe himself and his coworkers metaphorically as soldiers participating in their general's, the Lord God of hosts', triumphal procession."[30] Paul's claim in 4:5 summarizes this intricate picture in which he views his fellow workers and himself as conquered slaves who preach Christ Jesus as Lord. How can the captives in God's triumphal procession be the active participants of the dissemination of God's knowledge? This paradox is precisely what Paul wants to drive home: the antithetical nature of God's mission. More precisely, God achieves his mission through the least qualified and unlikely means. Thus, the captives are active participants in God's mission. Paul continues to expound this antithetical nature of God's activities in each major division in 3:1–7:16 (4:6-7, 10-12, 17), 8:1–9:15 (8:1-2, 9), and 10:1–13:10 (12:9-10; 13:4).

In 3:1–7:16, Paul develops three antitheses (4:6-7, 10-12, 17). First, God manifests his knowledge through worthless and fragile human agents. In utilizing a famous metaphor of "treasure in jars of clay" (4:7), Paul shows another paradoxical nature of God's ministry. The literary context indicates that the treasure pertains to God's knowledge in Christ (4:6), and the Greek adjective ὀστράκινος refers to something made of clay and denotes fragility.[31] Thus, Paul's illustration of treasure in clay jars conveys a sense that a relatively worthless, cheap, and breakable vessel contains the indescribably valuable treasure of the gospel. Just as Paul describes in 2:14 that God manifests his knowledge through captives or slaves whose value is often ignored in the eyes of conquerors, the image of vessels of clay in 4:7 continues to represent God's paradoxical way of ministry: God entrusts the treasure that contains the glorious and transforming message of the gospel to worthless and fragile human agents. Furthermore, the ἵνα clause in 4:7 explains the purpose of the divine paradox, stating, ἡ ὑπερβολὴ τῆς δυνάμεως ᾖ τοῦ θεοῦ καὶ μὴ ἐξ ἡμῶν. Therefore, in this passage, Paul expounds not only the nature of God's mission but also its purpose. God manifests his gospel through the most unqualified means so that the Corinthians would understand the centrality of God but not that of human agents in ministry.

Second, God manifests life through death. Building on the contrast of treasure and clay jars, Paul continues to explain the divine paradox in ministry. Since many captives who were led in triumphal procession were executed afterward, the Greek verb θριαμβεύω in 2:14 strongly connotes the sense of death.[32] While people celebrate the victory and lives of officials, the captives are destined to die. Paul develops this antithesis of life and death in ministry, particularly in 4:10-12, in which he brings the implicit image of life and death in 2:14 to the fore. In these verses, Paul repeatedly emphasizes

---

[30] Aus, *Imagery of Triumph and Rebellion*, 17. See also Barrett, *Second Epistle to the Corinthians*, 98.
[31] BDAG, s.v. "ὀστράκινος."
[32] On the connotation of suffering and death in Roman triumphal processions, see Hafemann, *Suffering and the Spirit*, 7-39; cf. Heilig, *Paul's Triumph*.

the purpose of carrying the death of Jesus. God manifests the life of Jesus (4:10, 11, 12) through his servants' deaths (4:10, 11).[33]

Third, God manifests glory through suffering. In 4:17, Paul describes that light momentary affliction produces for them an eternal weight of glory. In 1:8, Paul describes that his experience of affliction burdened him beyond comparison (καθ' ὑπερβολὴν), even to the point of death (cf. Barn 12:5). However, in 4:17 he has come to understand that affliction becomes a means to produce God's glory beyond comparison (καθ' ὑπερβολὴν).[34] In the imagery of God's triumphal procession in 2:14, one immediately senses an overtone of the captives' suffering and affliction in combination with their death and execution. However, Paul clarifies that God produces extraordinary glory through the least expected means—suffering and affliction (4:17).[35]

In 8:1-9:15, Paul continues to expound the divine paradox: God manifests wealth through poverty. In 8:1-2 and 8:9, he describes God's grace related to the paradoxical nature of God's activity in the ministry of the collection. In 8:1-2, God's grace given to the churches in Macedonia (8:1) pertains to two contrasts (8:2): Macedonians' joy in the midst of affliction and their poverty turning into a wealth of generosity. The world anticipates affliction turning to grief, bitterness, and poverty, leading to frugality. Nevertheless, the grace of God reveals the divine reality in which the Macedonian churches overcame the great ordeal of affliction with joy and triumphed over their deep poverty with riches of their generosity. Moreover, in 8:9, Paul brings the antithesis of poverty and wealth to the fore in the example of Christ by expounding the grace of the Lord Jesus Christ. Christ became poor so that the believers might become rich through his poverty; God manifests wealth through Christ's poverty. In the Greco-Roman world, where reciprocity and patronage play essential parts in social structure, the wealthy would give their clients some access to resources in return for their service and their homage to the patrons.[36] The society runs with the system that the poor, who are also weak within the society, obtain access to resources through the wealthy, who are social elites with power. However, people would not anticipate that the poor become rich through poverty, because people would have anticipated the link between the poor and weakness and the rich and power in their worldview. However, Christ brings riches through his poverty: Christ's poverty makes believers rich; his weakness indeed empowers others.

In 10:1-13:10, Paul mainly develops the paradox in 12:9-10 and 13:4: God manifests power through weakness. In the pinnacle of his defense in 12:7-10, Paul reaches the

---

[33] One should note Paul's careful language in 4:10-12. He repeatedly employs "divine passive" (4:10, 11) to indicate the centrality of God in this paradox of death and life in ministry.

[34] Harvey, *Renewal Through Suffering*, 63-64; Savage, *Power through Weakness*, 183.

[35] Moreover, in this divine paradox, Paul describes the antithesis of affliction and glory regarding temporality and eternity (4:18). Also, one should note the contrast between joy and affliction in 7:4. Although the text does not explicitly indicate that God manifests joy through the means of affliction, the antithesis of joy and affliction is noteworthy. In 7:4 Paul expresses his joy through Titus's report (7:6). The divine passive with the verb ὑπερπερισσεύω in 7:4 shows that God fills him with joy in all his affliction. Paul does not find joy in the suffering itself; however, God fills him with joy by redeeming all his affliction through Paul's relationship with the Corinthians. While affliction usually results in sorrow, Paul declares that his affliction resulted in joy.

[36] On ancient patronage system, see David A. deSilva, *Honor, Patronage, Kinship & Purity: Unlocking New Testament Culture* (Downers Grove, IL: InterVarsity Press, 2000), 121-56.

climax regarding his description of God's paradoxical nature in ministry: power through weakness.[37] Despite his plea to remove his thorn in the flesh (12:8), the Lord gave him an answer that weakness is a locus in which divine power is perfected and manifested (12:9). Therefore, Paul not only accepts his weaknesses (11:29; 12:6) but finds delight in his weaknesses, insults, distresses, persecutions, and difficulties for the sake of Christ because he has come to understand the core of ministry: God's strength resides in his weakness (12:10). Moreover, Paul further bolsters this paradox by providing a basis in Christ's weakness and power in 13:4. Just as power and weakness characterize Paul's life and ministry, he describes Christ's crucifixion and resurrection in light of power and weakness. Paul depicts his experience of weakness and power in light of Jesus's experience of death and resurrection.

From the very beginning of his arguments, Paul portrays the paradoxical nature of God's ministry. The captives are the active participants in God's mission (2:14). God always triumphs in Christ but through the least qualified and most unlikely means, so that people might attribute the triumph to God, recognizing the centrality of God in ministry (4:7). Therefore, Paul continues to explicate the paradoxical nature of God's activities in ministry. God manifests his glorious knowledge of the gospel in Christ through worthless and fragile human agents (4:7); God manifests life through death (4:10-12); God manifests glory through suffering (4:17); God manifests wealth through poverty (8:1-2, 9); and God manifests power through weakness (12:9-10; 13:4).

5.2.1.2 *Content of Ministry: Manifestation of God's Knowledge*

Regarding the content of God's activities, Paul employs a metaphor of aroma that manifests his knowledge (2:14b). Paul elucidates the content of God's knowledge in the following material, especially in 3:1-4:12: God's knowledge pertains to the credentials of his servants (3:1-6a) and the gospel of Christ (3:12-4:12).[38]

First, God manifests his knowledge regarding the credentials of his servants. In response to the criticism against the lack of commendation letter (3:1), Paul declares that the existence of the Corinthians serves as his commendation letter (3:2-3). In using a metaphor of letter-writing, Paul carefully crafts his language to convey God's intention of the existence of the Corinthians to disseminate his knowledge regarding the credentials of God's servants. Syntactically speaking, Paul elaborates his declaration, ἡ ἐπιστολὴ ἡμῶν ὑμεῖς ἐστε in 3:2a, with five circumstantial participial clauses in 3:2b–

---

[37] Some recognize the climax of his argument in 12:9-10; e.g., Long, *Ancient Rhetoric and Paul's Apology*, 217. See the MSR of generalization with climax in 8.2.2.3.

[38] One may question or even critique the notion that the idea of God's knowledge should be considered as one of the main themes because of the brevity of space Paul devotes to develop it. In fact, the description of God's knowledge concentrates in 3:12-4:12, and Paul spends more space explaining the activities of God's agents. However, as we will see discussed further in Chapter 6, Paul articulates God's knowledge as the gospel most prominently in 3:12-4:12. Moreover, as we will see in Chapter 7, 8:1-9:15 is essentially an exhortation in response to Paul's arguments in 3:1-7:3, and as we will see in Chapter 8, 10:1-13:10 substantiate Paul's discourse in 2:14-9:15. In other words, although the descriptions of divine knowledge concentrate in 3:12-4:12, structurally speaking, 3:12-4:12 is a part of the crucial discussion for the rest of Paul's discourse. Thus, I still argue that the notion of God's knowledge is one of the main themes of the letter based on the significance of Paul's arguments.

3: ἐγγεγραμμένη, γινωσκομένη, ἀναγινωσκομένη, φανερούμενοι, and ἐγγεγραμμένη.[39] In these participial clauses, Paul communicates God as the author of the commendation letter and his intention of writing. All participles are in the passive form, but the first (ἐγγεγραμμένη), third (φανερούμενοι), and fifth (ἐγγεγραμμένη) passive participles function as what grammarians call the "divine passive,"[40] whereas Paul specifies the agents of the second (γινωσκομένη) and third (ἀναγινωσκομένη) passive participles with the prepositional phrase, ὑπὸ πάντων ἀνθρώπων. The divine passives indicate that God authored the Corinthians as the letter of Christ and the people of the spirit of the living God. The second (γινωσκομένη) and third (ἀναγινωσκομένη) passive participles express that God intends the letter (i.e., the Corinthians) to commend his servants to all people. As the nature of the letter communicates, people read out the letter to acquire knowledge about the subject. Thus, in 3:1-3, God manifests his knowledge, particularly regarding the credentials of his servants.

Second, God manifests his knowledge as the gospel of Christ through divine paradox (3:12-4:12). In order to appreciate the ways in which Paul unpacks the content of God's knowledge as the gospel of Christ, one should understand the progression of his discussion in 3:12-4:12. After describing the ministerial credentials of the servants (3:1-6a) and the glorious character of the new covenant in contrast to the old covenant (3:6b-11), Paul begins to articulate God's knowledge as the gospel of Christ in 3:12-4:12. The old covenant reveals the limited knowledge of God (3:13-15), whereas the new covenant discloses God's full and transforming knowledge in Christ (3:16-18). On the one hand, the knowledge God communicated in the old covenant was limited because of the veil Moses assumed (3:14-15).[41] In these verses, Paul relates the reading of the old covenant and Moses to God's knowledge revealed in the Torah by employing ἀνάγνωσις and ἀναγινώσκω (cognates of γινώσκω), for the understanding and knowledge of God comes from the reading of the Scripture. On the other hand, God fully manifests his knowledge in the new covenant that transforms us into the same image of the Lord (3:18) because the veil is removed in Christ (3:14, 16). Thus, by repeatedly employing divine passives (3:14, 16, 18), Paul underscores that God manifests his full and transforming knowledge in the new covenant. He then continues to articulate God's knowledge as the gospel in 4:1-12. Paul clarifies that the veil still hides the gospel of the glory of Christ, the image of God (4:3, 4). However, God's servants proclaim Christ Jesus as Lord (4:5) and God gives the light of his glorious knowledge in Christ to our hearts (4:6), which is manifested through the divine paradox of power through weakness (4:7-12). Therefore, Paul's discussion progresses as follows: In Christ, God removed the veil that hid his knowledge (3:12-18); thus, he now fully manifests his knowledge, the gospel of the glory Christ (4:1-6) through the divine paradox (4:7-12). Therefore, God manifests the gospel of Christ as his knowledge.

---

[39] We find another participle, διακονηθεῖσα, in 3:3; however, this verb is an attributive participle, modifying ἐπιστολή, not an adverbial/circumstantial participle.

[40] E.g., Wallace, *Greek Grammar,* 437-38.

[41] Paul also describes a similar idea elsewhere that the Jews had the embodiment of knowledge and truth in the Law (Rom 2:20), but they are ignorant about God's righteousness (Rom 10:2, 3, 19).

5.2.1.3 Summary

Preliminary observations of 2:14 indicate that God's triumph and the manifestation of his knowledge are closely related, especially in relation to χάρις. My investigation of the literary context of 2 Corinthians confirms that Paul develops two realities of divine ministry based on the thesis statement in 2:14–17: the nature and content of God's activities in the ministry. First, building on the antithetical nature of God's triumph in 2:14, Paul consistently explicates the paradoxical nature of God's mission: God achieves his mission through the least qualified and most unlikely means. In 3:1–7:16, God entrusts the treasure of the gospel to worthless and fragile human agents (4:6–7), manifests the life of Jesus through his servants' death (4:10–12) and glory through their suffering (4:17). In 8:1–9:15, God manifests wealth through Christ's poverty (8:9; cf. 8:1–2). In 10:1–13:10, God manifests power through weakness (12:9–10; 13:4). Second, Paul unpacks a metaphor of aroma that manifests God's knowledge (2:14) in the following material: God manifests his knowledge regarding the credentials of his servants (3:1–6a) and the gospel of Christ (3:12–4:12). Having examined the roles of God as the ultimate agent in ministry, we will turn to investigate those of God's agents in ministry.

5.2.2 Agents of Ministry

Paul employs another metaphor of sacral incense to communicate the roles of God's agents in ministry in 2:14–17. He portrays them with two types of scent: ὀσμή (2:14, 16) and εὐωδία (2:15). The former pertains to their activities to people and the latter to God. In other words, he describes their activities in two directions: horizontal and vertical. Moreover, taking 2:14–17 as a literary unit, his discussion in 2:17 also indicates that the image of incense particularly concerns their activities regarding speech (i.e., the dissemination of God's knowledge by speaking God's word).

While scholars debate the backgrounds of 2:14–17, an analysis of Paul's use of ὀσμή and εὐωδία indicates at least two facts. Paul employs εὐωδία in relation to ministry to God and ὀσμή in relation to ministry to people.[42] Many scholars claim that ὀσμή usually refers either to a pleasant or an unpleasant odor while εὐωδία refers only to a pleasant odor.[43] Paul distinguishes these terms in 2:14–17. On the one hand, he employs ὀσμή to describe God's manifestation of knowledge to people through God's agents (2:14). As God's ὀσμή, they announce both life and death to people (2:16) because God's knowledge can be both pleasant and unpleasant (cf. 1 Cor 1:18). On the other hand, Paul employs εὐωδία in relation to his fellow workers, and his service and

---

[42] Identifications of historical backdrops go beyond the purpose of the present study; however, the OT and Greco-Roman contexts may point to possible Greco-Roman and Jewish traditions behind Paul's discussion in 2:14–17. The imagery of triumph was well known among the Corinthians; at the same time, ὀσμή and εὐωδία appear together in the context of the burnt offering in the LXX (e.g., Gen 8:21; Exod 29:18; Lev 1:9; cf. Phil 4:18). On this, see Aus, *Imagery of Triumph and Rebellion*; Long, "'God of This Age,'" 219–69.

[43] E.g., Furnish, *II Corinthians*, 175–76; Harris, *The Second Epistle to the Corinthians*, 248.

sacrifice directed to God (2:15),[44] because εὐωδία is always pleasing to God. Thus, Paul describes himself and his fellow workers as a pleasing sacrifice of Christ to God. Moreover, Paul relates these two directions of ministry to the activity of speech, for they speak God's word in Christ in the sight of God (2:17). Therefore, he continues to unpack it in each major division (3:1–7:16; 8:1–9:15; 10:1–13:10).

5.2.2.1 God's Agents As Χριστοῦ Εὐωδία

In 3:1–7:16, Paul repeatedly describes ministry in light of sacrificial image (4:13–5:10; 5:11–6:10; 6:14–7:1; 7:4–16). First, Paul views ministry as a pleasing sacrifice to God by explicating the sacrificial image of ministry, most prominently in 4:13–5:10. After describing the credentials of God's servants (3:1–6a) and the character of the new covenant (3:6b–11), Paul begins to proclaim God's knowledge, the gospel of Christ (3:12–4:12; 4:13–5:10; 5:11–7:3): God's servants speak God's word (3:12, 4:13; 5:11).[45] Particularly, in 4:13–5:10, Paul characterizes his response with allusions to the OT sacrificial image to indicate the goal, sphere, and nature of the ministry.

To begin, Paul desires the ministry to be a pleasing sacrifice and service to God. Not being discouraged by hardships (4:16; 5:6, 8), Paul and his fellow workers continue to speak God's word (4:13). Thus, he concludes the section (4:13–5:10) by declaring in 5:9, διὸ καὶ φιλοτιμούμεθα, εἴτε ἐνδημοῦντες εἴτε ἐκδημοῦντες, εὐάρεστοι αὐτῷ εἶναι. Paul expresses his strong ambition that their service and sacrifice will be pleasing to God.[46] Some lexical connections between εὐάρεστος (5:9) and δεκτός suggest Paul's development of the sacrificial imagery from 2:14–17. While εὐάρεστος occurs only in Wis 4:10 and 9:10 in the LXX, δεκτός, a synonym of εὐάρεστος, often appears in the LXX.[47] Paul employs εὐάρεστος and δεκτός synonymously in Phil 4:18, in which he describes the gift from the Philippians in equating ὀσμὴν εὐωδίας with θυσίαν δεκτήν and εὐάρεστον τῷ θεῷ. One finds δεκτός often used in the context of offering and sacrifice in the LXX (e.g., Exod 28:38; Lev 1:3–4). For instance, in Exod 28:38, δεκτός is used in the context of the high priest's responsibility and instruction so that sacred offerings may be acceptable to the Lord. In Lev 1:3–4, δεκτός is used to describe that

---

[44] Sacrificial imagery is found in both Roman triumphal processions and the OT. However, the OT sacrificial image seems prominent here. On sacrifice in the triumphal procession, see Aus, *Imagery of Triumph and Rebellion*, 11–16.
[45] See more discussion in Chapter 6.
[46] Paul communicates the same idea elsewhere. The Greek adjective, εὐάρεστος, is the term Paul often employs in his letters (nine times in the NT; eight times in the Pauline letters; once in Hebrews). He generally employs the term in relation to the ethical conduct (Eph 5:10; Col 3:20; Titus 2:9), but Rom 12:1–2 and 14:18 are particularly of help to support my reading of εὐάρεστος in 2 Cor 5:9. In Rom 12:1–2, Paul exhorts the Romans to present their bodies as a sacrifice to God, and he modifies the noun, θυσία with three adjectives: living, holy, and acceptable: ζῶσαν ἁγίαν εὐάρεστον. Furthermore, in Rom 14:18, Paul employs εὐάρεστος in connection not only with sacrifice but also with his service. He associates his duty as a bond-servant of Christ with the phrase, εὐάρεστος τῷ θεῷ in that verse. Thus, in the context of Romans, Paul views his service as a bond-servant of Christ as a pleasing sacrifice to God.
[47] Exod 28:38; Lev 1:3, 4; 17:4; 19:5; 22:19, 20, 21, 29; 23:11; Deut 33:16, 23, 24; Job 33:26; Prov 10:24; 11:1; 12:22; 14:9, 35; 15:8, 28a; 16:7, 13; 22:11; Isa 49:8; 56:7; 58:5; 60:7; 61:2; Jer 6:20; Mal 2:13; Sir 2:5; 3:17; 35:6.

the purpose of a burnt offering is to be acceptable before the Lord. In 2 Cor 5:9, Paul employs εὐάρεστος instead of δεκτός. The facts (1) that Paul employs both terms as near synonyms in Phil 4:18, and (2) that δεκτός connotes sacrificial images in the LXX suggest that Paul views his proclamation in light of a pleasing sacrifice to God.

Moreover, Paul evokes another OT sacrificial image in the metaphor of the house. He portrays the earthly house in which he and his coworkers experience suffering (5:1–2, 4) as the locus of sacrifice and worship. In 4:13–5:10, he makes use of an analogy of the house,[48] and he relates explicitly the house with a tent (σκῆνος) in 5:1 and 5:4. By doing so, he seems to relate σκῆνος, a cognate of σκηνή in 5:1 and 5:4, to the image of sacrifice and offering in the OT.[49] In the LXX, σκηνή and its cognates often refer to the tent or tabernacle (e.g., Exod 40:34–35; Lev 1:1, 3, 5), in which the sacrificial system operated.[50] By calling the earthly place σκῆνος in 5:1 and 5:4, Paul relates the place in which God's servants groan (5:2) to the very place in which worship of God takes place.

In addition, Paul alludes to another sacrificial image in explaining the suffering of God's servants in ministry that produces glory. Paul's emphasis on glory denotes the sacrificial background of his argument in 4:13–5:10. In contrasting momentary light affliction and eternal weight of glory in 4:17, Paul especially emphasizes the degree of eternal glory by employing the phrase καθ' ὑπερβολὴν εἰς ὑπερβολὴν. The Greek noun ὑπερβολή very much reflects Pauline language,[51] and he uses the term twice in 4:17 to highlight the result of suffering: It produces an eternal weight of glory beyond all measure and proportion.[52] In the OT context, God's glory filled the tabernacle (Exod 40:34–35), and the sacrifice and offering would result in the presence of God's glory (Lev 9:6, 23). Paul pictures that their suffering as a pleasing sacrifice in the earthly house of the tent will result in the exceeding glory of God, just as Israel encountered it through their sacrifice and offering in the tabernacle. Therefore, in 4:13–5:10, Paul expounds the ways in which God's servants function as a fragrance of Christ to God (2:15) in their ministry.

Second, related to the first point, Paul continues to view his ministry of the proclamation as a sacrifice to God in 5:11–7:3. In 5:11–7:3, he begins the section with two general statements: We persuade people (ἀνθρώπους πείθομεν), and we have been manifested to God (θεῷ δὲ πεφανερώμεθα). On the one hand, God's agents continue to manifest his knowledge by speaking, particularly of their sincerity in appealing to the conscience of the Corinthians (5:11–19). On the other hand, Paul regards the proclamation of the gospel as a manifestation to God. In other words, the participation of God's servants in the gospel through their speech has two dimensions: One is directed to God (4:16–5:10; 5:11), and the other is directed to people (5:11–7:3).

Moreover, Paul continues to portray himself and the Corinthians as the locus of sacrifice in 6:14–7:1. He gives five exhortations in 5:20–7:3. In the fourth exhortation in 6:14–7:1, he describes himself and the Corinthians as the temple of the living God

---

[48] Notice the repetition of house-related language: οἰκία (5:1); οἰκοδομή (5:1); οἰκητήριον (5:2); σκῆνος (5:1, 4); ἐνδημέω (5:6, 8, 9); ἐκδημέω (5:6, 8, 9).
[49] Paul employs σκηνή and σκῆνος only in 2 Cor 5:1, 4; 12:9 in the Pauline letters.
[50] R. E. Averbeck, "Sacrifice and Offerings," *Dictionary of the Old Testament: Pentateuch*, 706–33.
[51] It occurs eight times in the NT and is found only in the Pauline letters.
[52] BDAG, s.v. "ὑπερβολή."

(6:16) and urges them to cleanse themselves from all defilement and to perfect holiness (7:1). In 5:1–4, Paul relates the earthly house to the tent in which the sacrifice and worship take place. In 6:14–7:1, he further explicates that he and the Corinthians are the temple of the living God.[53] His exhortations regarding cleansing and perfection of holiness (7:1) evoke the image of ritual purity in the OT. Moreover, Paul seems to use the language of holiness in the cultic context only in 2 Cor 7:1.[54] Just as Paul views his ministry to be a pleasing sacrifice to God, he likewise expects the Corinthians to be the temple of the living God in which sacrifice to God takes place. Therefore, he continues to develop an overtone of the sacrificial image of ministry in 6:14–7:1.

Third, Paul's desire to present the Corinthians before God reflects a sacrificial overtone. In 7:4–16, Paul justifies his previous letter by explaining its reason (7:9–10) and purpose (7:12; cf. 2:4). In 2:4, Paul declares that the purpose of the previous letter was to inform his love; in 7:12, he further articulates that the purpose of the letter was to manifest the Corinthians' eagerness before God. Just as Paul views himself and his ministry as a sacrificial fragrance to God (2:15; 4:16–5:10; 5:11–6:10; 6:14–7:1), he desires to manifest (φανερόω; cf. 2:14) the Corinthians' eagerness before God through his ministry by the previous letter.

Similarly, in 8:1–9:15, Paul views the collection as a sacrifice to the Lord. He describes the participation of the Macedonian churches in the collection as self-sacrifice to the Lord (8:5), which finds its ultimate example in Christ's self-sacrifice (8:9). In Paul's understanding, the ministry to the saints is not simply the financial contribution; rather it is a self-sacrifice to the Lord first and then to people. In addition, this self-sacrifice goes both to the Lord and to people, denoting the two dimensions of the ministry to the saints.[55] Moreover, Paul repeats that glory is the purpose of the ministry to the saints (8:19; 9:13). Paul has characterized the ministry with glory (3:7, 8, 9, 10, 11, 18; 4:4, 6, 15, 17) and particularly we have seen that Paul's sacrifice and suffering in this world alludes to the OT sacrificial background in 4:13–5:10. Just as the sacrifice and offering would result in the presence of God's glory (Lev 9:6, 23), Paul's suffering will result in the exceeding glory of God (4:17). Likewise, Paul describes that the ministry to the saints will result in glory (8:19; 9:13) because he views the collection as the ministry in which participants sacrifice themselves to God. Thus, Paul portrays the ministry to the saints as a pleasing sacrifice to God, which results in glory.[56]

---

[53] In the LXX, ναός refers to the holy place and the holy of holies in which God dwells, and ἱερόν refers to the entire temple. Paul maintains the distinction in his letters (ναός in 1 Cor 3:16–17; 6:19; 2 Cor 6:16; Eph 2:21; 2 Thess 2:4; ἱερόν in 1 Cor 9:13). See Philip W. Comfort, "Temple," *DPL*, 923–25.

[54] Stanley E. Porter, "Holiness, Sanctification," *DPL*, 397–402.

[55] One of the most significant and earliest manuscripts 𝔓46 reads θεω instead of κυριω in 8:5. External evidence strongly supports κυρίῳ, but the variant tells us that the scribe(s) of 𝔓46 may have recognized sacrificial language here in light of 2:15 and 5:11, in which Paul depicts himself and his service as a sacrifice or manifestation to God. Thus, they may have attempted to change from κυριω to θεω. Also notice the word order of the phrase, τῷ κυρίῳ καὶ ἡμῖν. Paul prioritizes τῷ κυρίῳ first and adds ἡμῖν with an additive καί.

[56] Jim Wilson argues for the OT sacrificial context of 2 Cor 8–9, in which he demonstrates lexical studies, such as ἰσότης, χάρις, διακονία, λειτουργία, εὐχαριστία, εὐλογία, and ἐπιτελέω, and explores ideological connections to the OT sacrifice ("The Old Testament Sacrificial Context of Second Corinthians 8–9," *BBR* 27 [2017]: 363–80).

Finally, Paul relates his weakness to the tent imagery of the OT in the pinnacle of his defense in 12:9–10. Having received the Lord's answer to his plea for removal of his thorn (12:9a), Paul accepted his weaknesses, knowing that Christ's power may dwell in him (12:9b). The Greek word ἐπισκηνόω (ἐπί+σκηνόω) is a hapax legomenon in the NT; nevertheless, we have already seen in the previous literary context that Paul portrays his body as a tent with a cognate word, σκῆνος (5:1, 4), which evokes the imagery of tent and tabernacle in the OT. Thus, Paul once again alludes to the tent imagery in the pinnacle of his defense in 12:9.[57] Therefore, Paul describes his fellow workers' and his sacrificial service to God as Χριστοῦ εὐωδία in 2:15 and continues to develop the theme in 3:1–13:10.

5.2.2.2 God's Agents As Ὀσμή

While Paul views ministry in light of a vertical relationship with God (i.e., a fragrance of Christ to God), he also expresses a horizontal dimension of ministry with another metaphor of sacral incense, ὀσμή. God disseminates his knowledge to people (2:14, 16), especially through the speech of his agents (2:17). They speak God's word in Christ as the persons of sincerity and the persons from God in the sight of God. We have seen that the content of God's knowledge pertains to the credentials of his servants (3:1–6a) as well as the gospel of Christ (3:12–4:12), and they disseminate his knowledge through their speech. Paul unpacks the metaphor in 3:1–13:10 by developing mainly two activities that involve speech. God's servants proclaim the gospel and speak regarding their credentials.

First, God's agents proclaim the gospel (4:1–6; 5:18–20; cf. 10:4–5; 12:19).[58] In 4:1–6, in responding particularly to the shameful situation or the charge against Paul and his coworkers, Paul defends their conduct and stresses their role as slaves for Christ, who proclaim God's knowledge. In 4:4–5 Paul contrasts two agents and their activities. On the one hand, the god of this age has blinded the minds of the unbelievers that they might not see the light of the gospel of the glory of Christ, who is the image of God (4:4).[59] On the other hand, Christ's bond-servants preach Christ Jesus as Lord (4:5). We

---

[57] A good number of scholars claim that ἐπισκηνόω connotes the divine glory based on the idea of Shekinah (see an overview of the idea in Thrall, *Second Epistle of the Corinthians*, 2:829, citing Martin McNamara, *Targum and Testament: Aramaic Paraphrases of the Hebrew Bible: A Light on the New Testament* [Shannon: Irish University Press, 1972], 98–101). In light of the heavy emphasis on glory in 2 Cor 3, it is possible that Paul connotes the presence of divine glory in 12:9 (cf. Exod 40:34–35).

[58] Although the image is implicit, Paul's language in the letter metaphor (3:1–6) may also reflect the role of God's servants as speakers. In 3:2, Paul describes that the Corinthians are a letter of Christ: ὅτι ἐστὲ ἐπιστολὴ Χριστοῦ. Paul substantiates the statement with an attributive participial clause, διακονηθεῖσα ὑφ' ἡμῶν. The literal translation is "ministered by us," but the verb communicates the sense that God's servants function as couriers in the letter metaphor (Josephus employs the term in the same sense in *Ant.* 6.298 [cited in BDAG, s.v. "διακονέω"]). Also see William Baird, "Letters of Recommendation: A Study of II Cor 3:1–3," *JBL* 80 [1961]: 166–72 at 169–70. If so, Paul may have viewed himself and his coworkers as not only couriers of the letter but also speakers, since ancient letter couriers frequently read the letter out for the recipients (E. Randolph Richards, *Paul and First-Century Letter Writing: Secretaries, Composition, and Collection* [Downers Grove, IL: InterVarsity Press, 2004], 184–85).

[59] See the potential identification of the god of the age in Long, "'God of This Age,'" 219–69.

Table 5.1 The Parallel between 2:17 and 4:2, 5

2:17	4:2, 5
God's agents are a fragrance of Christ to *everyone*: to both those who are being saved and *those who are perishing*: Χριστοῦ εὐωδία ἐσμὲν τῷ θεῷ ἐν τοῖς σῳζομένοις καὶ ἐν τοῖς ἀπολλυμένοις (2:15)	While the gospel is veiled to *those who are perishing*: ἐν τοῖς ἀπολλυμένοις (4:3), God's agents commend themselves to *everyone's conscience*: τῇ φανερώσει τῆς ἀληθείας συνιστάνοντες ἑαυτοὺς πρὸς πᾶσαν συνείδησιν (4:2)
God's agents do not *peddle the word of God*: καπηλεύοντες τὸν λόγον τοῦ θεοῦ (2:17)	God's agents do not *corrupt the word of God*: δολοῦντες τὸν λόγον τοῦ θεοῦ (4:2)[60]
God's agents speak as *the person of sincerity and the person from God in the sight of God*: ἀλλ᾽ ὡς ἐξ εἰλικρινείας, ἀλλ᾽ ὡς ἐκ θεοῦ κατέναντι θεοῦ (2:17)	God's agents *commend themselves before God* [ἐνώπιον τοῦ θεοῦ] (4:2)
God's agents *speak in Christ*: ἐν Χριστῷ λαλοῦμεν (2:17)	God's agents *proclaim Christ Jesus as Lord*: κηρύσσομεν ἀλλ᾽ Ἰησοῦν Χριστὸν κύριον (4:5)

have already seen that the flow of Paul's argument in 3:12–4:12 equates God's knowledge with the gospel of Christ. Thus, as God's ὀσμή (2:14, 16, 17), God's agents disseminate his knowledge by proclaiming Christ Jesus as the Lord, the gospel (4:5). The lexical and thematic similarities of Paul's language between 2:17 and 4:2–5 are striking (see Table 5.1; comparable elements are italicized).

In addition, Paul further expounds that speaking God's word involves the ministry of reconciliation in 5:18–20. Paul declares that God gave his servants the ministry of reconciliation (5:18) and entrusted the word of reconciliation to them (5:19). Thus, God's servants persuade people (5:11), as ambassadors for Christ (5:20), by proclaiming the word of reconciliation (5:19–20). Once again, the conceptual and lexical parallels between 2:14–17 and 5:18–20 are strong (see Table 5.2; comparable elements are italicized).

Moreover, the parallels may also indicate an overtone of contrast between God's agents and counteragents. In 2:17, Paul describes the counteragents as those who peddle (καπηλεύω) God's word. In 5:18–20, he explains that God's agents are ministers

---

[60] While some scholars argue that the Greek word καπηλεύω should be construed in the sense of "adulterating," "watering down," or "falsifying" in light of the word δολόω in 2 Cor 4:2 and the LXX Isa 1:22 (e.g., Plummer, *Second Epistle*, 73), Hafemann rejects the claim by showing the lack of attestation of the semantic relationship between καπηλεύω and δολόω: They are not semantically related in the polemic against the Sophists and Hellenistic Judaism (*Suffering and Spirit*, 106–26). Thus, he concludes, "It is simply to suggest that these two statements, though parallel in function, nevertheless represent two *distinct* assertions, i.e., Paul wishes to deny that he is selling (καπηλεύοντες) *and* watering down (δολοῦντες) God's word" (ibid., 125). Hafemann may be right about his conclusion in light of the semantic connection; however, the literary structure challenges his view. In addition to the strong parallel between 2:17 and 4:2 (see Table 5:1), if 2:14–17 is the thesis statement of the letter in which Paul introduces the major theme of the letter, one expects that Paul will expound and unpack the meaning of 2:14–17 in the material that follows in 3:1–13:10. Therefore, although καπηλεύω and δολόω may not be semantically related outside the NT and the LXX, the literary structure (i.e., the MSR of particularization with contrast) indicates that Paul relates these terms in his discourse. Perhaps, this is why John Chrysostom later understood καπηλεύω and δολόω as near-synonyms in his homily, stating as follows: Ταῦτα δὲ καὶ ἔμπροσθεν περὶ ἑαυτοῦ ἔλεγεν, ὅτι οὐ κατὰ πρόσωπον ἔξη, οὐδὲ δολῶν καὶ καπηλεύων τὸν λόγον ἐκήρυττεν (*Hom. 2 Cor*, 23 at 11:6).

Table 5.2 The Parallel between 2:14–17 and 5:18–20

2:14–17	5:18–20
God always leads us into triumph in Christ: Τῷ δὲ θεῷ χάρις τῷ πάντοτε θριαμβεύοντι ἡμᾶς ἐν τῷ Χριστῷ (2:14)	*God reconciles us* to himself *through Christ*: τὰ δὲ πάντα ἐκ τοῦ θεοῦ τοῦ καταλλάξαντος ἡμᾶς ἑαυτῷ διὰ Χριστοῦ (5:18)
God's agents *speak the word of God*: τὸν λόγον τοῦ θεοῦ (2:17)[61]	God's agents *persuade men* (5:11) because God entrusted *the word of reconciliation* to God's servants: τὸν λόγον τῆς καταλλαγῆς (5:19)
God manifests his knowledge *through God's agents: δι᾽ ἡμῶν* (2:14)	God encourages *through God's agents: δι᾽ ἡμῶν* (5:20)

of reconciliation (καταλλάσσω). Both καπηλεύω and καταλλάσσω are employed in the context of business or merchandise outside the NT. However, while καπηλεύω frequently conveys a pejorative sense, καταλλάσσω often signifies reestablishment of good relations.[62] Thus, Paul may have intended to contrast between God's agents and counteragents in 5:18–20, implying that false apostles peddle God's word for their profit (2:17), whereas God's servants proclaim God's reconciliation to restore the relationship between God and people (5:20).

Furthermore, God's servants proclaim the gospel by destroying arrogance raised up against God's knowledge (10:4–6). In 2:17 Paul describes that God's agents speak God's word in Christ in the sight of God, so Paul declares God's word as the gospel in 3:1–7:16 and exhorts the Corinthians to respond to the gospel in 8:1–9:15.[63] In 10:1–13:10, Paul defends his status as a servant of Christ. I have shown parallels between 2:14–17 and 4:2, 5, and 5:18–20, and one finds another remarkable parallel between 2:14–17 and 12:19. In 12:19, responding to the perception of the Corinthians that Paul has been defending himself, Paul clarifies that he is speaking in Christ in the sight of God. The expression between 2:17 and 12:19 is verbatim (see Table 5.3).

The parallel suggests that the dissemination of God's knowledge involves both the proclamation of the gospel (3:1–7:16) and the defense of the status as a servant of Christ (10:1–13:10), for the literary context in 10:1–12:13 indicates that this arrogance against God's knowledge essentially pertains to the criticism against Paul that he is not a servant of Christ (10:7; 11:23). Thus, Paul attempts to eliminate the arrogance against God's knowledge by defending his credentials.[64] Both the proclamation and defense aim to manifest God's knowledge, the gospel of Christ.

---

[61] In 2:17, there is an ellipsis; Paul omits τὸν λόγον τοῦ θεοῦ in the latter sentence, but his readers were expected to supply the word in their cognition.
[62] Hans Windisch, "καπηλεύω," *TDNT* 3:603–5; Ceslas Spicq, "καπηλεύω," *TLNT* 2:81–87; Friedrich Büchsel, "καταλλάσσω," *TDNT*, 1:254–58; Ceslas Spicq, "καταλλαγή, καταλλάσσω," *TLNT*, 2:262–66.
[63] See more discussions in Chapters 6–7.
[64] Also, the military metaphor in 10:4–6 describes a convergence of God and his servants in ministry. God's agents are the soldiers for warfare; however, God is the source and purpose of the battle. Paul clearly communicates these two senses in 10:4–5. In 10:4, he describes God as the provider of their weapon (δυνατὰ τῷ θεῷ as a dative of possession or means), with which God's servants destroy the enemy's fortresses. However, the weapon is also used for God's service (δυνατὰ τῷ θεῷ as a dative of advantage).

Table 5.3 The Parallel between 2:17 and 12:19

2:17	12:19
κατέναντι θεοῦ ἐν Χριστῷ λαλοῦμεν	κατέναντι θεοῦ ἐν Χριστῷ λαλοῦμεν

In addition, Paul develops the theme of death and life as the outcome of the manifestation of God's knowledge, particularly in the ministry of proclamation in 3:1–7:16. In 2:16, Paul describes that the manifestation of God's knowledge presents death and life (2:16; cf. 1 Cor 1:18). We have already seen the antithesis of death and life regarding the divine paradox: The death of Christ's bond-servants is the means to produce life (4:10–12). Paul continues to develop the theme of death and life, particularly regarding the outcome of the proclamation of the gospel in 3:1–11, 4:13–5:10, 5:11–7:3, and 7:4–16.

In 3:1–11, Paul describes the qualifications of God's agents (3:1–6a) and superiority of the ministry of the new covenant (3:6b–11), in which he shows the outcome of each ministry: the letter (i.e., old covenant) kills but the Spirit gives life (3:6; cf. 1:18). Thus, Paul contrasts the outcome of the ministry of the life-giving Spirit (3:3, 6; cf. 1 Cor 15:45) with that of the ministry of death (3:6, 7) and condemnation (3:9).[65] In 4:13–5:10, developing his arguments regarding temporal affliction and eternal life, Paul expresses that suffering is an indivisible essence of ministry. However, he declares that the purpose of the groaning and suffering is to attain the life that conquers death: ἵνα καταποθῇ τὸ θνητὸν ὑπὸ τῆς ζωῆς (5:4). Paul seems to allude to Isa 25:8 and 1 Cor 15:54 (cf. Rev. 7:17; 21:4) and contrasts death with the victory through the Lord Jesus Christ. Thus, the ministry results in death and life. In 5:11–7:3, Paul emphasizes the antithesis in 5:14–17, 6:9 and 7:3. In 5:14–17, Paul underscores that the basis of his persuasion is grounded in Christ's death and resurrection so that God's servants participate in his death and life. In other words, the gospel of Christ (4:4–6) is manifested in his death and resurrection (5:14); thus, one's participation in his death and life is required as the outcome of the gospel (5:15–17). Indeed, in 6:9, he emphasizes the antithesis of death and life in the hardship catalog in 6:3–10. Grammatically speaking, all the descriptions of hardships revolve around the only indicative verb in the list, ζάω in 6:9, stating, ὡς ἀποθνῄσκοντες καὶ ἰδοὺ ζῶμεν. In other words, from the syntactical point of view, the catalog of suffering centers on the antithesis of death and life in 6:9: God's agents face suffering for the proclamation of the gospel to the point of death, but they continue to live. Interpreters usually do not pay attention to this fact; however, it makes sense why Paul highlights the antithesis of death and life in 6:3–10 when one considers the passage in light of the thesis statement in 2:16. Likewise, in 7:3, Paul highlights death and life as an outcome of his exhortations. Paul persuades the

---

[65] Paul contrasts the old covenant and the new covenant in four ways in 3:7–11: the ministry of death and the Spirit (3:7–8); the ministry of condemnation and righteousness (3:8); glory and surpassing glory (3:10); what fades away and what remains (3:11). He also contrasts Moses and Christ by giving an exposition on Exod 34 in 3:12–18.

Corinthians to be reconciled to God (5:20–6:10) and his servants (6:11–7:3), and he concludes that the outcome of the proclamation of the gospel (i.e., the ministry of reconciliation) is to share death and life together (7:3). In 7:4–16, Paul describes the reason for his previous letter (7:8–10). He does not regret that he has sent the letter to the Corinthian church (7:8), but rejoices that his previous letter led them to repentance (7:9) because his ministry through the letter to Corinthians made them sorrowful, however such godly sorrow produces a repentance to salvation, whereas the sorrow of the world produces death (7:10). Paul contrasts the outcome of the sorrow according to God and that of the world: salvation and death. In 2:15–16, life and death are related to salvation and destruction. Likewise, in 7:10, Paul declares that the sorrow and repentance caused by the letter produce life, whereas the sorrow of the world results in death.

Second, Paul articulates the credentials of God's agents. In 2:16b, Paul asks a rhetorical question: πρὸς ταῦτα τίς ἱκανός. However, as some scholars rightly raise their concern, Paul's statement in 2:17 does not seem to directly answer the question,[66] though the conjunction γάρ between 2:16b and 2:17 indicates the close relationship of the sentences. In other words, if Paul answers the question in 2:17, how is the description of God's agents speaking God's word (2:17) related to the question regarding the credentials for the ministry (2:16b)? When one understands 2:14–17 as the thesis statement of the letter, a clearer picture emerges. Speaking God's word as persons of sincerity and persons from God (2:17; cf. 1:12) is the answer to the question in 2:16b because their speech involves not only the manifestation of the gospel but also knowledge pertaining to their credentials. He particularly underscores their demeanor in ministry (ὡς ἐξ εἰλικρινείας) and source of their credentials (ὡς ἐκ θεοῦ) in 2:17,[67] and continues to unpack them in each major division that follows (3:1–7:16; 8:1–9:15; 10:1–13:10).

In 3:1–7:16, responding to the charge against self-commendation (3:1; 5:12), Paul speaks of the credentials of God's agents by explicating their source (3:1–6a; 5:11–19) and demeanor (4:2–9; 6:3–10). On the one hand, Paul underscores the source of their credentials (3:1–6a) and cause of their ministry (5:11–20a); namely, God's servants are people from God (ὡς ἐκ θεοῦ in 2:17). In 3:1–6a, Paul responds to the charge against the lack of commendatory letter (3:1) by underscoring God as the source of their credentials.[68] God is the author of their commendatory letter (3:2); thus, their adequacy directly comes from God (3:5–6). In 5:11–19, Paul once again makes a rejoinder to the accusation of self-commendation (5:12) and explains Christ's love and God as the cause of the ministry. Christ's love is the compulsion of their ministry (5:14), and God gave them the ministry of reconciliation (5:18, 19). Thus, Paul proclaims that all things come from God (5:18) and that God's servants are ambassadors for Christ (5:19), emphasizing God and Christ as the cause of the ministry.

---

[66] E.g., Hafemann, *Suffering and the Spirit*, 90.
[67] The Greek word, εἰλικρίνεια, refers to the quality of character. Thus, it is often translated as sincerity and purity of motive (BDAG, s.v. "εἰλικρίνεια"; Friedrich Büchsel, "εἰλικρινής, εἰλικρίνεια," *TDNT*, 2:397–398; Ceslas Spicq, "εἰλικρίνεια, εἰλικρινής," *TLNT*, 1:420–423). The Greek phrase, ἐκ θεοῦ in 2:17, indicates God as the source.
[68] The practice of commendatory letters was well known in the ancient world (e.g., Act 9:2; 22:5; Rom 16:1–2; Phil 2:29–30), and Paul himself occasionally writes such letters (Rom 16:1–2; Phil 2:29–30).

On the other hand, Paul emphasizes the demeanor of God's agents in ministry: they are people of sincerity (ὡς ἐξ εἰλικρινείας in 2:17). They do not commend themselves (3:1; 5:12). However, when they do (4:2; 6:4), they commend themselves as slaves (4:5) and servants (6:4) in order to show their integrity in ministry. In 4:2, Paul proclaims that God's agents renounce shameful hidden deeds by the manifestation of truth, commending themselves to every man's conscience in the sight of God. The literary context indicates that the manifestation of truth pertains to the gospel of Christ (4:4) and that they serve as bond-servants to proclaim Christ Jesus as Lord (4:5). In order to bolster his claim, Paul proceeds to explain the manner in which God's agents manifest the truth with the famous metaphor of "treasure in jars of clay" in 4:7-12, which includes the first hardship catalog in 4:8-9. In 6:3-4a Paul provides an introduction to the hardship catalog in 6:4b-10, in which he explains that the catalog functions to protect the ministry from those discrediting it (6:3) and to prove the manner in which God's agents are his servants (6:4a). Paul does not coincidentally and randomly include self-commendations in 4:2 and 6:4. Rather, he strategically asserts the claim in the context where two hardship catalogs are found (4:8-9 and 6:3-10) to insist and demonstrate their integrity in ministry. In fact, Fitzgerald rightly emphasizes that Paul's extensive use of *peristaseis* catalogs in 2 Corinthians is "grounded in the fact that he is concerned with showing the Corinthians that he is a person of integrity in whom they may have both confidence and pride. Since *peristaseis* catalogs were a traditional means of demonstrating virtue, it was natural that he should choose to employ them for this purpose."[69] Thus, Paul develops the notion of sincerity in the division of 3:1-7:16.

In 8:1-9:15, Paul continues to speak the credentials of God's agents: They are not peddlers of God's word (2:17).[70] By doing so, he demonstrates the credentials of the collection workers (i.e., Titus and two brothers) and bolsters his fellow workers' and his own credentials, especially regarding their sincerity of ministry (cf. 2:17). On the one hand, just as Paul unpacks the source and demeanor of God's agents in 3:1-7:16, he continues to describe those of Titus and two emissaries in 8:16-24. Concerning the source, Paul portrays God as the source of their credentials. God puts earnestness in Titus's heart (8:16), and the churches of God appointed these brothers as their apostles (8:19, 22; cf. 1:1) who are a glory of Christ (8:23). Regarding their demeanor, Paul underscores their integrity: Titus has earnestness in his heart (8:16, 17); the first brother is praised in his work in the gospel (8:18); the second brother has genuine earnestness tested by Paul and his fellow workers (8:22). On the other hand, Paul strengthens his fellow workers' and his own sincerity by sending those emissaries. In 8:20, Paul clarifies that the purpose of sending these workers is to prove their integrity in the ministry.

In 10:1-13:10, Paul continues to articulate the credentials of God's agents, particularly in the form of defense through a foolish boasting. In 3:1-9:15, Paul's discussions of credentials are not the main concern; rather, it strengthens the primary purpose of his arguments (i.e., the proclamation of the gospel in 3:1-7:16 and encouragement to participate in the collection in 8:1-9:15; see Chapters 6-7). However,

---

[69] Fitzgerald, *Cracks in an Earthen Vessel*, 206.
[70] See the discussion of καπηλεύω in 5.2.4.

in 10:1–13:10, Paul brings the arguments regarding the defense of his status being a servant of Christ to the fore as the primary subject to be dealt with. Thus, he develops his defense, especially engaging in a boasting competition (11:1–12:13), in equating his defense with speaking in Christ (12:19). Rhetorical criticism has well demonstrated the relationship between the act of speech and boasting.[71] Paul boasts in his sufferings (11:21b–29), in visions and revelations (12:1–5a), and weakness (11:30–33; 12:5b–10). Moreover, he continues to unpack the source of credentials (cf. ὡς ἐκ θεοῦ in 2:17) and demeanor in ministry (cf. ἐξ εἰλικρινείας in 2:17).

Regarding the source of the credentials, Paul consistently attributes them to the divine origin. In 10:1–11 Paul makes a rejoinder to the criticism against Paul's conduct (10:1–2, 10) and status as a servant of Christ (10:7) by underscoring the Lord as the source of his authority (10:8; cf. 13:10). In 10:12–18, Paul responds to his rivals' violation of the ministerial jurisdiction by emphasizing that God assigned the sphere of the ministry (10:13). Thus, God's agents do not commend themselves as the opponents do (10:12); the Lord commends them (10:17). When Paul is forced to engage in an empty boasting competition in 11:1–12:13, especially within the speech proper in 11:21b–12:10, he continues to attribute his credentials to divine origin. In 11:23, Paul insists that Christ is the source of his status: While false apostles, who disguise themselves as apostles of Christ (11:13), belong to Satan (11:16), Paul belongs to Christ as his servant (11:23a) who suffers more than anyone (11:23b–29).[72] When he boasts in visions and revelations (12:1–5a), he clarifies that they come from the Lord (12:4).[73] When Paul stresses and characterizes his qualifications with weakness (11:29–33; 12:5b–10), he insists that the Lord himself has given him the thorn in the flesh (12:7), the primary representation of his weakness (12:9–10).[74] Finally, in 12:14–13:10, Paul prepares the Corinthians for his visit and concludes his writing in 13:10 by revisiting the divine origin of the authority (cf. 10:8). Therefore, throughout 10:1–13:10, Paul consistently describes the divine source of the credentials.

In addition, Paul continues to speak of his integrity in 10:1–13:10. In 10:1–11, responding to the charge against his demeanor (10:1), Paul insists on his consistency of conduct toward the Corinthians (10:2). In 10:12–18, responding to the adversaries' violation of the ministerial jurisdiction, Paul underscores his coworkers' and his sincerity in ministry: They neither commend themselves (10:12–13, 17–18) nor take credit for others' labors (10:13–16). In 11:1–21b, making a rejoinder to the criticism against Paul's inferiority to the super-apostles (10:5), he insists that he has manifested the superiority of his knowledge (11:6; cf. 12:1–5) and demonstrated his financial independence (11:7–15), which he once again highlights (12:14–21) in the consequent ecclesial preparation for his future visit (12:14–13:10).

---

[71] E.g., Paul's speaking of credentials (λέγω in 11:21; λαλέω in 11:23) is closely related to his boasting (11:1–12:13). See also Witherington, *Conflict and Community in Corinth*, 432–41.

[72] The genitive case of Χριστός, in the phrases ἀποστόλους Χριστοῦ (11:13) and διάκονοι Χριστοῦ (11:23), are both understood to be a genitive of source or possession, indicating the divine origin of Paul's status as a servant of Christ.

[73] The genitive of κύριος, in the phrase ὀπτασίας καὶ ἀποκαλύψεις κυρίου in 12:1, functions as a genitive of source.

[74] The divine passive in 12:7, ἐδόθη μοι σκόλοψ τῇ σαρκί, indicates the divine origin of Paul's thorn in the flesh, his weakness.

Therefore, Paul expounds the thesis statement regarding the horizontal aspect of the ministry of God's agents (2:14, 16) in 3:1–13:10. As God's ὀσμή, his servants proclaim the gospel (4:1–6; 5:18–20; 10:4–5; 12:19) and speak their credentials (12:19), particularly regarding their source (3:1–6a; 5:11–20a; 8:16, 19, 22, 23; 10:8, 13, 17; 11:23, 12:4, 7, 9; 13:10) and integrity (4:2–9; 6:3–10; 8:16, 17, 18, 20, 22; 10:2, 12–13, 13–16, 17–18; 11:6, 7–15; 12:14–21). However, Paul qualifies these activities by placing them under God's dominion by saying κατέναντι θεοῦ (2:17; 12:9),[75] suggesting two facts. On the one hand, Paul and his fellow workers not only manifest God's knowledge, but also trust in his knowledge regarding their integrity: God is a witness to their ministry (11:11, 31; cf. 3:4). On the other hand, they are held accountable for their activities before God (4:2; 5:10; 7:12; 8:21).

5.2.2.3 Summary

In this section, I have argued that Paul portrays his fellow workers and himself as human agents of God's ministry in 2:14–17, and continues to unpack their roles in ministry in each major division in 3:1–13:10 (3:1–7:16; 8:1–9:15; 10:1–13:10). As Χριστοῦ εὐωδία (2:15), Paul describes the proclamation of the gospel (3:1–7:16), the collection (8:1–9:15), and the defense of the gospel (10:1–13:10) in light of a sacrifice to God. As God's ὀσμή (2:14, 16), Paul underscores that God's agents engage in the speeches regarding the proclamation of the gospel that present life and death (3:1–7:16) and their credentials (3:1–7:16; 8:1–9:15; 10:1–13:10).

Having described the ways in which Paul portrays God as ultimate agent and his servants as human agents of the ministry in 3:1–13:10, I now turn to another agent, Christ, as the intermediate agent of the ministry.

5.2.3 Christ as Intermediate Agent

Another essential protagonist of the ministry is Christ as the intermediate agent.[76] God leads his agents in triumph and disseminates his knowledge through them (2:14). God's agents proclaim God's word as a sacrificial incense to God and disseminate his knowledge to people (2:15–17). However, the ministry is only possible through Christ's intermediary roles. Thrall rightly emphasizes, "God's display of his power in the apostolic proclamation comes about through the agency of Christ."[77] However, I do not define "intermediate agency" in a narrow sense as grammarians do. For instance,

---

[75] BDAG, s.v. "κατέναντι."
[76] See recurrence of Christ, Lord, and Jesus in 4.2.2.3.
[77] Thrall, *Second Epistle of the Corinthians*, 1:196. Lim also notes an emphasis on an articular expression of ἐν τῷ Χριστῷ in 2:14 (cf. ἐν Χριστῷ in 2:17), arguing "the triumphal procession is none other than *the* triumphal procession carried out through the agency of the Messiah" ("Suffering of Christ," 78). Lim's observation also fits into Levinsohn's explanations regarding articular and anarthrous substantives. Levinsohn explains that reactivation of the global VIP (i.e., Very Important Participant throughout the letter) is indicated by articular reference (*Discourse Features*, 152). In the case of 2 Cor 2:14, Christ may be expressed with a definite article for reactivation because Paul just begins a new literary unit.

Wallace explains that the idea of intermediate agency is expressed with phrases such as ὑπό + genitives (through)[78] and διά + genitives (through).[79] Rather, I understand Christ's intermediary roles more broadly in terms of his essential involvement in the ministry, particularly in relation to God and his servants (see Figure 5.1).

As Figure 5.1 shows, Christ bridges between the ultimate agent and human agents. Sometimes, Paul describes their distinct roles in ministry, as we see in the imagery of God's triumphal procession in 2:14: God triumphs through Christ and manifests his knowledge through his agents.[80] At some points, the revelation of God and Christ overlap, as we see in the union between God's knowledge and Christ (2:14–16).[81] At some places, the roles of Christ and God's agents are intertwined, as we see the fusion between Christ and God's agents in the imagery of sacral incenses (2:15–16). Paul has laid out these intermediary roles in the thesis statement of the letter by repeating Χριστός with different expressions: ἐν τῷ Χριστῷ (2:14), Χριστοῦ (2:15), and ἐν Χριστῷ (2:17). Grammatically speaking, one could define the specific use of ἐν τῷ Χριστῷ (2:14), Χριστός (2:15), and ἐν Χριστῷ (2:17).[82] However, as Harris points out, the expression "ἐν Χριστῷ is almost a christological 'blank check' to be filled in with an amount appropriate in each context,"[83] even more so in the thesis statement of the letter, for it is intended to be expanded in the material that follows. Therefore, Paul continues to develop Christ's intermediary roles in relation to God's and his agents' activities in 3:1–13:10. I will particularly argue Christ's function based on the previous discussion (see 5.2.1 and 5.2.2).

Regarding the nature of the ministry (see 5.2.1.1), Paul describes it as paradoxical. However, Christ's intermediary role makes such a paradox possible: The agency of Christ enables to accomplish God's mission through the least qualified means (2:14). In the metaphor of treasure in clay jars (4:7), the union between the gospel of Christ (i.e., treasure) and God's agents (i.e., clay jars) enables the divine paradox. In 4:10–12, Jesus enables the paradox of death and life in the ministry, for God's agents carry Jesus's

---

[78] Wallace, *Greek Grammar*, 389.
[79] Ibid., 433–34.
[80] The opening blessing in 1:3–7 is another example that portrays the distinctive roles of God, Christ, and human agents in the theme of encouragement and affliction.
[81] For instance, Paul equates God's knowledge (2:14) with Χριστοῦ εὐωδία (2:15) and [Χριστοῦ] ὀσμή (ellipsis; 2:16); also, the literary context makes it clear that God's knowledge is Christ (4:4, 6; 10:5).
[82] The prepositional phrase ἐν τῷ Χριστῷ in 2:14 can be interpreted as an association (God triumphs in union with Christ), cause (God triumphs because of Christ), or means (God triumphs through Christ). Although the last option seems more likely, the other two alternatives do not diminish the significance of Christ's involvement in God's activity. Likewise, genitival expressions of Χριστοῦ εὐωδία (2:15) and [Χριστοῦ] ὀσμή (ellipsis; 2:16) can be subjective genitive (Christ offered a fragrance and an aroma), possessive genitive (a fragrance and an aroma that belong to Christ), genitive of source (a fragrance and an aroma from Christ), or genitive of means (God's agents are a fragrance and aroma by Christ). However, the theological implications of these construals point in the same direction: Christ's involvement in the ministry. In 2:14 ὀσμή refers to God's knowledge, but in 2:15–16 εὐωδία and ὀσμή refer to God's agents. How can God's knowledge, the gospel (2:14), become God's agents themselves (2:15–16)? It is precisely because of Christ's intermediate function in the ministry. Also, the prepositional phrase ἐν Χριστῷ in 2:17 can be construed as a cause (we speak because of Christ), standard (we speak according to the standard of Christ), or an association (we speak in union with Christ). All of the options are possible in light of the immediate literary context. However, they again indicate Christ's involvement in the proclamation of God's word.
[83] Harris, *Second Epistle to the Corinthians*, 255–56.

death for Jesus in order for Jesus's life to be manifested in them (4:11) and in the Corinthians (4:12). Likewise, the assurance of future resurrection in conformity to Jesus' resurrection (4:14) enables Paul and his fellow workers to endure hardships so that God can manifest extraordinary glory through their suffering (4:17). In 8:9, Jesus Christ became the ultimate example of the divine paradox of poverty and wealth, which serves as a basis for the exhortation for the collection (8:7–15) as well as an explanation for the testimony of the Macedonians, who overcame poverty with generosity and affliction with joy (8:1–2). In 12:7–10, Christ's grace and power enable Paul not only to boast about his weaknesses (12:9) but also to delight in life with weaknesses and hardships, for Christ already exemplified the paradox of power and weakness (13:4). Therefore, the agency of Christ plays the indispensable role in the divine paradox.

Similarly, God manifests his knowledge (see 5.2.1.2) through the agency of Christ. In 3:1–6a, God manifests his knowledge regarding the credentials of his servants. Paul emphasizes that God authored the Corinthians as the letter of Christ (3:3). The union between Christ and the Corinthians (3:3; cf. 2:15–16) enables the existence of the Corinthians to become the commendation letter (3:2–3). In 3:12–4:12, God manifests his knowledge as the gospel of Christ (4:4, 6) through the agency of Christ (3:14, 16), for the veil of God's knowledge in the old covenant is removed by the life and work of Christ (3:14, 16).

Regarding the sacrificial image of the ministry (see 5.2.2.1), Christ continues to play essential roles for their service to God. When Paul alludes to the OT sacrificial image in 4:13–5:10 to portray his coworkers' and his sacrificial service to God, an eschatological vision of Christ serves as a foundation for their ministry (5:6, 8, 10). Just as they speak God's word in Christ (2:17), Christ's eschatological presence (5:6, 8) and his eschatological judgment (5:10) serve as the reason for their sacrificial service to God (5:9). Likewise, this eschatological vision, expressed as the fear of the Lord (5:11a), becomes a basis for a sacrificial service of the proclamation to God (5:11b).[84] Moreover, when Paul views the collection as a sacrifice to the Lord (8:5), Christ's sacrificial model serves as the reason for their service (8:9), and such ministry aims for the glory of Christ (8:19) through obedience to the gospel of Christ (9:13). Thus, Christ is the reason, goal, and means of the ministry to the saints. Finally, when Paul alludes to the tabernacle in the OT in the pinnacle of his defense in 12:9, the fusion between Christ's grace and power and Paul's weakness defines his sacrificial service to God.

Regarding the proclamation of God's word (see 5.2.2.2), Christ is an indivisible element of Paul and his fellow workers' speech. Just as Paul describes God's knowledge as a fragrance and an aroma of Christ (2:14–16), he clarifies that Christ is the embodiment of God's knowledge and the content of the proclamation (4:4–6). Moreover, God's knowledge, the gospel of Christ (4:4), comes only through Christ's

---

[84] One may find the scarcity of the notion of Christ's agency in 6:14–7:3 (except 6:15) and 7:4–16. However, the nature of these passages explains the paucity of the idea. 6:14–7:3 is a series of consequent exhortations that flow from 3:1–6:13, and 7:4–16 is a continuation of the narrative from 2:12–13, which frames Paul's arguments in 3:1–7:3. Thus, these passages are not parts of Paul's main discourse regarding the ministry, particularly pertaining to the proclamation of the gospel.

death and resurrection (5:14–17). Thus, Paul emphasizes that one must be ἐν Χριστῷ (5:17); namely, to participate in his death and resurrection to acquire true knowledge of God. Furthermore, in the ministry of reconciliation (5:18–19), God uses his servants (δι' ἡμῶν in 5:20). However, the ministry also involves Christ, for he is the intermediate agent for God's reconciling work (διὰ Χριστοῦ in 5:18; ἐν Χριστῷ in 5:19). Thus, God's agents are ambassadors for Christ who urge the Corinthians to be reconciled to God (5:20). In 10:5, Paul underscores that God manifests his knowledge through his servants, who destroy all arrogance against God's knowledge and take every thought captive to the obedience to Christ (10:5), and he indeed attacks his opponents through his speech in chs 11–12. However, the obedience to Christ (10:5) qualifies his boasting. Paul's boasting must result in the Corinthians' obedience to Christ; thus, he is constrained not to go beyond that purpose. Just as Paul characterizes his speech with Christ (ἐν Χριστῷ) in 2:17, he continues to define his defense in light of Christ. Therefore, Paul consistently describes Christ's essential involvement in the proclamation of the gospel.

Likewise, Christ continues to play critical roles when God's servants speak of their credentials. Regarding the source of their credentials, when Paul responds to the charge against self-commendation (3:1; 5:12), Paul emphasizes that their adequacy as servants of the new covenant come directly from God (3:5–6) because God authored the letter of commendation for them, in which the fusion between Christ and the Corinthians takes place (3:3). Likewise, Paul underscores that God gave Paul and his coworkers the ministry of reconciliation (5:18–19) because the love of Christ urged them (5:14) and God has already reconciled them to himself through Christ (5:18). Paul describes the credentials of the collection workers as Christ's glory (8:23). When he responds to the charge against his status (10:7a; 11:23a), Paul highlights that Christ is the source of his authority (10:8; 13:10) and that the union with Christ (i.e., belonging to Christ; cf. 2:15–16) is the fundamental qualification for God's servant (10:7b; 11:23a; 12:2). When making a rejoinder regarding ministerial jurisdiction (10:12–18), God's assignment of the area is defined by the gospel of Christ (10:14). When he boasts in visions and revelations (12:1–5a), Paul describes Christ as the source (12:1) and introduces himself in the union with Christ (12:2; cf. 2:15–16).[85] When Paul identifies weakness as his identity as a servant of Christ (11:30–33; 12:5b–10), Christ is the source of his weakness: The Lord gave Paul the thorn in the flesh (12:7), and Christ's example of power and weakness (13:4) becomes that of Paul's experience of power and weakness (12:9).

Regarding the demeanor and integrity of God's servants, when Paul responds to the charge against self-commendation, he insists that he and his fellow workers do not commend themselves (3:1; 5:12); rather, they are servants of God (6:5). At the same time, they are also servants of Christ (11:23) because they are servants of the new covenant (3:6) in which God's knowledge is revealed through Jesus Christ (3:14, 16); thus, they proclaim him as Lord and themselves as slaves for Jesus (4:5).[86] When Paul

---

[85] The phrase ἐν Χριστῷ in 12:2 is construed as an association, particularly denoting a close relationship (see Wallace, *Greek Grammar*, 372).

[86] Regarding the prepositional phrase, διὰ Ἰησοῦν in 4:5, some early manuscripts, including two most significant witnesses 𝔓⁴⁶ and ℵ*, have Ιησου (genitive; through Christ) instead of Ἰησοῦν (accusative; for Christ). Perhaps, scribes of those manuscripts may have wanted to clarify Christ's intermediate role in the new covenant in the light of the literary context, particularly 3:14–18.

addresses his fellow workers' and his integrity in the ministry to the saints in chs 8–9, he sends qualified emissaries (i.e., Titus and two brothers in 8:16–24). In doing so, he bolsters their sincerity before not only the Corinthians but also Christ (8:20–21). When Paul addresses the charge against his inconsistency (10:1–2), Christ's meekness and gentleness (διὰ τῆς πραΰτητος καὶ ἐπιεικείας τοῦ Χριστοῦ) characterize his response. When he makes a rejoinder to the issue of ministerial boundaries in 10:12–18, he underscores that God's servants do not commend themselves (10:12–13) but boast in Christ (10:17–18).[87] When Paul defends his financial independence (11:7–15; 12:14–21), he describes his integrity as the truth of Christ (11:10) as a servant of Christ in contrast to false apostles (11:15).

Therefore, Christ plays essential roles in both the activities of God and his servants in the ministry. In other words, Christ's indispensable role as the intermediate agency connects God and his servants, enabling the divine paradox, their sacrificial service to God, and the manifestation of God's knowledge.

5.2.4 Counteragents of Ministry

Finally, Paul describes human counteragents in ministry, in 2:17, as those peddling the word of God: καπηλεύοντες τὸν λόγον τοῦ θεοῦ. The Greek word καπηλεύω is a *hapax legomenon* in the NT.[88] The verb, the cognate of κάπηλος attested twice in the LXX (Isa 1:22; Sir 26:29), is used in both neutral and derogatory senses. In the neutral sense, καπηλεύω means "to engage in retail trade,"[89] or "trade in."[90] In the pejorative sense, the word is often figuratively used to mean "to drive a petty trade,"[91] or "to peddle."[92] For instance, the word appears in the context where philosophers accuse those "who sell their teaching for money" (e.g., Plato, *Prot.* 313c; *Soph.* 231d; Lucian, *Hermot.* 59; Philostratus, *Vit. Apoll.* 1.13).[93] Therefore, καπηλεύω came to mean "to sell, to hawk, deceitfully, at illegitimate profit," or "to misrepresent a thing."[94] In this pejorative sense, Paul describes counteragents as peddlers of God's word in 2:17. Paul's description of counteragents reflects more than just financial overtones. He accuses them of their conduct and integrity regarding their ministry of God's word.[95] Thus, he continues to unpack their deceitful conduct and misrepresentation of God's knowledge in the material that follows in 3:1–13:10.

Regarding the deceitful conduct of counteragents, Paul describes that they rely on self-commendation rather than God's commendation (10:12, 17–18; cf. 3:1–6); thus,

---

[87] Paul alludes to Jer 9:24 in 2 Cor 10:17 (cf. 1 Cor 1:31). In the context of the book of Jeremiah, κύριος refers to God. However, in the literary context of 2 Corinthians, the title refers to Christ (e.g., 2 Cor 1:2, 14; 2:12; 4:5, 14).
[88] The cognate κάπηλος is attested twice in the LXX (Isa 1:22; Sir 26:29).
[89] Hans Windisch, "καπηλεύω," *TDNT* 3:603.
[90] BDAG, s.v. "καπηλεύω."
[91] LSJ, s.v. "καπηλεύω."
[92] BDAG, s.v. "καπηλεύω."
[93] Hans Windisch, "καπηλεύω," *TDNT* 3:603.
[94] Ibid. See also Ceslas Spicq, "καπηλεύω," *TLNT* 2:81–87.
[95] Notice the sharp contrast between God's agents and counteragents in 2:17, which indicates that Paul's emphasis is not simply on their fiscal deception but also on their integrity and conduct in their ministry of God's word.

they are not people from God (cf. ὡς ἐκ θεοῦ in 2:17). They class themselves beyond what the ministerial roles God has given them (10:12-13) and take credit for others' labor (10:15-16); thus, they are not people of sincerity (cf. ἐξ εἰλικρινείας in 2:17). As popular rhetors and philosophers in the ancient world competed against each other to attract students to their teaching,[96] counteragents compare and compete against one another in their ministry of God's word. Moreover, as the fiscal overtone of καπηλεύω implies, Paul accuses counteragents of deceitfully taking advantage of financial support from the Corinthian church (11:7-12, 20; 12:13-19). In contrast to God's servants, deceitful conduct of false apostles lacks both integrity and qualifications from God in their ministry.

Most importantly, they misrepresent God's word (2:17); they fail to disseminate God's knowledge (cf. 2:14-17) in three fashions: corruption of God's word (4:2), boasting in fallacious knowledge (5:16), and proclamation of another gospel (11:3-4, 13-15). First, they corrupt God's word (4:2): δολοῦντες τὸν λόγον τοῦ θεοῦ. Paul declares that God's servants do not adulterate or falsify God's word,[97] alluding to false apostles by way of contrast. Although καπηλεύω (2:17) and δολόω (4:2) are not synonyms, the parallel between 2:17 and 4:2 is remarkable (see Table 5.1). Moreover, one reads a similar expression in Lucian: οἱ φιλόσοφοι ἀποδίδονται τὰ μαθήματα ὥσπερ οἱ κάπηλοι, κερασάμενοί γε οἱ πολλοὶ καὶ δολώσαντες (Hermot. 59; cf. Isa 1:22). Philosophers are likened to wine retailers with the Greek word κάπηλος, the cognate of καπηλεύω, and many (πολλοί; cf. 2:17) adulterate (δολόω) the wine.

Second, false apostles boast in fallacious knowledge of the gospel. In 5:12, the purpose statement of his speaking ministry in the ἵνα clause indicates that his adversaries boast in external matters. The immediate literary context clarifies that their outwardly boasting specifically pertains to the knowledge of Christ (5:16), which is the embodiment of God's knowledge, the gospel of Christ (4:4, 6). While God's knowledge is revealed to hearts through the Spirit (1:22) and in Christ (4:6), adversaries boast in the external knowledge of Christ (5:16). For this reason, Paul must emphasize that the knowledge of Christ is not according to the historical information about Jesus (5:16) but according to participation in his death and resurrection (5:14-15, 17). Thus, as Paul describes that peddlers of God's word misrepresent God's knowledge (2:14-17), false apostles boast in the fallacious knowledge of God (5:12).

Third, false apostles proclaim another gospel (11:3-4, 13-15). Paul has implicitly accused his adversaries of falsifying God's word (4:2) and boasting false knowledge of Christ (5:12), and now he more explicitly attacks them regarding their misrepresentation of Jesus, the gospel (i.e., God's knowledge). Paul portrays counteragents' deceptive preaching by likening them to the serpent that deceived Eve (11:3-4; cf. Gen 3:4, 13) and describes them as false apostles, deceitful workers, and servants of Satan who disguise themselves as apostles of Christ (11:13-15). As hucksters deceitfully sell their merchandise (2:17), false apostles deceitfully sell another gospel to the Corinthians

---

[96] P.Oxy 2190, cited in both Furnish, *II Corinthians*, 480 and Christopher Forbes, "Comparison, Self-praise and Irony: Paul's Boasting and the Conventions of Hellenistic Rhetoric," *NTS* 32 (1986): 1-30 at 7; See also Thrall, *Second Epistle of the Corinthians*, 2:643.
[97] BDAG, s.v. "δολόω."

(11:3-4, 13-15).⁹⁸ Therefore, Paul continues to unpack counteragents' deceitful conduct and misrepresentation of God's knowledge in 3:1-13:10.⁹⁹

Moreover, as already implied from my previous discussions, Paul presents a stark contrast between God's agents and counteragents in the thesis (2:14-17) and continues to develop it in 3:1-13:10 in relation to the dissemination of God's word, the nature of their ministries, and the qualifications and integrity in their ministries.¹⁰⁰ While God's agents speak God's word in Christ before God, counteragents peddle his Word (2:17); God's agents disseminate God's knowledge through the proclamation and defense of the gospel (4:1-6; 5:18-20; 10:4-5; 12:19), whereas counteragents corrupt God's word (4:2), boast in fallacious knowledge (5:16), and proclaim another gospel (11:3-4, 13-15) for their own competition (10:12-18) and benefit (11:7-12, 20). While God's agents offer themselves to God as a pleasing sacrifice to God (2:15; 4:17; 5:1-2, 4, 9, 11; 6:16; 7:1, 12; 8:5, 9, 19; 9:13; 12:9), counteragents exalt themselves (11:20). While God's agents are people from God, counteragents are not (2:17); God's agents speak of the divine origins of their credentials (3:1-6a; 5:11-20a; 8:16, 19, 22, 23; 10:8, 13, 17; 11:23, 12:4, 7, 9; 13:10), whereas counteragents rely on self-commendation (10:12-18), disguising themselves as apostles of Christ (11:13) and servants of righteousness (11:15). While God's agents are people of sincerity, counteragents lack integrity in their ministry (2:17); God's agents demonstrate their integrity through their speech (4:2-9; 6:3-10; 8:16, 17, 18, 20, 22; 10:2, 12-13, 13-16, 17-18; 11:6, 7-15; 12:14-21), whereas counteragents violate the ministerial jurisdiction in boasting in others' labors (10:12-18). Moreover, while God's agents empower the Corinthians to become God's agents by encouraging them to respond to the gospel through their participation in the ministry to the saints (chs 8-9), counteragents take advantage of the Corinthians' financial support and exploit them (11:7-12, 20). Therefore, the thesis introduces the contrast between God's agents and counteragents to be further developed in 3:1-13:10.

---

⁹⁸ Although Paul's description of counteragents in 4:2 and 5:12 conveys a different sense in comparison to that of false apostles in 11:4 (i.e., falsifying God's knowledge and boasting in the false knowledge vs. preaching another Jesus and gospel), one finds remarkable similarities between 4:2, 5:12, and 11:4. In 4:2, Paul relates the act of falsifying God's word with craftiness (πανουργία). Likewise, in 11:4, Paul characterizes his rivals' proclamation of another gospel with craftiness (πανουργία). Moreover, he employs δολόω to describe his adversaries' deceitful conduct in 4:2, whereas he uses δόλιος, the cognate of δολόω, to call false apostles deceitful workers (ἐργάται δόλιοι) in 11:13. Later, in 12:16, Paul sarcastically describes himself as a crafty person (πανοῦργος) who took the Corinthians in deceit (δόλος) by employing πανοῦργος and ἱ ὅλος, the cognates of πανουργία and ἱ ολόω. In doing so, he consistently relates the false apostles with those terms. In addition, one observes a close relationship between Paul's description of his opponents boasting in the erroneous knowledge of Christ in 5:12-16 and his accusation of their preaching of another Jesus in 11:4. Because they boast in the fallacious knowledge of Christ, therefore, it inevitably results in the proclamation of another Jesus.

⁹⁹ It is possible that Paul's description in 11:20 serves as a summary of the deceptive conduct of counteragents.

¹⁰⁰ Long similarly identifies the MSR of recurrence of contrast with particularization, arguing "Throughout 2 Corinthians Paul's and his companinons' conduct is CONTRASTED with that of others sporadically (1:12; 2:17; 4:2; 5:12, etc.).... This contrast becomes most intense and PARTICULARIZED in chs 10-12..." ("2 Corinthians," 261-95 at 280-81).

5.3 Conclusion

In this chapter, I have argued two aspects of the literary structure: 2:14–17 as a literary unit and particularization with contrast as the MSR in relation to the letter as a whole. First, the discourse function, of conjunctive relation and thematic unity regarding agents, shows that 2:14–17 is an independent literary unit. Second, I have contended that 2:14–17 and 3:1–13:10 are structured according to particularization with contrast, for insights from rhetorical criticism, epistolary criticism, and thematic continuity between 2:14–17 and 3:1–13:10 indicate that 2:14–17 is the thesis statement of the letter. Particularly, I have spent significant space to argue the ways in which Paul develops the theme of four agents and their activities in the following material in 3:1–13:10: God as the ultimate agent, Paul and his fellow workers as human agents, Christ as the intermediate agent, and false apostles as human counteragents. God achieves his mission through paradoxes, which characterize the ministry (2:14–17; 4:6–7, 10–12, 17; 8:1–2, 9; 12:9–10; 13:4), and manifests his knowledge regarding the credentials of his servants (3:1–6a) and the gospel of Christ (3:12–4:12). As Χριστοῦ εὐωδία (2:15), Paul views that the ministry of the proclamation of the gospel (3:1–7:16), the collection (8:1–9:15), and the defense of the gospel (10:1–13:10) as a pleasing sacrifice to God. As God's ὀσμή (2:14, 16), Paul explains that God's agents manifest God's knowledge in their speeches regarding the proclamation of the gospel that presents life and death (3:1–7:16) and their credentials (3:1–7:16; 8:1–9:15; 10:1–13:10). Moreover, Christ's essential involvement in the activities of God and his servants makes the divine paradox, their sacrificial service to God, and the manifestation of God's knowledge possible. As peddlers of God's word (2:17), Paul continues to explain false apostles' lack of integrity (10:12–18; 11:7–12, 20; 12:13–19) and misrepresentation of God's knowledge (4:2; 5:12, 16; 11:3–4, 13–15) through a contrast with God's agents. Therefore, Paul consistently develops the major theme described in 2:14–17 in the material that follows in 3:1–13:10. Having discussed the literary structure of the thesis statement of the letter, we will now turn to the analysis of 3:1–7:16.

6

Arguments Pertaining to Content of Ministry: Proclamation of the Gospel (3:1–7:16)

In Chapter 5, I demonstrated that 2:14–17 is the thesis statement of the letter, introducing the key theme regarding agents in ministry to be developed in 3:1–13:10. In this chapter, I argue that the analysis of the literary structure of 3:1–7:16 reveals that Paul develops one of the major aspects of the ministry: the proclamation of the gospel. Therefore, I begin my study with a scrutiny of the segmentation of 3:1–7:16 and then explicate two MSRs in relation to the division as a whole: causation with particularization and substantiation. Specifically, the MSRs reveal that the main thrust of Paul's discourse in 3:1–7:16 pertains to the proclamation of the gospel.

6.1 Division of 3:1–7:16

Regarding the division of 3:1–7:16, I propose its main units and subunits as follows:

A. Basis for the Proclamation of the Gospel: Description of Ministry of New Covenant (3:1–11)
   1. Qualifications for Ministry (3:1–6a)
      a) Qualifications Regarding Commendation Letter (3:1–3)
      b) Qualifications Regarding Ministry of New Covenant (3:4–6a)
   2. Character of the New Covenant (3:6b–11)
      a) New Covenant of Life-Giving Spirit (3:6b)
      b) New Covenant of Surpassing Glory (3:7–11)
B. Content of the Proclamation of the Gospel (3:12–7:3)
   1. Descriptive Speech Regarding Theocentric Character of the Proclamation (3:12–4:12):
      a) General Statement (3:12): Bold and Plain Speech
      b) Basis: God's Unveiled Knowledge through Christ (3:13–18)
      c) Content: Sincerity, Christocentric Preaching, and Divine Paradox (4:1–12)
   2. Descriptive Speech Regarding Attitude toward the Proclamation: Courage Despite Suffering (4:13–5:10)
      a) General Statement: Proclamation of the Gospel with Courage Despite Suffering (4:13–16)

b) Reasons for the Attitude: Glory through Affliction and the Spirit as God's Down Payment (4:17–5:5)
c) Basis for the Attitude: Christ's Eschatological Presence and Judgement (5:6–10)
3. Hortatory Speech Regarding Persuasion of the Gospel of Reconciliation (5:11–7:3)
a) General Statement: Persuasion (5:11)
b) Basis: Regarding Credentials (5:12–19)
c) Content: Regarding Reconciliation with God and His Servants (5:20–7:3)
C. Outcomes of the Proclamation of the Gospel (7:4–16)
1. General Statement: Paul's Boasting, Encouragement, and Joy (7:4)
2. Reasons for Paul's Boasting, Encouragement, and Joy (7:5–12)
a) Occasion of Encouragement and Joy: Through Titus's Arrival and His Report Concerning the Corinthians' Response to Paul's Previous Letter (7:5–7)
b) Joy and Boasting through the Corinthians' Ministry to Titus (7:13–16)
3. Summary (7:13–16)

Concerning the segmentation of 3:1–7:16 as a whole, most scholars agree that 7:16 marks the ending of a section regardless of whether they view 3:1–7:16 as a literary unity or not, for they recognize an apparent shift between 7:16 and 8:1. However, only a few interpreters claim that 3:1 is the beginning of a major division.[1] Others maintain 2:14 as the beginning of a new literary unit based on their observations regarding topical continuities and structural relationships between 2:14–16a/17 and the following material within 3:1–7:16.[2] However, as demonstrated in Chapter 5, one finds thematic

---

[1] Witherington, *Conflict and Community in Corinth*, 375; Seifrid, *Second Letter to the Corinthians*, 96–97; cf. Plummer, *Second Epistle*, 75–76.

[2] For instance, regarding the topical connection between 2:14–17 and 3:1–3 or 3:1–6, Hafemann contends a topical continuity in 2:14–3:3 regarding "Paul's Sufficiency As an Apostle" (*2 Corinthians*, 37; idem, *Suffering and the Spirit*, 41–182), and Garland observes thematic continuities regarding the antithesis of life and death (2:16; 3:6) and the theme of sufficiency (2:16; 3:5–6; *2 Corinthians*, 138). Long argues that 2:14–3:18 is the second argument in *probatio*, which concerns "Paul's ministry of proclamation and the glory of the new covenant" (*Ancient Rhetoric and Paul's Apology*, 165–67; also, Martin, *2 Corinthians*, 185, though Martin treats 2:14–3:6 and 3:7–18 separately). Regarding structural relationships between 2:14–16a/17 and the following material, McDonald claims the function of 2:14–3:3 as an introduction of 2:14–7:1. Also, Collange argues that 2:14–17 constitutes themes developed in 2:14–7:4 (*Enigmes*, 324). Furnish similarly views 2:14–3:6 as an introduction to the discussions developed in 3:7–5:19 (*II Corinthians*, 185–86). Thrall argues that 2:14–17 introduces the main themes for 3:1–6:10 (*Second Epistle of the Corinthians*, 1:188–89). Likewise, Seifrid maintains that 2:14–17 describes the primary theme Paul develops in the body of the letter in 3:1–7:16 (*Second Letter to the Corinthians*, 84). Many follow Lambrecht's analysis that 2:14–4:6 is structured according to a chiasm; namely, 2:14–3:6, 3:7–18, and 4:1–6 form a concentric A-B-A' pattern ("Structure and Line of Thought in 2 Corinthians 2,14–4,6," in *Studies on 2 Corinthians*, ed. Reimund Bieringer and Jan Lambrecht, BETL 112 [Leuven: Leuven University Press; Uitgeverij Peeters, 1994], 257–94). Also see Barnett, *Second Epistle to the Corinthians*, 145; Garland, *2 Corinthians*, 137–38; Matera, *II Corinthians*, 68; Harris, *Second Epistle to the Corinthians*, 241; Guthrie, *2 Corinthians*, 152–53.

and lexical connections between 2:14–17 and 3:1–13:10; thus, 2:14–17 functions as the thesis of the entire letter.³ Moreover, insights from epistolary criticism, rhetorical criticism, and the discourse function of asyndeton suggest that 3:1 is the beginning of a new literary unit. First, the epistolary structure suggests that 3:1 is the beginning of a new section. As I have already discussed, the epistolary formula of thanksgiving introduces primary themes to be developed in the following material. Thus, one expects the beginning of a new section after the thanksgiving. Applying insights from the epistolary criticism, Seifrid indeed identifies 3:1 as the beginning of the body of the letter, noting a shift from "his apostolic labors to his theological concern for his addressees."⁴ Second, the insight from rhetorical criticism, especially its emphasis on rhetorical structure, suggests that 3:1 is the beginning of a section. In the rhetorical structure, proofs called *probatio* or *confirmatio* should follow *propositio* or *partitio*,⁵ which suggests that Paul begins his discourse after the thesis statement in order to develop the ideas he introduced in 2:14–17.⁶ Third, the presence of asyndeton suggests a break between 2:17 and 3:1. While the precise functions of asyndeton are still debated, grammarians claim that one of its functions is to signal a section or paragraph break.⁷ While the presence of asyndeton itself cannot serve as the conclusive evidence for the section break between 2:17 and 3:1, it may add another piece of evidence to the aforementioned observations.⁸ Therefore, I contend that 3:1 marks the beginning of a new literary unit.

---

³ To be more specific, while scholars argue for the thematic unity between 2:14–17 and 3:1–3 or 3:1–6 regarding adequacy or sufficiency of apostleship, my discussion in Chapter 5 demonstrated that Paul speaks of the credentials of God's servants throughout the letter; thus, the discussion pertaining to the commendation letter in 3:1–6 is just one of the qualifications Paul develops in 3:1–13:10.
⁴ Seifrid, *2 Corinthians*, 96.
⁵ Hans Dieter Betz, *Galatians: A Commentary on Paul's Letter to the Churches in Galatia*, Hermeneia (Philadelphia: Fortress, 1979), 128.
⁶ However, one should also note that while rhetoricians insist that rhetorical arguments are to follow the outlines of *partitio* in the same order (Long, *Ancient Rhetoric and Paul's Apology*, 86, citing Cicero, *Inv.* 1.33; Quintilian, *Inst.* 4.5.28), Paul's discourse in 3:1–13:10 does not exactly follow the thesis statement in the same order.
⁷ On asyndeton, see a succinct but helpful summary of grammarians' discussion in Long, *2 Corinthians*, 261–63. For instance, Wallace explains, "Asyndeton is a vivid stylistic feature that often occurs for emphasis, solemnity, or rhetorical value (staccato effect), or when there is an abrupt change in topic" (*Greek Grammar*, 658). Moreover, Levinsohn describes, "Asyndeton is the norm between *paragraphs* with different topics" (*Discourse Features*, 119). Thus, one often finds it at the shifts from the letter opening to the letter body, from the letter body to the letter closing, and from primary and secondary subject to another (ibid.). In addition, Levinsohn argues that asyndeton can indicate other relationships such as evaluations of previous material, summaries of previous material, and general to specific (ibid., 119–20).
⁸ Long, *2 Corinthians*, 64, 263. Also, the asyndeton in 3:1 may mark a general-specific relationship (Levinsohn, *Discourse Features*, 120), for Paul moves from the general statement (2:14–17) to particulars (3:1–13:10) or the general statement regarding the qualifications of God's agents (2:17) to a specific type of qualifications (i.e., commendation letter) in 3:1–6. Either way, it seems to mark a section break.

6.1.1 3:1–11

Scholars disagree with one another on the identification of the first main unit within 3:1–7:16.[9] However, I propose that 3:1–11 forms the first main unit on the basis of the observations of a shift of focus, the conjunction οὖν in 3:12, and the presence of the prenuclear participial clause with ἔχω (i.e., an adverbial/circumstantial participle that precedes the main clause) in 3:12. First, a shift of focus takes place between 3:1–11 and 3:12–7:3. Paul first describes the ministry of the new covenant regarding the qualifications for the ministry (3:1–6a) and character of the new covenant (3:6b–11), and then begins to expound the content of the proclamation of the gospel in 3:12–7:3.[10] This shift of topic suggests a section boundary between 3:11 and 3:12.

Second, related to the first point, the inferential conjunction οὖν supports a section break between 3:11 and 3:12.[11] Runge explains, "One often finds οὖν at high-level boundaries in the discourse, where the next major topic is drawn from and builds upon what precedes."[12] In the case of 3:1, Paul develops his arguments (3:12–7:3) based on the description of the new covenant (3:1–11).

Third, the presence of the prenuclear participial clause with ἔχω in 3:12 suggests a section break between 3:11 and 3:12. Discourse grammarians explain that prenuclear participial clauses provide background information. Levinsohn defines, "Anarthrous participial clauses that *precede* their nuclear [i.e., main] clause present information that is backgrounded. This means that the information they convey is of secondary importance vis-à-vis that of the nuclear clause. This claim does not hold for anarthrous participial clauses that follow their nuclear clauses. That is, lacking the article."[13] In the case of 3:12, the prenuclear participial clause with ἔχω provides an important

---

[9] Also, identifications of main units and subunits depend on one's analysis of the major divisions of the letter as a whole. For example, Plummer identifies 3:1–6:10 as the second main unit within 1:12–7:16 (*Second Epistle*, 75–201), while Guthrie thinks that 2:14–7:4 is the second main unit within 1:12–7:16 (*2 Corinthians*, 150–366). Barrett recognizes 2:14–3:3 as the first main unit within 2:14–7:4 (*Second Epistle to the Corinthians*, 95–109); Furnish claims 2:14–5:19 as the second main unit within the letter body in 1:12–9:15. Witherington maintains 3:1–6:13 as the first argument within the *probatio* in 3:1–13:4 (*Conflict and Community in Corinth*, 375–401), while Long argues that 2:14–3:18 is the second argument in the *probatio* in 2:1–9:15 (*Ancient Rhetoric and Paul's Apology*, 165–67). Seifrid identifies 3:18 as the first main unit within the letter body in 3:1–7:16 (*Second Letter to the Corinthians*, 96–187). Land claims 2:14–5:21 as one of the major divisions (i.e., the second division) of the letter (*Integrity of 2 Corinthians*, 115–17). Many maintain 2:14–4:6 to be the first main unit within 2:14–7:3/4 (e.g., Thrall, *Second Epistle of the Corinthians*, 1:188–320; Barnett, *Second Epistle to the Corinthians*, 145–226; Matera, *II Corinthians*, 68–105; Harris, *Second Epistle to the Corinthians*, 241–337).
[10] See further discussion in the MSR of causation with particularization in 6.2.1.
[11] Grammarians often understand the conjunction to be inferential (i.e., therefore; e.g., Wallace, *Greek Grammar*, 673), whereas discourse grammarians denote that οὖν marks both continuity and development (e.g., Runge, *Discourse Grammar*, 43–48).
[12] Runge, *Discourse Grammar*, 43, giving Rom 5:1 as an illustration. He describes that οὖν marks a transition from Paul's discussion of the means of justification to that of its consequence. However, one should not assume that οὖν always marks a major break. For instance, οὖν in 5:6 does not indicate the beginning of a new section; rather, it signals the conclusion of Paul's discourse in 4:13–5:10.
[13] Levinsohn, *Discourse Features*, 183 (italics are original). Also see Runge, *Discourse Grammar*, 243–68; Long, *Koine Greek Grammar*, 389.

background framework, equating the descriptions of the new covenant in 3:1-11 as τοιαύτην ἐλπίδα to prepare the audience for the main clause in 3:12: πολλῇ παρρησίᾳ χρώμεθα. In other words, having described the ministry of the new covenant in 3:1-11, Paul pauses for a moment for the first time by summarizing what he has described as hope in order to highlight the ways in which God's servants participate in the ministry of the new covenant.[14] Along with the conjunction οὖν, this "pause" stops the flow of his argument, which suggests a boundary between 3:11 and 3:12.

Regarding the subunits of 3:1-11, I demarcate the main unit into 3:1-6a and 3:6b-11 based on a topical shift from the qualifications (3:1-6a) to the character of ministry (3:6b-11). I agree with many scholars who identify a section break between 3:6 and 3:7,[15] for I identify the aforementioned thematic unity in 3:1-6a and 3:6b-11. In addition, it is possible to identify a break between 3:3 and 3:4,[16] for the presence of the conjunction δέ may mark a new development of Paul's discussion.[17] However, I identify 3:1-6a as a unit based on the thematic unity regarding qualifications for ministry. Paul begins 3:1 by discussing his and his fellow workers' qualifications regarding the commendation letter (3:1-3). He proceeds to clarify the source of the credentials (3:4-5), which is already inferred by the divine passive in 3:2-3. Then, he moves to discuss their qualifications regarding the new covenant (3:6a). Thus, the flow of his argument moves from a specific type of qualification (i.e., commendation letter in 3:1-3) to the general description of the qualifications for the ministry (i.e., the ministry of the new covenant in 3:6a), both of which directly come from God himself (3:4-5, 6a).[18] However, Paul shifts his focus from the qualifications to the character of the new covenant at 3:6b. He has already characterized the qualifications of God's servants with an allusion to the Decalogue in 3:3 (Exod 31:18). Beginning with the descriptive genitives that contrast the new and old covenants in 3:6b: οὐ γράμματος ἀλλὰ πνεύματος, he starts to describe more explicitly the glorious character of the new covenant for which God made Paul and his coworkers servants (3:6a) in 3:6b-11. The new covenant (3:6a) is characterized by the life-giving Spirit (3:6b) and surpassing glory (3:7-11). Therefore, Paul shifts his discussions from the qualifications (3:1-6a) to the character of the ministry of the new covenant (3:6b-11).

6.1.2 3:12-7:3

As I have already demonstrated a break between 3:11 and 3:12, I maintain that the second main unit (3:12-7:3) begins at 3:12. Regarding the ending of the unit, I concur with the majority of scholars who acknowledge a major break between 7:3 and 7:4 or

---

[14] Also see the discussions of the information structure (Runge, *Discourse Grammar*, 179-242) and word order (Long, *2 Corinthians*, xxxix-xliii).
[15] E.g., Furnish, *II Corinthians*, 185-86; Thrall, *Second Epistle of the Corinthians*, 1:217-37; Lambrecht, *Second Corinthians*, 37-49. Also, some rightly observe a transitional nature of 3:6 (e.g., Lambrecht, *Structure and Line of Thought*, 266).
[16] E.g., Barnett, *Second Epistle to the Corinthians*, 159-70; Seifrid, *Second Letter to the Corinthians*, 110-18.
[17] See my comments on δέ in 4.1.1.
[18] One can argue for this movement as the structural relationship of generalization.

7:4 and 7:5,[19] for Paul picks up the travel narrative (7:4/5–16), which he left off at 2:12–13.[20] Within 3:12–7:3, I will argue for three subunits: 3:12–4:12, 4:13–5:10, and 5:11–7:3.

6.1.2.1 3:12–4:12

Having already argued a break between 3:11 and 3:12, I also contend that 3:12–4:12 forms the first subunit within 3:12–7:3 based on the insight from the structural relationship of causation and the presence of the ὥστε + indicative verb construction in 4:12. To begin, the structural relationship of causation indicates a thematic unity regarding the theocentric character of the proclamation that ties 3:12–4:12 as a unit. Particularly, having a general statement in 3:12, Paul moves from the basis (3:13–18) to the content of the character (4:1–12).[21] Namely, Paul first asserts a general statement in 3:12—πολλῇ παρρησίᾳ χρώμεθα—and then explains God's knowledge, contrasting the ministries of the old and new covenant. Unlike the ministry of the old covenant, the proclamation of the new covenant reveals God's unveiled knowledge through Christ (3:13–18). Because of this knowledge, the proclamation is theocentric (4:1–12),[22] for God's servants do not corrupt God's word but manifest the truth (4:1–2); they proclaim Jesus Christ as Lord (4:3–6); and they proclaim through the divine paradox to manifest the surpassing greatness of God's power (4:7–12).[23]

Moreover, the ὥστε + indicative verb construction signals the ending of the unit, for it denotes a conclusion of an argument. Historically speaking, Robertson explains, "In the Attic Greek actual result was expressed by ὥστε and the indicative, while ὥστε and the inf. ('so as to') denoted a result naturally or necessarily following the preceding cause."[24] Levinsohn further advances the study by exploring the NT Greek, particularly in the Pauline epistles and concludes, "When ὥστε introduces an independent clause or sentence, it constrains it to be interpreted as the result of what has previously been stated (+Result)."[25] Likewise, Long claims that the ὥστε + indicative or imperative construction "concludes a broader argument; it focalizes content by way of generalizing or summarizing the preceding argument as a conclusion."[26] This is also the case in 2

---

[19] While a majority of scholars recognize 7:3 as the end of a section, some maintain 7:1 or 7:2 as the ending of a section. See more discussions in 6.1.4.

[20] E.g., Plummer, *Second Epistle*, 215–16; Barrett, *Second Epistle to the Corinthians*, 205–6; Thrall, *Second Epistle of the Corinthians*, 1:486–87. Also see the Survey of Literature in Chapter 2.

[21] Thus, 3:12 and 3:13–4:12 are structured according to particularization.

[22] Thus, 3:13–18 and 4:1–12 are structured accruing to causation. See my discussion below on the segmentation of the subunits within 3:12–4:12.

[23] See further discussion in 6.2.1.

[24] Archibald Thomas Robertson, *A Grammar of the Greek New Testament in the Light of Historical Research* (Bellingham, WA: Logos, 2006), 1000.

[25] Stephen H. Levinsohn, "'Therefore' or 'Wherefore': What's the Difference?," in *Reflections on Lexicography: Explorations in Ancient Syriac, Hebrew, and Greek Sources*, ed. Richard A. Taylor and Craig E. Morrison, Perspectives on Linguistics and Ancient Languages 4 (Piscataway, NJ: Gorgias, 2014), 325–43 at 325.

[26] Long, *Koine Greek Grammar*, 462. Also see his case study on this construction, idem, "Paul's Prophesying Isa 28:11 in Context: The Signs of Unbelievers and Believers in 1 Corinthians 14," in *Kingdom Rhetoric: New Testament Explorations in Honor of Ben Witherington III*, ed. T. Michael W. Halcomb (Eugene, OR: Wipf and Stock, 2013), 133–69 at 153–57.

Cor 4:12; ὥστε and the indicative of ἐνεργέω conclude Paul's discourse in two ways. On the one hand, it summarizes Paul's immediately preceding argument in 4:7–12; on the other hand, it signals the conclusion of his larger discourse in 3:12–4:12. Thus, I maintain 3:12–4:12 as a unit.

Regarding subunits within 3:12–4:12, I identify three units: 3:12, 3:13–18, and 4:1–12. First, I identify 3:12 as the first subunit, for it marks the beginning of the new section and functions as a general statement for 3:13–4:12.[27]

Second, the presence of Διὰ τοῦτο, the prenuclear participial clause in 4:1, and a contrast between the old and new covenants suggest that 3:13–18 is the second subunit within 3:12–4:12. To begin, Διὰ τοῦτο in 4:1 marks the break between 3:18 and 4:1. While the prepositional phrase is not a conjunction, it functions as a connective in Koiné Greek, linking separate sentences.[28] Furthermore, Runge adds, "The demonstrative pronoun τοῦτο reiterates a proposition from the preceding context. Thus, the clause introduced by διὰ τοῦτο is constrained to have a causal relation with the preceding discourse. It is similar to οὖν in that both indicate + development and + continuity, but διὰ τοῦτο offers a narrower semantic constraint than οὖν does."[29]

In other words, while οὖν often signals boundaries in the larger discourse,[30] διὰ τοῦτο marks a break in smaller sections, since the phrase connects sentences with the narrower causal relationship.[31] This applies to the context of 3:12–18 and 4:1–12. The ways in which the ministry of the new covenant proclaims God's knowledge (3:12–18) serves as a basis for the character of the proclamation (4:1–12). Therefore, the presence of Διὰ τοῦτο in 4:1 indicates 3:12–18 as a unit. Moreover, the prenuclear participial clause, ἔχοντες τὴν διακονίαν ταύτην καθὼς ἠλεήθημεν in 4:1 also suggests a unit boundary between 3:18 and 4:1. Summarizing his discussion in 3:12–18 as τὴν διακονίαν ταύτην in 4:1, Paul pauses for a moment for a transition.[32] In addition, a stark contrast between the ways in which the old and new covenants manifest God's knowledge suggests 3:13–18 as a unit. In this section, Paul contrasts Moses and Jesus. Particularly, he employs a contrastive device to emphasize the distinctive manner of Moses's and Jesus's ministry: οὐ καθάπερ (3:13) ... ἡνίκα δὲ ἐὰν (3:16). Regarding the construction, two comments need to be made. To begin, the οὐ ... δὲ construction indicates a sharp contrast between Moses and Jesus. While οὐ ... ἀλλά construction is a more commonly attested form in the NT, οὐ ... δὲ is an alternative form of construction.[33] Moreover,

---

[27] See further discussion in 6.2.1.
[28] Robertson, *Grammar*, 443.
[29] Runge, *Discourse Grammar*, 48–49.
[30] Ibid., 43. Also see my discussion on οὖν in 6.1.1.
[31] This explains why the prenuclear participial clause with ἔχω + οὖν signals a major break in 3:12 (3:1–11 and 3:12–7:3), whereas the prenuclear participial clause with ἔχω + Διὰ τοῦτο in 4:1 marks a smaller break within 3:12–4:12.
[32] See my discussion on the prenuclear participial clause in 6.1.1.
[33] Long, *2 Corinthians*, 18. Also see Runge's discussion on point/counterpoint set in *Discourse Grammar*, 92–100. Although Long contends that οὐ in 3:13 and ἀλλά in 3:14 forms a point/counterpoint set (*2 Corinthians*, 70, 74–75), I disagree with him. Rather, I contend that μή in 3:13 and ἀλλά in 3:14 forms a μή ... ἀλλά construction (i.e., another form of οὐ ... ἀλλά construction). In fact, Paul repeats μή ... ἀλλά construction in 3:14–15 (see other instances of Ἵ ή ... ἀλλά in 1 Cor 2:5; Mark 13:20; Luke 7:6b–7). See more discussion on this construction in Shawn I. Craigmiles, "Pragmatic Constraints of Ἀλλά in the Synoptic Gospels" [PhD diss., Asbury Theological Seminary, 2016]).

καθάπερ in 3:13 further strengthens the manner of contrast.[34] Paul underscores that Jesus's ministry (i.e., the ministry of the new covenant) is not like Moses's ministry (i.e., the ministry of the old covenant) whose veil remains over their hearts (3:13–15), but it manifests transforming glory, for the veil is removed in Christ (3:14, 16–18).[35] Therefore, these three observations suggest that 3:12–18 forms the second subunit within 3:12–4:12.

Third, the presence of Διὰ τοῦτο in 4:1, the prenuclear participle, a topical unity regarding the theocentric character of the proclamation, and the conjunctive relations suggest that 4:1–12 functions as a unit. As I have already discussed the function of Διὰ τοῦτο and the prenuclear clause, they mark a break between 3:18 and 4:1. In addition, a topic regarding the theocentric character of the proclamation unifies 4:1–12 as a unit. In this unit, Paul seems to present three different topics in 4:1–2, 4:3–6, and 4:7–12. However, each topic points to the theocentric character of the proclamation. In 4:1–2, Paul proclaims the courage and integrity of God's servants: οὐκ ἐγκακοῦμεν and ἀπειπάμεθα τὰ κρυπτὰ τῆς αἰσχύνης.[36] However, in 4:2, Paul underscores the theocentric character of the proclamation in two manners: God's servants do not corrupt God's word; they manifest the truth; and they commend themselves in the sight of God. Thus, putting God in the center of their ministry, they emphasize God-centeredness in their proclamation.

In 4:3–6, Paul also highlights the centrality of Jesus Christ in the proclamation. Paul and his coworkers preach Jesus Christ as Lord and themselves as the Corinthians' servants (4:5), for Christ is the embodiment of God's knowledge (4:6). However, if people do not understand the gospel of Christ, it is not because the gospel is veiled but because the god of this age has blinded the minds of unbelievers (4:3–4).[37]

In 4:7–12, Paul again emphasizes the theocentric character of the proclamation. He describes that the gospel is proclaimed through the divine paradox so that it manifests the surpassing greatness of God's power (4:7). Thus, Paul declares the divine power through weakness with the illustration of the treasure in clay jars in 4:7 and moves to

---

[34] Robertson, *Grammar*, 967 (cf. BDAG, s.v. "καθάπερ"). Robertson further argues that the suffix -περ signifies "urgency" (*Grammar*, 1154). Long explains that the suffix adds morphological emphasis (Long, *2 Corinthians*, 28).

[35] One should note Paul's skillful crafting of the language in the construction of οὐ καθάπερ (3:13) . . . ἡνίκα δὲ ἐὰν (3:16). In 3:13–15 (except 3:14c), Paul describes what the ministry of the new covenant does not do (i.e., what the ministry of the old covenant does), by employing καθάπερ at the beginning. Paul proceeds to describe what the ministry of the new covenant does in 3:16–19. However, he qualifies the latter description by the phrase ἡνίκα δὲ ἐὰν at the beginning of 3:16. In other words, Paul does not merely describe and contrast the ministry of the old and new covenants; instead, he moves from the description of the ministry of the old covenant to the condition of the new covenant: whenever one turns to the Lord, the veil is taken away (3:16). Thus, Paul implicitly challenges the Corinthians to turn to the Lord.

[36] Grammatically speaking, these two statements are the only indicatives in 4:1–2. The rest of the clauses modify these two indicative sentences. Thus, the courage and integrity of God's agents are central to the discussion in 4:1–2 from the point of the grammatical construction.

[37] The conjunctive relation in 4:3–6 indicates 4:3–6 as a unit within 4:1–12. Syntactically speaking, one finds only two sentences within 4:3–6: 4:3–4 and 4:5–6. The conjunction γάρ indicates that 4:5–6 supports the claim in 4:3–4.

substantiate the claim in 4:8–12.[38] While a number of scholars identify 4:7 as the beginning of a new unit,[39] and many observe stronger continuities either within 2:14–4:6 or within 4:7–5:10,[40] the theocentric character topically unifies 4:1–12. Particularly, the theme of the demotion of self and promotion of Jesus in the proclamation of the gospel (4:5) continues in Paul's discussion in 4:7–12: God's servants suffer to promote Jesus's life (4:11–12).

Furthermore, the topical unity is supported by the conjunctive relations as follows:

Διὰ τοῦτο: Courage and Integrity (4:1–2),
δέ: Christocentric Preaching (4:3–6),
δέ: Divine Paradox (4:7–11),
ὥστε + indicative: Conclusion (4:12).

Beginning with Διὰ τοῦτο in 4:1, Paul begins to describe the theocentric character of the proclamation in 4:1–2. The conjunction δέ in 4:3 suggests a new development in Paul's discussion; thus, he begins to explain another theocentric character in 4:3–6.[41] The conjunction δέ in 4:7 again signals a new development in Paul's argument regarding the theocentric character in 4:7–11. Finally, ὥστε + indicative concludes both the immediately preceding argument in 4:7–12 and the larger discourse in 3:12–4:12. Therefore, with these observations, I maintain 3:12–4:12 as a unit.

6.1.2.2 4:13–5:10

Regarding the beginning and ending of 4:13–5:10, scholars differ from one another regarding the identification of the beginning of a section.[42] However, many agree that 5:10 marks the ending of a unit due to an apparent shift of topic between 5:10 and 5:11

---

[38] Particularly, Paul explains this divine paradox in two ways. On the one hand, the hardship catalog (4:8–9) portrays "what God's servants do not" with repeated contrasts between cause and result. Despite affliction, perplexity, persecution, and assault, they are not crushed, not despairing, not forsaken, and not destroyed. On the other hand, Paul moves to describe "what God's servants do" in 4:10–12: they carry the death of Jesus in the body (4:10) in order for the life of Jesus to be manifested (4:11–12).

[39] E.g., Plummer, *Second Epistle*, 122–23; Barrett, *Second Epistle to the Corinthians*, 136–37; Furnish, *II Corinthians*, 252–53, 277–78; Fitzgerald, *Cracks in an Earthen Vessel*, 166–80; Thrall, *The Second Epistle of the Corinthians*, 1:320–21; Barnett, *Second Epistle to the Corinthians*, 227; Lambrecht, *Second Corinthians*, 71; Matera, *II Corinthians*, 105–106; Harris, *Second Epistle to the Corinthians*, 338; Martin, *2 Corinthians*, 230; Guthrie, *2 Corinthians*, 249–50.

[40] In the former analysis, Lambrecht's work is influential: 2:14–3:6, 3:7–18, and 4:1–6 form a chiastic structure ("Structure and Line of Thought," 257–94). In the latter case, many scholars identify that the theme of suffering unites 4:1–6 and 4:7–5:10 as a unit (e.g., Plummer, *Second Epistle*, 122–64; Matera, *II Corinthians*, 105–26).

[41] On discourse function of δέ, see my discussion in 4.1.1.

[42] For examples, some view 4:7–5:10 as a unit (e.g., Plummer, *Second Epistle*, 122–64; Furnish, *II Corinthians*, 252–305); some argue 4:12–5:10 as a unit (e.g., Baument, *Täglich Sterben*, 72, 81–83); some maintain 5:1–10 as a unit (e.g., Windisch, *Der zweite Korintherbrief*, 141; Héring, *Second Epistle*, 36–40; Barrett, *Second Epistle to the Corinthians*, 149–61); others claim that 4:16–5:10 is a unit (e.g., Barnett, *Second Epistle to the Corinthians*, 245–77; Garland, *2 Corinthians*, 238–67; Lambrecht, *Second Corinthians*, 80–90). See also a survey of the segmentation in 2 Cor 4–5 in Lindgård, *Paul's Line of Thought*, 73–74.

and the presence of οὖν in 5:11. In this section, I contend that 4:13–5:10 is the second subunit within 3:12–7:3.[43] Particularly, I will focus on five pieces of evidence that suggest 4:13 is the beginning of the unit: the presence of ὥστε + indicative in 4:12, the new development marker δέ (4:13), another statement that pertains to speech (4:13), the prenuclear participial clause with ἔχω (4:13), and insight from the structural relationship between 4:13–16 and 4:17–5:10.

First, the ὥστε + indicative in 4:12 indicates the ending of the first subunit (3:12–4:12); thus, 4:13 is the beginning of the second subunit.[44] Second, the presence of δέ suggests a new development.[45] Third, closely related to the second point, Paul's statement regarding the speech marks a shift from the first descriptive speech (3:12–4:12) to the second descriptive speech (4:13–5:10).[46] Fourth, the presence of a prenuclear participle clause in 4:13 signals a break between 4:12 and 4:13: ἔχοντες δὲ τὸ αὐτὸ πνεῦμα τῆς πίστεως κατὰ τὸ γεγραμμένον· Ἐπίστευσα, διὸ ἐλάλησα.[47] Previously, Paul employs prenuclear participial clauses with the verb ἔχω to denote unit boundaries (3:12; 4:1; cf. 3:4; 4:7).[48] In 4:13, he once again marks a boundary between 4:12 and 4:13 by another prenuclear participial clause with ἔχω. Moreover, the prenuclear participial clause in 4:12 differs from those in 3:12 and 4:1 regarding its function, which further suggests that 4:13 begins a new unit. Namely, the prenuclear participial clauses with ἔχω in 3:12 and 4:1 anaphorically provide background information, whereas that in 4:13 cataphorically does so. In other words, prenuclear participial clauses provide background information that is secondary significance in relation to the information the main clause presents. However, while the prenuclear participial clauses in 3:12 and 4:1 provide such information by summarizing the previous argument,[49] that in 4:13 presents background information by pointing forward to the immediately following context; that is, the quotation from Ps 115:1 LXX (cf. 116:10 MT). In 4:13, the prenuclear participle of ἔχω takes τὸ αὐτὸ πνεῦμα τῆς πίστεως as the direct object, which points to the following quotation: κατὰ τὸ γεγραμμένον· Ἐπίστευσα, διὸ ἐλάλησα.[50] Thus, the prenuclear participial clause in 4:12

---

[43] A few scholars identify 4:13–5:10 as a unit; see Kennedy, *Rhetorical Criticism*, 89–90; McCant, *2 Corinthians*, 46–51.
[44] See my discussion in 6.1.2.1.
[45] See my comments on δέ in 4.1.1.
[46] Also see my discussion above in 6.1.
[47] Also see my comments on 3:12 and 4:1.
[48] Also, these prenuclear participles are accompanied by an inferential conjunction οὖν (3:12) and a connective Διὰ τοῦτο (4:1).
[49] The prenuclear participle with ἔχω in 3:12 takes τοιαύτην ἐλπίδα as the direct object, summarizing the discussion in 3:1–11, and that of 4:1 takes τὴν διακονίαν ταύτην, encapsulating the argument in 3:12–18. Also, the function of the conjunction οὖν (3:12) and the connective Διὰ τοῦτο (4:1) support this move, for both mark a continuity with the preceding context (Runge, *Discourse Grammar*, 43–51, 56).
[50] The difficulty to understand the phrase hinges on one's construal of the phrase, τὸ αὐτὸ πνεῦμα τῆς πίστεως. Some argue that the phrase refers back to ζωή ἐν ὑμῖν in 4:12, for Paul's faith and life are linked. Thus, Paul contrasts apostles' spirit of faith and the Corinthians' spirit of life (Norbert Baumert, *Täglich Sterben Und Auferstehen: Der Literalsinn von 2 Kor 4,12-5,10*, SANT [Munich: Kösel-Verlag, 1973], 83–84; see also Schlatter, *Paulus*, 534; R. H. Strachan, *The Second Epistle of Paul to the Corinthians*, MNTC [London: Hodder and Stoughton, 1935], 96). However, since Paul does not employ πίστις in the preceding context in 3:1–4:12, many concur that the noun phrase τὸ αὐτὸ πνεῦμα τῆς πίστεως refers to the faith of the psalmist, which Paul introduces in the immediately following context with a unique OT quotation formula: κατὰ τὸ γεγραμμένον· Ἐπίστευσα, διὸ ἐλάλησα (e.g., Thrall, *Second Epistle of the Corinthians*, 338–39; Harris, *Second Epistle to the Corinthians*, 351).

Table 6.1 Anaphoric and Cataphoric Prenuclear Participial Clauses in 3:12, 4:1, and 4:13

	Secondary/Background Information	Primary Information
3:12	Discussion in 3:1–11 (Anaphorically Summarizing 3:1–11) Ἔχοντες οὖν τοιαύτην ἐλπίδα	πολλῇ παρρησίᾳ χρώμεθα
	Secondary/Background Information	Primary Information
4:1	Discussion in 3:12–18 (Anaphorically Summarizing 3:12–18) ἔχοντες τὴν διακονίαν ταύτην καθὼς ἠλεήθημεν	οὐκ ἐγκακοῦμεν
	Secondary/Background Information	Primary Information
4:13	ἔχοντες δὲ τὸ αὐτὸ πνεῦμα τῆς πίστεως (Cataphorically introducing the OT quotation) κατὰ τὸ γεγραμμένον· Ἐπίστευσα, διὸ ἐλάλησα,	καὶ ἡμεῖς πιστεύομεν, διὸ καὶ λαλοῦμεν

not only breaks the flow of the discourse with a pause but also signals a shift of topic by cataphorically providing the background information for the main statement in the same verse: καὶ ἡμεῖς πιστεύομεν, διὸ καὶ λαλοῦμεν (see Table 6.1).

Finally, the structural relationship between 4:13–16 and 4:17–5:10 indicates that 4:13–16 is an integral part of the discussion in 4:17–5:10, since they are structured according to particularization with substantiation: Paul substantiates his claim (4:13–16) by expounding its reasons (4:17–5:10).[51] Therefore, I contend that 4:13–5:10 is the second subunit within 3:12–7:3.

Regarding the subunits within 4:13–5:10, I demarcate it into 4:13–16, 4:17–5:5, and 5:6–10 on the basis of semantic and conjunctive relations, a thematic unity, and implications from the structural relationships within 4:13–5:10. To begin, I have already demonstrated that 4:13 is the beginning of the section, and I will further argue that the presence of γάρ in 4:15 and διό in 4:16 suggests that 4:13–16 is an independent unit. Grammatically speaking, 4:13–14 forms a single sentence, and γάρ in 4:15 indicates that Paul substantiates the claim in 4:15. In addition, διό in 4:16 marks an inferential conclusion of the preceding discussion. The Greek conjunction διό is derived from δι' ὅ (i.e., διά + the neuter relative pronoun ὅ).[52] Levinsohn explains its function as follows: "It [διό] typically introduces an expository or hortatory THESIS that is inferred from what has already been stated."[53] Thus, he concludes, "other passages containing διό should be exegeted in such a way that what follows is understood not as a new point of the argument but as part of the current point that follows inferentially from the context."[54] In other words, unlike οὖν that advances an argument,[55] διό does

---

[51] See further discussion on this relationship in 6.2.1.
[52] BDAG, s.v. "διό"; Long, *Koine Greek Grammar*, 495.
[53] Levinsohn, "'Therefore' or 'Wherefore'," 325–43 at 329. Thus, he describes that διό marks inference and continuity.
[54] Ibid., 330.
[55] Ibid., 327–28.

not make a new point in the argument.⁵⁶ In the context of 4:16, Paul does not move his argument to a new point; rather, he draws an inferential conclusion of 4:13–15. Therefore, 4:13–16 should be treated as a unit.

Furthermore, the presence of γάρ in 4:17 and οὖν in 5:6 suggests that 4:17–5:5 forms a unit. In 4:17, Paul begins to substantiate the claim in 4:13–16 by beginning with the conjunction γάρ,⁵⁷ which continues until 5:5, for Paul moves to a conclusion of his discussion by the conjunction οὖν in 5:6.⁵⁸

Finally, the conjunction οὖν in 5:6 and 5:11 and διό in 5:9, and a shift of topic between 5:10 and 5:11 indicate that 5:6–10 is a unit. As I have already discussed, the conjunction οὖν marks the advancement of an argument. In 5:6, οὖν indicates that Paul's argument moves to a conclusion of 4:13–5:10. Moreover, διό in 5:9 signals the inferential conclusion of 5:6–10. The segmentation is further supported by a shift of topic between 5:10 and 5:11. Employing another οὖν in 5:11, Paul begins to describe another response to the new covenant. Therefore, I argue that 4:13–5:10 consists of three units: 4:13–16, 4:17–5:5, and 5:6–10.

6.1.2.3 5:11–7:3

Concerning the segmentation of the third unit (5:11–7:3), many scholars view 5:11 as marking the beginning of a new unit.⁵⁹ However, they differ in their opinions on the ending of the unit.⁶⁰ In this section, I contend that 5:11–7:3 is a literary unit.⁶¹ Regarding its opening, the presence of οὖν, a prenuclear participial clause with οἶδα,, and a shift of topic signal that 5:11 is the beginning of a new literary unit. The Greek conjunction οὖν in 5:11 indicates that Paul proceeds to a next major topic,⁶² and the prenuclear participial clause with οἶδα in the same verse creates a pause in Paul's discourse, marking a unit boundary between 5:10 and 5:11.⁶³ Moreover, a shift of topic occurs between 4:13–5:10 and 5:11–7:3. Paul shifts his discussion regarding the attitude toward the proclamation (4:13–5:10) to hortatory speech regarding the persuasion of

---

⁵⁶ Also Long, *Koine Greek Grammar*, 495.
⁵⁷ Also see my discussion regarding γάρ in 4.2.1.2.
⁵⁸ See the discourse function of οὖν in 6.1.1. Also, some may question the ways in which 4:17–5:4 and 5:5 are related, since 5:5 begins with δέ. See my note in 6.2.1.
⁵⁹ See my note in 6.1.2.2.
⁶⁰ Some argue that 5:11–6:10 forms a unit (Plummer, *Second Epistle*, 164–201; Matera, *II Corinthians*, 126–56; Harris, *Second Epistle to the Corinthians*, 411–86); some maintain 5:11–21 as a unit (Barrett, *Second Epistle to the Corinthians*, 162–81; Seifrid, *Second Letter to the Corinthians*, 238–65); some claim that 5:11–19 is a unit (Furnish, *II Corinthians*, 305–337); some view 5:11–7:1 as a unit (Barnett, *Second Epistle to the Corinthians*, 277–358); some consider 5:11–21 to be a unit (Garland, *2 Corinthians*, 267–302; Lambrecht, *Second Corinthians*, 90–107); some argue that 5:11–15 forms a unit (Martin, *2 Corinthians*, 273–92); some maintain 5:11–7:1 as a unit (Long, *Ancient Rhetoric and Paul's Apology*, 165, 168–72).
⁶¹ Some scholars agree with this segmentation, though they think that 7:4 marks the ending of the unit (e.g., Thrall, *Second Epistle of the Corinthians*, 1:400–485; Guthrie, *2 Corinthians*, 293–366).
⁶² See my discussion on οὖν in 6.1.1.
⁶³ In 5:11, the prenuclear participial clause, Εἰδότες οὖν τὸν φόβον τοῦ κυρίου, is anaphoric (cf. 3:12; 4:1), which summarizes Paul's immediately preceding discussion regarding the eschatological judgement of Christ in 5:9–10 as the fear of the Lord. See my discussion on the function of the prenuclear participle in 6.1.1.

the gospel of reconciliation (5:11–7:3) with another statement regarding the speech in 5:11: ἀνθρώπους πείθομεν.⁶⁴

Regarding the ending of the unit, a majority of scholars identify 2:14–7:4 as a major unit, for they see a strong narrative continuity between 2:12–13 and 7:5–16.⁶⁵ In other words, a unity of topic and literary form between 2:12–13 and 7:5–16 suggests that 7:4 is the ending of a section. However, insights from other methodologies have led some scholars to different conclusions. On the one hand, scholars using rhetorical criticism view 7:1 as the end of a section. Witherington claims that 7:2 is the beginning of another argument after a digression in 6:14–7:1, for "each argument of a defense, if there were multiple arguments, could have a brief *narratio* or rehearsal of the facts to be dealt with in that particular argument, or it could allude to and build on the original *narratio*."⁶⁶ In contrast, Long contends that 6:14–7:1 is not a digression but a climax of Paul's argument in 3:14–7:1, yet he still views that 7:2 begins the narrative section in 7:2–16.⁶⁷ Likewise, McCant identifies 7:2 as the beginning of 7:2–16, for 7:2 recapitulates the preceding exhortation in 6:11–13 after the digression in 6:14–7:1.⁶⁸ However, their identification of the segmentation is not necessarily informed by the ancient rhetorical tradition; rather, it is based on their observation of a topical shift between 7:1 and 7:2.

On the other hand, epistolary criticism suggests that 7:2 is the end of a section. Viewing 1:1–7:16 as the letter of apologetic commendation, Belleville argues, "Πρὸς κατάκρισιν οὐ λέγω in 7.3 signals the formal transition from the body middle to the body closing section, and from the request section to the final section of confidence and appreciation, expressions characteristic of a Hellenistic letter of recommendation."⁶⁹ Nevertheless, comparing the closings of other Pauline letters, the transition that marks the closing of the letter in 7:3 is not apparent.⁷⁰

One difficulty in determining the ending of the segmentation pertains to the fact that 7:2, 7:3, and 7:4 begin with asyndeta; the lack of a conjunction at the beginning of each sentence in these verses poses a difficulty to construe the relationships with preceding and following context as well as a unit boundary. However, I argue that 5:11–7:3 is a literary unity based on four observations: a thematic unity regarding life and death in 5:11–7:3, a topical emphasis on speech in 3:12–7:3, lexical links within 3:1–7:3 and 7:4–16, and insight from the structural relationship within 5:11–7:3.⁷¹

---

⁶⁴ See more discussion on the MSR of causation with particularization in 6.2.1.
⁶⁵ E.g., Barrett, *Second Epistle to the Corinthians*, 95–204; Thrall, *Second Epistle of the Corinthians*, 1:188–485; Barnett, *Second Epistle to the Corinthians*, 137–364; Lambrecht, *Second Corinthians*, 37–128; Matera, *II Corinthians*, 65–170; Harris, *Second Epistle to the Corinthians*, 240–521; Guthrie, *2 Corinthians*, 150–366. Also, because of the smooth transition from 2:13 to 7:5, especially later partition theorists such as Bornkamm, Vielhauer, Suhl, and Schenke and Fischer regarded 1:1–2:13 and 7:5–16 as part of the letter of reconciliation (see a summary of their theories in Betz, *2 Corinthians 8 and 9*, 2–36).
⁶⁶ Witherington, *Conflict and Community in Corinth*, 407.
⁶⁷ Long, *Ancient Rhetoric and Paul's Apology*, 171–72.
⁶⁸ McCant, *2 Corinthians*, 67–68.
⁶⁹ Belleville, *Reflection of Glory*, 160.
⁷⁰ In fact, Belleville admits a number of peculiarities in the closing in 7:3–16 (ibid., 161–64).
⁷¹ Garland also views 7:3 as the ending of a unit, arguing that 7:4 functions as "a hinge-joint, ending the previous passage and beginning the next" (*2 Corinthians*, 347).

First, as I have already discussed the antithesis of death and life as the outcome of the manifestation of God's knowledge in 3:1–7:16 (see 5.2.2.2), the theme of death and life suggests 5:11–7:3 as a unit, for it frames Paul's argument in 5:11–7:3. Christ's death and resurrection and the participation of God's servants in them (5:14–17) are the foundation for the ministry of reconciliation (5:18–19). As a result, Paul and his fellow workers suffer for it to the point of death, but they continue to live (6:9; cf. 1:8–11), and Paul desires to share life and death with the Corinthians as the outcome of his proclamation of the reconciliation (7:3). Therefore, unlike scholars who identify 7:2 as the beginning of a new unit, I contend that Paul's discourse extends to 7:3.

Second, Paul's emphasis on speech suggests that 7:3 marks the ending of 3:12–7:3. After describing the ministry of the new covenant (3:1–11), Paul begins to proclaim the gospel in 3:12–7:3. Namely, God's servants articulate the theocentric character of the proclamation (3:12–4:12), explain their attitude toward the proclamation (4:13–5:10), and persuade the Corinthians to be reconciled to God (5:11, 5:20–6:10) and his servants (6:11–7:3).[72] Thus, their speech (3:12; 4:13; 5:11) characterizes each discussion, and, once again, Paul stresses his speech in 7:3 by employing the speech-related words λέγω and προεῖπον,

Third, related to the second point, the lexical connections within 3:1–7:3 and 7:4–16 suggest a break between 7:3 and 7:4. On the one hand, the lexical links between 3:1–7:2 and 7:3 indicate that 7:3 belongs to the preceding context. As I mentioned, the vocabularies pertaining to speech, λέγω and προεῖπον in 7:3, are more connected to the preceding context (3:1–7:3) than the following context (7:4–16). Moreover, Paul's employment of the word κατάκρισις (3:9; 7:3) supports this lexical connection within 3:1–7:3. Paul employs κατάκρισις to describe the character of the old covenant in 3:9 and employs the same term once again in 7:3 to reassure that the ministry of the new covenant does not condemn but rather proclaims the gospel of the reconciliation. On the other hand, lexical connections within 7:4 and 7:5–16 suggest that 7:4 belongs to 7:5–16. Some terms in 7:4 appear in 3:1–7:3 but not in 7:5–16,[73] and other terms in 7:4 occur in 7:5–16 but not in 3:1–7:3,[74] yet the cognates of these words are found in both 3:1–7:3 and 7:5–16.[75] However, the recurrence of χαρά (7:4, 13), its cognate χαίρω (7:7, 9, 13, 16), παράκλησις (7:4, 7, 13), and its cognate παρακαλέω (7:6 [twice], 7, 13) within 7:4–16 presents a strong case that 7:4 is more closely related to 7:5–16 than 3:1–7:3.[76]

Fourth, the structural relationship within 5:11–7:3 suggests that 7:2 is a part of the exhortation in 5:11–7:3. Paul moves from the description of the ministry of the reconciliation (5:11–19) to exhortations (5:20–7:3).[77] As he begins the section by declaring, ἀνθρώπους πείθομεν (5:11), he gives five consecutive exhortations to

---

[72] See more discussion in 6.2.1.
[73] These include παρρησία (3:12; 7:4) and θλῖψις (4:17; 6:4; 7:4).
[74] These include καύχησις (7:4, 14), παράκλησις (7:4, 7, 13), and χαρά (7:4, 13).
[75] The cognate of θλῖψις (θλίβω) occurs in 4:8 and 7:5; the cognates of καύχησις appear in both 3:1–7:3 and 7:5–16 (καύχημα in 5:12; καυχάομαι in 5:12; 7:14); the cognate of παράκλησις (παρακαλέω) appears in both units (5:20; 6:1; 7:6 [twice], 7, 13).
[76] In addition, the close proximity of θλῖψις (7:4) and θλίβω (7:5) adds another piece of evidence that 7:4 and 7:5–16 are lexically linked.
[77] Thus, 5:11–19 and 5:20–7:3 are structured according to causation.

persuade the Corinthians into reconciliations: be reconciled to God (5:20-21); do not receive the grace of God in vain (6:1-10); widen your heart (6:11-13); do not be partners with the unbelievers (6:14-7:1); make room for us (7:2-3). Thus, unlike scholars who maintain 7:2 as the beginning of the unit, the structural relationship suggests that 7:2 is a part of five consecutive exhortations in 5:20-7:3.

Therefore, having presented the aforementioned observations, I maintain that 7:3 is the ending of the unit. In addition, a thematic unity regarding the antithesis of life and death within 5:11-7:3, a topical emphasis on speech in 3:12-7:3, and lexical links within 3:1-7:3 indicate that 7:3 functions as a conclusion of 3:11-7:3.

Regarding the subunits within 5:11-7:3, I identify three units: 5:11, 5:12-19, and 5:20-7:3. To begin, three observations suggest that 5:11 is an independent subunit. First, the structural relationship within 5:11-7:3 suggests that 5:11 serves as a general statement for 5:12-7:3, in which Paul introduces the notion of persuasion as the primary concern for his following argument in 5:12-7:3.[78] Thus, Paul moves from a general statement (5:11) to particulars (5:12-7:3). In 5:11, Paul develops three aspects of speech by employing δέ twice as follows:

οὖν   We persuade people,
δέ   We are manifested to God,
δέ   I hope to be manifested in your consciences.

Paul develops three aspects of persuasion: The persuasion of people is at the same time sacrifice to God (see 5.2.2.1) as well as an appeal to the Corinthians' conscience. Then, he moves to explicate the content of this persuasion in the following verses in 5:12-7:3: He begins to persuade the Corinthians regarding the credentials (5:12-19) and the reconciliations (5:20-7:3). Second, the presence of asyndeton may mark the break between 5:11 and 5:12.[79] Third, the textual variant suggests a section break between 5:11 and 5:12. In some manuscripts,[80] scribes inserted γαρ at the beginning of 5:12. Although the external evidence is not strong, this may be another indication that scribes may have understood a break in the flow of Paul's argument; thus, they might have inserted the conjunction to clarify the relationship between 5:11 and 5:12. Thus, I maintain 5:11 as an independent subunit.

Moreover, I contend 5:12-19 and 5:20-7:3 as separate subunits. In fact, the break between 5:19 and 5:20 is not difficult to discern. The conjunction οὖν in 5:20 and a shift of literary form from a discursive text (5:11-19) to a series of exhortations (5:20-7:3) indicate that 5:11-19 and 5:20-7:3 are separate literary units. The conjunction οὖν in 5:20 shows that Paul moves his argument to the next major topic.[81] Indeed, this movement is supported by a shift of a literary form from the description of the gospel

---

[78] Thus, 5:11 and 5:12-7:3 is structured according to particularization.
[79] On asyndeton, see my discussion in 6.1.
[80] E.g., D² K L P 048. 33. 365. 630. 1175. 1241. 1505 𝔐 sa
[81] Some manuscripts, such as 𝔓⁴⁶, D*, F, G, Ψ, and b, omit οὖν in 5:20. However, the conjunction should be retained as it has stronger external evidence (𝔓³⁴, ℵ, B, C, D², K, L, P, 048., 33., 81., 104., 365., 630., 1175., 1241., 1505., 1739., 1881., 2464, 𝔐, vg, and sy). Also see my discussion on οὖν in 6.1.1.

as the ministry of reconciliation (5:11–19), in which God's servants persuade the Corinthians regarding their credentials, to five consecutive exhortations (5:20–7:3). To be more precise, Paul persuades the Corinthians (5:11) to be reconciled to God (5:20–21; 6:1–10) and to himself and his fellow workers (6:11–13; 6:14–7:1; 7:2–3). In the first two exhortations (i.e., reconciliation with God), Paul employs appeal formulas (5:20; 6:1); in the last three appeals (i.e., reconciliation with God's servants), he utilizes imperatives (6:13; 6:14; 7:2).[82] Therefore, 5:11–19 and 5:20–7:3 should be treated as discrete units.

6.1.3 7:4–16

Concerning the segmentation of 7:4–16, I have already demonstrated that 7:4 is the beginning of the unit. In addition, I maintain that 7:16 is the ending of the section, following a majority of scholars who recognize a major break between 7:16 and 8:1.[83] A shift of literary form and topic are especially of significance. First, Paul shifts from a travel narrative and a report from Titus (7:4–16) to exhortations (8:1–9:15).[84] Second, Paul shifts his arguments from the proclamation of the gospel (3:1–7:16) to the collection (8:1–9:15). Therefore, I treat 7:4–16 as a literary unit.[85]

Regarding the subunits within 7:4–16, I propose three units based on conjunctive relations, a shift of topic, and insights from the structural relationship: 7:4, 7:5–12, and 7:13–16. First, I maintain 7:4 is a discrete unit, for it serves as a general statement for 7:4–16.[86] Second, γάρ in 7:5, διὰ τοῦτο in 7:13, and a topical unity suggest that 7:5–12 is a unit. The conjunction γάρ in 7:5 indicates that the material in 7:5–12 provides supports for 7:4. Moreover, διὰ τοῦτο in 7:13 signals that the material in 7:13–16 functions as a conclusion of Paul's argument in 7:4–16.[87] Particularly, in 7:5–12, Paul explains the reasons for his encouragement and joy in affliction.[88] Within 7:5–12, one can demarcate the unit into two subunits: 7:5–7 and 7:8–12.[89] In the former, he

---

[82] One finds three more imperatives in 6:17; however, they are part of the OT allusions, which many scholars think are from Isa 52:11 and Ezek 20:34 (e.g., Peter Balla, "2 Corinthians," in *Commentary on the New Testament Use of the Old Testament*, ed. G. K. Beale and D. A. Carson [Grand Rapids: Baker Academic; Nottingham: Apollos, 2007], 753–84 at 770–71). Also see more discussions regarding the ways in which these exhortations are related in 6.2.1.

[83] Some scholars, however, view 8:1–9:15 as a part of a larger section. For instance, Witherington maintains that 8:1–9:15 belongs to the *probatio* in 3:1–13:4 (*Conflict and Community in Corinth*, 411–28); Long likewise claims that 8:1–9:15 is a part of the *probatio* in 2:1–9:15 (*Ancient Rhetoric and Paul's Apology*, 165, 173–77). Furnish categorizes 5:20–9:15 as appeals (*II Corinthians*, 338–453). Barnett maintains 7:5–9:15 as a major unit based on Paul's location: Paul was in Macedonia when Titus brought news about the Corinthian church (*Second Epistle to the Corinthians*, 364–450). Nonetheless, those scholars still recognize a major break between 7:16 and 8:1.

[84] See more discussions on the nature of 8:1–9:15 as exhortations in 7.2.2.

[85] Regarding the break between 7:16 and 8:1, see more discussion in 7.1.

[86] Therefore, 7:4 and 7:5–16 are structured according to particularization with substantiation.

[87] More precisely, 7:4–12 and 7:13–16 are structured according to summarization. In 7:13–16, Paul recapitulates his arguments by repeating some keywords used in 7:4–12: Titus (7:6, 13, 14), boasting (7:4, 14), encouragement (7:4, 6, 7, 13), and joy/rejoicing (7:4, 7, 9, 13, 16). On the function of διὰ τοῦτο, see my comment in 6.1.2.1.

[88] On the function of γάρ, see my comment in 4.2.1.2.

[89] The conjunction ὅτι in 7:8 signals a break between 7:7 and 7:8, for ὅτι introduces a causal clause to describe the reason for God's encouragement (7:4, 6–7).

describes the occasion in which God encouraged him through the coming of Titus and his report; in the latter, Paul underscores his joy by explaining the justification of the previous letter he sent to the Corinthians in 7:8–12. Thus, Paul was encouraged not only by Titus's arrival (7:4, 6–7) but also by what he learned from Titus's report (7:7), that the Corinthians rightly responded to his previous letter (7:8–12). Third, διὰ τοῦτο in 7:13 marks that Paul shifts his argument to a conclusion. Therefore, Paul's argument in 7:4–16 flows as follows: Paul makes a general statement (7:4) and moves to explain the reasons for his claim in 7:5–12, in which he explains the occasion (7:5–7) and the reason of his encouragement and joy (7:8–12); then, he summarizes his argument (7:13–16). Therefore, I maintain 7:4, 7:5–12, and 7:13–16 as units within 7:4–16.

Having discussed the segmentation of 3:1–7:16, I will turn to the study of the MSRs, for one must scrutinize both segmentation and structural relationships to understand the literary structure.

6.2 Major Structural Relationships in Relation to the Division as a Whole

Having identified main units and subunits of 3:1–7:16, my next task is to demonstrate the ways in which those main units and subunits are related to one another. In this section, I propose two MSRs in relation to the division as a whole: causation with particularization (3:1–11 and 3:12–7:3) and substantiation (3:1–7:3 and 7:4–16). These two MSRs reveal that the main thrust of Paul's discourse in this division pertains to the proclamation of the gospel.

6.2.1 Causation with Particularization (3:1–11 and 3:12–7:3)

I argue that 3:1–11 and 3:12–7:3 are structured according to causation with particularization, which shows that Paul's primary concern of 3:1–7:3 pertains to the proclamation of the gospel. On the one hand, Paul develops his claim (3:1–11) in the following material in 3:12–7:3 (particularization).[90] In 3:1–11, Paul emphasizes the divine origin of the qualifications that God made them adequate as servants of a new covenant, which is characterized by the life-giving Spirit and surpassing glory. In 3:12–7:3, Paul expounds the ways in which God's servants serve in the ministry of the new covenant through the proclamation of the gospel.[91] In doing so, Paul particularizes his claim in 3:1–12 in the following material in 3:12–7:3.

---

[90] More precisely, 3:1–11 and 3:12–7:3 are structured according to ideological particularization. See Bauer and Traina, *Inductive Bible Study*, 100–101.

[91] Also, see the discussion in 6.1.2 regarding the ways in which Paul develops his argument in relation to the proclamation of the gospel in 3:12–7:3. Paul moves from two descriptive speech (3:12–4:12 and 4:13–5:10) to hortatory speech (5:11–7:3). The fact that Paul begins each section with a speech related expression (πολλῇ παρρησίᾳ χρώμεθα in 3:12; ἐπίστευσα, διὸ ἐλάλησα in 4:13; ἀνθρώπους πείθομεν in 5:11) is a clear indication that Paul's primary concern pertains to speech, that is, the proclamation of the gospel. See more details in the following discussion.

On the other hand, the description of the ministry of the new covenant (3:1–11) serves as a basis for the proclamation of the gospel regarding the qualifications and character of the ministry (3:12–7:3). In other words, because God qualified his servants for the glorious ministry of the new covenant, Paul's following discussions in 3:12–7:3 (3:1–4:12; 4:13–5:10; 5:11–7:3) also reflect the character of the new covenant (causation).

First, in 3:12–4:12, because the ministry of the new covenant has the surpassing glory (3:6b–11), the proclamation not only reflects God's glorious and transforming knowledge (3:12–18) but also manifests God's knowledge as the gospel of the glory of Christ (4:4, 6). In 3:12–4:12, Paul particularly focuses on the theocentric character of the proclamation. Paul moves from a general statement (3:12) to a basis (3:12–18) and the content of the character of the proclamation (4:1–12). He begins the unit with a general statement by emphasizing πολλῇ παρρησίᾳ χρώμεθα (3:12). The noun παρρησία was a well-known term in relation to speech, which came to mean frankness, plainness, or courage.[92] Thus, Paul courageously and plainly expounds the character of their proclamation in 3:12–4:12, especially emphasizing the centrality of God and Christ in the proclamation, so Paul proceeds to explicate the ways in which the servants proclaim the gospel in 3:13–4:12.[93] In 3:13–18, Paul describes God's unveiled knowledge through Christ (3:13–18), which becomes a basis for his following discussion in 4:1–12. Paul insists that the servants proclaim God's knowledge according to the ministry of the new covenant; thus, their proclamation is contrasted with Moses's ministry, whose veil remains over people's hearts and hardens people's minds to understand God's knowledge (3:12–15). However, the veil is taken away through Christ; thus, this new revelation of God's knowledge through Christ transforms believers into the image of the glory of the Lord from glory to glory (3:14, 16–18). Then, Paul moves to describe the content of the theocentric character of the proclamation in 4:1–12. Their proclamation is characterized by their integrity before God, for they do not corrupt God's word but rather manifest the truth and commend themselves in the sight of God (4:1–2). In addition, it is characterized by the Christocentric preaching, for they proclaim Christ Jesus as the Lord and themselves as slaves (4:3–6). In addition, it is characterized by the divine paradox, for the proclamation is manifested through the divine power through their weakness so that it will manifest the surpassing greatness of God's power, in which God's servants suffer to manifest Christ's life (4:7–12). Thus, they boldly and clearly articulate the theocentric character of the proclamation in 3:12–4:12.

Second, in 4:13–5:10, because the ministry of the new covenant has the surpassing glory (3:6b–11), God's servants are courageous despite suffering, for they know that their suffering produces the surpassing eternal glory (4:13–5:10). In addition, because

---

[92] BDAG, s.v. "παρρησία"; Heinrich Schlier, "παρρησία, παρρησιάζομαι," *TDNT*, 5:871–86. Thus, many scholars understand the word in light of Paul's courage or boldness (e.g., Furnish, *II Corinthians*, 231; Lambrecht, *Second Corinthians*, 52). However, in the context of 3:12–4:12, the term may also connote the sense of plainness, since Paul expounds God's knowledge as the gospel of Christ (4:4–6). Moreover, he characterizes the proclamation with courage: οὐκ ἐγκακοῦμεν (4:1; cf. 4:16).

[93] Thus, 3:12–4:12 is structured according to particularization.

the new covenant is characterized by the life-giving Spirit (3:3, 6, 8), God has prepared his servants for suffering by giving the Spirit as a down payment (5:5). In this section, Paul particularly describes the attitude of the proclamation: They are courageous despite suffering in their proclamation, by moving from a general statement (4:13–16) to reasons (4:17–5:5) to the basis for the attitude (5:6–10). To begin, quoting from Ps 115:1 LXX (cf. 116:10 MT),[94] Paul begins the section by declaring Ἐπίστευσα, διὸ ἐλάλησα, καὶ ἡμεῖς πιστεύομεν, διὸ καὶ λαλοῦμεν (4:13). The context of Ps 114 and 115 LXX (116 MT) portrays the psalmist's suffering, and Paul incorporates the voice into his response to the new covenant that "he shares the sufferings with the psalmist and also his faith that enables him to speak (to bear witness to Christ) boldly."[95] Furthermore, similar to the way he characterizes his first response with courage, he repeatedly portrays the second response with courage. God's servants are not discouraged: οὐκ ἐγκακοῦμεν (4:16; cf. 4:1); rather, they are always courageous: Θαρροῦντες οὖν πάντοτε (5:6); θαρροῦμεν (5:8). Thus, Paul continues to describe the afflictions and sufferings in the following material in 4:17–5:10. In 4:17–5:5, he proceeds to substantiate the general statement. God's servants are not discouraged (4:16) because (1) affliction produces for them the surpassing glory (4:17–5:4) and (2) God prepared them for the suffering and gave them the Spirit as a down payment (5:5). To be more specific, beginning with the conjunction γάρ,[96] Paul describes the eternal glory in contrast to the temporal affliction in 4:17–18,[97] and then strengthens his claim through the analogy of house in 5:1–4, underscoring the contrast between temporal affliction and eternal life again.[98] Then, he moves to describe another reason for the courageous proclamation despite suffering in 5:5: God prepared us by giving us the Spirit as a down payment.[99] Thus, he concludes the section in 5:6–10, especially emphasizing Christ's eschatological presence (5:6, 8) and judgment (5:10), which serve as the foundation for their suffering. God's servants are not discouraged but rather courageous (4:16; 5:6, 8) despite suffering because they understand their affliction in light of these eschatological perspectives. Thus, they express their courageous attitude toward the proclamation in 4:13–5:10, for they know that suffering produces glory.

Third, because God qualified his agents as servants of the new covenant (3:6a), they persuade the Corinthians (5:11–7:3). In this section, Paul moves from descriptive speeches (3:12–4:12; 4:13–5:10) to hortatory speech,[100] and he develops his persuasion by moving from a general statement (5:11) to basis (5:12–19) and content of persuasion

---

[94] Note the difference between the MT and the LXX regarding their versification. The LXX of Ps 114:1–9 is the MT of Ps 116:1–9 (Balla, "2 Corinthians," 753–84 at 764).

[95] Ibid., 765.

[96] See my discussion of the discourse function of γάρ in 4.2.1.2.

[97] Grammatically speaking, 4:17–18 contains two sentences: 4:17–18a and 4:18b, in which the latter substantiates the former.

[98] Also, note Paul's employment of γάρ in 5:1, which indicates that the discussion in 5:1–4 strengthens the claim in 4:17–18. Thus, one can claim that 4:17–18 and 5:1–4 are structured according to substantiation.

[99] Note that 5:5 begins with δέ, which seems to mark a new development within 4:17–5:5. Namely, in 4:17–5:5, Paul presents two reasons to substantiate the claim made in 4:13–16, and δέ in 5:5 signals a new development because Paul moves from one reason (4:17–5:4) to another (5:5).

[100] Concerning the structural relationship within 3:12–7:3, one can identify a causational relationship between 3:12–5:10 and 5:11–7:3.

(5:20–7:3). In 5:11, Paul begins the section by asserting: ἀνθρώπους πείθομεν (cf. Gal 1:10).[101] He particularly persuades people concerning two matters: their credentials (5:12–19) and reconciliations (5:20–7:3), in which the former (5:12–19) serves as a basis for the latter (5:20–7:3). The love of Christ (5:13–16) is the cause, and God is the source of the ministry of reconciliation (5:17–19).[102] Therefore, Paul proceeds to persuade the Corinthians by giving five exhortations so that they might be reconciled to God (5:20–6:10) and his servants (6:11–7:3). In 5:20–21, God's servants, as ambassadors for Christ, urge the Corinthians to be reconciled to God. In 6:1–10, God's servants urge the Corinthians not to receive God's grace in vain (6:1). The immediate literary context indicates that God's grace is related to the ministry of reconciliation (5:19) and salvation (6:2; cf. Isa 49:8), and the broader context shows that God's grace is related to the proclamation of God's knowledge (2:14; 4:15), that is the gospel of Christ (4:4, 6). Therefore, the reception of God's grace signifies salvation, for it means that they accept the word of reconciliation as the gospel of Christ. In order to bolster the exhortation, Paul further provides proof of his coworkers' and his integrity through a catalog of suffering (6:3–10).

In 6:11–7:3, Paul shifts his exhortations from reconciliation with God (5:20–6:10) to that with his servants (6:11–7:3). Scholars often recognize parallels between 6:11–13 and 7:2–4 regarding Paul's plea for reciprocal affection; they observe that in 7:2–4, Paul resumes his appeal made in 6:11–13.[103] Thus, it does not impose a difficulty to construe Paul's pleas in 6:11–13 and 7:2–4 in relation to the reconciliation with God's servants. However, scholars ceaselessly debate the ways in which 6:14–7:1 is related to 6:11–13 and 7:2–4. Whether they maintain the unity of the letter or not, they at least agree that Paul's exhortations for separation from all defilements and for holiness in 6:14–7:1 differ from the exhortations in 6:11–13 and 7:2–4. Furthermore, interpreters recognize non-Pauline features in 6:14–7:1.[104] Thus, scholars espousing partition theories often conclude that the passage is an interpolation, whereas those maintaining a unity of the letter tend to view it as a digression.[105] However, I contend that Paul's plea in 6:14–7:1

---

[101] The expression is a well-known allusion to the rhetorical practice in Paul's day (Betz, *Galatians*, 54 n.103, citing Plato *Geog.* 452E, 458E, 462C, 453A, 454E; *Prot.* 352E; *Theaet.* 201A; Matt 27:20; 28:14; Acts 12:20; 14:19; 19:26; 18:4).

[102] See my discussion on his credentials in 5:11–19 in 5.2.2.2.

[103] For instance, Lambrecht argues that 6:11–13, 6:14–7:1, and 7:2–4 are chiastically structured as a-b-a'; thus, he observes parallels in 6:11–13 and 7:2–4 ("The Fragment 2 Corinthians 6.14–7,1: A Plea for Its Authenticity," in *Studies on 2 Corinthians*, ed. Reimund Bieringer and Jan Lambrecht, BETL 112 [Leuven: Leuven University Press; Uitgeverij Peeters, 1994], 531–49 especially at 535). See also Matera, *II Corinthians*, 157–59; Harris, *Second Epistle to the Corinthians*, 486.

[104] Scholars have identified a number of elements that suggest non-Pauline features, which include the lack of specific connections with the issues related to the Corinthian church; a large volume of hapax legomena for the NT (ἑτεροζυγέω; συμφώνησις; συγκατάθεσις; Βελιάρ; ἐτοχή; μολυσμός); employment of some Pauline terms (δικαιοσύνη; πιστός; σάρξ; πνεῦμα) in non-Pauline senses; unique phrases in Pauline literature (καθαρίσωμεν ἑαυτοὺς ἀπὸ παντὸς μολυσμοῦ σαρκὸς καὶ πνεύματος; ἐπιτελοῦντες ἁγιωσύνην); unique citation formulas; strong similarities between 6:14–7:1 and expressions and theology found in Qumran literature; incongruity between the exhortation in 6:14–7:1 and Paul's teaching on Christian freedom elsewhere (e.g., 1 Cor 5:10). On the overview of the debate, see Harris, *Second Epistle to the Corinthians*, 14–25).

[105] See Thrall, *Second Epistle of the Corinthians*, 1:26–36; Furnish, *II Corinthians*, 371–83; Witherington, *Conflict and Community in Corinth*, 402–406.

is congruous with both his immediate and larger discourse in the letter. Regarding the immediate context, as some interpreters have already noted, Paul's call for separation from unbelievers is an integral part of the exhortation for reconciliation,[106] for the separation is a prerequisite for the reconciliation. Moreover, others also show that Paul carefully selects the allusions to the OT contexts in 6:16–18, for they come "from similar contexts of warning against combining the worship and service of God with that given to other gods."[107] Thus, Paul's plea for separation is an essential part of the exhortation for reconciliation.

Furthermore, the broader literary context helps one understand the thrust of Paul's argument in 6:14–7:1, especially in relation to the purpose of reconciliation in three ways: God's servants and the Corinthians should be partners in ministry. To begin, as Paul characterizes ministry with partnership in 1:3–2:13, he revisits the notion in 6:14–7:1. As I have already discussed in 4.2.2.1, 1:3–2:13 and 2:14–13:10 are structured according to causation with particularization: Paul has developed the theme of mutuality and partnership in 1:3–2:13 and continues to develop it in 2:14–13:10. Since God's agents and the Corinthians are partners (κοινωνός) in suffering and encouragement (1:7), the Corinthians should not have partnership (κοινωνία) with unbelievers (6:14). Rather, Paul urges the Corinthians to be reconciled to his servants that they can be partners in their ministry. In fact, closely related to the theme of partnership, Paul has underscored the mutual character of ministry in 1:3–2:13. Just as Christ, Paul, his fellow workers, and the Corinthians mutually share suffering and divine encouragement (1:3–7), the Corinthians are co-participants in ministry (1:11), sharers of boasting (1:14), coworkers of joy (1:24), sharers of joy (2:3), love (2:4, 8), sorrow (2:5), and forgiveness (2:7, 10). Thus, Paul urges the Corinthians to be reconciled with God first (5:20–6:10) and then with his servants (6:11–7:3), so that the Corinthians may mutually share the ministry and become partners in the ministry.

In addition, Paul expects his ministry partners (i.e., the Corinthians) to pursue holiness (7:1) and for their ministry to be a pleasing sacrifice to God, which is how Paul views the ministry (see 5.2.2.1). Thus, Paul urges the Corinthians not only to separate themselves (6:14; 7:1) from unbelievers and all the defilement, but also to be the temple of the living God in which sacrifice to God takes place (6:16), and to perfect holiness (7:1). Because the purpose of reconciliation is to become partners in ministry, Paul expects the Corinthians to be holy so that their ministry will also be a pleasing sacrifice to God.

Finally, Paul's exhortations in 6:14–7:1 both encourage the Corinthians to be reconciled with God's servants and prepare them to participate in the collection as their ministry partners (8:1–9:15). Here, one finds Paul's skillful crafting of the structure of his arguments in 5:20–7:3 in light of his broader discourse. His exhortations for reconciliation in 5:20–7:3 not only stem from his arguments pertaining to the

---

[106] Hafemann, *2 Corinthians*, 278; Matera, *II Corinthians*, 160; Guthrie, *2 Corinthians*, 346.
[107] John W. Olley, "A Precursor of the NRSV? 'Sons and Daughters' in 2 Cor 6.18," *NTS* 44 (1998): 204–12 at 204; Garland, *2 Corinthians*, 336–41. These OT allusions include Lev 26:11–12 in 6:16b, Isa 52:11 and Ezek 20:34 in 6:17, and 2 Sam 7:14 and Deut 32:18–19 in 3:18. Also see Guthrie, *2 Corinthians*, 346–61.

proclamation of the gospel (3:1–5:19, especially 5:11–19), but also prepare the Corinthians for the next major argument in 8:1–9:15. Particularly, in 6:14–7:1, Paul stresses that the Corinthians should not have partnership (κοινωνία) with unbelievers (6:14) because they should rather be partners in the ministry to the saints (8:1–9:15). In fact, Paul calls the Corinthians' fiscal contribution κοινωνία in 9:13 (cf. κοινωνία in 8:4; κοινωνός in 8:23). Thus, Paul's plea for separation and holiness in 6:14–7:1 is consistent with both the immediate (5:20–7:3) and the broader literary context of the letter.

Therefore, in 3:1–7:3, Paul develops the ways in which God's servants participate in the ministry of the new covenant through the proclamation of the gospel (particularization) based on the description of the ministry of the new covenant (3:1–11; causation).

6.2.2 Substantiation (3:1–7:3 and 7:4–16)

Concerning the relationship between 3:1–7:3 and 7:4–16, I propose that they are structured according to substantiation. Namely, the description of outcomes of Paul's proclamation through the previous letter to the Corinthians in 7:4–16 strengthens Paul's discussion regarding the proclamation of the gospel in 3:1–7:3 in two manners. First, by describing the ways in which his previous letter ministered to the Corinthians and how the Corinthians responded to it, Paul provides an actual example of his ministry and its results (see also 4.2.1.4). In other words, Paul strengthens his arguments regarding the proclamation of the gospel (3:1–7:3) by grounding it in the history of his ministry to the Corinthians.

Second, Paul's discussion in 7:4–16 particularly strengthens the exhortations made in 5:20–7:3 by showing the results of an appropriate response to the ministry. To begin, Paul does not view the proclamation of the gospel (3:1–7:3) and the ministry through the previous letter (7:4–16) as separate entities. Instead, he portrays both as the proclamation of the gospel. As I have already demonstrated in Chapter 5 that 2:14–17 and 3:1–13:10 are structured according to particularization with contrast, we can say that Paul's discussion in 7:4–16 reflects some aspects of the thesis statement of the letter: sacrificial overtones (see 5.2.2.1) and death and life as the outcome of the manifestation of God's knowledge (see 5.2.2.2). Moreover, his discussion in 7:4–16 adds descriptions to the outcome of the proclamation of the gospel. Paul explains that an appropriate response to the proclamation results in boasting, encouragement, and joy.[108] Because the Corinthians responded to Paul's proclamation through the previous letter with sorrow and repentance that lead to salvation (7:8–10), Paul has boasting, encouragement, and joy (7:4, 13–16). In this way, Paul implicitly encourages the Corinthians to respond to the exhortations in 5:20–7:3, for history shows that positive outcomes are waiting when they respond to his exhortations.

Therefore, Paul's argument in 7:4–16 strengthens his discourse in 3:1–7:3 by (1) appealing to the history of ministry to the Corinthians and (2) showing not only that

---

[108] See also my discussion on χαρά and χαίρω in 3.2.1 and 3.2.2; encouragement in 4.2.2.2; boasting in 4.2.2.3.

Paul's previous letter is a form of proclamation of the gospel but also that the Corinthians' response to the proclamation in the past anticipates the positive outcomes when they respond to his exhortations in 5:20–7:3.

6.3 Conclusion

In this chapter, I scrutinized the literary structure of 3:1–7:16. First, I argued that 3:1–7:16 is the third major division of the letter and identified its main units and subunits. Second, I have demonstrated two MSRs in relation to the division as a whole. I have contended that 3:1–11 and 3:12–7:3 are structured according to causation with particularization. The description of the ministry of the new covenant in 3:1–11 functions as both a general statement and a basis for the ministry of the proclamation in 3:12–7:3. On the one hand, Paul makes a general statement in 3:1–11 regarding the ways in which God qualified him and his fellow workers as servants of the new covenant, and in 3:12–7:3 he develops the general statement, expounding the ways in which the qualified servants serve in the ministry of the new covenant through their proclamation of the gospel. The ministry of the new covenant is to articulate the theocentric character of the proclamation (3:12–4:12), to explain their attitude toward the proclamation (4:13–5:10), and to persuade the Corinthians of the gospel of the reconciliation (5:11–7:2). On the other hand, Paul frames his discussion in 3:12–7:3 regarding a causational relationship with 3:1–11. Because the ministry of the new covenant has the surpassing glory (3:6b–11), the proclamation of the gospel reflects God's glorious transforming knowledge (3:12–18); God's servants manifest God's knowledge as the gospel of the glory of Christ (4:4, 6); and their suffering in the proclamation produces the surpassing glory (4:13–5:10). Moreover, because the new covenant is characterized by the life-giving Spirit (3:3, 6, 8), God has prepared his servants for suffering by giving the Spirit as a down payment (5:5). In addition, because God qualified his servants for the new covenant (3:6a), they persuade the Corinthians (5:11–7:3).

I have also demonstrated that 3:1–7:3 and 7:4–16 are structured according to substantiation. Paul's discussion regarding his previous ministry to the Corinthians through the letter reinforces Paul's argument in 3:1–7:3 by grounding it in the history of his proclamation to the Corinthians and showing the positive outcomes of appropriate response to the proclamation of the gospel.

Having summarized the findings, one theological implication regarding the title of Paul's discourse in 3:1–7:3 needs to be drawn. I designate his discourse as "Arguments Pertaining to Content of Ministry," for as Paul underscores that God's agents disseminate God's knowledge through speech (2:14–17), he explicates the ways in which they speak God's word in 3:1–7:16. Furthermore, I call his discourse in 3:1–7:16 "Proclamation of the Gospel," for the MSRs have shown that Paul's primary concern in his argument in 3:1–7:16 pertains to the proclamation of the gospel, by

1. showing the movement from basis (3:1–11) to cause (3:12–7:3) and the movement from general (3:1–11) to particulars (3:11–7:3);

2. spending a significant amount of space to expound their ministry of speech (3:11–7:3); and
3. reinforcing his argument through the description of the outcomes of Paul's proclamation to the Corinthians (7:4–16).

Having scrutinized the literary structure of 3:1–7:16, I now turn to the analysis of 8:1–9:15.

7

Arguments Pertaining to Content of Ministry: Response to the Gospel (8:1–9:15)

In Chapter 6, I analyzed the segmentation of 3:1–7:16 and expounded MSRs in relation to the division as a whole, which reveal that the chief concern of Paul's discourse in 3:1–7:16 pertains to the proclamation of the gospel. In this chapter, I continue to analyze the literary structure of 8:1–9:15. I first scrutinize the segmentation of the division and then explicate the MSRs in relation both to the division as a whole and the letter as a whole. These MSRs reveal that (1) Paul's discussion in 8:1–9:15 is essentially hortatory, and (2) Paul invites the Corinthians to respond to the proclamation of the gospel (3:1–7:16) by participating in the collection (8:1–9:15).

7.1 Division of 8:1–9:15

Regarding the segmentation of 8:1–9:15, I contend its main units and subunits as follows:

A. Model for the Ministry to the Saints: Testimony of Macedonian Churches (8:1–6)
 1. God's Grace Given in the Macedonian Churches (8:1–2)
 2. The Macedonians' Response to God's Grace: Participation in the Collection (8:3–6)
  a) Manners of Their Participation (8:3–5)
  b) Result of Their Participation (8:6)
B. Exhortations: Abound in Grace and Complete Collection (8:7–15)
 1. Exhortation 1: Abound in Grace (8:7–9)
  a) Exhortation: Abound in Grace (8:7)
  b) Nature of the Exhortation: Not as a Command but as a Test of the Corinthians' Sincerity (8:8)
  c) Basis for the Exhortation: Christ's Example of Abounding Grace (8:9)
 2. Exhortation 2: Complete the Collection (8:10–15)
  a) Exhortation: Complete the Collection (8:10–11)
  b) Manner of the Collection: According to What They Have (8:12)
  c) Purpose of the Collection: Equality (8:13–15)

C. Descriptions of Collection Workers (8:16–9:5)
  1. Workers (8:16–24)
     a) Titus (8:16–17)
     b) Brother A (8:18–21)
     c) Brother B (8:22)
     d) Exhortation Regarding Workers (8:23–24)
  2. Rationale for Sending Workers (9:1–5)
     a) Introduction: Unnecessary Reminder by Acknowledgement of the Corinthians' Willingness (9:1–2)
     b) Purposes of Sending Brethren: Protection of Boasting and the Corinthians' Readiness (9:3–4)
     c) Conclusion: Necessary Reminder (9:5)
D. Theological Reasons for the Exhortations and Anticipated Outcomes of the Fulfillment of the Exhortations (9:6–15)
  1. Theological Reasons for the Exhortations (9:6–11a)
     a) God's Love for Cheerful Giver (9:6–7)
     b) God's Abundance of All Grace to the Corinthians (9:8–9)
     c) God's Provision and Enrichment for the Corinthians (9:10–11a)
  2. Anticipated Outcomes of the Fulfillment of the Exhortations (9:11b–14)
     a) Supply of the Need and Thanksgiving to God (9:11b–12)
     b) Glory to God (9:13)
     c) Longing for the Corinthians (9:14)
  3. Concluding Thanksgiving (9:15)

Concerning the beginning and ending of the division, I agree with the majority of scholars who recognize 8:1–9:15 as a literary unit.[1] Concerning the beginning of the division, I have already noted in Chapter 6 (6.1.4) that a shift of literary form from a travel narrative (7:4–16) to exhortations (8:1–9:15), and that of the topic from the proclamation of the gospel (3:1–7:16) to the collection (8:1–9:15), mark a unit boundary between 7:16 and 8:1. Moreover, I will add three more pieces of evidence, which bolster my claim that 8:1 begins a new literary unit: the presence of δέ, vocative address, and disclosure formula. First, a new development in Paul's discourse is marked by the conjunction δέ.[2] Second, Paul's vocative address, ἀδελφοί, in 8:1, also signals a shift in Paul's discourse.[3] Third, the presence of the disclosure formula in 8:1 indicates a major transition in Paul's argument.[4] While the disclosure formula generally denotes

---

[1] See my note on other scholars who propose different segmentations in 6.1.4.
[2] While δέ frequently signals a new development in Paul's discourse, one should note that δέ does not always mark a new development. For instance, δέ in 9:3 rather marks a contrast between Paul's statement between 9:1–2 and 9:3–4 within his argument in 9:1–5. Also see my comment on δέ in 4.1.1.
[3] See my comment on the vocative address in 3.1.
[4] Stanley E. Porter and Andrew W. Pitts define the formula, "The disclosure formula expresses the author's desire for the audience to know something, commands the audience to know something, or informs the audience of something in support of a statement or argument" (Porter and Pitts, "Disclosure Formula," 421–38 at 427); the definition is also cited by Weima, *Paul the Ancient Letter Writer*, 95.

a transition, it also signifies "major transitions *within* the body of the letter."[5] In fact, as noted, Paul transitions to another main aspect of the ministry in 8:1–9:15: response to the gospel.

Concerning the ending of the division, a shift of topic between 9:15 and 10:1 has been widely recognized. Moreover, I will provide four more pieces of evidence that further strengthen the observation: thanksgiving in 9:15, the MSR of *inclusio* (8:1 and 9:15), the presence of δέ in 10:1, and the appeal formula in 10:1.

First, thanksgiving in 9:15 sometimes signals a conclusion of a section (cf. Rom 7:25; 1 Cor 15:57).[6] Second, 8:1–9:15 is structured according to *inclusio* with χάρις and δίδωμι/δωρεά (8:1 and 9:15), which suggests that 8:1–9:15 forms a literary unit.7Third, a new development in Paul's discourse is signaled by δέ in 10:1.[8] Fourth, as Weima explains, "The primary function of the appeal formula is to signal a major transition in the text ... as more typically happens, a transition within the body of the letter,"[9] the appeal formula in 10:1 indicates a major transition in Paul's discourse. Therefore, following the majority of scholars, I maintain 8:1–9:15 as one of the major divisions in the letter. Having identified the beginning and ending of the division, I will turn to the main units and subunits within 8:1–9:15. I contend that 8:1–9:15 consists of four main units: 8:1–6, 8:7–15, 8:16–9:5, and 9:6–15.

7.1.1 8:1–6

Many scholars identify 8:1–15 or 8:1–24 as the first major unit of 8:1–9:15,[10] within which most treat 8:1–5/6/7 as a subunit.[11] However, five observations suggest that 8:1–6 is the first main unit: rhetorical disposition, grammar, a shift of a topic and literary form between 8:1–6 and 8:7–15, the presence of the conjunction ἀλλά in 8:7, and the insight from the MSR of comparative causation.

First, scholars employing rhetorical criticism frequently recognize 8:1–5/6 as a distinct literary unit in Paul's discourse in chs 8–9.[12] Second, grammar shows that 8:1–

---

[5] Ibid., 96 (italics original).
[6] Peter T. O'Brien, "Thanksgiving within the Structure of Pauline Theology," in *Pauline Studies: Essays Presented to Professor F. F. Bruce on His 70th Birthday*, ed. Donald Alfred Hagner and Murray J. Harris (Exeter: Paternoster; Grand Rapids: Eerdmans, 1980), 50–66 at 61.
[7] See more discussion on *inclusio* in 7.2.1.1.
[8] See note above and my comment on δέ in 4.1.1.
[9] Weima, *Paul the Ancient Letter Writer*, 93.
[10] E.g., those espousing 8:1–24 as a literary unit include Barrett, *Second Epistle to the Corinthians*, 216–31; Lambrecht, *Second Corinthians*, 135–44; Thrall, *Second Epistle of the Corinthians*, 2:520–62; Seifrid, *Second Letter to the Corinthians*, 317–47. Those treating 8:1–15 as a literary unit include Furnish, *II Corinthians*, 398–420; Garland, *2 Corinthians*, 363–90; Hafemann, *2 Corinthians*, 328–57; Harris, *Second Epistle to the Corinthians*, 554–94; Guthrie, *2 Corinthians*, 389–418.
[11] E.g., Matera (*II Corinthians*, 184–88), Martin (*2 Corinthians*, 428–36), and Land (*Integrity of 2 Corinthians*, 178–79) recognize 8:1–6 as a main unit within 8:1–9:15.
[12] Kennedy analyzes 8:1–6 as *narratio* (*Rhetorical Criticism*, 91); Betz identifies 8:1–5 as *exordium* (and 8:6 as *narratio*), especially emphasizing the genre called *exemplum* (*2 Corinthians 8 and 9*, 41–56); McCant likewise argues 8:1–5 as an *exemplum* (*2 Corinthians*, 78–81); Kieran J. O'Mahony maintains 8:1–6 as *exordium* (*Pauline Persuasion: A Sounding in 2 Corinthians 8-9*, JSNTSup 199 [Sheffield: Sheffield Academic, 2000], 165); Long judges 8:1–6 as *narratio* (*Ancient Rhetoric and Paul's Apology*, 176).

6 forms a syntactically single sentence, suggesting that this constitutes a literary unit.[13] Third, a shift of a topic and literary form takes place between 8:1-6 and 8:7-15. In 8:1-6, Paul describes God's grace given in the Macedonian churches (i.e., their participation in the collection; 8:1-5) and its result (8:6),[14] and in 8:7-15, he moves to exhortations toward the Corinthians.[15] The movement from a description (8:1-6) to exhortations (8:7-15) signals a unit boundary between 8:6 and 8:7. Fourth, the presence of the conjunction ἀλλά adds another piece of evidence that 8:1-6 is a literary unit. Paul begins 8:7 with ἀλλά, and scholars debate the function of the conjunction.[16] However, the flow of the literary context seems to indicate that Paul contrasts the sending of Titus (8:6) with his exhortation to abound in grace (8:7).[17] In other words, as a result of the Macedonians' participation in the collection (8:1-5), Paul and his fellow workers sent Titus to complete the collection among the Corinthians (8:6). However, Paul emphasizes that the Corinthians should finish the collection not because of their sending of Titus, but by their own abundance (8:7). This contrast between the sending of Titus (8:6) and the exhortation (8:7) suggests a unit boundary between 8:6 and 8:7. Fifth, the structural relationship of comparative causation (8:1-6 and 8:7-15) implies that 8:1-6 is a unit. Paul grounds his exhortations (8:7-15) in the Macedonians' positive example of participation in the collection (8:1-6). Thus, he motivates Corinthians with the testimony of the Macedonian churches (cause) and exhorts the Corinthians to participate in the ministry to the saints (effect) in the same way the Macedonians did (comparison). Hence, the structural relationship suggests the presence of a section boundary between 8:1-6 and 8:7-15. Therefore, I maintain 8:1-6 as the first main unit within 8:1-9:15.

Regarding the subunits of 8:1-6, I demarcate the unit into 8:1-2 and 8:3-6. To begin, topical unity and syntax indicate 8:1-2 as a unit. On the one hand, the topic of God's grace manifested in the Macedonians unifies 8:1-2 as a unit. Additionally, 8:1 and 2 are syntactically connected: Paul substantiates his claim made in 8:1 by an epexegetical clause introduced by ὅτι in 8:2. Moreover, the presence of the causal conjunction ὅτι in 8:3 further supports a unit boundary between 8:2 and 8:3. Thus, 8:1-2 forms a unit. In addition, 8:3-6 is a syntactically unified causal clause, which substantiates Paul's testimony regarding the Macedonians' response to God's grace (i.e., the participation in the collection; 8:1-2). For this reason, I maintain 8:1-2 and 8:3-6 as subunits.

---

[13] However, while Matera agrees to view 8:1-6 as a unit, he also acknowledges a problem of the segmentation. Nestle-Aland's *Novum Testament Graece* treats 8:1-6 as a unit, whereas UBS' *Greek New Testament* identifies 8:1-7 as a unit (*II Corinthians*, 185 n7; cf. Barnett, *Second Epistle to the Corinthians*, 389-404). Also, SBL's *Greek New Testament* includes 8:7 as a part of 8:1-6. This study follows Nestle-Aland's segmentation, for the conjunction ἀλλά in 8:7 seems to begin a new sentence when one considers a shift of topical and literary form between 8:1-6 and 8:7-15. See my discussion below.

[14] Some scholars argue that the εἰς τό + infinitive construction in 8:6 functions as a purpose clause (e.g., Long, *2 Corinthians*, 148); I maintain it as a result clause (so Robertson, *Grammar*, 1072).

[15] See more discussions regarding the nature of 8:7-15 in 7.1.2 and 7.2.

[16] Some postulate that ἀλλά indicates a contrast between what God enabled the Macedonians and the Corinthians to do (Plummer, *Second Epistle*, 237-38); others think that 8:7 is a transitional verse (Leitzmann, *Korinther I-II*, 134). Also see Harris, *Second Epistle to the Corinthians*, 574.

[17] On imperative substantival ἵνα clause in 8:7, see my discussion in 7.1.2.

7.1.2 8:7-15

Most scholars recognize that 8:15 marks the ending of a unit, for Paul begins to describe his emissaries for the collection in 8:16, which is also marked by a shift of literary form (i.e., thanksgiving in 8:16) and a new development marker δέ.[18] Nevertheless, they differ with one another on the identification of the unit's beginning. In this study, I argue that 8:7 begins a new unit; thus, 8:7-15 forms the second main unit within 8:1-9:15. I have already discussed in 7.1.1 that a shift of a topic and literary form between 8:1-6 and 8:7-15, the presence of the conjunction ἀλλά in 8:7, and the insight from the structural relationship of comparative causation suggest a unit boundary between 8:6 and 8:7. In addition to the aforementioned observations, I will further explicate that the literary form of 8:7-15 is hortatory in nature; hence, 8:7-15 forms an independent literary unit. Namely, (1) 8:7-15 consists of two exhortations (8:7, 11), and (2) the rest of the verses syntactically and semantically revolve around them.

To begin, I construe the ἵνα clause in 8:7b (ἵνα καὶ ἐν ταύτῃ τῇ χάριτι περισσεύητε) as an imperative. Harris provides a helpful taxonomy regarding the interpretive options.[19] First, some provide a certain verb to understand the ἵνα clause, such as βλέπετε,[20] παρακαλῶ,[21] θέλομεν,[22] or αἰτοῦμαι.[23] Second, some understand the ἵνα clause as a wish.[24] Third, most grammarians construe the ἵνα clause as a command.[25] I contend that the third option is the best option based on the flow of Paul's argument and his use of ὥσπερ construction elsewhere (Rom 6:19; 1 Cor 16:1). In 8:7 Paul employs περισσεύω twice and moves from the indicative (ὥσπερ . . . περισσεύετε) to the command (ἵνα . . . περισσεύητε).[26] Paul constructs this movement with the comparative conjunction ὥσπερ. In Rom 6:19 and 1 Cor 16:1, Paul employs a similar construction. In Rom 6:19, he moves from ὥσπερ + indicative to οὕτως + imperative by using the same verb παριστάνω: ὥσπερ γὰρ παρεστήσατε τὰ μέλη ὑμῶν δοῦλα τῇ ἀκαθαρσίᾳ καὶ τῇ ἀνομίᾳ εἰς τὴν ἀνομίαν, οὕτως νῦν παραστήσατε τὰ μέλη ὑμῶν δοῦλα τῇ δικαιοσύνῃ εἰς ἁγιασμόν. In 1 Cor 16:1, he similarly constructs his command, moving from ὥσπερ + indicative to οὕτως + imperative: ὥσπερ διέταξα ταῖς ἐκκλησίαις τῆς Γαλατίας, οὕτως καὶ ὑμεῖς ποιήσατε. In 8:7, it seems that Paul substitutes οὕτως with ἵνα.[27] Thus, interpreting the ἵνα clause as a command seems most likely. However, even if one insists on other interpretive possibilities, my point still stands: The ἵνα clause in 8:7b is hortatory in nature. Furthermore, Paul explicates the first exhortation (8:7b) in the second exhortation with an imperative verb (8:11): τὸ ποιῆσαι ἐπιτελέσατε.

---

[18] See my discussion on δέ in 4.1.1.
[19] Harris, *Second Epistle to the Corinthians*, 575.
[20] E.g., Barrett, *Second Epistle to the Corinthians*, 216.
[21] E.g., Plummer, *Second Epistle*, 238; Long, *2 Corinthians*, 151.
[22] E.g., Verlyn D. Verbrugge, *Paul's Style of Church Leadership Illustrated by His Instructions to the Corinthians on the Collection* (San Francisco: Mellen, 1992), 247–51; Wallace, *Greek Grammar*, 477 n82; Long *2 Corinthians*, 151.
[23] *Twentieth Century New Testament*.
[24] E.g., Lambrecht, *Second Corinthians*, 135.
[25] E.g., BDF §387(2); Robertson, *Grammar*, 994; Wallace, *Greek Grammar*, 477.
[26] So Harris, *Second Epistle to the Corinthians*, 575.
[27] So BDAG, s.v. "ὥσπερ."

In other words, Paul clarifies that to abound in the grace (8:7b) is to complete the collection (8:11).

In addition, other verses in 8:7-15 syntactically and semantically revolve around these two exhortations. First, Paul elaborates the first exhortation (8:7b) by a comparison (8:7a) and explanations regarding nature (8:8a), purpose (8:8b), and basis (8:9) of the first exhortation. The ὥσπερ clause in 8:7a syntactically depends on 8:7b, in which Paul utilizes a comparison between what the Corinthians abound in (8:7a) and what they should abound in (8:7b). Then, Paul underscores that the nature of the exhortation is not a command (8:8a) and describes that the purpose of the appeal is to test their sincerity of love (8:8b). Finally, he provides the grace of Jesus Christ as the ultimate example for the first exhortation with the conjunction γάρ (8:9; cf. Macedonians' abundance of grace in 8:1-5).[28] Thus, Paul's argument in 8:7-9 revolves around the exhortation in 8:7b. Second, his discourse in 8:10-15 likewise syntactically and semantically revolves around the second exhortation (8:11). Paul utilizes a comparison (8:10) and explains the means (8:12) and purpose (8:13-15) of the second plea. Paul frames his exhortation (8:11) with a comparison between what the Corinthians did last year (8:10) and what they should do now (8:11).[29] Then, he substantiates the exhortation (γάρ in 8:12 and 8:13) by explaining that their manner of giving should be according to what they have (8:12) and by emphasizing that the purpose of their participation in the collection is equality (8:13-15).

Therefore, I conclude that the literary form of 8:7-15 is an exhortation, for Paul's discourse in 8:7-15 centers on the two exhortations in 8:7b and 11. This observation further reinforces other pieces of evidence that suggest 8:7-15 as a literary unit. In addition, I identify 8:7-9 and 8:10-15 as subunits within 8:7-15 because of the observations already described.

7.1.3 8:16-9:5

Many exegetes insist that 8:16 marks a new literary unit. In fact, as I have mentioned, a shift of literary form from exhortations (8:7-15) to a thanksgiving (8:16), a shift of topic from the appeal for the abundance of grace and the completion of the collection (8:7-15) to the descriptions of his emissaries (8:16-9:15), and the conjunction δέ in 8:16 suggests that 8:16 begins a new literary unit. However, they disagree with one another on the identification of the unit ending. Some identify 8:24 as the ending,[30] and the others maintain the unit extends to 9:5.[31] In this study, I contend that 8:16-9:5 is a

---

[28] On the discourse function of γάρ, see my discussion in 4.2.1.2.

[29] Paul's use of δέ corresponds to the comparison between the past and present in 8:10-11. Building on the past (8:10), Paul moves to a new development in his discourse (i.e., the second exhortation) in 8:11. See my discussion on δέ in 4.1.1.

[30] E.g., Barrett, *Second Epistle to the Corinthians*, 216-31; Betz, *2 Corinthians 8 and 9*, 37-86; Scott, *2 Corinthians*, 181-84; Lambrecht, *Second Corinthians*, 135-36; McCant, *2 Corinthians*, 86-89; Land, *Integrity of 2 Corinthians*, 186-87; Thrall, *Second Epistle of the Corinthians*, 2:520-62; Seifrid, *Second Letter to the Corinthians*, 317-47. Because of the identification of the ending, it is not a surprise that some, such as Betz and Thrall, view ch. 8 and ch. 9 as separate letters.

[31] E.g., Plummer, *Second Epistle*, 246-56; Furnish, *II Corinthians*, 420-39; Garland, *2 Corinthians*, 390-404; Harris, *Second Epistle to the Corinthians*, 594-630; Guthrie, *2 Corinthians*, 418-44.

literary unit. In order to demonstrate my case, I first present a few pieces of evidence suggesting that 9:5 is the ending of a unit, and then I will discuss the subunits of 8:16–9:5 (8:16–24 and 9:1–5). Finally, I will show the ways in which 8:16–24 and 9:1–5 are related.[32]

To begin, a shift of topic and literary form between 8:16–9:5 and 9:6–15, the presence of the conjunction οὖν in 9:5 and ; P in 9:6, and the demonstrative pronoun οὗτος in 9:6 indicate that 9:5 marks the ending of the unit. First, Paul shifts his discussion from the descriptions of the collection workers (8:15–9:5) to theological reasons for the exhortations and anticipated outcomes of the fulfillment of the exhortations (i.e., the completion of the collection; 9:6–15). The topical shift is further marked by Paul's employment of an agricultural analogy that begins in 9:6. Second, the conjunction οὖν in 9:5 signals the ending of the unit (cf. 5:6).[33] Third, the presence of δέ in 9:6 suggests that Paul proceeds to a new development in his discourse, which suggests a unit break between 9:5 and 9:6. Fourth, the demonstrative pronoun οὗτος in 9:6 functions as a forward-pointing device, marking a break between 9:5 and 9:6.[34] Thus, these observations demonstrate that 9:5 is the ending of the unit.

Regarding the subunits within 8:16–9:5, I demarcate the main unit into two subunits: 8:16–24 and 9:1–5. On the one hand, a shift of topic between 8:16–24 and 9:1–5, the presence of περί and γάρ in 9:1, the conjunction οὖν in 8:24, and the insight from the structural relationships within 8:16–9:5 (generalization and causation) suggest that 8:16–24 is a unit. First, Paul shifts his discussion from the descriptions of the collection workers (8:16–24) to the reasons for sending them (9:1–5). Second, the presence of περί and γάρ in 9:1 strengthens the topical transition. The preposition περί + genitive shows a topical transition.[35] In addition, the conjunction γάρ signals that Paul's discourse transitions to substantiate his claim in 8:16–24.[36] Third, the conjunction οὖν in 8:24 marks the ending of the unit. While I have already discussed that οὖν can mark the beginning of a unit,[37] the same conjunction can also introduce a conclusion. Runge explains, "In the NT Epistles, it [οὖν] is regularly translated as 'therefore' to indicate that what follows the particle is either inferentially drawn or concluded from what precedes, hence + continuity."[38] In the case of 8:24, οὖν concludes the preceding material in 8:16–23.[39] Fourth, the structural relationships of generalization (8:16–22 and 8:23) and causation (8:16–23 and 8:24) suggest that 8:16–24 is a unit. After Paul describes his emissaries in 8:16–22, Paul concludes the description with a general statement concerning them in 8:23: Titus is Paul's partner and fellow worker; the

---

[32] Usually, I discuss the interrelationships between units in the second half of a chapter (i.e., under the Major Structural Relationships). However, it is necessary to deal with the relationship between 8:16–9:5 here.
[33] See my discussion on οὖν in 6.1.1.
[34] See my discussion on the discourse function of forward-pointing devices in 4.2.1.2. Also see Long, *2 Corinthians*, 173.
[35] On the function of περί, see BDAG, s.v. "περί" (1h); Wallace, *Greek Grammar*, 379.
[36] See the discourse function of γάρ in my discussion in 4.2.1.2.
[37] See my discussion on οὖν in 6.1.1.
[38] Runge, *Discourse Grammar*, 44.
[39] Also, see οὖν functioning in the same way in 5:16 and 9:5.

brethren are apostles of the churches, a glory of Christ.[40] In addition, the description of the workers (8:16-23) leads to the concluding exhortation in 8:24: to show them the proof of love and boasting.[41] These structural relationships suggest that Paul's final statement (8:23) and exhortation (8:24) conclude his discussion in 8:16-24.

On the other hand, in addition to the aforementioned evidence that marks 9:1 as the beginning and 9:5 as the ending of the unit, I further argue that 9:1-5 forms a syntactically and semantically unified unit. Paul begins 9:1 with μέν (9:1) ... δέ (9:3) construction. The acknowledgment of the Corinthians' willingness to participate in the collection (9:1-2) anticipates a corresponding sentence introduced by δέ in 9:3-4.[42] Then, in 9:5, Paul recapitulates what he describes in 9:1-4 by employing οὖν to signal the conclusion of the unit; thus, 9:1-5 forms a syntactically and semantically unified unit.[43]

Finally, the conjunctive relations and a topical connection between 8:16-24 and 9:1-5 suggest that they belong to the same unit. First of all, the discourse function of γάρ in 9:1 indicates that Paul's discussion in 9:1-5 substantiates or reinforces the previous argument in 8:16-24,[44] yet the more pressing question is how Paul's discussion in 9:1-5 substantiates the discussion in 8:16-24. The flow of the literary context in 9:1-5 shows that Paul's primary concern in 9:1-5 pertains to his explanations regarding the purpose for his sending of brothers. The μέν (9:1) ... δέ (9:3) construction is particularly of help to understand the thrust of the argument in 9:1-5. Levinsohn explains the discourse function of the construction as follows: "The presence of μέν not only anticipates a corresponding sentence containing δέ but frequently, in narrative, it also downgrades the importance of the sentence containing μέν. In particular, the information introduced with μέν is often a secondary importance in comparison with that introduced with δέ."[45] This is also true in 2 Cor 9:1-4: Paul's acknowledgement of the Corinthians' willingness to participate in the collection (9:1-2) is the secondary information. Instead, the emphasis is on Paul's justifications of the sending of the

---

[40] While I am inclined to understand the phrase, δόξα Χριστοῦ, as an apposition to the ἀπόστολοι ἐκκλησιῶν, Long argues that the phrase is a concluding exclamation, translating it as "Christ's glory!" in English (*2 Corinthians*, 164). If so, the final statement may be another piece of evidence that supports 1) 8:23-24 as the ending of the unit and 2) the structural relationship of generalization.

[41] Some manuscripts, including ℵ, read the verb ἐνδείκνυμι in the imperative form (ἐνδείξασθε), whereas NA[28], SBL, and other manuscripts, such as B, read the verb in the participle form (ἐνδεικνύμενοι). If one follows the latter variant, which I do, the participle should be understood as an imperative (Wallace, *Greek Grammar*, 650-51; cf. BDF §468).

[42] In 9:3-4, Paul explains three purposes of sending brethren signaled by two ἵνα clauses (9:3) and μή πως clause (9:4). On the function of πως as a conjunction in the form of μή πως, see BDAG, s.v. "πώς" (2a). BDF explains that μή is strengthened by πως and followed by the aorist subjunctive (§370).

[43] See my discussion on the function of οὖν in the previous paragraph. Long also argues that 9:1-5 forms an argumentative pattern known as an epicheireme (*2 Corinthians*, 172).

[44] Scholars espousing that 8:1-24 and 9:1-15 are separate letters argue that γάρ in 9:1 could be redactional (e.g., Thrall, *Second Epistle of the Corinthians*, 1:42). However, the majority of extant manuscripts (except for a few [C 1243 1874 1877]) include γάρ in their reading. Also see the discourse function of γάρ in my discussion in 4.2.1.2.

[45] Levinsohn, *Discourse Features*, 170. Although he notes Phil 1:15-17 as a counter-example (i.e., clauses introduced by μέν and δέ are equally significant), this is the case in 2 Cor 9:1-4.

brethren (9:3–4). Thus, Paul's primary concern in 9:1–5 pertains to his desire to explain the purposes of sending the brethren.⁴⁶ In fact, Paul has been concerned with sending his emissaries throughout the unit (8:17 [cf. 8:6], 18, 22; 9:3, 5). In sum, while some interpreters, including partition theorists, construe the μέν . . . δέ construction as a positive indication for the unit boundary between 8:24 and 9:1,⁴⁷ one should not downplay the function of γάρ in 9:1. Instead, both the μέν . . . δέ construction and γάρ indicate the organic relationship between 8:16–24 and 9:1–5. On the one hand, the μέν . . . δέ construction shows that the primary concern of Paul's argument in 9:1–5 is his explanations regarding the sending of the brethren, and γάρ in 9:1 relates his primary message in 9:1–5 to the description of the collection workers in 8:16–24.

7.1.4 9:6–15

Since I have already discussed the observations that suggest the beginning and ending of 9:6–15,⁴⁸ I will focus my discussion on the subunits within the fourth main unit. I identify three subunits: 9:6–11a, 9:11b–14, and 9:15.

Interpreters differ in their opinions on the segmentation of 9:6–15.⁴⁹ However, I maintain 9:6–11a and 9:11b–14 as separate units based on a topical unity by an agricultural illustration, Paul's flow of argument marked by δέ in 9:6, 8, and 10,⁵⁰ a shift of topic from theological reasons for the exhortations (9:6–11a) to the anticipated outcomes of the fulfillment of the exhortations (9:11b–14), and insight from the

---

[46] As mentioned above, Paul summarizes his discussion (9:1–4) in 9:5.
[47] For instance, Betz states, "The presence of the particle μέν means that γάρ ('for') need not refer to anything preceding. Rather, it refers to that which follows without connection to what has gone before. In fact, the δέ which one would expect to follow μέν is found in in v3. In conclusion, it is likely that 9:1 constitutes the beginning of a new letter" (*2 Corinthians 8 and 9*, 90).
[48] On 9:15 as the ending of the division, see my discussion in 7.1; on 9:6 as the beginning of a unit, see in 7.1.3.
[49] Some maintain 9:6–10 and 9:11–15 as subunits (e.g., Furnish, *II Corinthians*, 446–53; Barnett, *Second Epistle to the Corinthians*, 436; Land, *Integrity of 2 Corinthians*, 191; cf. O'Mahony, *Pauline Persuasion*, 165); some understand 9:6–9 and 9:10–15 as subunits (e.g., Lambrecht, *Second Corinthians*, 144–45; Matera, *II Corinthians*, 204–12; Thrall, *Second Epistle of the Corinthians*, 2:563; Martin, *2 Corinthians*, 467); some view 9:6–7, 9:8–11, and 9:12–15 as subunits (Guthrie, *2 Corinthians*, 446–61); some analyze 9:6 and 9:7–14, and 9:15 as subunits (Betz, *2 Corinthians 8 and 9*, 88–90); some demarcate 9:6–15 into 9:6–12 and 9:13–15 (Long, *Ancient Rhetoric and Paul's Apology*, 176); and others identify 9:6–11 and 9:12–15 as subunits (Harris, *Second Epistle to the Corinthians*, 631–60; Seifrid, *Second Letter to the Corinthians*, 352).
[50] Land also argues 9:6–10 as a unit based on the conjunctive relationship of δέ; he respectively identifies 9:6–10 and 9:11–15 as a unit. The former pertains to the message of "the sowing the seed God supplies," and the latter is the response to it (*Integrity of 2 Corinthians*, 191). While I agree that δέ plays an important role in the identification of the unit, I disagree with his segmentation. Most importantly, it is difficult to demarcate the sentence between 9:10 and 9:11, for 9:11 is not an independent sentence but a verbless dependent clause. Thus, scholars have offered many options to understand the nominative participle πλουτιζόμενοι in 9:11, and many construe it as the future indicative (see a summary of the scholarly debate in Harris, *Second Epistle to the Corinthians*, 644–45). However, the participle should be treated as a part of 9:10 as a postnuclear participle, elaborating that God's provision and growing the harvest of the Corinthians' righteousness pertains to their enrichment for liberality (on postnuclear participle, see Runge, *Discourse Grammar*, 262–63; Levinsohn, *Discourse Feature*, 185–86; Long, *Koine Greek Grammar*, 333–34).

structural relationship between 9:6–11a and 9:11b–14. First, Paul begins to employ an analogy of sowing and reaping in 9:6, which extends to 9:11a.[51]

Second, within the agricultural imagery in 9:6–11a, the conjunction δέ in 9:6, 8, and 10 signals the ways in which Paul develops the analogy. Namely, he develops three arguments regarding the reasons for the Corinthians' participation in the collection as follows:

δέ God loves a cheerful giver (9:6–7),
δέ God abounds in all grace to the Corinthians (9:8–9),
δέ God provides and enriches the Corinthians (9:10–11a).[52]

More specifically, the conjunction δέ seems to mark a new development in two ways. On the one hand, Paul explains the ways in which God is involved in the collection. In 9:6–7, Paul stresses that God's love for a cheerful giver (9:7b) serves as the foundation of how one participates in the giving (i.e., harvest in proportion to sowing [9:6]; one's willingness of giving [9:7a]).[53] In 9:8–9, he underscores God as the source of giving, for God can abound in all grace to the Corinthians. In 9:10–11a, Paul highlights God's provision and enrichment for the Corinthians. Thus, δέ seems to indicate the development of Paul's thought regarding the ways in which God is involved in the collection.[54]

On the other hand, δέ suggests a new development regarding Paul's argumentative move from general to particular.[55] In 9:6–7, Paul expresses a general statement or maxim by employing the third person as the subjects of the sentence (ὁ σπείρων; ὁ σπείρων; ἕκαστος); he does not directly address the Corinthians.[56] In 9:8–9, Paul begins to address the Corinthians, stating that God can abound in all grace to them, yet his statement remains somewhat general, for he employs all the inclusive terms particularly in 9:8 (see the underlined words): δυνατεῖ δὲ ὁ θεὸς <u>πᾶσαν</u> χάριν περισσεῦσαι εἰς ὑμᾶς, ἵνα ἐν <u>παντὶ πάντοτε πᾶσαν</u> αὐτάρκειαν ἔχοντες περισσεύητε εἰς <u>πᾶν</u> ἔργον ἀγαθόν.[57] In 9:10–11a, Paul further particularizes his statement in 9:8–9

---

[51] Harris, emphasizes Paul's agricultural imagery, viewing 9:6–11 as a unit (*Second Epistle to the Corinthians*, 631). However, my analysis identifies 9:11a as the ending of the unit. On the reason for such a segmentation, see my discussion below on the topical shift and the structural relationship.

[52] Cf. Land, *Integrity of 2 Corinthians*, 191.

[53] One should note the close relationship between 9:6 and 9:7a. Although 9:6 expresses a general principle that one's harvest is in proportion to one's sowing, people know that such a principle is not always true; how one sows does not guarantee how one reaps. Sometimes people sow much but harvest little (Hag 1:6; cf. Jer 12:13; Hos. 8:7). However, in God's ministry, one's manner of giving corresponds to its result. Therefore, Paul goes on to underscore the significance of one's willingness in 9:7a, for God loves a cheerful giver (9:7b).

[54] Also note Paul's use of grammar to highlight God as the subject. In 9:7b, 8, and 10, God is the subject of the sentence. In 9:11a, while the Corinthians are the subject, the divine passive underscores God as the agent.

[55] Thus, 9:6–11a is structured according to particularization.

[56] Scholars debate if Paul's statement in 9:6 represents a general idea or addresses to the Corinthians. However, Land convincingly argues that the former is the case based on the flow of Paul's argumentation (*Integrity of 2 Corinthians*, 189–91).

[57] On quantitative emphasis, see Long, *2 Corinthians*, 174–75, 275.

by explicating how God's abundance of grace (9:8) is embodied in the Corinthians: God's provision and enrichment for the Corinthians. Thus, in 9:6–11a, the conjunction δέ marks a new development regarding the move from general to particular. At least, δέ in 9:6, 8, and 10 shows that Paul's new argument begins in 9:6 and continues to 9:10. However, one may question where his argument ends. The third and fourth points will explain why I maintain 9:11a as the ending of the unit.

Third, Paul shifts his discussion from theological reasons for the exhortations (i.e., the completion of the collection; 9:6–11a) to the anticipated outcomes of the fulfillment of the exhortations (9:11b–14). Paul has explicated what God does in the Corinthians' completion of the collection in 9:6–11a and moves to elucidate what the results of their completion will be in 9:11b–14: supply of the need (9:12), thanksgiving to God (9:11b, 12), glory to God (9:13), and longing for the Corinthians (9:14).

Fourth, related to the third point, Paul's shift of topic is further supported by the insight from the structural relationship between 9:6–11a and 9:11b–14. Namely, 9:6–11a and 9:11b–14 are structured according to causation. Paul's explanation of what God does in the Corinthians' completion of the collection (9:6–11a) leads to the outcomes described in 9:11b–14. In other words, the Corinthians' giving does not automatically guarantee all the outcomes listed in 9:11b–14; rather, God causes these results. This movement from cause (9:6–11a) to effect/result (9:11b–14) is semantically and pragmatically signaled by a relative pronoun clause in 9:11b: ἥτις κατεργάζεται δι' ἡμῶν εὐχαριστίαν τῷ θεῷ. On the one hand, the relative pronoun clause semantically highlights the nature or essence of God's enrichment for the Corinthians' liberality. The pronoun ὅστις functions as the qualitative use of an indefinite relative pronoun, which "can usually be translated intensively ('the very one who,' 'who certainly,' 'who indeed')."[58] On the other hand, the relative pronoun clause pragmatically underscores the cause/effect relationship between 9:11a and 9:11b. Regarding the functions of relative pronoun clauses, Ernest D. Burton explains two basic functions:

> All relative clauses whether adjective or adverbial may be distinguished as either restrictive or explanatory. A restrictive clause defines its antecedent, indicating what person, thing, place, or manner is signified. An explanatory clause adds a description to what is already known or sufficiently defined. The former *identifies*, the latter *describes*.[59]

In 9:11b, the relative pronoun clause with the indefinite relative pronoun ὅστις functions as a nonrestrictive relative pronoun clause, since ἥτις does not identify the antecedent noun ἁπλότης. Instead, it describes the antecedent noun. Levinson further explicates that nonrestrictive relative clauses can be categorized into appositional and continuative.[60] In the continuative use, especially in non-narrative arguments, which is the case in 9:11b, the statement that precedes the relative pronoun becomes a ground

---

[58] Wallace, *Greek Grammar*, 344.
[59] Ernest D. Burton, *Syntax of Moods and Tenses in the New Testament Greek*, 3rd ed. (Edinburgh: T&T Clark, 1898), 119 (italics original), cited in Long, *Koine Greek Grammar*, 173.
[60] Levinsohn, *Discourse Features*, 191.

for another assertion.[61] In other words, the continuative use of the nonrestrictive relative pronoun clause in 9:11b indicates that Paul's statement in 9:10–11a serves as a basis for that in 9:11b: God's provision and enrichment for Corinthians' liberality leads into thanksgiving to God.[62] Hence, combined, both the semantical emphasis on the indefinite relative pronoun and the pragmatic function of the nonrestrictive relative pronoun support my observation regarding a shift from cause (9:6–11a) to effect/result (9:11b–14).[63] Therefore, Paul's framing of the unit with an agricultural analogy, his development of arguments with the conjunction δέ in 9:6, 8, and 10, a shift of topic between 9:6–11a and 9:11b–14, and the structural relationship of causation suggest that 9:6–11a and 9:11b–14 are respective units.

Finally, I treat 9:15 as an independent unit, for Paul's thanksgiving concludes the entire division (8:1–9:15).[64] Having discussed the segmentation of 8:1–9:15, I will turn to the second aspect of the literary structure: the MSRs.

7.2 Major Structural Relationships

Having analyzed the segmentation of 8:1–9:15, my next task is to demonstrate (1) the ways in which the main units (8:1–6; 8:7–15; 8:16–9:5; 9:6–15) are related to one another within the division (8:1–9:15), and (2) the ways in which the division (8:1–9:15) is related to the entire letter. The MSRs in relation to the division as a whole indicate that Paul's discourse in 8:1–9:15 is hortatory in nature, and the MSR in relation to the letter as a whole shows that his discussion in 8:1–9:15 is an invitation to the Corinthians to respond to the proclamation of the gospel (3:1–7:16) through the completion of the collection (8:1–9:15).

7.2.1 In Relation to Division as a Whole (8:1–9:15)

Regarding the MSRs in relation to the division as a whole, I will expound five MSRs: *inclusio*, recurrence, comparative causation, instrumentation, and substantiation. I will conclude this section by summarizing the findings and drawing a theological implication of the MSRs. They indicate that Paul's discourse in 8:1–9:15, which is characterized by the notion of grace, centers on the exhortations in 8:7–15; thus, the argument in this division is hortatory in nature.

---

[61] Ibid., 192–93.
[62] Garland also observes that 9:11a summarizes Paul's argument in 9:6–10, and 9:11b introduces the theme of thanksgiving (*2 Corinthians*, 412–13).
[63] Interestingly, some manuscripts read εἰ τις instead of ἥτις ($\mathfrak{P}^{46}$ D* 326 b; Ambst). While the variant seems most likely to have arisen from the confusion of vowels (i.e., itacism), scribes may have thought a break between 9:11a and 9:11b, for the flow of Paul's argument marks an ending at 9:11a. Thus, they may have begun a new sentence in 9:11b.
[64] Also see my comments regarding 9:15 as the ending of the division in 7.1.

7.2.1.1 Inclusio (8:1–9:15)

I propose that 8:1–9:15 is structured according to *inclusio*. Paul frames the division with χάρις and δίδωμι/δωρεά (8:1 and 9:15). Paul begins the division with the description of the grace (χάρις) God has given (δίδωμι) in the churches of Macedonia (8:1) and concludes it with the thanksgiving (χάρις) to God for his gift (δωρεά).[65] In Chapter 1, I described three categories of structural relationships: recurrence, semantic, and rhetorical structures. I explained the nature of rhetorical structures, which pertain to the arrangement of material within the text; writers typically combine rhetorical structures with semantic relationships to reinforce and develop those semantic relationships.[66] However, the rhetorical structure of *inclusio* in 8:1–9:15 bolsters not only other semantic structures but also recurrence structure. Namely, the *inclusio* seems to be combined with recurrence structure with χάρις and δίδωμι (its cognates; 7.2.1.2), semantic structures of comparative causation (7.2.1.3), and substantiation (7.2.1.5).

The ministry to the saints begins with the grace God gives (8:1),[67] and the ministry results in thanksgiving to God for his gift: χάρις τῷ θεῷ ἐπὶ τῇ ἀνεκδιηγήτῳ αὐτοῦ δωρεᾷ (9:15). Thus, moving from the grace of God (8:1) to the grace to God (9:15), Paul explains that God's grace enables the ministry of grace (i.e., the collection), which leads to their thanksgiving to God, emphasizing the centrality of God (more discussions follow).

7.2.1.2 Recurrence

Related to the *inclusio*, one finds the recurrence structure with χάρις and δίδωμι (and its cognates) in 8:1–9:15. These words frequently occur in 8:1–9:15 to emphasize and develop Paul's discourse regarding the ministry to the saints in light of grace and gift-giving. I have already indicated in Chapters 3 and 4 that χάρις and its cognates characterize Paul's discourse in the book. In 8:1–9:15, one especially finds the cluster of the occurrences of the word (8:1, 4, 6, 7, 9, 16, 19; 9:8, 14, 15).[68] Particularly, Paul employs χάρις to refer to the ministry to the saints (8:1, 4, 6, 7, 9, 19; 9:8, 14, 15). Likewise, δίδωμι and its cognates (δότης; δωρεά) recur in 8:1–9:15 (δ ίδωμι in 8:1, 5, 10, 16; 9:9; δότης in 9:7; δωρεά in 9:15).[69] Paul underscores the notion of giving, especially in relation to God's grace. Thus, being closely related to one another, these terms characterize Paul's discourse in 8:1–9:15.

---

[65] In the NT, δωρεά, the cognate of δίδωμι, is always employed to refer to God's or Christ's gift to people ("δῶρον, δωρέομαι, δώρημα, δωρεά," *TDNT* 2:167).

[66] Bauer and Traina, *Inductive Bible Study*, 116.

[67] The genitive in the phrase τὴν χάριν τοῦ θεοῦ in 8:1 is subjective genitive: God gives grace, which is further bolstered by the attributive/adjectival participle δεδομένην.

[68] The term χάρις appears ten out of eighteen times in 2 Corinthians (8:1, 4, 6, 7, 9, 16, 19; 9:8, 14, 15; cf. 1:2, 12, 15; 2:14; 4:15; 6:1; 12:9; 13:13); εὐχαριστία appears two out of three (9:11, 12; cf. 4:15; εὐχαριστέω in 1:11); χαρά occurs one out of four (8:2; cf. 1:24; 2:3; 7:4, 13; χαίρω in 2:3; 6:10; 7:7, 9, 13, 16; 13:9, 11).

[69] The verb δίδωμι appears five out of thirteen times in Second Corinthians (8:1, 5, 10, 16; 9:9; cf. 1:22; 5:5, 12, 18; 6:3; 10:8; 12:7; 13:10; παραδίδωμι in 4:11); δότης (9:7) is a *hapax legomenon* in the NT; δωρεά occurs once in 9:15; δωρεάν appears once in 11:7.

7.2.1.3 Comparative Causation (8:1–6 and 8:7–15)

Regarding the relationship between 8:1–6 and 8:7–15, many scholars recognize their close connection.[70] I argue that these units are structured according to comparative causation (8:1–6 and 8:7–15).[71] On the one hand, Paul's discussion moves from cause (8:1–6) to effect (8:7–15). Paul shares the testimony of Macedonian churches (8:1–6) to motivate the Corinthians to participate in the collection according to his exhortations in 8:7–15.

On the other hand, Paul presents two models for the Corinthians to follow (comparison): the Macedonian churches and Christ, especially in relation to the notion of grace. First, Paul compares the ways in which the divine grace works through agents between the Macedonian churches and the Corinthians. Namely, he explicates the vertical and horizontal dimension of the divine grace manifested among the Macedonians (8:1–6) and uses them as an example for his exhortations to the Corinthians (8:7–15). In 8:1–6, Paul first describes the vertical dimension of God's grace: God's grace enabled the Macedonian churches to overcome affliction with joy and poverty with their liberality (8:1–2). Then, he continues to explicate the horizontal dimension of God's grace: The Macedonians were eager to participate in the χάρις, that is, the participation in the ministry to the saints (8:4).[72] Thus, Paul and his fellow workers encouraged Titus to finish the χάρις (i.e., the collection) among the Corinthians (8:6). In other words, God has given the grace to the Macedonians (vertical) so that they became agents to pass God's grace to others, especially by participating in the ministry to the saints (horizontal). In 8:7–15, Paul similarly underscores these dimensions of grace. Paul emphasizes that his exhortations to abound in χάρις (8:7b; 8:11) is grounded in the grace of Jesus Christ (8:9). In other words, Christ's manifestation of grace to the Corinthians (vertical) enables the Corinthians to abound in grace to others (horizontal; i.e., the collection). Thus, by giving the testimony of the Macedonian churches (8:1–6), Paul shows the manner in which the divine grace was given to and mediated through the Macedonians, and he continues to emphasize the vertical and horizontal dimension of the divine grace in his exhortations to the Corinthians (8:7–15).

Second, Paul describes that God's grace is manifested as self-sacrifice and willingness in the example of the Macedonians (8:1–6) and Christ (8:9) and utilizes their examples for his exhortations to the Corinthians (8:7–15). In 8:1–6, Paul underscores that the divine grace is particularly manifested in the Macedonians' self-sacrifice. Their

---

[70] E.g., among the scholars employing rhetorical criticism, Kennedy (*Rhetorical Criticism*, 91) and Long (*Ancient Rhetoric and Paul's Apology*, 176) identify 8:1–6 as *narratio*; Betz maintains 8:1–5 as *exordium* and 8:6 as *narratio* (*2 Corinthians 8 and 9*, 41–56); O'Mahony understands 8:1–6 as *exordium* (*Pauline Persuasion*, 165); however, they disagree with one another on the identification of the rhetorical disposition. Others also acknowledge that the testimony of the Macedonian churches functions as an example or a rhetorical *synkrisis* and *exemplum* for the following discourse (e.g., Plummer, *Second Epistle*, 232–38; Witherington, *Conflict and Community in Corinth*, 412; McCant, *2 Corinthians*, 78–81; Harris, *Second Epistle to the Corinthians*, 558).

[71] Regarding the function of ἀλλά in 8:7, the conjunction indicates a subtle contrast between the sending of Titus (8:6) and the exhortation to abound in grace (8:7; see my discussion in 7.1.1). However, the overall relationship between 8:1–6 and 8:7–15 is comparative causation.

[72] The two nouns, τὴν χάριν καὶ τὴν κοινωνίαν, should be construed as appositional; thus, καὶ seems to function epexegetically (Plummer, *Second Epistle*, 236; Harris, *Second Epistle to the Corinthians*, 566).

participation in the grace (i.e., their giving) is not a mere fiscal contribution but rather self-sacrifice to the Lord and to people (8:5), which finds its ultimate example in Christ (8:9). Paul emphasizes that Christ's grace pertains to his sacrifice: He was rich, but he became poor for the Corinthians so that they might become rich through his poverty (8:9). Pointing to these examples of the divine grace, especially in relation to self-sacrifice, Paul shows the Corinthians the ways in which they should abound in the grace and finish the collection (8:7b, 11).

Therefore, Paul utilizes the testimony of the Macedonian churches (1) to show the model of the vertical and horizontal dimensions of the divine grace, and (2) to illustrate self-sacrifice as the manifestation of the grace (8:1–6), which finds its ultimate example in Christ's sacrifice (8:9), and he invites the Corinthians to follow these examples (8:7–15).

7.2.1.4 Instrumentation (Description of Means; 8:7–15 and 8:16–9:5)

Regarding the relationship between 8:7–15 and 8:16–9:5, these units are structured according to instrumentation (description of means). The description of the emissaries for the collection in 8:16–9:5 has two functions. On the one hand, as I have already discussed in Chapter 5 (see 5.2.2.2), Paul describes the credentials of the collection workers (8:16–9:5, especially 8:16–24) through which he strengthens his and his fellow workers' integrity (8:20). Thus, some scholars recognize the function of the unit as commendation.[73] On the other hand, the description of the collection workers in 8:16–9:5 has another function. Paul describes them in order to explicate the means by which the ministry to the saints will be accomplished. In other words, Paul's discussion moves from exhortations (8:7–15) to the description of the emissaries through whom the Corinthians are to participate in the ministry to the saints (8:16–9:5).

7.2.1.5 Substantiation (8:7–15 and 9:6–15)

I propose that 8:7–15 and 9:6–15 are structured according to substantiation.[74] By providing reasons for his exhortations made in 8:7–15 (9:6–11a) and showing the anticipated outcomes of the fulfillment of the exhortations (9:11b–14), Paul strengthens his exhortations (8:7–15). Paul explains why the Corinthians should abound in grace (8:7b) and complete the collection (8:11): because God loves a cheerful giver (9:6–7), because God can make all grace abound to them (9:8–9), and because God provides and enriches the Corinthians' liberality (9:10–11a). In explaining these, Paul strengthens his exhortations by highlighting the centrality of God in the collection. The Corinthians' bountiful and cheerful giving ultimately aims to please God, who cares about the ways in which they participate in the ministry (9:6–7). Moreover, God is the source of the grace (i.e., giving; 9:8–9); thus, he provides and enriches the Corinthians (9:10–11a).[75]

---

[73] E.g., Kennedy, *Rhetorical Criticism*, 92; Betz, *2 Corinthians 8 and 9*, 70–82.
[74] More precisely, it is hortatory substantiation. Bauer and Traina explain, "*Hortatory substantiation* occurs when the writer moves from an exhortation, or a passage characterized by exhortation, to the reason why (i.e., the cause) the exhortation should be obeyed: you ought to obey *A* because of *B*" (*Inductive Bible Study*, 107).
[75] Also see my discussion on God's grace in 7.2.1.2.

Furthermore, Paul continues to explain the anticipated outcomes of their completion of the collection in 9:11b–14: The Corinthians abound in grace (8:7b) and complete the collection (8:11) because their completion of the financial contribution will supply the need and produce thanksgiving to God (9:11b–12), because their abundance of grace will lead the saints to glorify God for the Corinthians' obedience and liberality (9:13), and because their support will create the recipients' longing for the Corinthians (9:14). Paul's descriptions of these anticipated outcomes reinforce his exhortations, encouraging the Corinthians to have the confidence to fulfill his exhortations. Unlike farming in the real world, in which bountiful sowing does not guarantee bountiful harvests (e.g., Hag 1:6; Jer 12:13; Hos. 8:7), Paul is confident that the Corinthians' response to the gospel through their financial support to the saints will result in spiritual and material harvests. Their giving will lead believers into worship (i.e., thanksgiving [9:11a–12] and glory [9:13] to God). Their gift will strengthen the partnership among the believers, for it not only provides the need for the saints (9:11b) but also creates their affection for the Corinthians (9:14).[76] In doing so, Paul therefore bolsters his exhortations to the Corinthians (8:7–15).

7.2.1.6 Summary and Theological Implication

In this section, I have demonstrated five MSRs in relation to the division as a whole: *inclusio*, recurrence, comparative causation, instrumentation, and substantiation. The *inclusio* and recurrence structure show that grace and giving characterize Paul's argument in 8:1–9:15. Comparative causation (8:1–6 and 8:7–15) reveals (1) that the notion of grace particularly pertains to the vertical and horizontal dimension of the divine grace and self-sacrifice, and (2) that the move from comparative cause (8:1–6) to comparative effect (8:7–15) shows Paul's strategy to present the testimony of the Macedonians (8:1–6) as a positive example to prompt the Corinthians to fulfill Paul's exhortations (8:7–15). Thus, the focus of Paul's discourse centers on his exhortations (8:7–15). Furthermore, instrumentation (8:7–15 and 8:16–9:5) and substantiation (8:7–15 and 9:6–15) reinforce Paul's exhortations (8:7–15) by describing the means, reasons, and outcomes of the ministry to the saints.[77] Therefore, these MSRs in relation to the division as a whole indicate that his exhortations (8:7–15) are central to his argument in 8:1–9:15.

7.2.2 In Relation to Letter as a Whole (3:1–7:16 and 8:1–9:15): Comparative Causation (3:1–7:16 and 8:1–9:15)

Regarding the ways in which 8:1–9:15 is related to the rest of the letter, the majority of scholars, except for a few partition theorists, hold to the integrity of chs 1–9, recognizing

---

[76] See my discussion on partnership in 4.2.2.2 and 6.2.1.
[77] Also note that scholars employing rhetorical criticism, though they disagree with one another on their analysis of rhetorical disposition, find *propositio* in 8:7–15. Kennedy identifies 8:8–9 as preparation for *propositio* and 8:10–11 as *propositio* (*Rhetorical Criticism*, 91–92), Betz identifies 8:7–8 as *propositio* (*2 Corinthians 8 and 9*, 56–60); O'Mahony maintains 8:7 (8) as *propositio* (*Pauline Persuasion*, 165); Long contends that 8:7–9 is *partitio* (*Ancient Rhetoric and Paul's Apology*, 176).

that Paul's argument shifts to the exhortation in chs 8–9.[78] In this section, I particularly claim that 3:1–7:16 and 8:1–9:15 are structured according to comparative causation. On the one hand, Paul moves from the indicatives (3:1–7:16) to imperatives (8:1–9:15).[79] Paul exhorts the Corinthians to participate in the ministry to the saints (8:1–9:15) because of the proclamation of the gospel (3:1–7:16). Implications from the analyses of MSRs within 3:1–7:16 and 8:1–9:15 and examples from other Pauline letters support this movement. First, the MSRs of 3:1–7:16 as a whole and 8:1–9:15 as a whole show that Paul's discourse in 3:1–7:16 is indicative in nature and that in 8:1–9:15 is hortatory in nature. As I have already discussed in 6.3, one significant implication of the analyses of the MSRs of causation (3:1–11 and 3:12–7:3) and substantiation (3:1–7:3 and 7:4–16) is that the thrust of Paul's discourse in 3:1–7:16 revolves around 3:12–7:3, in which Paul underscores the proclamation of the gospel. Moreover, as I just summarized, the MSRs in relation to 8:1–9:15 as a whole show that Paul's discourse revolves around his exhortations (8:7–15); thus, the division is hortatory in nature.[80] Therefore, Paul's argument moves from indicative statements regarding the proclamation of the gospel (3:1–7:16) to imperative statements regarding the collection (8:1–9:15).

Second, the structural relationship in other Pauline letters attests to a similar movement from indicatives to imperatives. For instance, in Paul's undisputed letters, the shift from statements in indicatives to exhortations and imperatives are common (except for 1 Corinthians). In Romans, Paul moves from the exposition of the gospel (chs 1–11) to the exhortations regarding Christian living according to the gospel (chs 12–15).[81] In Galatians, Paul moves from his argument for the freedom of justification by faith (chs 1–4) to exhortations regarding life according to freedom in faith (chs 4/5–6).[82] In Philippians, Paul shifts from the report concerning his situation in relation to the gospel (1:12–26) to exhortation regarding the conduct worthy of the gospel

---

[78] On the history of interpretation regarding the integrity of chs 1–9, as well as that of chs 8–9, see Harris, *Second Epistle to the Corinthians*, 25–29.

[79] Bauer and Traina categorize this type of causation as hortatory causation, describing, "*Hortatory causation* occurs when a writer moves from a statement in the indicative (i.e., a claim or statement of fact) to a command, or exhortation, in the imperative: because A is so, therefore you ought to do B" (*Inductive Bible Study*, 106).

[80] Also see my discussion in 7.1.2 that Paul's argument in 8:7–15 is hortatory in nature, for it syntactically and semantically revolves around his two imperatival statements in 8:7b and 8:11.

[81] E.g., Ernst Käsemann, *Commentary on Romans*, trans. Geoffrey W. Bromiley (Grand Rapids: Eerdmans, 1980), 323; James D. G. Dunn, *Romans 9–16*, WBC 38B (Dallas: Word, 1988), 705–8; Joseph A. Fitzmyer, *Romans: A New Translation with Introduction and Commentary*, AB 33 (New York: Doubleday, 1993), 637; Luke Timothy Johnson, *Reading Romans: A Literary and Theological Commentary*, Reading the New Testament Series (Macon, GA: Smyth & Helwys, 2001), 187–88; Cranfield, *Epistle to the Romans*, 2:593–96; Craig S. Keener, *Romans*, New Covenant Commentary Series 6 (Eugene, OR: Cascade, 2009), 142; cf. Robert Jewett, *Romans*, Hermeneia (Minneapolis: Fortress, 2007), 724–899.

[82] Although scholars have debated as to where Paul's exhortation begins, many still recognize the movement from indicatives to imperatives (on the survey of options, see Otto Merk, "Der Beginn Der Paränese Im Galaterbrief," *ZNW* 60 (1969): 83–104). For instance, Betz recognizes 5:1–6:10 as the *exhortatio* (*Galatians*, 253–311); Richard N. Longenecker maintains 4:12–6:10 as the exhortations (*Galatians*, WBC 41 [Dallas: Word, 1990], 184–284); Dunn claims that 5:13–6:10 is the exhortation (*The Epistle to the Galatians*, BNTC [Peabody, MA: Hendrickson, 1993], 284–333); J. Louis Martyn identifies 5:13–6:10 as the exhortation (*Galatians: A New Translation with Introduction and Commentary*, AB 33A [New York: Doubleday, 1997], 468, 480–558).

(1:27–4:20).⁸³ In 1 Thessalonians, Paul again moves from indicatives (chs 1–3) to exhortations (chs 4–5).⁸⁴ Even in Paul's shortest letter, Philemon, one observes a movement from statements in indicatives (4–7) to exhortation (8–20).⁸⁵ Moreover, this movement from theological and historical arguments in indicatives to exhortations in imperatives is frequently observed in Paul's disputed letters.⁸⁶ In 2 Corinthians, Paul similarly shifts his arguments concerning the proclamation of the gospel (3:1–7:16) to the exhortation to respond to the gospel (8:1–9:15). Particularly, Paul insists that the collection is the response to the proclamation of the gospel. In 3:11–7:3, Paul emphasizes that the content of the proclamation is the gospel of Christ (4:4, 6), and he clarifies that the Corinthians' response in the ministry to the saints is indeed the obedience to the Corinthians' confession of the gospel of Christ (9:13). The proclamation of the gospel requires the recipients' response; Paul invites the Corinthians to respond to the proclamation of the gospel (3:1–7:16) through participating in the ministry to the saints (8:1–9:15).

On the other hand, Paul's discourse in 3:1–7:16 and his exhortation in 8:1–9:15 are structured according to comparison, especially regarding (1) the ways in which Paul describes both the proclamation of the gospel (3:1–7:16) and the participation in the ministry to the saints (8:1–9:15), and (2) the results of both ministries. First, Paul describes both the proclamation of the gospel (3:1–7:16) and the ministry to the saints (8:1–9:15) by employing the terms διακονία, χάρις and their cognates. In 3:1–7:16, Paul employs διακονία (3:7, 8, 9 [twice]; 4:1; 5:18; 6:3, 4) and its cognates (διακονέω in 3:3 and διάκονος in 3:6; cf. λειτουργία in 9:12) to describe the proclamation of the gospel.

---

⁸³ Although interpreters differ in their opinions on the ending of the exhortation, they at least recognize the shift from indicatives (1:12–26) to imperatives (1:27). For instance, Peter T. O'Brien (*The Epistle to the Philippians*, NIGTC [Grand Rapids: Eerdmans, 1991], 143–312) and Gerald F. Hawthorne (*Philippians*, WBC 43 [Nashville: Nelson, 2004], 65–150) maintain 1:27–2:18 as the exhortation; John H. P. Ruemann claims that 1:27–3:1 is the paraenesis (*Philippians: A New Translation with Introduction and Commentary*, AB 33B [New Haven: Yale University Press, 2008, 261–459).

⁸⁴ E.g., Abraham J. Malherbe, *The Letter to the Thessalonians: A New Translation with Introduction and Commentary*, AB 32B (New York: Doubleday, 2000), 216–17; Charles A. Wanamaker, *The Epistles to the Thessalonians*, NIGTC (Grand Rapids: Eerdmans, 1990), 146–204; cf. F. F. Bruce, (*1 & 2 Thessalonians*, WBC 45 [Dallas: Word, 1982], 77–78) recognizes 4:1 as the beginning of the paraenetic division of the letter; however, he does not agree that the exhortation introduced by οὖν does not follow the discussion in chs 1–3.

⁸⁵ While some scholars differ in their opinions on the identification of the ending of the exhortation, they at least agree that Paul's plea begins in 8. For instance, Peter T. O'Brien (*Colossians, Philemon*, WBC 44 [Dallas: Word, 1982], 284–303), Dunn (*Colossians and Philemon*, 322–43), and R. McL. Wilson (*Colossians and Philemon*, ICC [London: T&T Clark, 2005], 345–61) identify 8–20 as the plea, whereas Michael F. Bird maintains 8–22 as the plea (*Colossians and Philemon*, New Covenant Commentary Series 12 [Eugene, OR: Cascade, 2009], 137–43).

⁸⁶ To give some examples, in Ephesians, Paul moves from the theological discussion regarding God's work through Christ (chs 1–3) to the exhortation to walk in a manner worthy of the calling (chs 4–6; e.g., Barth, *Ephesians 1–3*, 53; Andrew T. Lincoln, *Ephesians*, WBC 42 [Dallas: Word, 1990], xxxvi; Ernest Best, *A Critical and Exegetical Commentary on Ephesians*, ICC [Edinburgh: T&T Clark, 1998], 353–55; cf. Stephen E. Fowl, *Ephesians: A Commentary*, NTL [Louisville: Westminster John Knox, 2012], 125–27). In Colossians, Paul proclaims God's reconciling work in Christ (1:15–2:5) and then begins to employ imperatives to exhort the Colossians to walk in Christ according to the tradition of Christ Jesus the Lord (2:6, 8, 16, 18; 3:1, 2, 5, 8, 9, 12, 15, 16, 18, 19, 20, 21, 22, 23, 24; 4:1, 2, 5) in 2:6–4:6 (cf. James D. G. Dunn, *Colossians and Philemon*, NIGTC [Grand Rapids: Eerdmans, 1996], 136–43).

Likewise, in 8:1–9:15, Paul employs διακονία (8:4; 9:1, 12, 13) and its cognate διακονέω (8:19, 20) to describe the fiscal contribution to the saints.[87] Moreover, Paul also portrays both the proclamation of the gospel and the collection with the term χάρις. In 3:1–7:16, Paul employs χάρις (4:15; 6:1) in relation to the proclamation of the gospel. In 4:15, χάρις signifies the proclamation of the gospel;[88] in 6:1, Paul employs χάρις in relation to the acceptance of the word of reconciliation as the gospel of Christ.[89] Similarly, in 8:1–9:15, Paul employs χάρις to depict the collection (8:1, 4, 6, 7, 9, 19; 9:8, 14).[90] While Paul elsewhere calls the financial contribution λογεία (1 Cor 16:1), he deliberately describes the collection as διακονία and χάρις, portraying both the proclamation of the gospel and the collection not as separate ministries but as different parts of the same ministry.

Second, Paul underscores that both the proclamation of the gospel (3:1–7:16) and the ministry to the saints (8:1–9:15) result in thanksgiving and glory to God. In 4:15, Paul underlines that the ministry of χάρις (i.e., the proclamation of the gospel) will result in thanksgiving (εὐχαριστία). Likewise, in 9:11–12, Paul emphasizes that the ministry of χάρις (i.e., the collection) will produce thanksgiving (εὐχαριστία). Thus, both the proclamation and the collection aim to produce thanksgiving to God. Furthermore, both ministries will also result in glory to God. In responding to the glorious new covenant (3:6b–11), God's servants proclaim the gospel of the glory of Christ (4:4), that is the knowledge of God's glory (4:6); therefore, the ministry of χάρις (i.e., the proclamation of the gospel) causes thanksgiving to overflow into the glory of God (4:15), even when facing sufferings and afflictions, for they produce an eternal glory beyond comparison (4:17). Similarly, Paul underscores that the ministry of χάρις (i.e., the collection) is for the glory of the Lord (8:19); thus, the completion of the collection will result in the glory to God (9:13). Therefore, Paul does not view the proclamation of the gospel and the ministry to the saints as separate ministries. Instead, he views both under the same ministry by (1) describing both with the same terms, and (2) emphasizing that both share the same purpose and results: thanksgiving and glory to God.

---

[87] Also see my discussion on the theme of service/work (συνυπουργέω; διακονέω; διάκονος; διακονία; δοῦλος; καταδουλόω; ἐνεργέω; συνεργός; κατεργάζομαι; συνεργέω; ἐργάζομαι; ἔργον; ἐργάτης) in 4.2.2.3.

[88] Three observations should be noted regarding this statement. First, the MSRs in ch. 6 demonstrate that the focus of Paul's discourse in 3:1–7:16 pertains to the proclamation of the gospel. Thus, Paul's use of χάρις in 4:15 should be understood in light of Paul's primary purpose of the discourse. In fact, the immediate literary context (4:13–15) shows that χάρις is related to the proclamation (4:13). Second, the immediately preceding literary context clarifies that the content of Paul's proclamation is the gospel of Christ (4:4, 6). Third, the noun phrase in 4:15, ἡ χάρις πλεονάσασα διὰ τῶν πλειόνων, further suggests that χάρις signifies the proclamation of the gospel: the agents (διὰ τῶν πλειόνων) contribute to the growth of χάρις. This corresponds to Paul's emphasis on God's agents and their work as discussed in Chapter 5. Also, while the Greek in 4:15 has triggered a number of exegetical debates among the scholars, I translate the ἵνα clause in 4:15, ἵνα ἡ χάρις πλεονάσασα διὰ τῶν πλειόνων τὴν εὐχαριστίαν περισσεύσῃ εἰς τὴν δόξαν τοῦ θεοῦ, as follows: "so that the grace, which abounds by many, may cause thanksgiving to overflow into the glory of God." I construe πλεονάσασα as an intransitive verb and περισσεύσῃ as a transitive verb, taking τὴν εὐχαριστίαν as a direct object (see a summary of scholarly opinions in Thrall, *Second Epistle of the Corinthians*, 1:344–47; Harris, *Second Epistle to the Corinthians*, 356–57).

[89] See my discussion in 6.2.1.

[90] Also see my discussion on χάρις in 3.2.1.

7.3 Conclusion and Theological Implication

In this chapter, I analyzed the literary structure of 8:1–9:15. First, I argued the segmentation of 8:1–9:15. Second, I demonstrated the MSRs in relation both to the division as a whole and the letter as a whole. On the one hand, I expounded five MSRs in relation to the division as a whole: *inclusio*, recurrence, comparative causation, instrumentation, and substantiation. These structural relationships reveal that Paul's discourse centers on his exhortations in 8:7–15; thus, the division is hortatory in nature. On the other hand, I have demonstrated comparative causation as the MSR in relation to the letter as a whole (3:1–7:16 and 8:1–9:15). The comparative causation shows that Paul's discourse shifts from the proclamation of the gospel in indicatives (3:1–7:16) to exhortations for the collection in imperatives (8:1–9:15), yet Paul describes both the proclamation and the collection in comparison. He depicts both ministries with the same terms (διακονία, χάρις, and their cognates). Furthermore, he underscores that both ministries share the same purpose and results (i.e., thanksgiving and glory to God).

Before concluding this chapter, one significant implication from the aforementioned findings needs to be drawn regarding the designation of Paul's discourse in 8:1–9:15. The stated observations have led me to title it "Arguments Pertaining to Content of Ministry: Response to the Gospel." I will highlight two observations that are especially of significance for this designation. First, I titled Paul's argument in 8:1–9:15 as "Arguments Pertaining to Content of Ministry," for the MSR of comparative causation (3:1–7:16 and 8:1–9:15) shows the continuation of the discourse between 3:1–7:16 and 8:1–9:15. By depicting both the proclamation of the gospel and the collection with the same terms (i.e., διακονία and χάρις) and their cognates and highlighting the same purpose and result of the two, Paul views both activities as different aspects of the same ministry. Thus, just as Paul expounds the content of ministry as the proclamation of the gospel in 3:1–7:16, he continues to describe the content of ministry as the ministry to the saints (i.e., the collection) in 8:1–9:15.

Second, I designate Paul's discourse as "Response to the Gospel," for the MSR of comparative causation (3:1–7:16 and 8:1–9:15), especially the move from indicatives to imperatives, reveals that the exhortations in 8:1–9:15 are Paul's invitation for the Corinthians to respond to the gospel proclaimed by God's servants (3:1–7:16). The gospel of Christ, which is the manifestation of God's knowledge (4:4, 6), requires the recipients' response. Just as Paul and his fellow workers respond to the ministry of the new covenant (3:1–11) by proclaiming the gospel (3:11–7:3), they invite the Corinthians to respond to the gospel through the collection (8:1–9:15), for their abundance in grace and completion of the fiscal contribution to the saints manifest their obedience to their confession of the gospel of Christ (9:13). Therefore, these observations have led me to designate his discussion in 8:1–9:15 as "Arguments Pertaining to Content of Ministry: Response to the Gospel." Having scrutinized the literary structure of 8:1–9:15, I will next turn to the analysis of the final chapters: 10:1–13:10.

8

Arguments Pertaining to Content of Ministry: Defense of the Gospel (10:1–13:10)

In Chapter 7, I scrutinized the literary structure of 8:1–9:15. I argued the segmentation of 8:1–9:15 and demonstrated MSRs in relation to both the division as a whole and the letter as a whole. They show (1) that the division is hortatory in nature because Paul's exhortations (8:7–15) are central to his discourse in 8:1–9:15, and (2) that Paul's discourse moves from indicatives (3:1–7:16) to imperatives (8:1–9:15). In this chapter, I continue to analyze the literary structure of 10:1–13:10. I first demonstrate the segmentation of the division and then explicate the MSRs in relation to both the division as a whole and the letter as a whole. These MSRs reveal (1) that Paul's discourse in 10:1–13:10 centers on the defense of his status as a servant of Christ, which is directly related to the defense of the gospel, and (2) that Paul does not view the proclamation of the gospel (3:1–7:16), the exhortation to respond to the gospel (8:1–9:15), and the defense of the gospel (10:1–13:10) as separate entities but as different aspects in the same ministry.

8.1 Division of 10:1–13:10

Regarding the segmentation of 10:1–13:10, I analyze its main units and subunits as follows:

A. Basis for Consequent Ecclesial Preparation for Impending Visit: Foolish Boasting (10:1–12:13)
   1. Basis for Foolish Boasting (10:1–18)
      a) Offense against Paul's Status (10:1–11)
      b) Offense against Paul's Authority: Sphere of Boasting (10:12–18)
   2. Content of Foolish Boasting (11:1–12:13)
      a) Justification for Foolish Boasting (11:1–21a)
      b) Speech Proper (11:21b–12:10)
      c) Conclusion (12:11–13)
B. Consequent Ecclesial Preparation for Impending Visit (12:14–13:10)
   1. Basis for Ecclesial Preparation for Impending Visit (12:14–21)
      a) Announcement of Impending Visit (12:14a)
      b) Parent-child Relationship (12:14b–18)
      c) Upbuilding Relationship (12:19–21)

2. Content of Ecclesial Preparation for Impending Visit (13:1–10)
   a) Announcement of Imending Visit (13:1)
   b) Warning, Command, and Prayer (13:2–9)
   c) Intent of Visit (13:10)

Concerning the beginning and ending of the division, as I previously stated, a majority of scholars recognize a topical shift between ch. 9 and ch. 10, for they recognize an abrupt change of a topic and tone in Paul's argument.[1] Moreover, I have also noted that thanksgiving in 9:15, the MSR of *inclusio* (8:1 and 9:15), the presence of δέ in 10:1, and the appeal formula in 10:1 further strengthen the observation (see 7.1). Moreover, some rhetorical critics recognize a shift of literary form, identifing 10:1 as the beginning of *refutatio* or defense.[2] Regarding the ending of the division, I have also argued in 3.1 that the Greek adjective λοιπός in 13:11, the vocative use of ἀδελφός in 13:11, and the epistolary formula of the letter closing suggest that 13:11–13 is an independent literary unit; thus, 13:10 marks the ending of the division. In addition, the implication of the MSR of *inclusio* within 10:1–13:10 adds another piece of evidence to the aforementioned observations. Paul frames the division with a statement regarding his impending visit (10:1–2; 13:10), which suggests that his discourse ends at 13:10.[3] Therefore, I maintain 10:1–13:10 as the fifth division of the letter, and I will turn to the main units of 10:1–13:10 that are 10:1–12:13 and 12:14–13:10.

8:1.1 10:1–12:13

Regarding the first main unit of the division, while I posit that 10:1–12:13 forms the first main unit, a majority of scholars recognize 10:1–18 and 11:1–12:13 as independent literary units.[4] However, the MSR of causation with particularization (10:1–18 and 11:1–12:13) suggests that 10:1–12:13 is the first main unit. Namely, Paul both establishes the bases (10:1–18) for his foolish boasting (11:1–12:13) and begins to defend his status as a servant of Christ in 10:1–18 and fully develops it in 11:1–12:13.[5] Thus, I claim that 10:1–12:13 is the first main unit.

---

[1] See the summaries of the history of the interpretation in Thrall, *Second Epistle of the Corinthians*, 1:5–20; Harris, *Second Epistle to the Corinthians*, 29–51. Also, the change of tone is especially apparent in Paul's use of the intensive/emphatic use of αὐτός with ἐγώ and Παῦλος. Long describes, "The subject of 10:1 is emphasized in nearly every way possible: two unnecessary additional pronouns (Αὐτὸς and ἐγώ), an unnecessarily self-identified explicit subject Παῦλος, and elaboration in a relative clause that includes correlative emphasis (μὲν. . .δὲ; *2 Corinthians*, 185).
[2] McCant, *2 Corinthians*, 101; Long, *Ancient Rhetoric and Paul's Apology*, 178.
[3] See my discussion in 8.2.1.1.
[4] E.g., Furnish, *II Corinthians*, 454–556; Scott, *2 Corinthians*, 193–241; Matera, *II Corinthians*, 213–90; Harris, *Second Epistle to the Corinthians*, 663–879; Seifrid, *Second Letter to the Corinthians*, 373–459; cf. Barnett recognizes 10:1–11 and 10:12–12:13 as units (*Second Epistle to the Corinthians*, 456–582); McCant (*2 Corinthians*, 101–56) and Thrall (*Second Epistle of the Corinthians*, 2:595–857) identify 10:1–18 and 11:1–12:18 as units; Guthrie claims that 10:1–11, 10:12–18, and 11:1–12:13 are independent units (*2 Corinthians*, 465–606); Long understands 10:1–11:15 as *refutatio* and 11:16–12:10 as self-adulation (*Ancient Rhetoric and Paul's Apology*, 178–90).
[5] See my discussion on causation with particularization in 8.2.1.3.

Defense of the Gospel (10:1–13:10) 169

Moreover, scholars differ in their opinions on the ending of Paul's speech: Some identify 12:10,[6] and others recognize 12:13 as the ending of the speech.[7] However, five observations suggest that 12:13 marks the ending of 10:1–12:13: a topical shift between 10:1–12:13 and 12:14–13:10, the insight from the structural relationships within 11:1–12:13 (i.e., generalization [11:1–12:10 and 12:11–13]; *inclusio* [11:1 and 12:11]; recurrence [11:1, 16, 17, 19, 21, 23; 12:6, 11]), and the interjection ἰδού in 12:14. First, Paul shifts a topic from foolish boasting (10:1–12:13) to the consequent ecclesial preparation for his impending visit (12:14–13:10). In 10:1–12:13, Paul engages in the foolish boasting, in which he repeatedly employs the terms καυχάομαι (10:8, 13, 15, 16, 17 [twice]; 11:12, 16, 18 [twice], 30 [twice]; 12:1, 5 [twice], 6, 9) and καύχησις (11:10, 17), but these terms do not appear in 12:14–13:10.[8] Instead, Paul begins to describe his plan to visit the Corinthians (12:14, 20; 13:1, 2, 10).

Second, the structural relationship of generalization within 11:1–12:13 (11:1–12:10 and 12:11–13) shows that Paul's discussion in 12:11–13 marks the ending of the unit. In 12:11–13, Paul concludes his foolish boasting by providing a general description of the preceding arguments in 11:1–12:10, especially highlighting three reasons that forced him to engage in the foolish boasting. Paul was forced to become foolish (12:11; cf. 11:1, 16, 17, 19, 21; 12:6); he is not inferior to the super-apostles (12:11–12; cf. 11:5); and he did not receive the financial support from the Corinthians (12:13; cf. 11:7–15).[9]

---

[6] E.g., Witherington claims that Paul begins to resort to *amplificatio* in 12:11–13:4, preparing for *peroratio* in 13:5–10 (*Conflict and Community in Corinth*, 442–71); Land argues that 12:11–18 forms a unit based on the topical unity regarding the financial discussion (*Integrity of 2 Corinthians*, 218–21); Long claims that Paul moves his discussion to *peroratio* in 12:11–13:10 (*Ancient Rhetoric and Paul's Apology*, 186–97); Martin follows Long's argument (*2 Corinthians*, 542–646).

[7] See my note above.

[8] Thus, 10:1–12:13 is structured according to recurrence regarding καυχάομαι and its cognate. See my discussion below.

[9] Moreover, Paul's enigmatic statement in 12:12 regarding signs and wonders seems to refer to Paul's boasting as well (10:1–12:13). While scholars debate over the meaning of the phrase σημείοις τε καὶ τέρασιν καὶ δυνάμεσιν in 12:12, the phrase σημεῖον and τέρας appears as a common phrase in the LXX (e.g., Exod 7:3; Deut 6:22; Isa 8:18) as well as in the NT (e.g., Mark 13:22; John 4:48; Acts 2:22). Since Paul does not employ the same phrase elsewhere in 2 Corinthians, some interpreters construe the phrase as miracles based on other occurrences in the NT, especially in relation to the term δυνάμεσιν (e.g., Harris, *Second Epistle to the Corinthians*, 875). However, the syntax, the literary context of 2 Corinthians, and a close parallel to Rom 15:18–19 may also suggest that the phrase σημείοις τε καὶ τέρασιν καὶ δυνάμεσιν pertains to the divine power in Paul's defense of the status. First, grammarians argue that the phrase τε καὶ marks the equality and sameness of the groups (Levinsohn, *Discourse Features*, 106–11; Long, *Koine Greek Grammar*, 284–85). Besides, σημεῖον, τέρας, and δύναμις are used in the dative plural form to modify the verb, κατεργάζομαι. Thus, Paul seems to consider these elements referring to the same kind of reality, through which God has performed the signs of apostleship, for κατεργάζομαι in 12:12 is expressed in the divine passive. Second, while Paul employs σημεῖον and τέρας only in 12:12, he consistently employs δύναμις in relation to the divine power in the context of 2 Corinthians (1:8; 4:7; 6:7; 12:9). Thus, it is also likely true that δύναμις in 12:12 refers to the divine power; thus, σημεῖον, τέρας, and δύναμις altogether point to the same reality of the divine power. Third, if we take the closest parallel to Rom 15:18–19, where Paul employs the same vocabularies (κατεργάζομαι, σημεῖον, τέρας, and δύναμις) into consideration, these terms in 12:12 appear to be related to the proclamation of the gospel, just as in Rom 15:18–19. Fourth, the literary context indicates that Paul's primary concern in 10:1–12:13 pertains to the defense of his status as a servant of Christ; thus, it is appropriate to construe 12:12 in light of Paul's central message regarding the defense of the status. Therefore, considering these observations together, it is reasonable to argue that σημεῖον, τέρας, and δύναμις may not necessarily refer to miracles Paul performed only; rather, they also seem to refer to God's power manifested in Paul's weakness in his defense of the status.

In fact, a subsequent correction or an apology called *epidiorthosis* was not uncommon in rhetorical practice.[10] By emphasizing these reasons, Paul concludes his boasting by reminding the Corinthians of his reluctancy but the necessity to have boasted like a fool in 11:1–12:10. Therefore, the insight from the structural relationship of generalization suggests that 12:13 marks the ending of the unit.

Third, the structural relationship of *inclusio* (11:1 and 12:11) suggests that 11:1–12:13 is an independent unit. Paul seems to frame 11:1–12:13 regarding the notion of foolishness, for the unit begins with the noun ἀφροσύνη (11:1) and ends with its adjective form, ἄφρων (12:11).

Fourth, related to *inclusio*, 11:1–12:13 is structured according to recurrence regarding the notion of foolishness (ἀφροσύνη in 11:1, 17, 21; ἄφρων in 11:16 [twice], 19; 12:6, 11).[11] However, these terms do not appear in 12:14–13:10, which suggests that 11:1–12:13 forms a unit. Moreover, 10:1–12:13 is structured according to recurrence regarding the theme of boasting (καυχάομαι in 10:8, 13, 15, 16, 17 [twice]; 11:12, 16, 18 [twice], 30 [twice]; 12:1, 5 [twice], 6, 9; καύχησις in 11:10, 17), which suggests that 12:13 signals the ending.[12]

Fifth, the presence of the interjection ἰδού in 12:14 further suggests a unit boundary between 12:13 and 12:14. Runge describes ἰδού and other interjections (e.g., ἀμήν; ἀληθῶς/ἀληθείας; οὐαί ὑμῖν; ὃς ἔχει ὦτα ἀκούειν ἀκουέτωas) as "attention-getters" and treats them as forward-pointing devices.[13] Thus, he explains, "They have the effect of creating a break in the flow of the discourse that would not otherwise have been so noticeable."[14] In the case of 12:14, Paul employs this attention-getting device to signal a major break in his argument.[15] Therefore, these observations suggest that 10:1–12:13 is an independent unit, within which I identify two subunits: 10:1–18 and 11:1–12:13.

Regarding the structural relationship of generalization, 11:1–12:10 and 12:11–13 are structured according to ideological generalization, which summarizes some significant aspects of the discussion. See Bauer and Traina, *Inductive Bible Study*, 103–4. One could view this structure as summarization; however, Paul's description in 12:11–13 does not involve "a point-by-point recapitulation" (ibid., 110) of the preceding argument in 11:1–12:10 (e.g., the description does not include the notion of weakness, which is one of the major themes in his speech in 11:1–12:10). Also see my note under my discussion of summarization in 3.2.2.

[10] Basil of Caesarea, *Hom. Hex.* 9.7.63C; Augustine, *Serm.* 339 c. 1, cited in Rowe, "Style," 141. However, some identify 12:11 as *epidiorthosis* (BDF, §495[3]; Harris, *Second Epistle to the Corinthians*, 871), and others maintain 12:11–13 (Furnish, *II Corinthians*, 554) and 12:11–18 (McCant, *2 Corinthians*, 153) as *epidiorthosis*.

[11] Cf. εὐφραίνω in 2:2; σωφρονέω in 5:13; φρόνιμος in 11:19; παραφρονέω in 11:23.

[12] I have argued in 4.2.2.3 that the letter is structured according to the recurrence regarding the theme of boasting. Paul employs καυχάομαι and its cognates twenty-nine times in the letter (1:12, 14; 5:12 [twice]; 7:4, 14 [twice]; 8:24; 9:2, 3; 10:8, 13, 15, 16, 17 [twice]; 11:10, 12, 16, 17, 18 [twice], 30 [twice]; 12:1, 5 [twice], 6, 7). However, these terms most frequently occur in 10:1–12:13 (i.e., nineteen times).

[13] Runge, *Discourse Grammar*, 122–24.

[14] Ibid., 124. Also see my discussion on the demonstrative pronoun αὕτη in 1:12 as a forward-pointing device in 4.1.2.2.

[15] To be more precise, ἰδού is the aorist middle imperative of εἶδον (BDAG, s.v. "ἰδού"). Paul does not employ this form to signal a unit boundary in his letters (Rom 9:33; 1 Cor 15:51; 2 Cor 5:17; 6:2 [twice], 9; 7:11; Gal 1:20). However, he employs ἴδε (the aorist active imperative of εἶδον) to signal a major unit boundary in Gal 5:2, which many commentators identify as the beginning of a new literary unit (e.g., Martyn, *Galatians*, 476; Keener, *Galatians*, 443). Interestingly, some later manuscripts (999 [the thirteenth century] and 1891 [the tenth century]) replaced ἴδε in Gal 5:2 with ἰδού, leaving the impression that the scribes seem to have wanted to correct the grammar.

8.1.1.1 10:1-18

As indicated, many interpreters recognize 10:1-18 as a unit. Two observations particularly suggest that 10:1-18 forms the first subunit: a shift of topic between 10:1-18 and 11:1-12:13 and the implication from the structural relationship of generalization within 10:12-18. First, Paul transitions his argument from the basis for foolish boasting (10:1-18) to the content of foolish boasting (11:1-12:13). In 10:1-18, Paul describes the causes that force him to engage in the boasting competition, which Paul regards as foolish (11:1-12:13). Paul's adversaries question his status as a servant of Christ (10:1-11) and undermine his authority, especially regarding his ministerial jurisdiction (10:12-18). Thus, Paul's discussion in 10:1-18 forms a topical unity regarding the descriptions of the causes that have led him into a foolish boasting. Then, in 11:1-12:13, Paul begins to boast, especially by employing the terms ἀφροσύνη (11:1, 17, 21) and ἄφρων (11:16 [twice], 19; 12:6, 11), which characterize his boasting as foolish. Thus, one observes a shift of topic between 10:18 and 11:1.[16]

Second, an implication from the structural relationship of generalization within 10:12-18 suggests a unit boundary between 10:18 and 11:1. In 10:12-18, Paul begins to talk about the sphere of his authority (10:8), especially regarding the ministerial jurisdiction, and concludes his discussion with a general statement in 10:17-18, which identifies the essential character of his discussion in 10:12-18. One should boast in the Lord; one should be commended by the Lord.[17] This general statement functions as a conclusion of Paul's discussion in 10:12-18; thus, it suggests a unit boundary between 10:18 and 11:1. Therefore, I claim 10:1-18 as a unit.

Regarding the subunits within 10:1-18, I identify two units: 10:1-11 and 10:12-18, though I admit that 10:7-11 functions as a transitional section.[18] To begin, a topical unity suggests that 10:1-11 is an independent literary unit. Paul consistently implies the offense against his status throughout his discussion in 10:1-11, which suggests a topical unity in these verses. His adversaries accuse Paul of the timidity and inconsistency of his behaviors when he is present with and absent from the Corinthians (10:1, 11),[19] which led them to question Paul and his fellow workers' status as God's servants, for they appear to be walking/conducting according to the flesh (10:2). Moreover, this charge is particularly related to Paul's physical presence (10:10), for his opponents judge matters based on outward appearance (10:7a). Therefore, they doubt their status, thinking that they do not belong to Christ (10:7b). Thus, the topical unity regarding the offenses against the status of God's agents unifies 10:1-11.

---

[16] See further discussion in 8.2.1.3. Also, see my note on the structural relationship of *inclusio* (11:1-12:13) in 8.1. The structural relationship suggests a section boundary between 10:18 and 11:1. Moreover, the expression, Ὄφελον ἀνείχεσθέ μου μικρόν τι ἀφροσύνης in 11:1, conveys a sense of wish. If so, it may function similar to the appeal formula (see 7.1); thus, it marks a break between 10:18 and 11:1 (see the summary of scholarly debates on ὄφελον in 11:1 in Harris, *Second Epistle to the Corinthians*, 732).

[17] Thus, 10:12-16 and 10:17-18 are structured according to identificational generalization (see Bauer and Traina, *Inductive Bible Study*, 103).

[18] For this reason, some understand 10:7 as the beginning of a new unit (Barrett, *Second Epistle to the Corinthians*, 254-69).

[19] It is possible to construe that 10:1 and 10:11 are structured according to *inclusio* regarding the charge against Paul's inconsistency and timidity.

Furthermore, a topical unity regarding the offense against the ministerial jurisdiction also signals 10:12–18 as a unit. Paul begins to contrast himself and his fellow workers with their enemies who engage in a competition (10:12), violate the ministerial jurisdiction and boast in others' labors (10:13–16), and commend themselves (10:12, 17–18).[20] These contrastive descriptions regarding the adversaries suggest a topical unity.

Finally, 10:1–11 and 10:12–18 are structured according to substantiation, especially regarding the notion of Paul's authority. The presence of γάρ in 10:12 signals that the material in 10:12–18 strengthens Paul's discussion in 10:1–11.[21] In response to the charge against the status that Paul and his fellow workers do not belong to Christ (10:7b), Paul begins to respond to the offense by boasting about the authority God has granted his servants (10:8). In 10:12–18, Paul particularly strengthens the notion of the authority in relation to the ministerial jurisdiction. God used Paul and his fellow workers, but not his opponents, to preach the gospel to the Corinthians. However, their adversaries are violating the divine authority by boasting in others' labors (10:13–16). For these reasons, I maintain 10:1–11 and 10:12–18 as subunits within 10:1–18, while viewing 10:7–11 as a transitional section. Now I turn to the segmentation of 11:1–12:13.

8.1.1.2 11:1–12:13

Scholars disagree with one another regarding the identification of the beginning and the ending of Paul's speech.[22] However, I maintain that 11:1–12:13 is a unit. I have already discussed various observations regarding this segmentation: a shift of topic from the basis (10:1–18) to the content of foolish boasting (11:1–12:13) and the structural relationship of generalization within 10:12–18 suggest that 11:1 is the beginning of a unit (see 8.1.1.1). In addition, a topical shift from Paul's foolish boasting (10:1–12:13) to consequent ecclesial preparation for the impending visit (12:14–13:10), the insight from the structural relationships within 11:1–12:13 (i.e., generalization [11:1–12:10 and 12:11–13]; *inclusio* [11:1 and 12:11]; recurrence [11:1, 16, 17, 19, 21, 23; 12:6, 11]), and the interjection ἰδού in 12:14 suggest that 12:13 marks the ending of the unit (see 8.1). Thus, in this section, I focus on the identification of subunits within 11:1–12:13: 11:1–11:21a, 11:21b–12:10, and 12:11–13.

Regarding the first subunit (11:1–11:21a), four observations suggest that 11:1–21a is a unit: a topical unity, Paul's statement regarding speech in 11:21b, a shift of literary

---

[20] It is possible to construe 10:12 and 17 as being structured according to *inclusio* regarding self-commendation (So Harris, *Second Epistle to the Corinthians*, 727).

[21] On the discourse function of γάρ, see my discussion in 4.2.1.2. Also, one could view the conjunction γάρ in 10:8 beginning a unit. However, since Paul frames 10:1 and 11 regarding the charge against his timidity and inconsistency, I regard 10:1–11 as a unit, though, as I said above, 10:7–11 functions as a transitional unit. The difficulty pertains to the fact that Paul begins 10:7 with an asyndeton.

[22] As noted above in 8.1.1, many view 11:1 as the beginning of Paul's foolish boasting. However, some argue that 11:16 is the beginning of the speech (Lambrecht, *Second Corinthians*, 187–210; Thrall, *Second Epistle of the Corinthians*, 2:708–857; Martin, *2 Corinthians*, 542–620; cf. Long, *Ancient Rhetoric and Paul's Apology*, 186–90).

form, and the presence of δέ in 11:21b suggest that 11:1–21a forms a unit. First, a topical unity regarding the justification for the foolish boasting unifies 11:1–21a as a unit. In fact, giving a kind of preliminary justification called *prodiorthosis* was a conventional rhetorical technique with which rhetors attempt "to prepare the audience for a shocking or offensive statement."[23] In 11:1–21a, Paul prepares the audience for his speech proper (11:21b–12:10) by providing its justifications. After giving an introductory statement regarding the foolish boasting (11:1), Paul begins to explain the reasons that justify his boasting competition (11:21b–12:10). Paul is forced to boast like a fool because the adversaries have deceived the Corinthians by preaching another Jesus, a different spirit, and a different gospel (11:2–4), because they consider Paul inferior to the super-apostles (11:5–6), and because they criticize his financial independence (11:7–15). Then, Paul restates and develops the general statement (11:1) in 11:16–21a. Thus, this topical coherence suggests that 11:1–21a is a unit.

Second, Paul's statement in 11:21b, ἐν ᾧ δ' ἄν τις τολμᾷ, ἐν ἀφροσύνῃ λέγω, τολμῶ κἀγώ, indicates that his speech proper begins at 11:21b; thus, it marks a unit boundary between 11:21a and 11:21b. Related to the first observation, Paul has prepared his audience for his foolish boasting in 11:1–21a, and now he begins to "speak in foolishness."

Third, a shift of literary form from the justification of the defense (11:1–21a) to comparison with rivals (11:21b–23a) marks a break between 11:21a and 11:21b. As mentioned, Paul demonstrates justifications for his foolish boasting in 11:1–21a. Now, Paul begins to compare himself with his adversaries in 11:21b–23.[24] Thus, the change of the literary form further suggests a break between 11:21a and 11:21b.

Finally, the presence of δέ in 11:21b further supports the shift between 11:21a and 11:21b. As seen in many places in the previous discussions, δέ often marks a new development in Paul's discourse. Given the convergence of the aforementioned observations, the presence of δέ in 11:21b seems to add another piece of evidence that suggests a unit boundary between 11:21a and 11:21b. Therefore, I maintain 11:1–21a as a unit.

Concerning the beginning of 11:21b–12:10, I have already discussed the observations that signal a unit boundary between 11:21a and 11:21b. Also, many interpreters agree that 12:10 marks the ending of the unit.[25] Two pieces of evidence are particularly of significance for such a segmentation: the insight from the structural relationship of interchange (11:23b–12:10) and the presence of διό in 12:10. First, having made a general statement regarding his status as a servant of Christ (11:21b–23a), Paul begins to develop the content of boasting speech 11:23b–12:10, which is structured according to interchange (i.e., A-B-A-B arrangement) as follows:

---

[23] Galen O. Rowe, "Style," in *Handbook of Classical Rhetoric in the Hellenistic Period, 330 B.C.–A.D. 400*, ed. Stanley E. Porter (Leiden: Brill, 1997), 121–57; BDF, §495(3).

[24] The comparison begins with a general statement in 11:21b and moves to a point-by-point comparison regarding the Jewish heritage with which both Paul and his rivals were innately born (11:22) and their status as servants of Christ (11:23a). Ancient rhetoricians often employed a point-by-point comparison (Menander Rhetor, 2.3, 381.31–32; 386.10–13; 2.10, 416.2–4; 417.5–9, cited in Keener, *1–2 Corinthians*, 232–33).

[25] See my note above.

A: Boast in Suffering (11:23b–11:29)
B: Boast in Weakness (11:30–33)
A: Boast in Visions and Revelations (12:1–5a)
B: Boast in Weakness (12:5b–10)

Therefore, this rhetorical structure implies that 12:10 marks the ending of the unit.[26]

Second, the conjunction διό signals that 12:10 draws an inferential conclusion of the speech proper in 11:21b–12:10. As I have already discussed in 6.1.2.2, διό usually does not move his argument to a new point as οὖν does; instead, it draws an inferential conclusion. In 12:9–10, Paul employs both οὖν (12:9) and διό (12:10).[27] Thus, while οὖν in 12:9 signals the conclusion of his discussion regarding the thorn in the flesh (12:7–9), διό in 12:10 indicates that Paul draws an inferential conclusion of the entire speech (11:21b–12:10).

Finally, along with 11:1–21a and 11:21b–12:10, I identify 12:11–13 as a unit, for a topical shift between 10:1–12:13 and 12:14–13:10, the insight from the structural relationship of generalization, *inclusio*, and recurrence, and the ἰδού in 12:14 suggest that 12:13 is the ending of the unit (see 8.1.1). Therefore, I maintain three subunits within 11:1–12:13: 11:1–21a, 11:21b–12:10, and 12:11–13. Having analyzed the segmentation of 10:1–12:13, I now turn to the analysis of 12:14–13:10.

8.1.2 12:14–13:10

Since I have already demonstrated the identifications of the beginning (12:14) and ending of the unit (13:10; see 3.1 and 8.1), I will focus on the subunits of 12:14–13:10.

Some consider that 12:19 is the beginning of the new unit.[28] However, two observations are especially of significance to suggest that 12:14–21 and 13:1–10 form respective units: Paul's second announcement of the third visit in 13:1 and the insight from the structural relationship of causation (12:14–21 and 13:1–10). First, Paul restates his third visit in 13:1 (cf. 12:14), which suggests a unit boundary. Guthrie calls the parallel statement in 12:14 and 13:1 "Parallel Introductions."[29] Furthermore, the statements in 12:14 and 13:10 are not merely parallel. Paul skillfully crafts his language to underscore his impending visit. In 12:14, he states his readiness to visit the Corinthians (Ἰδοὺ τρίτον τοῦτο ἑτοίμως ἔχω ἐλθεῖν πρὸς ὑμᾶς), but in 13:1, he announces that he is coming (Τρίτον τοῦτο ἔρχομαι πρὸς ὑμᾶς). Shifting the expression from the readiness to come (12:14) to actual coming (13:1), Paul builds up his arguments within 12:14–13:10.[30]

---

[26] See more discussion in the MSR of causation with the particularization in 8.2.1.2.
[27] Also see my discussion of οὖν in 6.1.1.
[28] E.g., Plummer, *Second Epistle*, 365–79; Barrett, *Second Epistle to the Corinthians*, 326–41; McCant, *2 Corinthians*, 157–72; Thrall, *Second Epistle of the Corinthians*, 2:857–900; Martin, *2 Corinthians*, 646–87.
[29] George H. Guthrie, *The Structure of Hebrews: A Text-Linguistic Analysis*, NovTSup 73 (Leiden: Brill, 1994), 104–5; idem, *2 Corinthians*, 629n1.
[30] Moreover, it seems intentional that Paul re-announces the third visit in 13:1a in relation to his allusion to Deut 19:15 in 13:1b, for his third visit seems to function as the witness for his impending potential discipline over the Corinthians.

Second, the insight from the structural relationship of causation further supports a shift of emphasis between 12:14–21 and 13:1–10. Namely, Paul establishes the basis for the ecclesial preparation for the impending visit in 12:14–21. Paul will come to the Corinthians as their parent (12:14–18), who is also responsible for the spiritual well-being of his children through discipline (13:1–10). He insists that his argument is for the Corinthians' upbuilding (12:19); thus, he will not execute the discipline out of self-interest (12:19; 13:1–10). He describes his possible mourning over many of those who sinned in the past and never repented (12:21); thus, he will not spare them when he visits them (13:2). Therefore, Paul establishes the ground for his preparation for the impending visit in 12:14–21 and then proceeds to prepare the Corinthians by a warning (13:1–4), a command to test themselves (13:5–6), and prayers (13:7–9) so that he does not have to carry out his stern discipline over them (13:10).[31] For these reasons, I maintain that 12:14–21 and 13:1–10 as subunits within 12:14–13:10.

8.1.2.1 12:14–21

Regarding the subunits within 12:14–21, I demarcate it into 12:14a, 14b–18 and 12:19–21 based on thematic unities. In this section, after announcing his visit in 12:14a, Paul attempts to establish the basis for his impending visit in two fashions. On the one hand, he emphasizes his parent-child relationship with the Corinthians in 12:14–18, in which he clarifies his financial integrity. Thus, he insists that his intention of the visit is to seek and love the Corinthians but not to exploit them (12:14–15), and then substantiates his claim by appealing to his financial integrity in the past (12:16–18).

On the other hand, he shifts a topic from his parent-child relationship to his upbuilding relationship with the Corinthians in 12:19–21. The shift is apparent because his statement in 12:19, κατέναντι θεοῦ ἐν Χριστῷ λαλοῦμεν, clearly ties to the proclamation of the gospel (i.e., defense of the gospel here) as I have already discussed it (see 5.2.2.2 and Table 5.3). Thus, in 12:20–21 he substantiates the claim in 12:19; Paul underscores that the vice list in 12:20 and his possible morning over the unrepented in 12:21 will be consequences if he does not defend the gospel (12:19). Therefore, I identify two subunits within 12:14–21.

8.1.2.2 13:1–10

Regarding the subunits within 13:1–10, I identify three units: 13:1, 2–9, and 10 according to thematic unities. After announcing his visit once again in 13:1, in 13:2–9 Paul proceeds to prepare the Corinthians for the upcoming visit by warning that he will not spare them (13:2–4), giving command to test themselves (13:5–6), and offering prayers that they may not do anything wrong and that they may become mature (13:7–9). Then, Paul concludes the section by clarifying that the intent of his visit is to build up but not tear down (13:10). Having analyzed the segmentation of 10:1–13:10, I will

---

[31] See more discussion in 8.2.1.4.

turn to the second part of the literary structure: the MSRs in relation to both the division as a whole and the letter as a whole.

8.2 Major Structural Relationships

Having established the segmentation of 10:1–13:10, I will turn to demonstrate (1) the ways in which the main units and subunits within 10:1–13:10 are related to one another, and then (2) discuss the ways in which Paul's discourse in 10:1–13:10 is related to the rest of the letter. The MSRs in relation to the division as a whole show that while the locutionary purpose of Paul's argument regarding foolish boasting (10:1–12:13) aims to establish grounds to prepare and exhort the Corinthians for his impending visit (12:14–13:10), the perlocutionary purpose of his discourse pertains to the defense of his status as a servant of Christ in order to defend the gospel for the Corinthians' salvation. The MSRs in relation to the letter as a whole indicate that Paul views his arguments both in 3:1–9:15 and 10:1–13:10 as related aspects of the same ministry.

8.2.1 In Relation to Division as a Whole

Regarding the MSRs in relation to the division as a whole, I will expound four MSRs: *inclusio*, instrumentation (statement of purpose), causation with particularization and contrast, and causation. *Inclusio*, instrumentation (statement of purpose), and causation indicate that the primary purpose of Paul's discourse in 10:1–13:10 pertains to Paul's impending visit. Causation with particularization and contrast (10:1–18 and 11:1–12:13) shows that Paul's boasting (10:1–12:13) centers on the defense of his status as a servant of Christ.

8.2.1.1 *Inclusio (10:1–13:10)*

I propose that 10:1–13:10 is structured according to a conceptual *inclusio*. Paul frames the division regarding statements of his desire not to impose discipline on the Corinthians when he is present with them (10:1–2; 13:10). Thus, the *inclusio* shows that the primary concern of Paul's discourse in 10:1–13:10 pertains to his impending visit (10:1, 10; 12:14; 13:10), especially regarding the exercise of the discipline over some Corinthians according to the authority God has given to him (10:8; 13:10; cf. 12:19). The *inclusio* further reinforces the semantic structure of instrumentation (10:1–13:9 and 13:10; see 8.2.1.2) and causation (10:1–12:13 and 12:14–13:10; see 8.2.1.4)

8.2.1.2 *Instrumentation (Statement of Purpose; 13:10)*

Closely related to the *inclusio*, I observe instrumentation (statement of purpose) in 13:10. At the end of the division, Paul states, διὰ τοῦτο ταῦτα ἀπὼν γράφω, ἵνα παρὼν μὴ ἀποτόμως χρήσωμαι κατὰ τὴν ἐξουσίαν ἣν ὁ κύριος ἔδωκέν μοι εἰς οἰκοδομὴν καὶ οὐκ εἰς καθαίρεσιν. Some commentators take this sentence as the purpose statement of the entire letter.³² While such possibility is not excluded, I view the statement more closely related to his discussion in 10:1–13:10, for Paul's statements regarding his reluctancy to exercise stern discipline in 10:1–2 and 13:10 frame the division (thus, *inclusio*).

Thus, *inclusio* and instrumentation (10:1–2 and 13:10) indicate Paul's understanding of the divine authority on two levels. On the one hand, Paul does not desire to discipline the Corinthians if possible (10:2; 13:10), although he is ready and capable of doing so (10:1–6). Instead, as their parent (12:14), he seeks to love them (12:15); thus, he wants to exercise the authority for their upbuilding but not for their destruction (10:8; 13:10; cf. 12:19). On the other hand, while he does not want to experience disappointment and humiliation by them or to mourn over their sins (12:20–21), when he must execute the discipline over his spiritual children as their parent, he insists that his discipline is for their upbuilding, though they may feel that they are being torn down (10:18; 13:10; cf. 12:19).

Moreover, the *inclusio* and instrumentation suggest that Paul does not regard the punishment as the most effective way to edify the Corinthians, for he emphasizes his reluctancy both in the beginning and ending of the division (10:1–2; 13:10). Savage's observations on 10:5–6 and 1:23–2:11 further reinforce this point:

> In 2 Corinthians 10:5–6 we read that Paul withholds the use of force until the thoughts of his converts are taken captive for obedience to Christ. Presumably then he will punish, but only his opponents. The same sequence is found in the early chapters of the epistle ... (1:23–2:11). On this evidence it would seem that Paul feels he can more successfully foster true obedience by withholding punishment than by unleashing it.³³

Therefore, Paul's concluding statement in 13:10 serves as the purpose statement of his argument in 10:1–13:10 in light of the *inclusio* (10:1–2; 13:10).

8.2.1.3 Causation with Particularization and Contrast (10:1–18 and 11:1–12:13)

Regarding the relationship between 10:1–18 and 11:1–12:13, some scholars treat Paul's discussion in 10:1–18 and 11:1–12:13 as separate topics, paying less attention to the ways in which each discussion is related.³⁴ Others attempt to scrutinize the relationships

---

³² E.g., Matera, *II Corinthians*, 310.
³³ Savage, *Power through Weakness*, 68.
³⁴ E.g., Scott categorizes Paul's arguments based on topics: the opponents' accusation against Paul (10:1–18); Paul's boasting (11:1–12:13); and Paul's preparation for his third visit (12:14–13:10; *2 Corinthians*, 193); Barnett demarcates Paul's arguments according to the various groups of his opponents: they are "those who regard him as spiritually powerless (10:1–11), the 'superlative' apostles (10:12–12:13), and the morally wayward (12:20–13:3)" (*Second Epistle to the Corinthians*, 479–80).

between 10:1-18 and 11:1-12:13.³⁵ While their attempts to analyze the relationships between these units are commendable, commentators do not fully develop their analyses, and those using rhetorical criticism disagree on the identification of the segmentation.³⁶ Therefore, in this section, I will demonstrate how Paul's discussion between 10:1-18 and 11:1-12:13 is related. Namely, I argue that 10:1-18 and 11:1-12:13 are structured according to causation with particularization and contrast. Although this MSR does not pertain to the relationship between main units (i.e., 10:1-12:13 and 12:14-13:10), I decided to include the analysis of this structural relationship as one of the MSRs, for it controls the bulk of the division (i.e., almost 80 percent of the material in 10:1-13:10—sixty-four out of eighty-two verses). In 10:1-18, Paul describes the causes that force him to engage in the boasting competition (causation), and in 11:1-12:13, he further explains the causes described in 10:1-18 (particularization). Moreover, Paul begins to defend his status as a servant of Christ in 10:1-12 and fully develops it in 11:1-12:13 (particularization). Paul also develops his arguments in the way of contrast between himself and his adversaries who influence the Corinthians (contrast).

On the one hand, in 10:1-18, Paul describes two fundamental offenses that force him to boast like a fool in 11:1-12:13 (causation). One is the offense against Paul's status (10:7). In 10:1-11, Paul implies his accusers' offense against him (10:1, 2, 7, 10); however, these charges boil down to the offense against his status: Paul does not belong to Christ (10:7b). His timidity and meekness when present and his inconsistency of behavior (10:1; 10; cf. 1:15-22) have led his opponents to regard that he is walking according to the flesh (10:2), failing to meet their "standard,"³⁷ for they evaluate him based on their superficial judgment (10:7a). Therefore, the adversaries have come to question his status as a servant of Christ (10:7b).

The other is the offense against Paul's authority. Paul begins to respond to the offense by boasting in the divine authority (10:8), and particularly in 10:12-18, he criticizes the accusers' behaviors, all of which are related to the offense against the authority. Namely, they undermine the divine authority. Based on their self-commendation (10:12, 17-18), they violate the ministerial jurisdiction and boast in others' labor (10:13-16), for they compete with each other in their ministry (10:12). Thus, Paul is forced to respond to their offense through a foolish boasting in 11:1-12:13. At the same time, in 10:12-18,

---

[35] E.g., Some argue that 10:1-6 functions as a letter opening (Furnish, *II Corinthians*, 459) or an introduction (Seifrid, *Second Letter to the Corinthians*, 373), preparing the audience for the following discussion. Some identify 10:1-6 as *exordium*, getting the attention of the audience (Peterson, *Eloquence and the Proclamation of the Gospel in Corinth*, 84), though some claim that 10:1-11 functions as *exordium* in the form of *insinuatio* (Hans-Georg Sundermann, *Der Schwache Apostel Und Die Kraft Der Rede: Eine Rhetorische Analyse von 2 Kor 10-13*, Europäische Hochschulschriften XXIII 575 [Frankfurt: Lang, 1996], 86; Thrall, *Second Epistle of the Corinthians*, 2: 597-98). Others discuss or infer structural relationships. For instance, Garland argues that Paul's discussion in 10:12-18 establishes the ground for his boasting (*2 Corinthians*, 450); Matera posits, "the theme of 'boasting,' with which this unit [10:1-18] concludes, prepares for Paul's foolish boasting in 11:1-12:13" (*II Corinthians*, 216); and Harris implies a contrastive relationship: Paul rebukes self-praise (10:1-18), but he boasts like a fool (11:1-12:13; *Second Epistle to the Corinthians*, 729).

[36] However, rhetorical critics bring helpful insights as well. See some affinities between my analysis and rhetorical criticism in my discussion below in 8.2.2.

[37] The expression, κατὰ σάρκα in 10:2, refers to the human standard in 2 Corinthians (1:17; 5:16; 11:18).

Paul also establishes the ground for his following speech (11:1–12:13). Because God has granted him the authority to preach the gospel to the Corinthians (10:8), unlike his adversaries (10:12, 17–18), Paul does have a basis to boast before the Corinthians (11:1–12:13). Although he is reluctant to do so, his boasting is not beyond his measure; rather, it is proper within the sphere God assigned him (10:13–16).

Moreover, these two offenses are closely related. Because the enemies undermine Paul's authority by violating the ministerial jurisdiction and trying to compete with Paul (10:12–18), they began to teach the Corinthians their standard for what God's servants should be (10:1, 2, 10) based on outward judgement (10:7) and to lead them to suspect Paul's status, questioning if he indeed belongs to Christ (10:7b). Therefore, the offenses against his status (10:1–11) and authority (10:8, 11–18) cause Paul to engage in a boasting competition (11:1–12:13); thus, Paul repeats that he is forced to do so (11:1–21a; 12:1, 11).

On the other hand, Paul additionally develops his discussion in 11:1–12:13 in two manners (particularization). First, Paul unpacks some details of the offenses against his status and authority in 11:1–12:13. While the opponents question Paul's status (10:7b) based on superficial judgment (10:1, 2, 7, 10), he further explains in 11:1–12:13 that their criticism arises from their perception of Paul being inferior to super-apostles (11:5; 12:11) due to his contemptible speech (11:6; cf. 10:10) and their construal of Paul's financial independence (11:7–15; 12:13).[38] Thus, they question if Paul is a servant of Christ (11:23). Likewise, while Paul describes the offense against his authority in 10:12–18, he adds some details in 11:1–12:13. While the adversaries compete with each other (10:12) and boast in others' labors (10:13–16), Paul further describes that they want to be regarded as equal with Paul and his fellow workers (11:12). While the opponents came with self-commendation (10:12, 17–18), Paul continues to clarify that they disguise themselves as apostles of Christ (11:13–15). Thus, they violate the ministerial jurisdiction (10:13–16) by deceiving the Corinthians and leading them astray from Christ (11:3) through the proclamation of the false gospel (11:4). As a result, they exploit the Corinthians (11:20). Therefore, Paul's discussion in 11:1–12:13 develops the description of the offenses mentioned in 10:1–18.

Second, Paul begins his defense in 10:1–18 and fully develops it in 11:1–12:13. In response to the charge against his status (10:7b), Paul begins to defend it, insisting that he belongs to Christ (10:7b) and that he is consistent in his words and actions (10:11).[39] Therefore, Paul proceeds to expound it in 11:1–12:10. In fact, the structural relationships within 11:1–12:13 indicate that the defense of his status as a servant of Christ centers on Paul's speech. The structural relationships of causation (11:1–21a and 11:21b–

---

[38] As many scholars have already pointed out, the opponents seem to have considered Paul's weak physical presence (10:10) and his inability of speech (11:6) incompatible with his status. See the discussion on the rhetorical expectations in Keener, *1–2 Corinthians*, 218–19. Also, they regarded Paul's financial independence as an indication of his inferior status, for not only those who worked with their hands were often considered to be in a lower social stratum, but also his rejection of benefactions meant the rejection of friendship (Barnett, *Second Epistle to the Corinthians*, 513–14; Keener, *1–2 Corinthians*, 228–29; Martin, *2 Corinthians*, 529–30).

[39] Also note that the λογίζομαι in 10:7b and 10:11 is in the imperative form, denoting Paul's emphasis on the statement.

12:10), particularization (11:21b–23a and 11:23b–12:10), interchange (A: 11:24–29; B: 11:30–33; A: 12:1–5a; B: 12:5b–10), and generalization (11:1–12:10 and 12:11–13) are particularly helpful to trace the primary emphasis on Paul's discourse in 11:1–12:13. To begin, 11:1–21a and 11:21b–12:10 are structured according to causation, for Paul gives justifications/basis for his fool's boasting in 11:1–21a, preparing the audience for the speech proper in 11:21b–12:10.

Furthermore, Paul's boasting speech proper is structured according to particularization (11:21b–23a and 11:23b–12:10). In 11:21b–23a, Paul gives a general statement for the following material in 11:23b–12:10 regarding his status. He begins to compare himself with the adversaries regarding hereditary status: He has the same Jewish heritage with which both he and his rivals were innately born (11:22). However, he declares in 11:23a that he is a servant of Christ more than anyone else: διάκονοι Χριστοῦ εἰσιν; παραφρονῶν λαλῶ, ὑπὲρ ἐγώ.[40] This status is not hereditary (11:22); thus, Paul proceeds to show the ways in which he is a superior servant of Christ over his rivals in 11:23b–12:10 (cf. 10:7b). Therefore, particularization indicates that Paul's primary concern is to defend his status as a servant of Christ (11:23b).

Moreover, 11:23b–12:10 is structured according to interchange as follows:

A: Boast in Suffering (11:23b–11:29)
B: Boast in Weakness (11:30–33)
A: Boast in Visions and Revelations (12:1–5a)
B: Boast in Weakness (12:5b–10)[41]

Structuring his speech according to interchange (A-B-A-B arrangement), Paul skillfully crafts his argument by contrasting his boastings according to human standard (A) and his boasting in weakness (B).[42] The list of the hardships in 11:23b–29, called the *peristaseis* catalog, demonstrates the proof of Paul's servanthood, for "*Peristaseis* catalogs serve to legitimate the claims made about a person and show him to be virtuous because *peristaseis* have a revelatory and probative function in regard to character."[43] Likewise, his experience of visions in 12:1–5a demonstrates that he is superior to the adversaries even according to their standard.[44] However, he concludes

---

[40] Note Paul's expressions of κἀγώ (11:21, 22 [three times]) and ὑπὲρ ἐγώ (11:23a). His argument moves from the qualifications his rivals can compete (κἀγώ; 11:22) to the areas they cannot (ὑπὲρ ἐγώ; 11:23a).

[41] Also, Paul's defense of status as well as his ministry of the speech reaches its climax at 12:9-10. See my discussion in 8.2.2.3.

[42] Moreover, Paul begins each section (11:21b-29; 11:30-33; 12:1-5a; 12:5b-10) with a general statement (11:21b-23a; 11:30; 12:1; 12:5b) and develops the general statement (11:23b-30; 11:31-33; 12:2-5a; 12:6-10).

[43] Fitzgerald, *Cracks in an Earthen Vessel*, 203; also see 47-201; Cf. 2 Cor 4:8-9; 6:3-10; 12:10; Rom 8:35; 1 Cor 4:9-13. Likewise, in 12:10, at the climax of the defense of his status, Paul once again enumerates his afflictions as loci of God's power in weakness. See also my discussion regarding the ways in which Paul utilizes the *peristaseis* catalogs of 4:8-9 and 6:3-10 to reinforce his ministerial credentials in 5.2.2.2.

[44] Plummer, *Second Epistle*, 339; Windisch, *Zweite Korintherbrief*, 368. Also see the list of scholars who interpret Paul's experience as a response to his enemies who boast about their own experience in the survey of the history of the research of 2 Cor 12:1-10 in Lisa M. Bowens, *An Apostle in Battle: Paul and Spiritual Warfare in 2 Corinthians 12:1-10*, WUNT 2/433 (Tübingen: Mohr Siebeck, 2017), 3-6.

each argument (11:23b-29; 12:1-5a) with the discussions regarding weakness (11:30-33; 12:5b-10). In structuring his argument in this way (i.e., A-B-A-B), Paul reinforces a contrast between A (11:23b-29; 12:1-5a) and B (11:30-33; 12:5-10), underscoring that weakness is not incompatible with his status as a servant of Christ. While showing his superior experience of sufferings (11:23b-29) and visions (12:1-5a), he insists that he does not boast according to the standard with which the opponents judge him; rather, he boasts in his weaknesses (11:30-33; 12:5b-10) so that the divine power may be manifested in his weaknesses (12:9-10).[45]

Finally, 11:1-12:10 and 12:11-13 are structured according to generalization.[46] These four structural relationships (causation, particularization, interchange, and generalization) within 11:1-12:13 show that Paul's primary concern in his discourse in 11:1-12:13 pertains to the defense of his status as a servant of Christ (cf. 10:7b; 11:23b). Causation indicates that Paul's discourse in 11:1-21a establishes bases for his speech proper in 11:21b-12:10. Particularization demonstrates that Paul's emphatic statement regarding his stature as a servant of Christ (11:23a) serves as a thesis-like statement, and the following material in 11:23b-12:10 shows the ways in which he is so. Thus, the primary concern of his speech proper pertains to the defense of Paul's status as a servant of Christ (11:23a; cf. 10:7b). Interchange in 11:23b-12:10 reveals a strong contrast between human boastings (suffering and revelations) and Paul's boasting (weakness), emphasizing that weakness is not incompatible with his status as a servant of Christ, for divine power will be manifested through weaknesses. Generalization summarizes salient points of his arguments in 11:1-12:10. Thus, Paul's argument in 11:1-12:13 essentially develops his earlier claim in 10:7b regarding his status that he belongs to Christ.

In addition, as my discussion implies, Paul develops his argument in 10:1-12:13 by a contrast between himself and his enemies who criticize Paul and influence some of the Corinthians. Essentially, the contrast involves the opponents' criticism against Paul's status and his defense of the status (see my discussion in 5.2.4).

Therefore, 10:1-18 and 11:1-12:13 are related in three manners. First, Paul describes the offenses (10:1-18) that force him to engage in a boasting competition (11:1-12:13; causation). Second, Paul explains the details of those offenses and develops his defense of the status (10:7b) in 11:1-12:13 (particularization). Third, Paul develops his defense by way of contrast between himself and his adversaries (contrast).

8.2.1.4 Causation (10:1-12:13 and 12:14-13:10)

Regarding the relationship between Paul's discussion on foolish boasting (10:1-12:13) and the consequent ecclesial preparation for his impending visit (12:14-13:10), many

---

[45] In fact, David Alan Black convincingly argues based on his study in Pauline letters, especially the Corinthian Correspondence, that Paul creates the doctrine of weakness for the first time in history by employing ἀσθένεια and its cognates with a positive theological meaning, for no other authors in Classical Greek, LXX, or the rest of the NT do so (*Paul, Apostle of Weakness: Astheneia and Its Cognates in the Pauline Literature*, 2nd ed. [Eugene, OR: Pickwick, 2012]).

[46] See my discussion in 8.1.1.

scholars do not pay close attention to the organic relationship between 10:1–12:13 and 12:14–13:10. Some provide explanations,[47] especially those using rhetorical criticism.[48] However, as I previously mentioned (see 8.2.1.3), commentators do not fully develop their analyses, and the flexibility of *peroratio* allows rhetorical critics to identify its various segementation. Nevertheless, the MSR of causation shares some elements with those in *peroratio*, such as Paul's self-reflection, recapitulation of the arguments, admonitions to make the decision, and emotional appeal.[49] The major difference is that *peroratio* presupposes that aforementioned elements refer back to the entire speech, whereas the MSR of causation shows Paul's discussion in 12:14–13:10 more closely related to his argument in 10:1–12:13. Therefore, in this section, I claim that Paul's discourse on foolish boasting (10:1–12:13) and consequent ecclesial preparation for the impending visit (12:14–13:10) are structured according to causation. As the *inclusio* structure (see 8.2.1.1) shows, the chief concern of Paul's discourse in 10:1–13:10 pertains to his impending visit (10:1, 10; 12:14; 13:10). However, Paul must defend his status first (10:1–12:13), for they were questioning Paul's financial integrity (12:14–18) and seeking the proof of Paul's status as a servant of Christ (13:3a), particularly regarding his weakness (13:3b–4). Thus, Paul proceeds to defend his status (10:7b; 11:23a; see 8.2.1.3) so that he can prepare the Corinthians for his future visit (12:14–13:10). In other words, while Paul has the impending visit in mind from the beginning of the discussion (10:1–13:10), establishing his status is necessary to prepare the Corinthians for the successful visit so that he can come to the Corinthians as a parent to seek and love them (12:14–18) and exercise the discipline when needed (13:1–10). This is why, in his discussion in 12:14–13:10, Paul consistently refers back to his previous argument in 10:1–12:13 to show that he has already addressed those criticisms (i.e., his financial integrity [12:14–18], his status [13:3a], and his weakness [13:3b–4, 9]).[50] Moreover, he turns their charges against him and asks the Corinthians to examine themselves (13:5–6). Therefore, in 12:19, Paul corrects the perception of the Corinthians that he has been defending himself for his own interest;[51] rather, he insists that his speech (10:1–12:13) is for their upbuilding (cf. 10:8; 13:10) because without their proper recognition of Paul's status, he can neither build a loving relationship with the Corinthians (12:14–18) nor exercise the discipline (13:1–10) for their upbuilding.

---

[47] E.g., Matera rightly implies that Paul's argument in 10:1–12:13 serves as a basis for his discussion in 12:14–13:10 (*II Corinthians*, 291).

[48] They understand the last section of the letter as *peroratio*, which summarizes the arguments (i.e., the proofs) and appeals to the emotions of the audience. Witherington understands 13:5–10 as *peroratio* (*Conflict and Community in Corinth*, 471–73); Long (*Ancient Rhetoric and Paul's Apology*, 190–97) and Martin (*2 Corinthians*, 621) identify 12:11–13:10 as *peroratio*; Peterson claims that 12:19–13:10 is *peroratio* (*Eloquence and the Proclamation of the Gospel in Corinth*, 157–59); Sundermann (*Schwache Apostel und die Kraft der Rede*, 47–48, 214), and Thrall (*Second Epistle of the Corinthians*, 2:871) posit that 13:1–10 functions as *peroratio*.

[49] See Long, *Ancient Rhetoric and Paul's Apology*, 190–97.

[50] Lambrecht similarly notes the presence of a number of similar motifs in both chs 10 and 13 (*Second Corinthians*, 158–59).

[51] The present tense verb δοκεῖτε in 12:19 denotes, "the present of past action still in progress" (Robertson, *Grammar*, 879).

Therefore, Paul's discussion on foolish boasting (10:1–12:13) establishes a basis for the consequent ecclesial preparation for his impending visit (12:14–13:10).[52]

8.2.2 In Relation to the Letter as a Whole

In this section, I will present three MSRs in relation to the letter as a whole: recurrence of causation (3:1–9:15 and 10:1–13:10), substantiation with particularization and instrumentation (description of means; 3:1–9:15 and 10:1–13:10), and generalization with climax (12:9–10). The first indicates a formal relationship between 3:1–9:15 and 10:1–13:10; the second and third show the conceptual connection between 3:1–9:15 and 10:1–13:10.[53]

8.2.2.1 Recurrence of Causation (3:1–9:15 and 10:1–13:10)

I posit that 3:1–9:15 and 10:1–13:10 are structured according to recurrence of causation. In 3:1–9:15, Paul moves from the proclamation of the gospel (3:1–7:16) to the

---

[52] In addition, 10:1–12:13 and 12:14–13:10 may be structured according to comparison regarding its purpose of ministry. Paul repeats οἰκοδομή in 12:19 and 13:10. In 12:19, Paul corrects the perception of the Corinthians and emphasizes that the proclamation of the gospel (i.e., the defense of the gospel) aims for upbuilding so that the Corinthians can avoid all the vices listed in 12:20–21. In 13:10, Paul clarifies that his impending visit is for the Corinthians' upbuilding. Paul consistently explains that ministries of both the proclamation of the gospel and apostolic visit have the same purpose: οἰκοδομή.

[53] Scholars sometimes discuss the comparison regarding the lexical and thematic continuities between chs 1–9 and chs 10–13 (e.g., Barnett, *Second Epistle to the Corinthians*, 19–23; Garland, *2 Corinthians*, 40–44; Harris, *Second Epistle to the Corinthians*, 44–51). However, many of the affinities are actually implied from the MSRs of causation with particularization (1:3–2:13 and 2:14–13:10; see 4.2.2.1), recurrence (see 4.2.2.3), and particularization with contrast (2:14–17 and 3:1–13:10; see ch. 5). For instance, in 4.2.2.1, I have demonstrated that Paul introduces the notion of divine encouragement and suffering in 1:3–2:13, which is further developed in 10:1–13:10, especially in his discussion in 11:21b–12:10 (i.e., the catalog of suffering; divine encouragement in his struggle with the thorn in the flesh). Also, my discussions on the recurrence structure regarding the themes of service/work, boasting, grace/joy/forgiveness/thanksgiving, love, and Christ imply the continuities regarding these themes in Paul's discussion between 3:1–9:15 and 10:1–13:10 (see 4.2.2.3). Likewise, in ch. 5, I have demonstrated the ways in which Paul develops the thesis statement of the letter (2:14–17) in the following material in 3:1–13:10 regarding the paradoxical nature of God's mission, the manifestation of God's knowledge, the sacrificial overtone, the theme of death and life, the credentials of God's agents, Christ's intermediary role, false apostles' lack of integrity, and misrepresentation of God's knowledge (see 5.2). Thus, Paul's discourse in 3:1–9:15 and 10:1–13:10 naturally share some affinities. Particularly, I have shown the link between 2:17 and 12:19 in which Paul employs the verbatim expression: κατέναντι θεοῦ ἐν Χριστῷ λαλοῦμεν (2:17; 12:19). Also, I have shown that Paul's discourse in 3:1–7:16 centers on the proclamation of the gospel (ch. 6). Thus, the parallel suggests that Paul does not view the proclamation of the gospel (3:1–7:16) and the defense of the gospel (10:1–13:10) as separate entities; rather, he understands that both are indispensable aspects of the ministry to disseminate God's knowledge. Paul insists in 10:4–5 that he destroys speculations and every arrogance raised up against God's knowledge and takes every thought captive to the obedience of Christ (10:4–5). The immediate literary context in 10:1–13:10 indicates that this arrogance against God's knowledge essentially pertains to the criticism against Paul's status (10:7; 11:23). At the same time, the broader literary context shows that God's knowledge is closely related to the gospel of Christ (2:14; 4:4–6). Thus, Paul defends his status in order to eradicate any harm against God's knowledge, the gospel. So, in Paul's understanding, the repudiation of criticism against his status is a form of the proclamation of the gospel. In other words, because Paul develops the thesis statement (2:14–17) in the material in 3:1–13:10, his discourse in 3:1–7:16 and 10:1–13:10 functions as the particulars of the thesis statement; thus, they naturally share affinities.

exhortation to respond to the gospel (8:1–9:15; see 7.2.2). Likewise, in 10:1–13:10, Paul moves from foolish boasting (10:1–12:13) to consequent ecclesial preparation for the impending visit (12:14–13:10; see 8.2.1.4). Therefore, in both 3:1–9:15 and 10:1–13:10, Paul moves from arguments in the indicatives to exhortations in the imperatives; thus, 3:1–13:10 is structured according to recurrence of hortatory causation.[54] The recurrence structure points to the occasion of Paul's writing of 2 Corinthians, since Paul urges the Corinthians to fulfill his exhortations in both 8:1–9:15 and 12:14–13:10 before his arrival (9:3–5; 12:14, 20, 21; 13:1, 2, 10).

8.2.2.2 Substantiation with Particularization and Instrumentation (Description of Means; 3:1–9:15 and 10:1–13:10)

Paul's discourse in 3:1–9:15 and 10:1–13:10 are structured according to substantiation with particularization and instrumentation (description of means). As I have noted at the beginning of this chapter, the majority of scholars admit the abrupt change and tone in Paul's discourse in chs 10–13, attributing the change to partition theories and/ or to different historical situations.[55] Consequently, many do not consider the ways in which Paul's discourse in 3:1–9:15 and 10:1–13:10 are conceptually connected,[56] yet interpreters employing rhetorical criticism attempt to understand the thought connections between chs 1–9 and 10–13.[57] However, as I have repeatedly pointed out, they disagree with one another on the rhetorical disposition of the letter. Their insights are helpful for understanding the literary form of Paul's discussion in 10:1–12:13 as the

---

[54] On hortatory causation, see Bauer and Traina, *Inductive Bible Study*, 106.
[55] See the history of the interpretation in Thrall, *Second Epistle of the Corinthians*, 1:5–20; Harris, *Second Epistle to the Corinthians*, 29–51; Vegge, *2 Corinthians*, 7–34.
[56] Nevertheless, some scholars do discuss the thought connection between chs 1–9 and 10–13. For instance, Harris argues that the overarching purpose of writing is to prepare the Corinthians for the impending visit; thus, Paul's discourse in each section (i.e., chs 1–7; 8–9; 10–13) prepares for the next (Harris, *Second Epistle to the Corinthians*, 44–45, 51–54). Essentially, Harris understands the movement in the letter as causation. However, I disagree with his analysis for a few reasons. First, his understanding seems to be based on his interpretation that Paul's statement in 13:10 serves as a general statement for the entire letter; thus, he concludes that the preparation for the impending visit is the ultimate purpose of the writing. However, as I have shown in 8.2.1.1, Paul's statement in 13:10 is more closely related to his discourse in chs 10–13, for 10:1–2 and 13:10 forms *inclusio*.

Second, the purpose of the writing should be distinguished from the central message of the writing. The purpose of the writing arises from the historical situation and informs the ways in which Paul crafts his arguments in the letter. In other words, the primary message of the writing is the means to achieve the purpose of the writing. However, as I have argued in Chapter 1, the historical issues can be explored after one has gained understanding of Paul's train of thought and argument on the basis of the text itself. Thus, this study focuses on the message of the letter but not the purpose of the letter, which arose from the historical situations, though they are closely related.

Third, from the beginning, Paul identifies not only the Corinthians but also all the saints in Achaia as the recipients of the letter (1:1); thus, Paul has a wider audience in mind in his writing. Narrowing the purpose of the letter to the preparation for his imminent visit to the Corinthians ignores other audiences described in 1:1. Thus, Paul's concern seems much broader than his visit.
[57] E.g., Young and Ford understand that chs 10–13 form *peroratio* (*Meaning and Truth in 2 Corinthians*, 36); Witherington considers chs 10–13 as a part of *refutatio* (*Conflict and Community in Corinth*, 429–70); Long identifies 10:1–11:15 as *refutatio* (*Ancient Rhetoric and Paul's Apology*, 178–86). Also see my survey of the literature in Chapter 2.

defense (i.e., *refutatio*) and the ways in which the defense is related to the rest of his discourse in the letter. Thus, in this section, incorporating the insights from rhetorical criticism, I will provide plausible explanation regarding the ways in which Paul's discourse in 3:1–9:15 and 10:1–13:10 are conceptually related. Namely, Paul substantiates his discussion in 3:1–9:15 by defending his status as a servant of Christ in 10:1–13:10 (substantiation) through the means of foolish boasting (instrumentation [description of means]). Moreover, Paul reinforces his discourse in 3:1–9:15 by developing two themes regarding weakness and financial integrity: He introduces these themes in 3:1–9:15 and develops them in 10:1–13:10 (particularization). In other words, in order for Paul's proclamation (3:1–7:16) and exhortation (8:1–9:15) to be accepted and practiced by the Corinthians, they must properly recognize his status and authority (10:1–13:10), but Paul anticipates criticism against his standing; thus, he defends them in 10:1–13:10.

However, one might question Paul's arrangement of his arguments in the letter. While he usually establishes a ground first and moves to make an argument (e.g., see 8.2.2.1), in 3:1–13:10, Paul makes his argument first in 3:1–9:15 and then moves to substantiate his discourse by explaining its basis in 10:1–13:10, yet he skillfully arranges his materials in this order, for the charges against Paul's status in 10:1–13:10 have direct connections to his discussions in 3:1–9:15. Essentially, in 10:1–13:10, Paul's opponents undermine his status (10:7a; 11:23a) because of (1) his weakness (10:1, 2, 7, 10; 11:6; 13:3–4) and (2) his financial independence (11:7–15; 12:13, 14–18; see 8.2.1). However, at the same time, these accusations could also arise from Paul's previous discourse in 3:1–9:15. Therefore, while I do not deny that the charges against Paul in 10:1–13:10 arose from the historical Paul and his historical relationship with the Corinthians, I also argue that his defense in 10:1–13:10 functions as responses to the anticipated objections to his proclamation and exhortation in 3:1–9:15. In fact, responding to the potential opposition to orators' own arguments is one of the functions in *refutatio*.[58] More specifically, the movement from 3:1–9:15 to 10:1–13:10 is similar to one type of *insinuatio*. Timothy J. Christian describes that an orator might place a refutation at the beginning when the audience is favored towards the orator, whereas an orator might refute the opposing orator at the end of the speech when the rival already has the audiences' favor.[59] The latter is exactly the case in 2 Corinthians.

Regarding the anticipated criticism against Paul, he develops two responses. First, Paul extensively defends his timidity and weakness (10:1, 2, 7, 10; 11:6; 13:3–4) in 10:1–13:10 (esp. 11:21b–12:10; 13:3–4) because the Corinthians might misunderstand the paradoxical nature of his proclamation and exhortation in 3:1–9:15 as a sign of weakness. As I have demonstrated in 5.2.1.1, Paul describes that the nature of the ministry is a divine paradox. God entrusts the treasure of the gospel to worthless and fragile human agents (4:6–7); he manifests the life of Jesus through the death of his

---

[58] Long, *Ancient Rhetoric and Paul's Apology*, 89.
[59] Timothy J. Christian, "*Paul and the Rhetoric of Insinuatio: How and Why 1 Cor 15 Functions Rhetorically as the Climax to 1 Corinthians*" (Asbury Theological Seminary, PhD diss., 2019), 162–284. In fact, Witherington identifies 2 Cor 10–13 as *insinuatio* (*Conflict and Community in Corinth*, 429–32).

servants (4:10–12); he produces glory through their suffering (4:17). Moreover, one finds the ultimate example of such a paradox in Christ: God manifests wealth through Christ's poverty (8:9; cf. 8:1–2). However, Paul is afraid that the Corinthians might depreciate such nature; they might misunderstand his fragility (4:16–7), self-demotion (4:10–12), suffering (4:17; cf. 4:13–5:10), and Christ's meekness (8:9) as signs of weakness (10:1, 2, 7, 10; 11:6; 13:3–4). Therefore, in 10:1–13:10 Paul has to defend the point that weakness is indeed a locus of divine power. Moreover, he develops the theme of boldness. Despite the potential misperception of the paradoxical nature of the ministry, Paul emphasizes that the ministry is, rather, characterized by boldness (3:12; 4:1, 16; 5:6, 8; 10:1, 2, 12; 11:21). In 3:1–7:16, Paul characterizes the proclamation of the gospel with boldness (3:12; 4:1, 16; 5:6, 8; cf. 7:16). Paul declares that God's servants boldly and plainly articulate the theocentric character of the proclamation, stating, πολλῇ παρρησίᾳ χρώμεθα (3:12) and that he and his fellow workers are not discouraged: οὐκ ἐγκακοῦμεν (4:1). Moreover, he repeatedly describes the attitude toward the proclamation with courage and boldness. They are not discouraged: οὐκ ἐγκακοῦμεν (4:16); rather, they are always courageous: Θαρροῦντες οὖν πάντοτε (5:6); θαρροῦμεν (5:8). In 10:1–13:10, Paul continues to develop the theme (10:1, 2, 12; 11:21). Responding to the charge against Paul's timidity (10:1, 10), he warns them that he will show his boldness (θαρρέω; 10:2, 11) through stern discipline (13:1–10). Moreover, while God's servants are not bold (τολμάω) to compare themselves with others, such as their opponents (10:12), Paul boldly dares to (τολμάω) speak in foolishness (11:21b) that he is the servant of Christ (11:23b) because his rivals force him to do so (12:11).[60] Therefore, Paul extensively defends the compatibility of being weak and a servant of Christ by developing the theme of boldness in 10:1–13:10 in order to address the potential criticism against the paradoxical nature of the proclamation (3:1–7:16) and participation in the gospel (8:1–9:15).

Second, Paul repeatedly defends his financial integrity in 10:1–13:10 (esp. 11:7–15; 12:13, 14–18) because the Corinthians might misinterpret his motive behind the exhortations regarding the collection in 8:1–9:15. While Paul clarifies that the purposes of the collection are equality (8:14–15), the supply of others (8:14–15; 9:12), and thanksgiving and glory to God (9:11–13), Paul anticipates the criticism against his financial standing; thus, Paul defends himself by developing the theme regarding his financial integrity in 10:1–13:10. In 2:17, Paul describes that God's agents do not peddle God's word; thus, he sends qualified emissaries for the collection in order to avoid anyone discrediting his administration of the collection (8:19–20). In 10:1–13:10, he continues to expound and defend his financial integrity in 10:1–13:10 (esp. 11:7–15; 12:13, 14–18) in order to bolster his sincerity in the ministry to the saints (8:1–9:15). Therefore, on the one hand, Paul's defense in 10:1–13:10 is the response to the criticism

---

[60] While the thematic links regarding the character of Paul's discourse between 3:1–7:16 and 10:1–13:10 are readily observable, one should also note the lexical connections. Paul employs θαρρέω in 5:6, 8; 10:1, 2 in a similar sense (cf. 7:16). Moreover, Paul employs θαρρέω and τολμάω in the close semantic proximity in the same sentence (10:2) and continues to utilize τολμάω to describe the character of his speech (10:12; 11:21). Thus, while θαρρέω and τολμάω are not cognates, they share similar semantic meaning.

Defense of the Gospel (10:1–13:10) 187

that would have arisen from the historical relationship between him and the Corinthian church. On the other hand, the defense functions as responses to the anticipated objections toward his previous argument in 3:1–9:15.

8.2.2.3 Generalization with Climax (12:9–10)

Paul's statement in 12:9–10 serves as a general statement (generalization), reaching the apex of his discourse in the letter (climax).[61] While one could argue that 12:9–10 is the climax of his defense in 10:1–12:13, the themes he revisits in these two verses pertain to his entire discourse (i.e., 1:1–13:13) rather than his defense (i.e., 10:1–12:13); thus, I posit 12:9–10 as the general statement of the letter as a whole. To put it another way, Paul begins the content of the arguments pertaining to ministry with the thesis statement in 2:14–17 and expounds it in 3:1–13:10 (see Chapter 5). Now, in 12:9–10, Paul concludes and encapsulates significant aspects of his message in a general way regarding the themes of speech, grace, divine paradox, sacrifice, divine encouragement and suffering, qualifications for ministry, and boasting.[62]

First, Paul's speech comes to an end in 12:9–10. Paul articulates that God's agents will disseminate God's knowledge through their speech (2:14–17); thus, he has developed his speech in the material that follows: Paul proclaimed the gospel (3:1–7:16), encouraged the Corinthians to respond to the gospel (8:1–9:15), and defended the gospel (10:1–12:13); 12:9–10 concludes his speech.[63] Second, Paul begins his discourse (1:2) as well as the thesis with χάρις (2:14) and concludes with χάρις (12:9), revisiting the theme developed throughout the letter (12:9; see recurrence of χάρις in chs 3–4).[64] Third, the antithesis of power and weakness in 12:9–10 (cf. 13:4) underscores the notion of divine paradox that is introduced in 2:14–15 and developed in the material that follows (4:6–7, 10–12, 17; 8:1–2, 9). Fourth, the dwelling of Christ's power in weakness in 12:9–10 highlights the sacrificial image introduced in 2:15 and expounded in the following material (4:13–5:10; 5:11–6:10; 6:14–7:1; 7:4–16; 8:5; 8:19; 9:13; 12:9). Fifth, Paul's reception of encouragement from the Lord in the midst of suffering from his thorn in the flesh in 12:9 points to the theme of divine encouragement and suffering (1:3–7; 3:12; 4:1, 6–9; 4:13–5:10; 5:20–7:3; 7:4–16; 11:21b–12:10; see 4.2.2.2). Sixth, since the reception of grace that enabled his weakness to become a locus of the divine power not only serves as the divine qualification for Paul's ministry, 12:9–10 points to the theme of the qualifications for the ministry, which is introduced

---

[61] Some scholars also identify 12:9 and 12:10 as the climax (e.g., Long, *Ancient Rhetoric and Paul's Apology*, 190). Some also identify 12:10 as a summary statement (e.g., Lim, "*Sufferings of Christ*," 189–90). Long also identifies the MSR of 12:1–10 in relation to the letter as a whole as recurrence of cruciality with generalization and climax ("2 Corinthians," 261–95 at 282–83). While I think that his identification of cruciality should rather be designated as contrast, I agree that Paul's discussion, especially in 12:9–10, reaches its climax with a general statement of the letter as a whole (see my discussion below).

[62] Therefore, it is ideological generalization; Bauer and Traina, *Inductive Bible Study*, 101–102. Also see my note regarding the difference between generalization and summarization in 3.2.2.

[63] As noted above, 12:11–13 is *epidiorthosis*; thus, 12:10 marks the ending of his speech proper.

[64] The word does not show up after 12:9 until the closing (13:13). Also, one could argue that 2:14–12:10 is structured according to *inclusio* regarding χάρις.

in 2:17 and developed throughout the letter (3:1–6a; 5:11–20a; 8:16, 19, 22, 23; 10:8, 13, 17; 11:23, 12:4, 7, 9; 13:10). Seventh, the notion of boasting reaches its conclusion at 12:9 (1:12, 14; 5:12; 7:4, 14; 8:24; 9:2, 3; 10:8, 13, 15, 16, 17; 11:10, 12, 16, 17, 19, 30; 12:1, 5, 6, 9; recurrence in 4.2.2.3). Therefore, Paul's discussion in 12:9–10 concludes and revisits the major aspects of his discourse.

In addition, his discourse reaches its climax in 12:9–10 in the sense that the Lord Jesus Christ directly affirms some of the aforementioned themes; 12:9 is the only place in which Paul recounts the direct quotation from Christ in the letter. In fact, Lim argues that Paul's discussion in 11:23–12:10 is grounded in the story of Christ, particularly the antithesis of power and weakness (12:9–10; 13:3–4).[65]

First, Paul's ministry of the gospel reaches its apex in Christ's reply in 12:9. Paul has proclaimed the gospel (3:1–7:16), urged the Corinthians to respond to the gospel (8:1–9:15), and defended the gospel (10:1–12:13). In 12:9, the Lord's answer indicates that the gospel of Christ is not only the object he proclaims and defends; it has also become his identity, for his weakness that manifests divine power is grounded in Christ's death and resurrection (13:3–4). Thus, Barnett correctly writes, "Thus the Lord's reply to Paul's prayer for the removal of the thorn/stake is given in terms of the very gospel of the death and resurrection of Christ that the apostles proclaimed."[66] Second, the theme of χάρις also reaches its climax in Christ's direct answer to Paul's plea in 12:9. Paul's discourse pertaining to the content of ministry begins with God's χάρις (2:14) and culminates in Christ's χάρις. Third, Paul's discussion of the divine qualifications for ministry reaches its apex in Christ's affirmation in 12:9 that Paul's weakness indeed becomes his qualification as a servant of Christ. Fourth, the theme of divine encouragement and suffering reaches its pinnacle in Christ's answer in 12:9 that Paul received the divine encouragement from the Lord himself so that the torment from his thorn in the flesh (12:7), though he would have to continue to struggle with it, would not undermine his status as a servant of Christ. Instead, he would find delight in it, knowing his weakness becomes a locus of divine power. Therefore, Paul's discussion in 12:9–10 serves as a general statement as well as a climax of his discourse in the letter.

8.3 Conclusion and Theological Implication

In this chapter, I scrutinized the literary structure of 10:1–13:10. First, I demonstrated the segmentation of 10:1–13:10. Second, I demonstrated the MSRs in relation to the division as a whole and the letter as a whole. On the one hand, I expounded four MSRs in relation to the division as a whole: *inclusio*, instrumentation (statement of purpose), causation with particularization and contrast, and causation. These MSRs reveal the two foremost concerns of Paul's discourse in 10:1–13:10. First, *inclusio*, instrumentation

---

[65] Lim, "*Sufferings of Christ*," 158–96. In addition, I advance Lim's argument by demonstrating the ways in which Jesus' Passion and crucifixion echo and even shape Paul's argument in 2 Cor 12:7–10 (Kei Hiramatsu, "Echoes of Jesus' Cross in Second Corinthians 12:7–10," *Asbury Journal* 77 [2022]: 267–88.)

[66] Barnett, *Second Epistle to the Corinthians*, 573.

(statement of purpose), and causation (10:1–12:13 and 12:14–13:10) indicate that the notion of Paul's impending visit centers on his discourse in 10:1–13:10. Framing the division with the notion of his impending visit (*inclusio*; 10:1–2; 13:10) and inserting the purpose statement of the division (instrumentation: 13:10) show that Paul is concerned with his third visit, especially regarding the exercise of the discipline over some of the Corinthians according to the divine authority (10:8; 13:10; cf. 12:19), though Paul understands that withholding the discipline is the better way to edify the Corinthians. Second, causation with particularization and contrast (10:1–12:13) shows that Paul's boasting focuses on the defense of his status as a servant of Christ, which is directly connected to the defense of the gospel, for he spends significant space on the argument regarding his foolish boasting (i.e., almost 80 percent of the material in 10:1– 13:10; sixty-four out of eighty-two verses). Paul moves from the bases (10:1–18) to the content of foolish boasting (11:1–12:13). In 10:1–18, while he describes the causes that force him to engage in the boasting (10:1–18), he also establishes grounds for his boasting speech, especially in 10:12–18 (causation). In addition, Paul moves his discussion from general (10:1–18) to specifics (11:1–12:13; particularization) in two ways. While he unpacks the details of the offenses in 11:1–12:13, he also fully develops the defense of his status as a servant of Christ (10:7b; 11:21b–12:10). Thus, the MSR of causation with particularization indicates that Paul's boasting in 10:1–12:13 centers on the defense of his status (10:7b; 11:23a).

On the other hand, I demonstrated that the MSRs of recurrence of causation, substantiation with particularization and instrumentation (description of means), and generalization with climax in relation to the letter as a whole. The first indicates a formal relationship between 3:1–9:15 and 10:1–13:10, and the second and third show a conceptual connection between 3:1–9:15 and 10:1–13:10. Particularly, the MSRs of substantiation with particularization and instrumentation (description of means) and generalization with climax are significant. First, Paul's defense of status (10:1–13:10) reinforces Paul's proclamation of the gospel (3:1–7:16) and exhortation to respond to the gospel (8:1–9:15) by addressing the potential objections that might arise from his discourse in 3:1–9:15. Paul especially defends himself against the charge concerning his weakness (10:1, 2, 7, 10; 11:6; 13:3–4) and financial integrity (11:7–15; 12:13, 14– 18), both of which attribute to the charge against his status (10:7a; 11:23a) because he is afraid that the Corinthians might misunderstand the paradoxical nature of the ministry (4:6–7, 10–12, 17; 8:9) and the motive behind his administration of the collection (8:20–21). Therefore, Paul proceeds to address the anticipated criticism in 10:1–13:10.

Second, Paul's discussion in 12:9–10 revisits the significant aspects of his discourse in the letter regarding the themes of speech, grace, divine paradox, sacrifice, divine encouragement and suffering, qualifications for ministry, and boasting. Moreover, his discourse reaches its apex in 12:9–10 in the sense that the themes of the divine paradox, grace, the ministry of the gospel, the divine qualifications for the ministry, and divine encouragement and suffering culminate in the Lord's direct answer to Paul's plea in 12:9.

Having summarized my analysis, two implications need to be drawn regarding the designation of Paul's discourse in 10:1–13:10 and the theological significance of the relationship between the proclamation and exhortation (3:1–9:15) and the defense of the gospel (10:1–13:10). Regarding the title of the division, two observations are particularly important. First, I designate Paul's discourse in 10:1–13:10 "Arguments Pertaining to Content of Ministry," for the MSR of substantiation with particularization and instrumentation (3:1–9:15 and 10:1–13:10) shows that Paul's defense is the indivisible aspect of the ministry, for it strengthens his proclamation (3:1–7:16) and exhortation (8:1–9:15) by addressing the potential objections against his arguments in 3:1–9:15. Thus, Paul does not view his discourse in 3:1–9:15 and 10:1–13:10 as separate entities. Instead, he understands that both are essential aspects of the same ministry that disseminates God's knowledge. Thus, just as Paul expounds the content of ministry in 3:1–9:15, he continues to describe the content of ministry as the defense of the gospel in 10:1–13:10.

Second, I designate Paul's discourse in 10:1–13:10 as "Defense of the Gospel" based on the MSR of causation with particularization and contrast. Paul's devotion of approximately four-fifths of the space in 10:1–13:10 to the argument pertaining to his boasting (10:1–12:13) reveals the theological significance on the topic. The MSR of causation with particularization and contrast (10:1–18 and 11:1–12:13) shows that Paul's boasting centers on the defense of his status as a servant of Christ. Moreover, the contrast between Paul and his opponents shows that Paul's defense of the status is interconnected to the defense of the gospel; thus, the Corinthians' salvation. Namely, his rivals deceived the Corinthians' mind and led them astray from their devotion to Christ (11:3) at least in five ways. First, they violated the divine authority and the ministerial jurisdiction in commending themselves (10:12–18) and disguising themselves as apostles of Christ (11:13–15). Second, they preached another Jesus (i.e., another gospel; 11:4). Third, they accused Paul of being inferior to the super-apostles (11:5–6). Fourth, they charged against Paul's financial independence and integrity (11:7–15). Fifth, they concluded that Paul is weak (11:21a) and that he is not a servant of Christ (11:23a). Thus, Paul has to defend his status as a servant of Christ, for the Corinthians' salvation is at stake; denying Paul's status as a servant of Christ (10:7; 11:23) means denying the gospel he proclaims, for Christ speaks through him (13:3–4). Thus, he insists that his defense is not for his own interest because he has been forced to boast (11:1, 16, 17, 19, 21; 12:6, 11) and his boasting is for the Corinthians' upbuilding (12:19; cf. 10:8; 13:10). Therefore, while the MSR of causation (10:1–12:13 and 12:14–13:10) shows that the locutionary purpose of establishing his status through extensive defenses (10:1–12:13) aims to prepare and exhort the Corinthians for his impending visit (12:14–13:10), the perlocutionary purpose of the defense is to defend the gospel for the Corinthians' salvation. For these reasons, I designate Paul's argument as "Arguments Pertaining to Content of Ministry: Defense of the Gospel."

Regarding the relationship in Paul's discourse between 3:1–9:15 and 10:1–13, the MSR of substantiation with particularization with instrumentation (description of means) demonstrated that Paul does not view the proclamation of the gospel (3:1–7:16), the exhortation to respond to the gospel (8:1–9:15), and the defense of the gospel (10:1–13:10) as separate entities. Instead, he understands all of them as distinct but closely related aspects of the ministry, for the defense of the status (10:1–13:10) reinforces his proclamation of the gospel (3:1–7:16) and exhortations (8:1–9:15).

Moreover, one should draw an important theological implication: the relationship between thanksgiving and edification. While the dissemination of God's knowledge is accomplished through the speech in the form of the proclamation (3:1–7:16) and defense of the gospel (10:1–13:10), the former produces thanksgiving (εὐχαριστία; 4:15; cf. 9:11–12) and the latter produces edification (οἰκοδομή; 10:8; 12:19; 13:10). In 4:15, Paul underlines that the ministry of χάρις (i.e., the proclamation of the gospel) will result in thanksgiving.[67] Likewise, Paul emphasizes that the ministry to the saints will produce thanksgiving (9:11–12; see also my discussion in comparative causation in 7.2.2). In 12:19, Paul emphasizes that his defense is for their edification/upbuilding; likewise, in 13:10, he clarifies that his authority is for their edification/upbuilding. However, these seemingly distinct results are essential and indivisible aspects in Paul's theology. His discussion in 1 Cor 14 is particularly helpful in making my point. In 1 Cor 14:16–17, Paul juxtaposes thanksgiving (εὐχαριστέω) and edification (οἰκοδομέω) in the context of discussing the outcome of the ministry by the gift of tongues and prophecy (cf. Eph 4:29; Col 2:7). While Paul affirms the gift of tongues and its ministry (1 Cor 14:2, 4–5, 13–14, 18, 22, 26–28), which results in thanksgiving (1 Cor 14:16–17), he repeatedly emphasizes that the ministry should produce the edification of the church (1 Cor 14:3–5, 12, 17, 26). Thus, in Paul's understanding, thanksgiving and edification must go together. Likewise, in 2 Corinthians, he understands that thanksgiving (4:15; cf. 1:11; 2:14; 9:11, 12, 15) and the edification of the church (2 Cor 10:8; 12:19; 13:10) go together especially in relation to the gospel. In fact, the idea of edification (οἰκοδομή; 10:8; 12:19; 13:10) in Paul's argument in 10:1–13:10 seems to be related to the Corinthians' salvation, for Paul boasts about the divine authority (10:8) to defend his status for the Corinthians' salvation (10:1–12:13). Likewise, he will exercise discipline according to the authority over some of the Corinthians whose salvation is at stake, for they sinned in the past and have not repented (12:21; 13:2). Therefore, Paul proclaims the gospel in 3:1–7:16, exhorts to respond to the gospel in 8:1–9:15, and edifies the church by defending his status to protect the gospel and the Corinthians' faith in 10:1–13:10. Having analyzed the literary structure of 10:1–13:10, I turn to the conclusion of this study.

---

[67] See my discussion in 7.2.2.

9

Conclusion

In this study, I investigated the literary structure of 2 Corinthians by analyzing its two major components: the division of the letter and the identification of MSRs. In this chapter, I first summarize the findings of this study (9.1–6) and then provide a brief discussion of the theological implications that arise from my investigation (9.7). Finally, I conclude this study by suggesting further areas of research (9.8).

9.1 Summary of Argument

The need for the present study emerges from two unresolved yet related issues in the study of the NT. First, there is no scholarly consensus regarding both the literary structure and central theme of the letter. Second, the study of the literary structure and primary message of the letter lacks a hermeneutical model, which incorporates insights from various methodologies in order to understand the meaning of the text in its final form best. Therefore, this study has attempted to demonstrate that an inductive and integrative approach offers a way past this impasse. Thus, allowing the literary context of 2 Corinthians in its canonical form to point to all relevant and significant aspects of the text to be explored, I have analyzed the literary structure of 2 Corinthians, particularly paying special attention to the ways in which Paul's discourse within and between main units and subunits is related to communicating a message (i.e., MSRs) by incorporating insights from topical, epistolary, rhetorical, literary, and linguistic analysis so as to draw a fuller picture of the development of Paul's discourse as presented in the letter. This study aimed to show a more suitable and helpful literary structure for 2 Corinthians and to demonstrate an inductive and integrated approach as a better-founded and more advantageous methodology.

Therefore, in Chapter 1, I began my investigation by introducing the hermeneutical model of this study, Inductive Bible Study, and described theoretical foundations. In order to investigate the literary structure of 2 Corinthians, I described the categories of major structural relationships: recurrence, contrast, comparison, climax, particularization, generalization, causation, substantiation, cruciality, summarization, interrogation, preparation/realization (introduction), instrumentation, interchange, and *inclusio*. Then, I discussed the advantages of employing these categories for the study of 2 Corinthians.

In Chapter 2, before reapplying these categories to the text of 2 Corinthians, I surveyed the history of research into the literary structure and the central theme of the letter. The survey indicated three facts. First, there is a paucity of scholarly consensus regarding the literary structure and the primary message of the letter; thus, the survey called for a study of a more suitable and helpful literary structure of the letter as well as a demonstration of the primary message of the letter. Second, the disagreements in understanding the literary structure and central theme of the letter arise from the applications of multifarious methodologies. Five general approaches have been suggested as of now: topical analysis, epistolary criticism, rhetorical criticism, literary criticism, and discourse analysis. However, while each methodology addresses some significant aspects of the literary structure and the principal message of the letter, I pointed out that each methodology does not draw a complete picture on its own unless its insights are intentionally incorporated into the construal of the literary structure and central theme of the text. Third, the survey showed the relevant issues that must be addressed in my investigation of the literary structure and the principal message of 2 Corinthians:

1. The existence of discrete topical units within the letter and historical issues behind them;
2. the relevance of epistolary types, features, and structure;
3. the significance of rhetorical species and its dispositions;
4. the function of narrative substructures within some passages;
5. the existence of literary designs (e.g., chiasm) and their function;
6. the relevance of linguistically cohesive ties in Paul's discourse; and
7. the interrelationships between units (1:1–2; 1:3–11; 1:12–2:13; 2:14–7:4 [and 6:14–7:1]; 7:5–16; 8:1–9:15; 10:1–13:10; 13:11–13) and their relevance to the understanding of the central theme of the letter.

In Chapters 3–8, therefore, on the basis of the priority of the literary context of 2 Corinthians in its final form, I employed the aforementioned insights from various methodologies to investigate the segmentation of each major division and the MSRs in relation to the division as a whole and the letter as a whole (see 9.2).

While scholars have proposed various overarching themes of the letter, this study indicated that the analysis of the MSRs with insights from various methodologies points to Paul's theology of ministry as the central concern of the book. In addition to the recurring theme of service/ministry and work being most prominent throughout the letter (see 4.2.2.3/9.2.2.5), the salutation (1:1–2) prepares his audience that Paul will develop theological discourse. His discussion on the character of ministry (1:3–2:13) establishes a basis for the material that follows (2:14–13:10), leading to the thesis statement of the letter regarding the agents in ministry (2:14–17), which he develops in the rest of the letter (3:1–13:10). According to the thesis statement (2:14–17), Paul expounds his arguments regarding the proclamation of the gospel (3:1–7:16), which leads to the consequent exhortations regarding the response to the gospel (8:1–9:15). Moreover, he reinforces the proclamation (3:1–7:16) and exhortations (8:1–9:15) by defending his status as a servant of Christ to protect the gospel for the sake of the Corinthians' salvation (10:1–13:10). Then, the closing (13:11–13) recapitulates the major aspects of his discourse. Therefore, the analysis of the literary structure indicates that the discourse on Paul's theology of ministry is the central concern of the letter.

9.2 Overview of Division and Major Structural Relationships in Relation to the Letter as a Whole

9.2.1 Division of the Letter

Salutation	Arguments Pertaining to Basis for Ministry: Character of Ministry	Arguments Pertaining to Content of Ministry				Closing
		2:14–13:10				
		Thesis Statement	Proclamation of the Gospel	Response to the Gospel	Defense of the Gospel	
1:1–2	1:3–2:13	2:14–17	3:1–7:16	8:1–9:15	10:1–13:10	13:11–13

The following is the more detailed overview of the division of the letter:

I. Salutation (1:1–2; ch. 3)
II. Arguments Pertaining to Basis for Ministry: Character of Ministry (1:3–2:13; ch. 4)
   A. Mutuality of Suffering and Encouragement (1:3–7)
      1. Description of God's Character and Mutuality of Suffering and Encouragement (1:3–5)
      2. Mutuality of Suffering and Encouragement in Relationship between Paul and the Corinthians (1:6–7)
   B. Examples and Reasons for Mutuality of Suffering and Encouragement: Mutuality of Ministry and Boasting (1:8–2:11)
      1. Mutuality of Encouragement and Ministry (1:8–11)
         a) God's Deliverance from Affliction as a Testimony of Divine Encouragement in Suffering (1:8–10)
         b) Mutuality of Ministry: the Corinthians' Cooperation in Ministry (1:11)
      2. Mutuality of Boasting (1:12–2:11)
         a) Mutuality of Boasting: Integrity of Paul's Conduct as His Boasting (1:12–14)
         b) Mutuality of Joy in Paul's Defense of Change of Travel Plan (1:15–2:2)

c) Mutuality of Joy, Love, Sorrow, and Forgiveness in Paul's Defense of Previous Letter (2:3–11)
  C. Transitional Travel Narrative (2:12–13)
III. Arguments Pertaining to Content of Ministry: Thesis Statement (2:14–17; ch. 5)
IV. Arguments Pertaining to Content of Ministry: Proclamation of the Gospel (3:1–7:16; ch. 6)
  A. Basis for the Proclamation of the Gospel: Description of Ministry of New Covenant (3:1–11)
    1. Qualifications for Ministry (3:1–6a)
      a) Qualifications Regarding Commendation Letter (3:1–3)
      b) Qualifications Regarding Ministry of New Covenant (3:4–6)
    2. Character of New Covenant (3:6b–11)
      a) New Covenant of Life-Giving Spirit (3:6b)
      b) New Covenant of Surpassing Glory (3:7–11)
  B. Content of the Proclamation of the Gospel (3:12–7:3)
    1. Descriptive Speech Regarding Theocentric Character of the Proclamation (3:12–4:12)
      a) General Statement (3:12): Bold and Plain Speech
      b) Basis: God's Unveiled Knowledge through Christ (3:13–18)
      c) Content: Sincerity, Christocentric Preaching, and Divine Paradox (4:1–12)
    2. Descriptive Speech Regarding Attitude toward the Proclamation: Courage Despite Suffering (4:13–5:10)
      a) General Statement: Proclamation of the Gospel with Courage Despite Suffering (4:13–16)
      b) Reasons for the Attitude: Glory through Affliction and the Spirit as God's Down Payment (4:17–5:5)
      c) Basis for the Attitude: Christ's Eschatological Presence and Judgment (5:6–10)
    3. Hortatory Speech Regarding Persuasion of the Gospel of Reconciliation (5:11–7:3)
      a) General Statement: Persuasion (5:11)
      b) Basis: Regarding Credentials (5:12–19)
      c) Content: Regarding Reconciliation with God and His Servants (5:20–7:3)
  C. Outcomes of the Proclamation of the Gospel (7:4–16)
    1. General Statement: Paul's Boasting, Encouragement, and Joy (7:4)
    2. Reasons for Paul's Boasting, Encouragement, and Joy (7:5–12)
      a) Occasion of Encouragement and Joy: Through Titus's Arrival and His Report Concerning the Corinthians' Response to Paul's Previous Letter (7:5–7)
      b) Joy and Boasting through the Corinthians' Ministry to Titus (7:13–16)
    3. Summary (7:13–16)

V. Arguments Pertaining to Content of Ministry: Response to the Gospel (8:1–9:16; ch. 7)
  A. Model for the Ministry to the Saints: Testimony of Macedonian Churches (8:1–6)
    1. God's Grace Given in the Macedonian Churches (8:1–2)
    2. The Macedonians' Response to God's Grace: Participation in the Collection (8:3–6)
      a) Manners of Their Participation (8:3–5)
      b) Result of Their Participation (8:6)
  B. Exhortations: Abound in Grace and Complete Collection (8:7–15)
    1. Exhortation 1: Abound in Grace (8:7–9)
      a) Exhortation: Abound in Grace (8:7)
      b) Nature of the Exhortation: Not as a Command but as a Test of the Corinthians' Sincerity (8:8)
      c) Basis for the Exhortation: Christ's Example of Abounding Grace (8:9)
    2. Exhortation 2: Complete the Collection (8:10–15)
      a) Exhortation: Complete the Collection (8:10–11)
      b) Means of the Collection: According to What They Have (8:12)
      c) Purpose of the Collection: Equality (8:13–15)
  C. Descriptions of Collection Workers (8:16–9:5)
    1. Workers (8:16–24)
      a) Titus (8:16–17)
      b) Brother A (8:18–21)
      c) Brother B (8:22)
      d) Exhortation Regarding Workers (8:23–24)
    2. Rationale for Sending Workers (9:1–5)
      a) Introduction: Unnecessary Reminder by Acknowledgement of the Corinthians' Willingness (9:1–2)
      b) Purposes of Sending Brethren: Protection of Boasting and the Corinthians' Readiness (9:3–4)
      c) Conclusion: Necessary Reminder (9:5)
  D. Theological Reasons for the Exhortations and Anticipated Outcomes of the Fulfillment of the Exhortations (9:6–15)
    1. Theological Reasons for the Exhortations (9:6–11a)
      a) God's Love for Cheerful Giver (9:6–7)
      b) God's Abundance of All Grace to the Corinthians (9:8–9)
      c) God's Provision and Enrichment for the Corinthians (9:10–11a)
    2. Anticipated Outcomes of the Fulfillment of the Exhortations (9:11b–14)
      a) Supply of the Need and Thanksgiving to God (9:11b–12)
      b) Glory to God (9:13)
      c) Longing for the Corinthians (9:14)
    3. Concluding Thanksgiving (9:15)
VI. Arguments Pertaining to Content of Ministry: Defense of the Gospel (10:1–13:10; ch. 8)

A. Basis for Consequent Ecclesial Preparation for Impending Visit: Foolish Boasting (10:1–12:13)
    1. Basis for Foolish Boasting (10:1–18)
      a) Offense against Paul's Status (10:1–11)
      b) Offense against Paul's Authority: Sphere of Boasting (10:12–18)
    2. Content of Foolish Boasting (11:1–12:13)
      a) Justification for Foolish Boasting (11:1–21a)
      b) Speech Proper (11:21b–12:10)
      c) Conclusion (12:11–13)
  B. Consequent Ecclesial Preparation for Impending Visit (12:14–13:10)
    1. Basis for Ecclesial Preparation for Impending Visit (12:14–21)
      a) Announcement of Impending Visit (12:14a)
      b) Parent-child Relationship (12:14b–18)
      c) Upbuilding Relationship (12:19–21)
    2. Ecclesial Preparation for Impending Visit (13:1–10)
      a) Announcement of Impending Visit (13:1)
      b) Warning, Command, and Prayer (13:2–9)
      c) Intent of Visit (13:10)
VII. Closing (13:11–13; ch. 3)

9.2.2 Major Structural Relationships in Relation to the Letter as a Whole

9.2.2.1 Preparation/Realization with Inclusio (1:1–2 and 1:3–13:10 with 13:11, 13) in 3.2.1

The salutation in 1:1–2 prepares readers by providing a threefold background for Paul's discourse pertaining to ministry in 1:3–13:10: writers, recipients, and greeting. In addition, the greeting of χάρις and εἰρήνη frames the entire letter as *inclusio* (1:2; 13:11, 13).

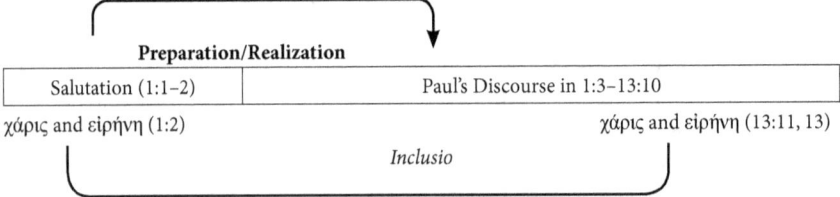

9.2.2.2 Summarization (1:3–13:10 and 13:11–13) in 3.2.2

The closing (13:11–13) concludes the letter by recapitulating major elements of Paul's discourse pertaining to the ministry in 1:3–13:10, in which Paul revisits not only the notions of χάρις (and its cognates, χαίρω and χαρά), peace, and love but also those of the divine encouragement (1:3–2:13), the gospel of reconciliation (5:11–7:3), the ministry to the saints (8:1–9:15), the defense of his status (10:1–12:13), and his impending visit (12:14–13:10).

Conclusion

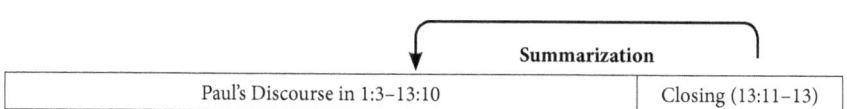

9.2.2.3 Causation with Particularization (1:3–2:13 and 2:14–13:10) in 4.2.2.1

The discussions in 1:3–2:13 serve as a basis for the following arguments in 2:14–13:10: Because Paul understands his ministry and his relationship with the Corinthians in light of mutuality, *therefore*, his discourse in 2:14–13:10 also reflects the theme (causation). Moreover, he introduces the themes regarding not only mutuality but also encouragement in suffering and agents in ministry in 1:3–2:13 and continues to develop them in 2:14–13:10 (particularization).

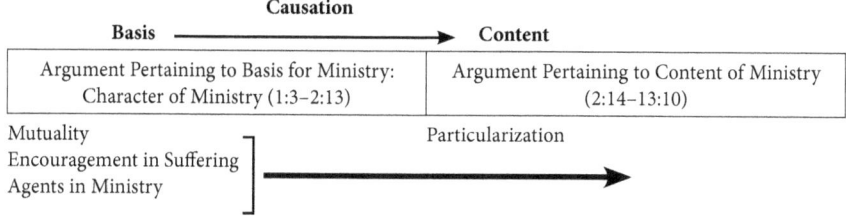

9.2.2.4 Recurrence of Particularization (1:3–2:13 and 2:14–13:10) in 4.2.2.2

Paul's discourse in both 1:3–2:13 and 2:14–13:10 moves from a general statement (1:3–7; 2:14–17) to particulars (1:8–2:13; 3:1–13:10; recurrence of particularization). Paul underscores God as the ultimate agent, Christ as the mediator, and Paul and his fellow workers as God's agents of divine encouragement in 1:3–7 and continues to develop the theme in light of mutuality. Likewise, he underscores God as the ultimate agent, Christ as the intermediate agent, God's servants as God's agents, and false apostles as counteragents in 2:14–17 and continues to expound the theme in 3:1–13:10.

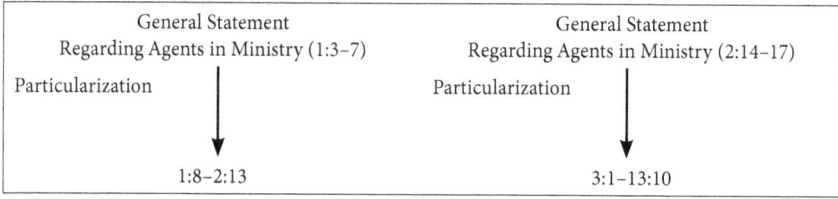

9.2.2.5 Recurrence in 4.2.2.3

The themes of service/work, boasting, grace/joy/forgiveness/thanksgiving, love, and Christ/Jesus/Lord repeatedly appear in Paul's discourse throughout the letter.

- Service/work (συνυπουργέω; διακονέω; διάκονος; διακονία; δοῦλος; καταδουλόω; ἐνεργέω; συνεργός; κατεργάζομαι; συνεργέω; ἐργάζομαι; ἔργον; ἐργάτης): 1:6, 11,

24; 3:3, 6 7, 8, 9; 4:1, 2, 12, 17; 5:5, 18; 6:1, 3, 4; 7:10, 11; 8:4, 19, 20, 23; 9:1, 8, 11, 12, 13; 10:11; 11:3, 8, 13, 15, 23; 12:12, 16
- Boasting (καύχησις; καύχημα; καυχάομαι): 1:12, 14; 5:12; 7:4, 14; 8:24; 9:2, 3; 10:8, 13, 15, 16, 17; 11:10, 12, 16, 17, 19, 30; 12:1, 5, 6, 9
- Grace/joy/forgiveness/thanksgiving (χάρις; χαρά; εὐχαριστέω; εὐχαριστία): 1:2, 11, 12, 15, 24; 2:3, 7, 10, 14; 4:15; 6:1, 10; 7:4, 7, 9, 13, 16; 8:1, 2, 4, 6, 7, 9, 16, 19; 9:8, 11, 12, 14, 15; 12:9, 13; 13:9, 11, 13
- Love (ἀγάπη; ἀγαπάω): 2:4, 8; 5:14; 6:6; 7:1; 8:7, 8, 24; 9:7; 11:11; 12:15, 19; 13:11, 13
- Christ/Jesus/Lord (Χριστός; Ἰησοῦς; κύριος)
  - Χριστός: 1:1, 2, 3, 5, 19, 21; 2:10, 12, 14, 15, 17; 3:3, 4, 14; 4:4, 5, 6; 5:10, 14, 16, 17, 18, 19, 20; 6:15; 8:9, 23; 9:13; 10:1, 5, 7, 14; 11:2, 3, 10, 13, 23; 12:2, 9, 10, 19; 13:3, 5, 13
  - Ἰησοῦς: 1:1, 2, 3, 14, 19; 4:5, 6, 10, 11, 14; 8:9; 11:4, 31; 13:5, 13
  - κύριος: 1:2, 3, 14; 2:12; 3:16, 17, 18; 4:5, 14; 5:6, 8, 11; 6:17, 18; 8:5, 9, 19, 21; 10:8, 17, 18; 11:17, 31; 12:1, 8; 13:10, 13

9.2.2.6 Particularization with Contrast (2:14–17 and 3:1–13:10) in 5.2

Paul's discussion in 2:14–17 serves as a thesis statement of the letter, introducing the major topic regarding agents in ministry (i.e., God, Christ, God's agents, and counteragents), which Paul develops in 3:1–13:10 (cf. 4.2.2.2). Paul also presents a stark contrast between God's agents and counteragents regarding the dissemination of God's word, the nature of their ministries, and the qualifications and integrity in their ministries (2:14–17) and continues to develop it in 3:1–13:10.

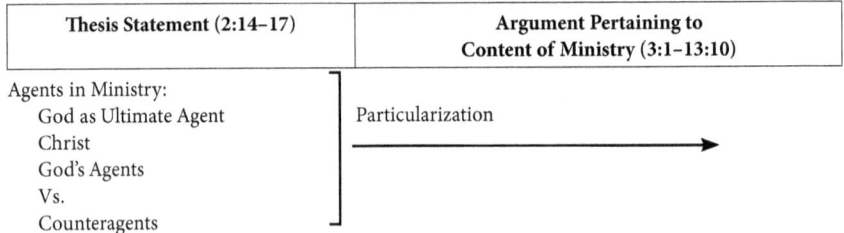

9.2.2.7 Comparative Causation (3:1–7:16 and 8:1–9:15) in 7.2.2

Paul moves from the indicatives (3:1–7:16) to the imperatives (8:1–9:15; causation): Paul exhorts the Corinthians to participate in the ministry to the saints (8:1–9:15) because of the proclamation of the gospel (3:1–7:16). In addition, Paul's discourse in 3:1–7:16 and his exhortation in 8:1–9:15 are structured according to comparison, for (1) Paul describes both the proclamation of the gospel (3:1–7:16) and the participation in the ministry to the saints (8:1–9:15) with the terms, διακονία (and its cognates; 3:3, 6, 7, 8, 9; 4:1; 5:18; 6:3, 4; 8:4, 19, 20; 9:1, 12, 13) and χάρις (and its cognates; 4:15; 6:1; 8:1, 4, 6, 7, 9, 19; 9:8, 14), and (2) he emphasizes that both ministries result in thanksgiving (4:15; 9:11, 12) and glory (3:7, 8, 9, 10, 11, 18; 4:4, 6, 15, 17; 8:19, 23; 9:13).

Conclusion

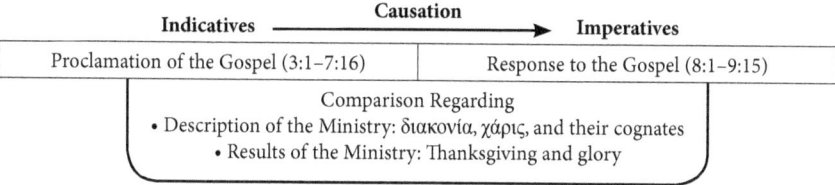

9.2.2.8 Recurrence of Causation (3:1–9:15 and 10:1–13:10) in 8.2.2.1

The discussions in both 3:1–9:15 and 10:1–13:10 move from indicatives (cause; 3:1–7:16; 10:1–12:13) to exhortations (effect; 8:1–9:15; 12:14–13:10).

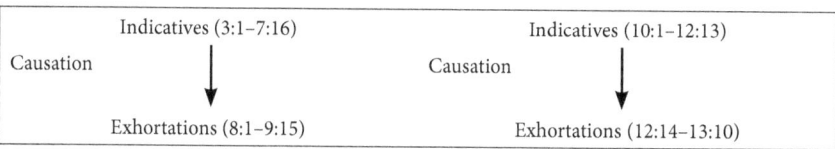

9.2.2.9 Substantiation with Particularization and Instrumentation (Description of Means; 3:1–9:15 and 10:1–13:10) in 8.2.2.2

The defense of the gospel (10:1–13:10) strengthens the discussion in 3:1–9:15 (substantiation) through the means of boasting (instrumentation). Moreover, Paul's defense in 10:1–13:10 reinforces his discourse in 3:1–9:15 by developing two themes regarding weakness and financial integrity: He introduces these themes in 3:1–9:15 and develops them in 10:1–13:10 (particularization) in order to address the potential objections that might arise from his discourse in 3:1–9:15.

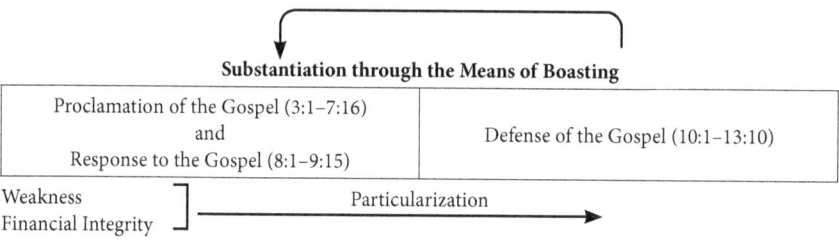

9.2.2.10 Generalization with Climax (12:9–10) in 8.2.2.3

Paul's statement in 12:9–10 serves as a general statement (generalization), recapitulating the significant aspects of his discourse in a general way regarding the themes of speech, grace, divine paradox, sacrifice, divine encouragement and suffering, qualifications for ministry, and boasting (generalization). Moreover, his discourse reaches its apex in 12:9–10 in the sense that the themes of the divine paradox, grace, the ministry of the gospel, the divine qualifications for the ministry, and divine encouragement and suffering culminate in the Lord's direct answer to Paul's plea in 12:9 (climax).

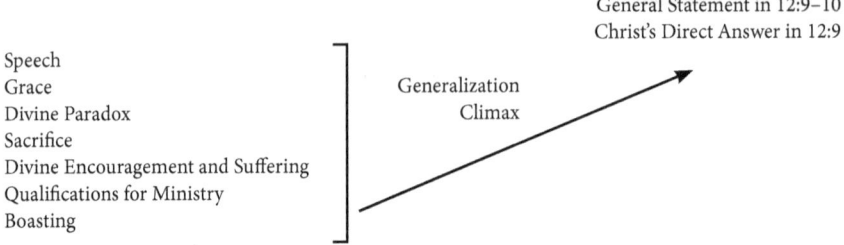

9.3 Overview of Division and Major Structural Relationships of 1:3–2:13 (ch. 4)

In addition to the segmentation and MSRs in relation to the letter as a whole, this study presents those of each division (1:3–2:13; 3:1–7:16; 8:1–9:15; 10:1–13:10) except for 1:1–2, 2:14–17, and 13:11–13 due to their brevity. The following is the overview of the segmentation and MSRs of each division.

9.3.1 Division of 1:3–2:13

Arguments Pertaining to Basis for Ministry: Character of Ministry				
1:3–2:13				
Mutuality of Suffering and Encouragement		Examples and Reasons for Mutuality of Suffering and Encouragement		Transitional Travel Narrative
1:3–7		1:8–2:11		
Description of God's Character and Mutuality of Suffering and Encouragement	Mutuality of Suffering and Encouragement in Relationship between Paul and the Corinthians	Mutuality of Encouragement and Ministry	Mutuality of Boasting	
1:3–7	1:6–7	1:8–11	1:12–2:11	2:12–13

9.3.2 Major Structural Relationships in Relation to the Division as a Whole: Particularization and Causation with Substantiation (1:3–7 and 1:8–2:13) in 4.2.1

The blessing in 1:3–7 serves as a general statement as well as a theological basis regarding the theme of mutuality for the following discussion in 1:8–2:13, in which Paul continues to develop the theme (particularization and causation). At the same time, Paul's discussion in 1:8–2:13 provides examples and reasons for the general statement (substantiation).

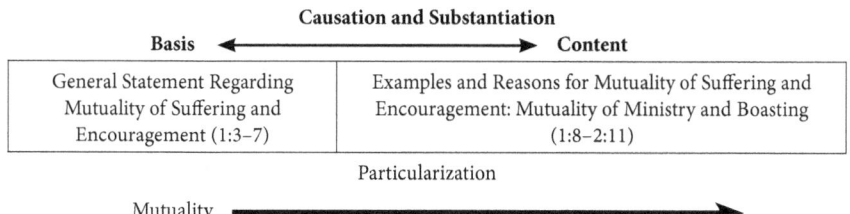

9.4. Overview of Division and Major Structural Relationships of 3:1–7:16 (ch. 6)

9.4.1 Division of 3:1–7:16

Arguments Pertaining to Content of Ministry: Proclamation of the Gospel							
3:1–7:16							
Basis for the Proclamation of the Gospel: Description of Ministry of New Covenant		Content of the Proclamation of the Gospel				Outcomes of the Proclamation of the Gospel	
3:1–11		3:12–7:3				7:4–16	
Qualifications for Ministry	Character of New Covenant	Descriptive Speech Regarding Theocentric Character of Proclamation	Descriptive Speech Regarding Attitude toward the Proclamation: Courage Despite Suffering	Hortatory Speech Regarding Persuasion of the Gospel of Reconciliation	General Statement: Paul's Boasting, Encouragement, and Joy	Reasons for Paul's Boasting, Encouragement, and Joy	Summary
3:1–6a	3:6b–11	3:12–4:12	4:13–5:10	5:11–7:3	7:4	7:5–12	7:13–16

9.4.2 Major Structural Relationships in Relation to the Division as a Whole

9.4.2.1 Causation with Particularization (3:1–11 and 3:12–7:3) in 6.2.1

The description of the ministry of the new covenant (3:1–11) functions as a basis for the following arguments (3:12–7:3): Because God qualified God's servants for the glorious ministry of the new covenant (3:1–11), *therefore*, Paul's following discussions in 3:12–7:3 also reflect the character of the new covenant (causation). In addition, the discussion moves from general (3:1–11) to particulars (3:12–7:3; particularization): Paul describes the qualifications and character of new covenant (3:1–11) and expounds the ways in which God's servants serve in the ministry of the new covenant through the proclamation of the gospel (3:12–7:3).

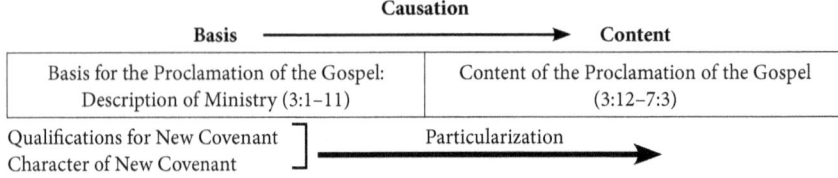

9.4.2.2 Substantiation (3:1–7:3 and 7:4–16) in 6.2.2

The description of outcomes of Paul's proclamation through the previous letter to the Corinthians in 7:4–16 strengthens Paul's discussion regarding the proclamation of the gospel in 3:1–7:3 by (1) appealing to the history of ministry to the Corinthians, and (2) showing not only that Paul's previous letter is a form of proclamation of the gospel but also that the Corinthians' response to the proclamation in the past anticipates the positive outcomes when they respond to his exhortations in 5:20–7:3.

	Substantiation
Basis and Content of the Proclamation of the Gospel (3:1–7:3)	Outcomes of the Proclamation of the Gospel (7:4–16)

9.5 Overview of Division and Major Structural Relationships of 8:1–9:15 (ch. 7)

9.5.1 Division of 8:1–9:15

Arguments Pertaining to Content of Ministry: Response to the Gospel 8:1–9:15									
Model for the Ministry to the Saints: Testimony of Macedonian Churches		Exhortations: Abound in Grace and Complete Collection		Descriptions of Collection Workers		Theological Reasons for the Exhortations and Anticipated Outcomes of the Fulfillment of the Exhortations		
8:1–6		8:7–15		8:16–9:5		9:6–15		
God's Grace Given in the Macedonian Churches	Macedonians' Response to God's Grace: Participation in the Collection	Abound in Grace	Complete the Collection	Workers	Rationale for Sending Workers	Theological Reasons	Anticipated Outcomes	Thanksgiving
8:1–2	8:3–6	8:7–9	8:10–15	8:16–24	9:1–5	9:6–11a	9:11b–14	9:15

9.5.2 Major Structural Relationships in Relation to the Division as a Whole

9.5.2.1 Inclusio (8:1–9:15) in 7.2.1.1

The division is framed with χάρις and δίδωμι/δωρεά (8:1 and 9:15): The ministry to the saints begins with the grace given by God (8:1) and results in thanksgiving to God for his gift (9:15).

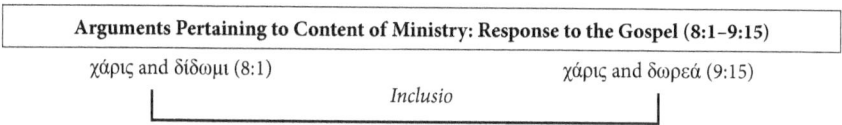

9.5.2.2 Recurrence in 7.2.1.2

The words χάρις and δίδωμι (and its cognates) recur throughout the division (χάρις: 8:1, 4, 6, 7, 9, 16, 19; 9:8, 14, 15; δίδωμι in 8:1, 5, 10, 16; 9:9; δότης in 9:7; δωρεά in 9:15).

9.5.2.3 Comparative Causation (8:1–6 and 8:7–15) in 7.2.1.3

Paul's discussion moves from cause (8:1–6) to effect (8:7–15), in which he shares the testimony of Macedonian churches (8:1–6) to motivate the Corinthians to participate in the collection according to his exhortations in 8:7–15 (causation). Paul also presents the Macedonian churches (8:1–6) and Christ (8:9) as models for the Corinthians to follow regarding the vertical and horizontal dimension of the divine grace and self-sacrifice as the manifestation of the grace (comparison).

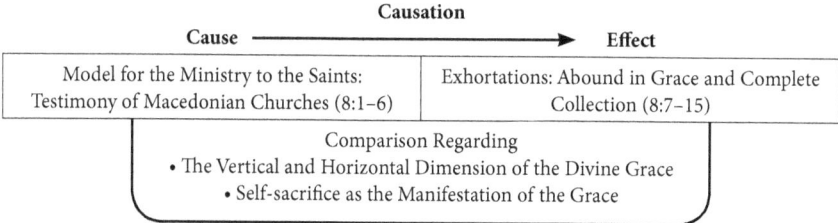

9.5.2.4 Instrumentation (Description of Means; 8:7–15 and 8:16–9:5)

The discussions regarding the collection workers in 8:16–9:5 describe the means through which the Corinthians are to participate in the ministry to the saints according to the exhortations in 8:7–15.

Instrumentation (Description of Means)	
Exhortations: Abound in Grace and Complete Collection (8:7–15)	Descriptions of Collection Workers (8:16–9:5)

9.5.2.5 Substantiation (8:7–15 and 9:6–15)

The discussion in 9:6–15 strengthens the exhortations in 8:7–15 by providing theological reasons for the exhortations and anticipated outcomes of the fulfillment of the exhortations.

	Substantiation
Exhortations: Abound in Grace and Complete Collection (8:7–15)	Theological Reasons for the Exhortations and Anticipated Outcomes of the Fulfillment of the Exhortations (9:6–15)

9.6 Overview of Division and Major Structural Relationships of 10:1–13:10 (ch. 8)

9.6.1 Division of 10:1–13:10

Arguments Pertaining to Content of Ministry: Defense of the Gospel			
10:1–13:10			
Basis for Consequent Ecclesial Preparation for Impending Visit: Foolish Boasting		Consequent Ecclesial Preparation for Impending Visit	
10:1–12:13		12:14–13:10	
Basis for Foolish Boasting	Content of Foolish Boasting	Basis for Ecclesial Preparation for Impending Visit	Ecclesial Preparation for Impending Visit
10:1–18	11:1–12:13	12:14–21	13:1–10

9.6.2 Major Structural Relationships in Relation to the Division as a Whole

9.6.2.1 Inclusio (10:1–13:10) in 8.2.1.1

The division is framed with the statements regarding Paul's desire not to impose discipline on the Corinthians when he is present with them (10:1–2; 13:10).

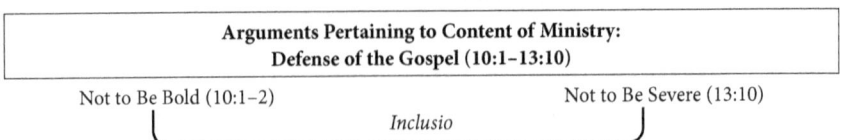

9.6.2.2 Instrumentation (Statement of Purpose; 13:10) in 8.2.1.2

Paul's message in 13:10 functions as a purpose statement of the division (10:1–13:10) regarding his reluctancy to exercise stern discipline over the Corinthians.

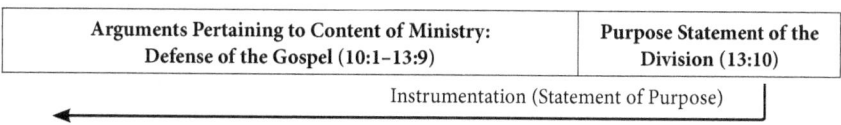

9.6.2.3 Causation with Particularization and Contrast (10:1–18 and 11:1–12:13) in 8.2.1.3

Paul's discussion in 10:1–18 serves as a basis for his discourse in 11:1–12:13 by describing the causes that force him to engage in the boasting competition (causation). At the same time, he continues to elaborate the causes in 11:1–12:13 (particularization). In addition, Paul begins to defend his status as a servant of Christ in 10:1–11 and fully develops it in 11:1–12:13 (particularization) through the contrast between himself and his adversaries.

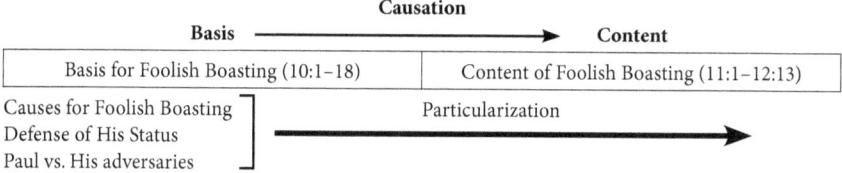

9.6.2.4 Causation (10:1–12:13 and 12:14–13:10) in 8.2.1.4

Paul's defense of his status as a servant of Christ (10:1–12:13) serves as a basis for his consequent preparation for his impending visit (12:14–13:10).

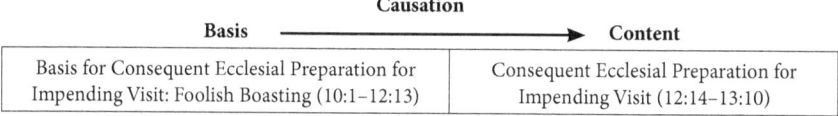

9.7 Theological Implications: Paul's Theology of Ministry and Weakness

As I stated in Chapter 1, the purpose of this study is not only to propose that an inductive and integrative approach presents a more suitable and helpful literary structure for 2 Corinthians but also to demonstrate the relevance of studying the literary structure for understanding the theology of the letter. However, due to the limited space, I have focused on the former. While another volume would be needed to draw out the full implications of this study, I provide a brief discussion regarding significant theological implications regarding Paul's theology of theocentric ministry and weakness.

Regarding these theological implications, other scholars have also reached similar conclusions through their historical–critical and lexical study. Savage argues that the reconstruction of the Hellenistic cultural influence on the Corinthians indicates that Paul responds to the egocentrism, such as self-exalting, self-boasting, and exploiting others by insisting on a Christ-centered perspective. Thus, he concludes that the heart of what it means to Paul to be a minister of Christ is best found in his paradoxical teaching in 12:10, for weakness is an affirmation of apostolic office as well as a locus in which divine power is manifested (see 2.2.1.3). Black likewise argues based on his lexical study of ἀσθένεια and its cognates that Paul develops the doctrine of weakness for the first time in history (see note in 8.2.1.3).

On the one hand, my study adds its own confirmation of those observations through a different methodology; thus, these different approaches reinforce the legitimacy of the theological implications for the theology of 2 Corinthians. On the other hand, my study makes its own contribution to the understanding of the theological message of the letter regarding its methodology and content. First, the following theological implications are not the result of the exegetical works on certain key passages or terms in the letter; instead, these observations are consistently and coherently indicated throughout Paul's discourse in the letter. Thus, the literary context of the letter as a whole supports them. Second, while other scholars suggest various theological conclusions (see Chapter 2), no proposals have drawn theological implications regarding Paul's theology of ministry in depth as this study does by weaving related themes together to show their organic connections.

9.7.1 Paul's Theology of Ministry

The dynamics of the literary structure of 2 Corinthians not only points to the central concern of the letter but also informs Paul's theology of ministry, for the study of form illumines its content. Namely, the study of the literary structure of 2 Corinthians provides clear indications regarding Paul's understanding of theocentric ministry in relation to its qualifications, its role, its purpose, its manner, its nature, and its Christology.

Regarding Paul's understanding of qualifications for ministry, it is theocentric, for the qualifications have their origin in God, which is evinced by the manner and character of God's servants in ministry. This divine origin of the qualifications is indicated throughout the letter. I have noted that the salutation (1:1–2) prepares the audience for Paul's entire discourse in 1:3–13:10, in which Paul highlights the divine origin of apostleship (1:1). This emphasis is further indicated in the second division (1:3–2:13). I noted that Paul's discussion regarding the character of ministry (1:3–2:13) establishes a basis for his main discourse in 3:1–13:10, in which he presents that God's encouragement enabled Paul to become the agent of the divine encouragement to others (1:3–7) and supports it by his integrity of conduct (1:12–2:11). Moreover, the notion is further developed in the rest of the letter in 2:14–13:10. I have argued that 2:14–17 is the thesis of the letter, in which he emphasizes the qualifications of God's agents regarding their sincerity and divine origin, which is evinced by his sincerity of speaking God's word (2:17). According to the movement from general (2:14–17) to particular (3:1–13:10), Paul continues to explicate divine qualifications (3:1–6a; 5:11–19; 8:16, 19, 22; 10:8; 17; 11:23a; 12:4, 7; 13:10), testified by his integrity (4:2–9, 6:3–10; 8:16, 17, 18, 20, 22; 10:2, 12–18; 11:7–15; 11:23b–29; 12:9–10, 14–21). Therefore, Paul's understanding of ministry is theocentric, for its qualifications have divine origin.

In addition, his understanding of ministerial function is theocentric, for the ministry promotes God's knowledge, the gospel of Christ. This primary ministerial function is indicated throughout the letter. I noted that Paul's discussion in 1:3–2:13 establishes a basis for his discourse in 3:1–13:10. I also discussed that Paul's skillful crafting of the structure by framing his argument in 2:14–7:3 with the discussions regarding the proclamation of the gospel through the previous letter (2:3–11 and 7:4–16) reinforces this argument, in which Paul shows that his previous proclamation was meant to protect the Corinthians from Satan's scheme (2:11) and produce godly sorrow into salvation (7:9–10). In this way, the history of Paul's proclamation establishes a ground for his discourse in 2:14–7:3 by presenting his interest in the promotion and protection of the gospel. This paramount purpose is particularly articulated and developed in 2:14–13:10. In the thesis statement (2:14–17), Paul clarifies that one of the primary functions of the ministry is to disseminate God's knowledge through their speech. Thus, according to the movement from general (2:14–17) to particulars (3:1–13:10), Paul expounds the ways in which God's servants disseminate God's knowledge. On the one hand, God's servants promote God's knowledge by proclaiming it as the gospel of Christ (3:1–7:16). On the other hand, he promotes God's knowledge by destroying arrogance and obstacles against it (10:4–6) through his defense (10:1–13:10). Thus, his ministry is theocentric because it promotes God's knowledge.

Furthermore, his understanding of ministerial purpose is theocentric, for the ministry produces other agents of God. This chief purpose is also indicated throughout the letter. In 1:3–2:13, Paul emphasizes that God's agents and the Corinthians share ministry. I argued that Paul's discussion regarding the character of the ministry (1:3–2:13) establishes a basis as well as introduces major themes to be developed in 2:14–13:10, particularly by emphasizing the mutual character in ministry. By understanding his previous relationship with the Corinthians in light of mutuality, Paul leads the audience to his arguments in 2:14–13:10. According to the causal move from general (1:3–2:13) to particulars (2:14–13:10), Paul and his fellow workers proclaim the gospel as God's agents in persuading the Corinthians to be reconciled to God and his servants (5:11–7:3) so that he can urge them to respond to the gospel by becoming God's agents through their partnership in the ministry to the saints (8:1–9:15). Thus, his emphasis on the mutual character of ministry (1:3–2:13) is further expressed as the reconciliation (5:11–7:3) and partnership in the ministry to the saints (8:1–9:15). Moreover, Paul reinforces this purpose in 10:1–13:10 by defending his financial integrity (11:7–15; 12:14–18) so that the Corinthians would understand that the collection is not meant to benefit him but rather to reproduce God's agents. Thus, his ministry is theocentric, for it produces other Christian workers for God.

In addition, Paul's understanding of the manner of ministry is theocentric, for the divine paradox in ministry points to the centrality of God. This idea of God-centeredness is indicated throughout the letter. I have noted that Paul's discussion on the character of the ministry (1:3–2:13) introduces major themes to be developed in

2:14–13:10, among which is the antithesis regarding divine encouragement and suffering (1:3–7). Paul supports the theme by the testimony of his affliction in Asia, in which he underscores not only the antithesis of God's deliverance and Paul's affliction but also the centrality of God, for he would not trust in himself but in God (1:8–11). The theme of God-centeredness through the divine paradox is articulated in 2:14–13:10. In the thesis statement in 2:14–17, Paul continues to express the manifestation of God's knowledge through the paradox in the imagery of God's triumphal procession and to develop the theme in the rest of the letter (4:6–7, 10–12, 17; 8:1–2, 9; 12:9–10; 13:4) according to the movement from general (2:14–17) to particulars (3:1–13:10). The purpose of the divine paradox is to point to the centrality of God in ministry, manifesting God's knowledge (2:14–17), God's power (4:6–7; 13:4), Jesus's life (4:10–12), glory to God (4:17), the grace of God and Christ (8:1–2, 9), and Christ's power (12:9–10). Thus, Paul's theology of ministry is theocentric, for he understands that God executes his ministry through a divine paradox so that it points to the centrality of God and Christ in ministry.

Moreover, Paul understands that the nature of the ministry is theocentric, for the ministry is worship of God. This primary nature is indicated throughout the letter as well. Paul begins and concludes the letter with benedictions (χάρις in 1:2 and 13:13), expressing his response to God's gracious saving activity. This emphasis on worship is further indicated in 1:3–2:13, in which he expresses introductory blessing, praising God's merciful character and encouragement (1:3–7), which serves as a general statement for the discussion in 1:8–2:13. Moreover, I have noted that Paul's discussion in 1:3–2:13 characterizes the rest of Paul's discourse in 2:14–13:10. One aspect of the worship is articulated in the thesis statement (2:14–17) regarding the sacrificial overtone of ministry. As Χριστοῦ εὐωδία, Paul describes the ministry as a pleasing sacrifice to God (2:15); thus, according to the movement from general (2:14–17) to particulars (3:1–13:10), he continues to expound this aspect in 3:1–13:10 (4:13–5:10; 5:11–6:10; 6:14–7:1; 7:4–16; 8:5; 8:19; 9:13; 12:9). Therefore, Paul's understanding of ministry is theocentric in the sense that he views it as a pleasing sacrifice to God. Moreover, another aspect of the nature of worship is indicated in 3:1–13:10. First, I have noted that Paul's discussions in 3:1–7:16 and 8:1–9:15 share the same purpose that the ministry of the proclamation (3:1–7:16) and the collection (8:1–9:15) result in thanksgiving and glory to God (4:15; 8:19; 9:13). Thus, the ministry is theocentric, for it results in worship in giving thanks and glory to God. Furthermore, this nature is reinforced by Paul's defense of the gospel in 10:1–13:10. There, he highlights that the purpose of the defense is the Corinthians' edification (10:8; 12:19; 13:10). As I noted, Paul understands that thanksgiving and edification are indispensable aspects of worship (1 Cor 14); thus, the defense strengthens the nature of the ministry. Therefore, Paul recognizes that the ministry is theocentric, for it is a worship to God in the sense that Paul views the ministry as a pleasing sacrifice to God, in the sense that he understands the ministry of the proclamation and the collection results in worship with thanksgiving and glory to God, and in the sense that the ministry of the defense edifies the worship.

Finally, Paul acknowledges the theocentric character of ministry by presenting Christ's essential roles in ministry as the intermediate agent, for Christ is the basis, means, and goal of the ministry. This notion is emphasized from the beginning to the end of the letter not only by the recurring references to Christ, but also by the structural features. I noted that the salutation (1:1–2) prepares the audience for Paul's discourse in 1:3–13:10 by, among other things, presenting Christ as the sender of the apostle (1:1) and by characterizing the entire letter with the grace of the Lord Jesus Christ (1:2). Moreover, Paul concludes the letter (13:11–13) by the grace of the Lord Jesus Christ; thus, *inclusio* of Christ's grace frames the entire letter. The emphasis of Christ as the mediator of the ministry is additionally indicated in 1:3–2:13 by presenting Christ as the mediator of the divine encouragement and suffering (1:3–7) whose function is further supported by the following discussion in 1:8–2:13. Moreover, Paul articulates Christ as the intermediate agent in the thesis statement in 2:14–17, whose roles enable the ministry by bridging between the ultimate agent (God) and his agents. Thus, according to the movement from general (2:14–17) to particulars (3:1–13:10), Paul expounds Christ's intermediate roles in ministry. Through the agency of Christ, God manifests the divine paradox (2:14; 4:7, 10–12, 14, 17; 8:9; 12:7–10) and manifests his knowledge (2:14; 3:2–3, 14, 16). The sacrificial service of God's agents (2:15) finds its foundation (5:6, 8, 10, 11a; 8:9; 12:9) and its goal in Christ (8:5, 19; 9:13). As ambassadors for Christ (5:20), God's servants proclaim the gospel of Christ (4:4–6) based on his death and resurrection (5:14–17) and destroy obstacles against the gospel in taking them to the obedience to Christ (10:5), based on the qualifications that come from Christ (3:3; 5:14; 18; 8:23; 10:8, 14, 17–18; 11:30–33; 12:1, 2, 5b–10; 13:4, 10); thus, they commend themselves as slaves and servants of Christ (4:5; 11:23). Therefore, Paul's understanding of ministry is theocentric, for Christ's intermediary roles indicate his involvement in every aspect of the ministry.

Therefore, the theological implication that arises from the dynamics of the literary structure of 2 Corinthians have shown Paul's understanding of theocentric ministry in relation to its qualifications, its role, its purpose, its manner, its nature, and its mediator. To put it another way, while the counteragents rely on self-commendation (10:12, 18) and lack their integrity in their ministry (2:17; 10:12, 17–18; 11:7–12, 20), Paul has the divine qualifications and lives up to them by his integrity. While the counteragents demote God's knowledge (2:17; 4:2; 5:16; 11:3–4, 13–15), Paul promotes it. While the counteragents exploit the Corinthians (11:7–12, 20), Paul empowers them to become God's agents in ministry. While the counteragents focus on themselves, boasting about external matters (5:12), others' labors (10:13, 15, 16), and themselves (11:18), and by competing with each other (10:12, 18; 11:12), Paul boasts about his weakness through which divine power is manifested, placing God and Christ in the center of his ministry. While the counteragents exalt themselves (11:20), Paul praises and worships God through his sacrificial service, thanksgiving, glory, and edification. While the counteragents are servants of Satan (11:13–15), Paul is a servant of Christ who is the basis, means, and goal of the ministry.

9.7.2 Paul's Theology of Weakness

Related to the theology of ministry, the literary structure of 2 Corinthians also has another theological implication regarding Paul's understanding of weakness, for weakness defines Paul's identity and characterizes his ministry. This emphasis is, in fact, indicated throughout the letter. To begin, I demonstrated that Paul's statement in 12:9–10 serves as a general and climactic statement of the letter, in which he shows that weakness defines his identity as a servant of Christ based on Christ's weakness (13:4). Thus, his status of weakness in Christ serves as a theological foundation for his discourse in the letter. Moreover, the climactic statement of his defense in 12:10 reveals that weakness is a larger category that encompasses all types of difficulties in ministry, such as suffering and persecution. Thus, weakness defines not only his identity as a servant of Christ, but also his ministry that involves all sorts of hardship in ministry, through which God manifests his power. In addition, I have also noted that Paul's defense in 10:1–13:10 as a whole reinforces his discourse in 2:14–9:15.

Moreover, this notion of the divine power through weakness is further expressed in his discussion in 1:3–2:13 in the form of the antithesis between divine encouragement and suffering (1:3–7), which is substantiated by his testimony of affliction in Asia (1:8–11). Just as the affliction becomes a locus of God's encouragement (1:3–7), Paul's affliction became a means to manifest the divine power of deliverance. Thus, the antithesis of divine encouragement and suffering is a form of divine power through weakness. I noted that Paul's arguments pertaining to the character of ministry (1:3–2:13) serves as a basis for his following arguments and introduces major themes to be developed in the rest of the letter. Therefore, on the one hand, the history of Paul's ministry (1:8–11) paves a way to his message in 2:14–9:15: Because the history of Paul's ministry provides an example of the divine power through weakness (1:8–11), Paul continues to proclaim the gospel and exhorts the Corinthians in the divine power through weakness (2:14–9:15). On the other hand, Paul continues to expound the theme of divine encouragement and suffering (3:12; 4:1, 6–9; 4:13–5:10; 5:20–7:3; 7:4–16; 11:21b–12:10). To put it another way, Paul reinforces his discourse in 2:14–9:15 by defining his identity as a servant of Christ and his ministry with the divine power through weakness (10:1–13:10), and by presenting an actual example of the divine power through weakness via his testimony in the form of divine encouragement and suffering (1:3–11).

Furthermore, the theme of divine power through weakness continues to be indicated in 2:14–9:15. In the thesis statement (2:14–17), Paul expresses the divine paradox that the captives are active participants in God's triumphal procession; God achieves his ministry through the least qualified and the unlikely means. The strong conquer the weak, but the mighty God manifests his knowledge through the weak. Then, when moving from general (2:14–17) to particulars (3:1–9:15), Paul develops the proclamation (3:1–7:16) and exhortations (8:1–9:15) in relation to the divine paradox of power through weakness (4:6–7, 10–12, 17; 8:1–2, 9). God reveals his power through human weakness in the sense that God entrusts his glorious, life-giving, and transforming knowledge, the gospel of Christ to fragile and worthless human agents whose suffering and death manifest Jesus's life (3:12–4:12), in the sense that God produces glory through affliction (4:13–5:10), in the sense that Christ's example of becoming the weak serves (8:9; cf. 8:1–5) as a model for the ministry to the saints (8:1–9:15).

Therefore, weakness defines and characterizes his identity and ministry, for it is a locus in which the divine power is manifested. To put it another way, the structure of 2

Corinthians points to Paul's theology of weakness, for it informs Paul's understanding of God and Christology, anthropology, missiology, ethics/ecclesiology. Weakness is a platform where the divine power is exhibited in the world (God and Christology). At the same time, the paradox of divine power through human weakness presupposes the nature of human agents as fragile and worthless beings (4:6–7) susceptible to suffering, affliction, and difficulties (4:10–12; 4:13–5:10; 6:3–10; 11:23–29; 12:5a–10; anthropology). However, God's mission is accomplished through such a paradox (missiology), and Christ's weakness becomes a model for the ways in which Christians should partner with each other and have fellowship (8:9; cf. 8:1–2; ethics/ecclesiology).

9.8 Further Areas of Research

The study of the literary structure of 2 Corinthians leaves us a few further areas of research. First, as I have repeated in my discussion, the identification of the MSRs is not the end of the exegesis. Because one cannot separate the form from the content, the study of the form must inform that of the content and *vice versa*. Therefore, individual passages in 2 Corinthians should be studied in light of the literary structure presented by this study.

Second, having investigated the text of 2 Corinthians in its final form, one can and should use these insights to explore historical questions of the letter (e.g., the reconstruction of Paul's opponents and the course of the events between Paul and the Corinthians), for these issues can be best approached when one understands Paul's train of thought and argument on the basis of the text itself.

Third, this study demonstrated the inductive and integrative approach as a better hermeneutical model for the study of the text in its final form; thus, one can and should employ this methodology for the analysis of other books of the Bible.

Bibliography

Abrams, Meyer Howard. *A Glossary of Literary Terms*. 4th ed. New York: Holt, Rinehart & Winston, 1981.

Achtemeier, Elizabeth R. *Minor Prophets I*. NIBCOT 17. Peabody, MA: Hendrickson, 1996.

Achtemeier, Paul J. *Mark*. Proclamation Commentaries. Philadelphia: Fortress, 1975.

Alary, Laura D. "Good Grief: Paul as Sufferer and Consoler in 2 Corinthians 1:3–7: A Comparative Investigation." PhD diss., University of St. Michael's College, 2003.

Allo, Ernest Bernard, ed. *Saint Paul: Seconde Épître aux Corinthiens*. Paris: Gabalda, 1937.

Alter, Robert. *The Art of Biblical Narrative*. New York: Basic Books, 1981.

Amador, J. David Hester. "Re-Reading 2 Corinthians: A Rhetorical Approach." Pages 276–95 in *Rhetorical Argumentation in Biblical Texts: Essays from the Lund 2000 Conference*. Edited by Anders Eriksson, Thomas H. Olbricht, and Walter G. Übelacker. Emory Studies in Early Christianity 8. Harrisburg, PA: Trinity, 2002.

Amador, J. David Hester. "Revisiting 2 Corinthians: Rhetoric and the Case for Unity." *NTS* 46 (2000): 92–111.

Amador, J. David Hester. "The Unity of 2 Corinthians: A Test Case for a Re-Discovered and Re-Invented Rhetoric." *Neot* 33 (1999): 411–32.

Anderson, Janice Capel. *Matthew's Narrative Web: Over, and Over, and Over Again*. JSNTSup 91. Sheffield: JSOT Press, 1994.

Arnold, Bill T. "Samuel, Books Of." *Dictionary of the Old Testament: Historical Books*, 865–77.

Arthur, Kay. *How to Study Your Bible*. Eugene, OR: Harvest House Publishers, 1994.

Auerbach, Erich. *Mimesis: The Representation of Reality in Western Literature*. Translated by Willard R. Trask. Garden City, NY: Doubleday, 1957.

Aune, David E. *The New Testament in Its Literary Environment*. LEC 8. Philadelphia: Westminster, 1987.

Aune, David E. *The Westminster Dictionary of New Testament and Early Christian Literature and Rhetoric*. Louisville: Westminster John Knox, 2003.

Aus, Roger David. *Imagery of Triumph and Rebellion in 2 Corinthians 2:14–17 and Elsewhere in the Epistle: An Example of the Combination of Greco-Roman and Judaic Traditions in the Apostle Paul*. Studies in Judaism. Lanham, MD: University Press of America, 2005.

Averbeck, R. E. "Sacrifice and Offerings." *Dictionary of the Old Testament: Pentateuch*, 706–33.

Bachmann, Philipp. *Der Zweite Brief des Paulus an die Korinther*. Edited by Theodor Zahn. Kommentar Zum Neuen Testament 8. Leipzig: Deichert, 1909.

Baird, William. "Letters of Recommendation: A Study of II Cor 3:1–3." *JBL* 80 (1961): 166–72.

Balla, Peter. "2 Corinthians." Pages 753–84 in *Commentary on the New Testament Use of the Old Testament*. Edited by G. K. Beale and D. A. Carson. Grand Rapids; Nottingham: Baker Academic; Apollos, 2007.

Barnes, Kevin Bryan. "A Bible Study about Studying Bible: An Introduction to Inductive Bible Study." DMin diss., Asbury Theological Seminary, 2018.

Barnett, Paul W. *The Second Epistle to the Corinthians*. NICNT. Grand Rapids: Eerdmans, 1997.

Barnett, Paul W. "Apostle." *DPL*, 45–51.

Barrett, C. K. *A Commentary on the Second Epistle to the Corinthians*. BNTC. London: Black, 1973.

Barth, Karl. *The Resurrection of the Dead*. Translated by H. J. Stenning. New York: Fleming H. Revell, 1933.

Barth, Markus. *Ephesians 1–3: Introduction, Translation, and Commentary on Chapters 1–3*. AB 34. Garden City, NY: Doubleday, 1974.

Bates, W. H. "The Integrity of II Corinthians." *NTS* 12 (1965): 56–69.

Batstone, William W. "The Antithesis of Virtue: Sallust's 'Synkrisis' and the Crisis of the Late Republic." *Classical Antiquity* 7 (1988): 1–29.

Bauer, David R. "Chiasm." *NIDB* 1:587–88.

Bauer, David R. "Inductive Biblical Study: History, Character, and Prospects in a Global Environment." *The Asbury Journal* 68 (2013): 6–35.

Bauer, David R. *The Structure of Matthew's Gospel: A Study in Literary Design*. JSNTSup 31; BLS 15. Sheffield: Almond Press, 1988.

Bauer, David R., and Robert A. Traina. *Inductive Bible Study: A Comprehensive Guide to the Practice of Hermeneutics*. Grand Rapids: Baker Academic, 2011.

Baumert, Norbert. *Täglich Sterben und Auferstehen: Der Literalsinn von 2 Kor 4,12-5,10*. SANT. Munich: Kösel-Verlag, 1973.

Baur, Ferdinand Christian. *Paul, the Apostle of Jesus Christ: His Life and Work, His Epistles and His Doctrine: A Contribution to the Critical History of Primitive Christianity*. Edited by Eduard Zeller. Translated by Allan Menzies. 2 vols. Theological Translation Fund Library. London: Williams and Norgate, 1875.

Beale, G. K. *The Book of Revelation*. NIGTC. Grand Rapids: Eerdmans, 1999.

Beasley-Murray, George R. *John*. 2nd ed. WBC 36. Dallas: Word, 1999.

Beekman, John, John Callow, and Michael Kopesec. *The Semantic Structure of Written Communication*. 5th ed. Dallas: Summer Institute of Linguistics, 1981.

Belleville, Linda L. *Reflections of Glory: Paul's Polemical Use of the Moses-Doxa Tradition in 2 Corinthians 3.1-18*. JSNTSup 52. Sheffield: JSOT Press, 1991.

Belleville, Linda L. *2 Corinthians*. The IVP New Testament Commentary. Downers Grove, IL: InterVarsity Press, 1996.

Berlin, Adele. *The Dynamics of Biblical Parallelism*. Rev. and exp. ed. Grand Rapids: Eerdmans, 2008.

Bernard, J. H. "The Second Epistle to the Corinthians." Pages 1–119 in *The Expositor's Greek Testament*. Edited by W. Robertson Nicoll. Vol. 5 of. London: Hodder and Stoughton, 1903.

Best, Ernest. *A Critical and Exegetical Commentary on Ephesians*. ICC. Edinburgh: T&T Clark, 1998.

Betz, Hans Dieter. *Der Apostel Paulus und die Sokratische Tradition: Eine Exegetische Untersuchung zu seiner Apologie 2 Korinther 10-13*. BHT 45. Tübingen: Mohr, 1972.

Betz, Hans Dieter. *Galatians: A Commentary on Paul's Letter to the Churches in Galatia*. Hermeneia. Philadelphia: Fortress, 1979.

Betz, Hans Dieter. *2 Corinthians 8 and 9: A Commentary on Two Administrative Letters of the Apostle Paul*. Edited by George W. MacRae. Hermeneia. Philadelphia: Fortress, 1985.

Bird, Michael F. *Colossians and Philemon*. New Covenant Commentary Series 12. Eugene, OR: Cascade, 2009.

Black, David Alan. *Paul, Apostle of Weakness: Astheneia and Its Cognates in the Pauline Literature*. 2nd ed. Eugene, OR: Pickwick, 2012.
Blass, Friedrich, Albert Debrunner, and Robert Walter Funk. *A Greek Grammar of the New Testament and Other Early Christian Literature*. Chicago: University of Chicago Press, 1961.
Blomberg, Craig L. "The Structure of 2 Corinthians 1-7." *CTR* 4 (1989): 3–20.
Bonneau, Guy. "À La Vie, à La Mort: Le Conflit à Corinthe et Ses Enjeux Théologiques En 2 Co 2,14-7,4." *ScEs* 51 (1999): 351–66.
Booth, Wayne C. "Metaphor as Rhetoric: The Problem of Evaluation." Pages 47–70 in *On Metaphor*. Edited by Sheldon Sacks. Chicago: University of Chicago Press, 1978.
Booth, Wayne C. *The Rhetoric of Fiction*. Chicago: University of Chicago Press, 1961.
Bornkamm, Günther. *Geschichte und Glaube*. 2 vols. Munich: Kaiser, 1971.
Bornkamm, Günther. "The History of the Origin of the So-Called Second Letter to the Corinthians." *NTS* 8 (1962): 258–64.
Bowens, Lisa M. *An Apostle in Battle: Paul and Spiritual Warfare in 2 Corinthians 12:1-10*. WUNT 2/433. Tübingen: Mohr Siebeck, 2017.
Breck, John. *The Shape of Biblical Language: Chiasmus in the Scriptures and Beyond*. Crestwood, NY: St. Vladimir's Seminary Press, 1994.
Breytenbach, Cilliers. "Paul's Proclamation and God's 'Thriambos': (Notes on 2 Corinthians 2:14–16b)." *Neot* 24 (1990): 257–71.
Bright, John. *The Authority of the Old Testament*. Grand Rapids: Baker, 1975.
Bruce, F. F. *The Acts of the Apostles: The Greek Text with Introduction and Commentary*. NICNT. Grand Rapids: Eerdmans, 1952.
Bruce, F. F.. *1 & 2 Thessalonians*. WBC 45. Dallas: Word, 1982.
Burton, Ernest D. *Syntax of Moods and Tenses in the New Testament Greek*. 3rd ed. Edinburgh: T&T Clark, 1898.
Campbell, Constantine R. *Verbal Aspect and Non-Indicative Verbs: Further Soundings in the Greek of the New Testament*. Studies in Biblical Greek 15. New York: Lang, 2008.
Campbell, Douglas A. *Paul: An Apostle's Journey*. Grand Rapids: Eerdmans, 2018.
Chevallier, Max-Alain. "L'argumentation de Paul dans 2 Corinthiens 10 à 13." *RHPR* 70 (1990): 3–15.
Christian, Timothy J. "Paul and the Rhetoric of Insinuatio: How and Why 1 Cor 15 Functions Rhetorically as the Climax to 1 Corinthians." PhD diss., Asbury Theological Seminary, 2019.
Chronis, Harry L. "The Torn Veil: Cultus and Christology in Mark 15:37–39." *JBL* 101 (1982): 97–114.
Classen, Carl Joachim. *Rhetorical Criticism of the New Testament*. Boston: Brill, 2002.
Cohen, Ted. "Metaphor and the Cultivation of Intimacy." Pages 1–10 in *On Metaphor*. Edited by Sheldon Sacks. Chicago: University of Chicago Press, 1978.
Collange, Jean-François. *Enigmes de la Deuxième Épître de Paul aux Corinthiens: Etudes Exégétique de 2 Cor. 2,14-7,4*. SNTSMS 18. Cambridge University Press, 1972.
Comfort, Philip W. *New Testament Text and Translation Commentary: Commentary on the Variant Readings of the Ancient New Testament Manuscripts and How They Relate to the Major English Translations*. Carol Stream, IL: Tyndale House, 2008.
Constantineanu, Corneliu. *The Social Significance of Reconciliation in Paul's Theology: Narrative Readings in Romans*. LNTS 421. London: T&T Clark, 2010.
Craigmiles, Shawn I. "Pragmatic Constraints of Ἀλλά in the Synoptic Gospels." PhD diss., Asbury Theological Seminary, 2016.
Craigie, Peter C. *Psalm 1–50*. WBC 19. Dallas: Word, 1983.

Cranfield, C. E. B. *A Critical and Exegetical Commentary on the Epistle to the Romans*. Repr. 2 vols. ICC. London: T&T Clark, 2004.
Culpepper, R. Alan. *Anatomy of the Fourth Gospel: A Study in Literary Design*. FF. Philadelphia: Fortress, 1983.
Dana, H. E., and Julius R. Mantey. *A Manual Grammar of the Greek New Testament*. New York: Macmillan, 1927.
Danker, Frederick W. *II Corinthians*. ACNT. Minneapolis: Augsburg, 1989.
Danker, Frederick W., Walter Bauer, and William Arndt. *A Greek-English Lexicon of the New Testament and Other Early Christian Literature*. 3rd ed. Chicago: University of Chicago Press, 2000.
Denney, James. *The Second Epistle to the Corinthians*. The Expositor's Bible. New York: Armstrong and Son, 1894.
deSilva, David A. *Honor, Patronage, Kinship & Purity: Unlocking New Testament Culture*. Downers Grove, IL: InterVarsity Press, 2000.
Dewey, Joanna. *Markan Public Debate: Literary Technique, Concentric Structure, and Theology in Mark 2:1-36*. SBLDS 48. Chico, CA: Scholars Press, 1980.
Duff, Paul Brooks. "Metaphor, Motif, and Meaning: The Rhetorical Strategy Behind the Image 'Led in Triumph' in 2 Corinthians 2:14." *CBQ* 53 (1991): 79–92.
Duff, Paul Brooks. "2 Corinthians 1–7: Sidestepping the Division Hypothesis Dilemma." *BTB* 24 (1994): 16–26.
Dunn, James D. G. *Colossians and Philemon*. NIGTC. Grand Rapids: Eerdmans, 1996.
Dunn, James D. G. *The Epistle to the Galatians*. BNTC. Peabody, MA: Hendrickson, 1993.
Dunn, James D. G. *Romans 9–16*. WBC 38B. Dallas: Word, 1988.
Eberhardt, Charles R. *The Bible in the Making of Ministers: The Scriptural Basis of Theological Education: The Lifework of Wilbert Webster White*. New York: Association, 1949.
Enos, Richard L. "Ciceronian Dispositio as an Architecture for Creativity in Composition: A Note for the Affirmative." *Rhetoric Review* 4 (1985): 108–10.
Evans, Christopher F. *The Theology of Rhetoric: The Epistle to the Hebrews*. Friends of Dr. Williams's Library 42. London: Dr. William's Trust, 1988.
Finzel, Hans. *Observe, Interpret, Apply: How to Study the Bible Inductively*. GroupBuilder Resources. Wheaton, IL: Victor, 1994.
Fitzgerald, John T. *Cracks in an Earthen Vessel: An Examination of the Catalogues of Hardships in the Corinthian Correspondence*. SBLDS 99. Atlanta: Scholars Press, 1988.
Fitzgerald, John T. "Paul, the Ancient Epistolary Theorists, and 2 Corinthians 10–13: The Purpose and Literary Genre of a Pauline Letter." Pages 190–200 in *Greeks, Romans, and Christians: Essays in Honor of Abraham J. Malherbe*. Edited by Abraham J. Malherbe, David
L. Balch, Everett Ferguson, and Wayne A. Meeks. Minneapolis: Fortress, 1990.
Fitzmyer, Joseph A. *Romans: A New Translation with Introduction and Commentary*. AB 33. New York: Doubleday, 1993.
Forbes, Christopher. "Comparison, Self-Praise and Irony: Paul's Boasting and the Conventions of Hellenistic Rhetoric." *NTS* 32 (1986): 1–30.
Fowl, Stephen E. *Ephesians: A Commentary*. NTL. Louisville: Westminster John Knox, 2012.
Fowler, Robert M. *Loaves and Fishes: The Function of the Feeding Stories in the Gospel of Mark*. SBLDS 54. Chico, CA: Scholars Press, 1981.
France, R. T. *The Gospel of Mark*. NIGTC. Grand Rapids: Eerdmans, 2002.

Freedman, William. "The Literary Motif: A Definition and Evaluation." *Novel* 4 (1971): 123–31.

Freeman, Maria. "Study with an Open Mind and Heart: William Rainey Harper's Inductive Method of Teaching the Bible." PhD diss., The University of Chicago, 2005.

Frye, Northrop. *Anatomy of Criticism: Four Essays*. Princeton: Princeton University Press, 1957.

Fuller, Daniel P. *The Inductive Method of Bible Study*. Pasadena, CA: Fuller Theological Seminary, 1955.

Funk, Robert W. *Language, Hermeneutic, and Word of God: The Problem of Language in the New Testament and Contemporary Theology*. New York: Harper & Row, 1966.

Furnish, Victor Paul. *II Corinthians*. AB 32A. Garden City, NY: Doubleday, 1984.

Garland, David E. *2 Corinthians*. NAC 29. Nashville: Broadman & Holman, 1999.

Genette, Gérard. *Narrative Discourse: An Essay in Method*. Translated by Jane E. Lewin. Ithaca, NY: Cornell University Press, 1980.

Georgi, Dieter. *Die Geschichte der Kollekte des Paulus für Jerusalem*. TF 38. Hamburg-Bergstedt: Reich, 1965.

Gesenius, Wilhelm. *Gesenius' Hebrew Grammar*. Edited by E. Kautzsch. Translated by A. E. Cowley. 2nd ed. Oxford: Clarendon, 1910.

Goudge, Henry Leighton. *The Second Epistle to the Corinthians*. 2 vols. WC 43. Methuen: London, 1928.

Graham, Mary Creswell. *Inductive Bible Study Explained*. Rev. ed. Mary L. Graham, Institute of International Studies, 1995.

Grimes, Joseph E. *The Thread of Discourse*. Janua Linguarum Series Minor 207. Hague: Mouton, 1975.

Gros Louis, Kenneth R. R. "Some Methodological Considerations." Pages 2:13–24 in *Literary Interpretations of Biblical Narratives*. Edited by James Stokes Ackerman and Thayer S. Warshaw. Vol. 2. Nashville: Abingdon, 1974.

Guthrie, George H. *2 Corinthians*. BECNT. Grand Rapids: Baker Academic, 2015.

Guthrie, George H. *The Structure of Hebrews: A Text-Linguistic Analysis*. NovTSup 73. Leiden: Brill, 1994.

Hafemann, Scott J. *2 Corinthians*. The NIV Application Commentary. Grand Rapids: Zondervan, 2000.

Hafemann, Scott J. *Suffering and the Spirit: An Exegetical Study of II Cor. 2:14-3:3 Within the Context of the Corinthian Correspondence*. WUNT 2/19. Tübingen: Mohr Siebeck, 1986.

Hagner, Donald A. *Matthew 1–13*. WBC 33A. Dallas: Word, 1993.

Hansen, G. Walter. "Rhetorical Criticism." *DPL*, 822–26.

Harper, William Rainey. *A Critical and Exegetical Commentary on Amos and Hosea*. ICC. New York: Scribner's Sons, 1905.

Harris, Murray J. *The Second Epistle to the Corinthians*. NIGTC. Grand Rapids: Eerdmans, 2005.

Harvey, A. E. *Renewal Through Suffering: A Study of 2 Corinthians*. SNTW. Edinburgh: T&T Clark, 1996.

Hawthorne, Gerald F., and Ralph P. Martin. *Philippians*. WBC 43. Nashville: Nelson, 2004.

Hays, Richard B. *The Faith of Jesus Christ: An Investigation of the Narrative Substructure of Galatians 3:1-4:11*. SBLDS 56. Chico, CA: Scholars Press, 1983.

Heilig, Christoph. *Paul's Triumph: Reassessing 2 Corinthians 2:14 in Its Literary and Historical Context*. BTS 27. Leuven: Peeters, 2017.

Heinrici, C. F. Georg. *Das Zweite Sendschreiben des Apostel Paulus an die Korinthier*. Berlin: Hertz, 1887.

Heiny, Stephen B. "2 Corinthians 2:14–4:6: The Motive for Metaphor." Pages 1–22 in *Society of Biblical Literature 1987 Seminar Papers*. SBLSPS 26. Atlanta: Society of Biblical Literature, 1987.

Hellerman, Joseph H. *Reconstructing Honor in Roman Philippi: Carmen Christi as Cursus Pudorum*. SNTSMS 132. New York: Cambridge University Press, 2005.

Hendricks, Howard G., and William Hendricks. *Living by the Book*. Chicago: Moody, 1991.

Héring, Jean. *The Second Epistle of Saint Paul to the Corinthians*. London: Epworth, 1967.

Hilgenfeld, Adolf. *Historisch-Kritische Einleitung in Das Neue Testament*. Leipzig: Fues, 1875.

Hillers, Delbert R. *Micah*. Hermeneia. Philadelphia: Fortress, 1984.

Hiramatsu, Kei. "Echoes of Jesus' Cross in Second Corinthians 12:7–10." *Asbury Journal* 77 (2022): 267–88.

Holtzmann, Heinrich J. "Das Gegenseitige Verhältniss der Beiden Korintherbriefe." *ZWT* 22 (1879): 455–92.

Hubbard, Moyer V. *2 Corinthians*. Teach the Text Commentary. Grand Rapids: Baker Books, 2017.

Hughes, Frank W. "The Rhetoric of Reconciliation: 2 Corinthians 1.1–2.13 and 7.5–8.24." Pages 246–61 in *Persuasive Artistry: Studies in New Testament Rhetoric in Honor of George A. Kennedy*. Edited by Duane F. Watson. JSNTSup 50. Sheffield: Sheffield Academic, 1991.

Hughes, Philip E. *Paul's Second Epistle to the Corinthians*. NICNT. Grand Rapids: Eerdmans, 1962.

Hunter, Patricia Pauline. "Application of the Inductive Method of Bible Study in the Christian College." Master Thesis, Fuller Theological Seminary, 1960.

Hyldahl, Niels. "Die Frage Nach Der Literarischen Einheit Des Zweiten Korintherbriefes." *ZNW* 64 (1973): 289–306.

Ibita, Ma. Marilous S. "The Unity of Paul's Narrative World in 2 Corinthians 1-7: N. Petersen's Narrative-Critical Approach and the Coherence of 2 Corinthians." Pages 17–42 in *Theologizing in the Corinthian Conflict: Studies in the Exegesis and Theology of 2 Corinthians*. Edited by Reimund Bieringer, Ma. Marilou S. Ibita, Dominika Kurek-Chomycz, and Thomas A. Vollmer. BTS 16. Leuven: Peeters, 2013.

Jennings, William Henry. "The Inductive Method of Bible Study: A Uniquely Appropriate Tool for Lay Evangelists." DMin diss., Columbia Theological Seminary, 1988.

Jensen, Irving L. *Independent Bible Study: Using the Analytical Chart and the Inductive Method*. Chicago: Moody Press, 1963.

Jewett, Robert. "The Redaction of I Corinthians and the Trajectory of the Pauline School." *JAARSup* 44 (1978).

Jewett, Rober. *Romans*. Hermeneia. Minneapolis: Fortress, 2007.

Johnson, Lee Ann. "The Epistolary Apostle: Paul's Response to the Challenge of the Corinthian Congregation." PhD diss., University of St. Michael's College, 2002.

Johnson, Luke Timothy. *Hebrews: A Commentary*. NTL. Louisville: Westminster John Knox, 2006.

Johnson, Luke Timothy.. *Reading Romans: A Literary and Theological Commentary*. Reading the New Testament Series. Macon, GA: Smyth & Helwys, 2001.

Käsemann, Ernst. *Commentary on Romans*. Translated by Geoffrey W. Bromiley. Grand Rapids: Eerdmans, 1980.

Keener, Craig S. *Acts: An Exegetical Commentary*. 4 vols. Grand Rapids: Baker Academic, 2012–2015.
Keener, Craig S. *1–2 Corinthians*. NCBC. Cambridge: Cambridge University Press, 2005.
Keener, Craig S. *Galatians: A Commentary*. Grand Rapids: Baker Academic, 2018.
Keener, Craig S. *Romans*. New Covenant Commentary Series 6. Eugene, OR: Cascade, 2009.
Kennedy, George A. *New Testament Interpretation Through Rhetorical Criticism*. Chapel Hill: University of North Carolina Press, 1984.
Kingsbury, Jack Dean. *The Christology of Mark's Gospel*. Philadelphia: Fortress, 1983.
Kistemaker, Simon J. *II Corinthians*. New Testament Commentary. Grand Rapids: Baker Books, 1997.
Kittel, Gerhard, and Gerhard Friedrich, eds. *Theological Dictionary of the New Testament*. Translated by Geoffrey W. Bromiley. 10 vols. Grand Rapids: Eerdmans, 1964.
Klauck, Hans-Josef. *Ancient Letters and the New Testament: A Guide to Context and Exegesis*. Translated by Daniel P. Bailey. Waco, TX: Baylor University Press, 2006.
Klöpper, Albert. *Kommentar Über das Zweite Sendschreiben des Apostel Paulus an die Gemeinde Zu Korinth*. Berlin: Reimer, 1874.
Koester, Craig R. *Hebrews: A New Translation with Introduction and Commentary*. AB 36. New Haven: Yale University Press, 2001.
Korner, Ralph J. *The Origin and Meaning of Ekklēsia in the Early Jesus Movement*. Ancient Judaism and Early Christianity 98. Leiden; Boston: Brill, 2017.
Korner, Ralph J. "Paul's Corinthian Ekklēsia: A Non-Misogynistic, Sacred 'Location' for Jewish Manumission Ethics?" Presentation in Power and Authority Working Group at Annual Meeting of the Pacific Northwest Region of the Society of Biblical Literature, Virtual Meeting, May 13–14, 2022.
Kuist, Howard Tillman. *These Words Upon Thy Heart: Scripture and the Christian Response*. Richmond, VA: John Knox, 1947.
Lambrecht, Jan. "The Fragment 2 Corinthians 6.14–7,1: A Plea for Its Authenticity." Pages 531–49 in *Studies on 2 Corinthians*. Edited by Reimund Bieringer and Jan Lambrecht. BETL 112. Leuven: Leuven University Press; Uitgeverij Peeters, 1994.
Lambrecht, Jan. *Second Corinthians*. Edited by Daniel J. Harrington. SP 8. Collegeville, MN: Liturgical Press, 1999.
Lambrecht, Jan. "Structure and Line of Thought in 2 Corinthians 2,14–4,6." Pages 257–94 in *Studies on 2 Corinthians*. Edited by Reimund Bieringer and Jan Lambrecht. BETL 112. Leuven: Leuven University Press; Uitgeverij Peeters, 1994.
Land, Christopher D. *The Integrity of 2 Corinthians and Paul's Aggravating Absence*. Sheffield: Sheffield Phoenix, 2015.
Lane, William L. *Hebrews 9–13*. WBC 47B. Dallas: Word, 1991.
Lane, William L. *Hebrews 1–8*. WBC 47A. Dallas: Word, 1991.
Lee, Mason. "'Now Is the Acceptable Time; Now Is the Day of Salvation': Reading 2 Corinthians 5:11–6:2 in Light of Its Narrative Structure." *ResQ* 56 (2014): 1–13.
Levinsohn, Stephen H. *Discourse Features of New Testament Greek: A Coursebook on the Information Structure of New Testament Greek*. 2nd ed. Dallas: SIL International, 2000.
Levinsohn, Stephen H. "'Therefore' or 'Wherefore': What's the Difference?" Pages 325–43 in *Reflections on Lexicography: Explorations in Ancient Syriac, Hebrew, and Greek Sources*. Edited by Richard A. Taylor and Craig E. Morrison. Perspectives on Linguistics and Ancient Languages 4. Piscataway, NJ: Gorgias, 2014.
Liddell, Henry George, Robert Scott, Henry Stuart Jones. *A Greek-English Lexicon*. 9th ed. with revised supplement. Oxford: Clarendon, 1996.

Liefeld, Walter L. *New Testament Exposition: From Text to Sermon*. Grand Rapids: Zondervan, 1984.

Lietzmann, Hans. *An Die Korinther I–II*. HNT 9. Tübingen: Mohr Siebeck, 1949.

Lim, Kar Yong. "Generosity from Pauline Perspective: Insights from Paul's Letters to the Corinthians." *Evangelical Review of Theology* 37 (2013): 20–33.

Lim, Kar Yong. *"The Sufferings of Christ Are Abundant in Us" (2 Corinthians 1:5): A Narrative-Dynamics Investigation of Paul's Sufferings in 2 Corinthians*. LNTS 399. London: T&T Clark, 2009.

Lincoln, Andrew T. *Ephesians*. WBC 42. Dallas: Word, 1990.

Lindgård, Fredrik. *Paul's Line of Thought in 2 Corinthians 4:16–5:10*. WUNT 2/189. Tübingen: Mohr Siebeck, 2005.

Lohr, Charles H. "Oral Techniques in the Gospel of Matthew." *CBQ* 23 (1961): 403–35.

Long, Fredrick J. *Ancient Rhetoric and Paul's Apology: The Compositional Unity of 2 Corinthians*. SNTSMS 131. Cambridge: Cambridge University Press, 2004.

Long, Fredrick J. "'The God of This Age' (2 Cor. 4:4) and Paul's Empire-Resisting Gospel." Pages 219–269 in *The First Urban Churches*. Edited by James R. Harrison and Laurence L. Welborn. Vol. 2 of WGRWSup 7. Atlanta: SBL Press, 2016.

Long, Fredrick J *In Step with God's Word: Interpreting the New Testament with God's People*. GlossaHouse Hermeneutics & Translation Series 1. Wilmore, KY: GlossaHouse, 2017.

Long, Fredrick J. *Koine Greek Grammar: A Beginning-Intermediate Greek Exegetical and Pragmatic Handbook*. Wilmore, KY: GlossaHouse, 2015.

Long, Fredrick J. "Major Structural Relationships: A Survey of Origins, Development, Classifications, and Assessment." *The Journal of Inductive Biblical Studies* 1 (2014): 23–58.

Long, Fredrick J. "Paul's Prophesying Isa 28:11 in Context: The Signs of Unbelievers and Believers in 1 Corinthians 14." Pages 133–69 in *Kingdom Rhetoric: New Testament Explorations in Honor of Ben Witherington III*. Edited by T. Michael W. Halcomb. Eugene, OR: Wipf and Stock, 2013.

Long, Fredrick J. *2 Corinthians: A Handbook on the Greek Text*. Baylor Handbook on the Greek New Testament. Waco, TX: Baylor University Press, 2015.

Long, Fredrick J. "Vital Relations and Major Structural Relationships Heuristic Approaches to Observe and Explore Biblical and Other Discourse." *The Journal of Inductive Biblical Studies* 4 (2017): 92–128.

Long, Fredrick J. "2 Corinthians." Pages 261–95 in *Discourse Analysis of the New Testament Writings*. Edited by Todd A. Scacewater. Dallas: Fontes, 2020.

Longenecker, Richard N. *Galatians*. WBC 41. Dallas: Word, 1990.

Longman, Tremper, III. "Inclusio." *Dictionary of the Old Testament: Wisdom, Poetry & Writings*, 323–25.

Louw, Johannes P., and Eugene A. Nida, eds. *Greek-English Lexicon of the New Testament: Based on Semantic Domains*. 2nd ed. New York: United Bible Societies, 1989.

Lund, Nils Wilhelm. *Chiasmus in the New Testament: A Study in the Form and Function of Chiastic Structures*. Peabody, MA: Hendrickson, 1992.

Mack, Burton L. *Rhetoric and the New Testament*. GBS. Minneapolis: Fortress, 1989.

Malcolm, Matthew R. *Paul and the Rhetoric of Reversal in 1 Corinthians: The Impact of Paul's Gospel on His Macro-Rhetoric*. SNTSMS 155. Cambridge: Cambridge University Press, 2013.

Malherbe, Abraham J. *The Letter to the Thessalonians: A New Translation with Introduction and Commentary*. AB 32B. New York: Doubleday, 2000.

Martin, Ralph P. *2 Corinthians*. 2nd ed. WBC 40. Waco, TX: Zondervan Academic, 2014.

Martyn, J. Louis. *Galatians: A New Translation with Introduction and Commentary.* AB 33A. New York: Doubleday, 1997.

Matera, Frank J. *II Corinthians: A Commentary.* NTL. Louisville: Westminster John Knox, 2003.

Mattill, A. J., Jr. "The Value of Acts as a Source for the Study of Paul." Pages 76–98 in *Perspectives on Luke-Acts.* Edited by Charles H. Talbert. Association of Baptist Professors of Religion Special Studies Series 5. Danville, VA: Association of Baptist Professors of Religion, 1978.

McCant, Jerry W. *2 Corinthians.* Readings: A New Biblical Commentary. Sheffield: Sheffield Academic, 1999.

McConville, Gordon J. "Micah, Book Of." *Dictionary of the Old Testament: Prophets,* 544–54.

McDonald, James I. H. "Paul and the Preaching Ministry: A Reconsideration of 2 Cor. 2:14–17 in Its Context." *JSNT* 17 (1983): 35–50.

McNamara, Martin. *Targum and Testament: Aramaic Paraphrases of the Hebrew Bible: A Light on the New Testament.* Shannon: Irish University Press, 1972.

Menzies, Allan. *The Second Epistle of the Apostle Paul to the Corinthians: Introduction, Text, English Translation and Notes.* London: Macmillan, 1912.

Merk, Otto. "Der Beginn der Paränese im Galaterbrief." *ZNW* 60 (1969): 83–104.

Merkle, Benjamin L. "The Abused Aspect: Neglecting the Influence of a Verb's Lexical Meaning on Tense-Form Choice." *BBR* 26 (2016): 57–74.

Meyer, Ben F. *Reality and Illusion in New Testament Scholarship: A Primer in Critical Realist Hermeneutics.* Collegeville, MN: Liturgical Press, 1994.

Mitchell, Margaret M. *Paul and the Rhetoric of Reconciliation: An Exegetical Investigation of the Language and Composition of 1 Corinthians.* Louisville: Westminster John Knox, 1993.

Mitchell, Margaret M. "Rhetorical and New Literary Criticism." Pages 615–33 in *The Oxford Handbook of Biblical Studies.* Edited by J. W. Rogerson and Judith Lieu. Oxford: Oxford University Press, 2006.

Muilenburg, James. "Form Criticism and Beyond." *JBL* 88 (1969): 1–18.

Murphy, Rowland E. *Proverb.* WBC 22. Dallas: Word, 1998.

Nida, Eugene A. *Exploring Semantic Structures.* International Library of General Linguistics 11. Munich: Fink, 1975.

O'Brien, Peter T. *Colossians, Philemon.* WBC 44. Dallas: Word, 1982.

O'Brien, Peter T. *The Epistle to the Philippians.* NIGTC. Grand Rapids: Eerdmans, 1991.

O'Brien, Peter T. *Introductory Thanksgivings in the Letters of Paul.* NovTSup 49. Leiden: Brill, 1977.

O'Brien, Peter T. "Thanksgiving within the Structure of Pauline Theology." Pages 50–66 in *Pauline Studies: Essays Presented to Professor F. F. Bruce on His 70th Birthday.* Edited by Donald Alfred Hagner and Murray J. Harris. Exeter; Grand Rapids: Paternoster; Eerdmans, 1980.

Olley, John W. "A Precursor of the NRSV? 'Sons and Daughters' in 2 Cor. 6.18." *NTS* 44 (1998): 204–12.

Olson, Stanley N. "Confidence Expressions in Paul: Epistolary Conventions and the Purpose of 2 Corinthians." PhD diss., Yale University, 1976.

O'Mahony, Kieran J. *Pauline Persuasion: A Sounding in 2 Corinthians 8–9.* JSNTSup 199. Sheffield: Sheffield Academic, 2000.

Osiander, Johann E. *Commentar über den zweiten Brief Pauli an die Korinthier.* Stuttgart: Besser, 1858.

Pak, Luke Kyungwhan. "Teaching the Inductive Bible Study Method of Bible Interpretation to Adults: A Comparison of Three Instructional Approaches." PhD diss., University of North Texas, 1996.

Perelman, Chaïm, and Lucie Olbrechts-Tyteca. *The New Rhetoric: A Treatise on Argumentation*. Translated by John Wilkinson and Purcell Weaver. Notre Dame: University of Notre Dame Press, 1969.

Perelman, Chaïm, and Lucie Olbrechts-Tyteca. *La Nouvelle Rhétorique: Traité de l'Argumentation*. Paris: Presses universitaires de France, 1958.

Perrin, Norman. "Interpretation of the Gospel of Mark." *Int* 30 (1976): 115–24.

Petersen, Norman R. *Literary Criticism for New Testament Critics*. GBS. Philadelphia: Fortress, 1978.

Petersen, Norman R. *Rediscovering Paul: Philemon and the Sociology of Paul's Narrative World*. Philadelphia: Fortress, 1985.

Peterson, Brian K. *Eloquence and the Proclamation of the Gospel in Corinth*. SBLDS 163. Atlanta: Scholars Press, 1998.

Philip, Comfort W. "Temple." *DPL*, 923–25.

Plummer, Alfred. *A Critical and Exegetical Commentary on the Second Epistle of St. Paul to the Corinthians*. ICC. Edinburgh: T&T Clark, 1915.

Porter, Stanley E. "Holiness, Sanctification." *DPL*, 397–402.

Porter, Stanley E. ed. *Handbook of Classical Rhetoric in the Hellenistic Period, 330 B.D.– A.D. 400*. Leiden: Brill, 1997.

Porter, Stanley E. "Holiness, Sanctification." *DPL*, 397–402.

Porter, Stanley E. *Verbal Aspect in the Greek of the New Testament: With Reference to Tense and Mood*. Studies in Biblical Greek 1. New York: Lang, 1989.

Porter, Stanley E. *Idioms of the Greek New Testament*. 2nd ed. Sheffield: JSOT Press, 1999.

Porter, Stanley E, ed. *Paul and Ancient Rhetoric: Theory and Practice in the Hellenistic Context*. New York: Cambridge University Press, 2016.

Porter, Stanley E. *Paul in Acts*. Library of Pauline Studies. Peabody, MA: Hendrickson, 2001.

Porter, Stanley E. "The Portrait of Paul in Acts." Pages 124–38 in *The Blackwell Companion to Paul*. Edited by Stephen Westerholm. Blackwell Companions to Religion. Malden, MA: Wiley-Blackwell, 2011.

Porter, Stanley E., and Craig A. Evans. *Dictionary of New Testament Background: A Compendium of Contemporary Biblical Scholarship*. Downers Grove, IL: Inter Varsity Press, 2000.

Porter, Stanley E., and Andrew W. Pitts. "The Disclosure Formula in the Epistolary Papyri and in the New Testament: Development, Form, Function, and Syntax." Pages 421–38 in *The Language of the New Testament: Context, History, and Development*. Linguistic Biblical Studies 6. Edited by Stanley E. Porter and Andrew W. Pitts. Brill, 2013.

Porter, Stanley E., and Dennis L. Stamps, eds. *Rhetorical Criticism and the Bible*. JSNTSup 195. London: Sheffield Academic, 2002.

Powell, Mark Allan. *What Is Narrative Criticism?* GBS. Minneapolis: Fortress, 1990.

Ramsay, William Mitchell. *The Bearing of Recent Discovery on the Trustworthiness of the New Testament*. London: Hodder and Stoughton, 1915.

Reed, Jeffrey T. *A Discourse Analysis of Philippians: Method and Rhetoric in the Debate Over Literary Integrity*. JSNTSup 136. Sheffield: Sheffield Academic, 1997.

Resseguie, James L. *Narrative Criticism of the New Testament: An Introduction*. Grand Rapids: Baker Academic, 2005.

Reumann, John H. P. *Philippians: A New Translation with Introduction and Commentary.* AB 33B. New Haven: Yale University Press, 2008.

Richards, E. Randolph. *Paul and First-Century Letter Writing: Secretaries, Composition, and Collection.* Downers Grove, IL: InterVarsity Press, 2004.

Rillera, Andrew R. "Paul's Philonic Opponent: Unveiling the One Who Calls Himself a Jew in Romans 2:17." PhD diss., Duke University, 2021.

Robbins, Vernon K. *Exploring the Texture of Texts: A Guide to Socio-Rhetorical Interpretation.* Valley Forge, PA: Trinity Press International, 1996.

Robbins, Vernon K. "Sociorhetorical Interpretation (SRI) and Inductive Bible Study (IBS): Outlines of Mark, the Lord's Prayer, and the Son's Prayer in John 17." *The Journal of Inductive Biblical Studies* 1 (2014): 182–222.

Robertson, Archibald Thomas. *A Grammar of the Greek New Testament in the Light of Historical Research.* Bellingham, WA: Logos, 2006.

Rolland, Philippe. "La Structure Littéraire de La Deuxième Épître Aux Corinthiens." *Bib* 71 (1990): 73–84.

Rowe, Galen O. "Style." Pages 121–57 in *Handbook of Classical Rhetoric in the Hellenistic Period, 330 B.C.–A.D. 400.* Edited by Stanley E. Porter. Leiden: Brill, 1997.

Runge, Steven E. *Discourse Grammar of the Greek New Testament: A Practical Introduction for Teaching and Exegesis.* Lexham Bible Reference Series. Peabody, MA: Hendrickson, 2010.

Ruskin, John. *The Elements of Drawing and the Elements of Perspective.* New York: Dutton, 1907.

Ruskin, John. *The Elements of Drawing in Three Letters to Beginners.* London: Smith, Elder, and Company, 1857.

Sampley, J. Paul. "Paul, His Opponents in 2 Corinthians 10–13, and the Rhetorical Handbooks." Pages 162–177 in *The Social World of Formative Christianity and Judaism: Essays in Tribute to Howard Clark Kee.* Edited by Jacob Neusner, Peder Borgen, Ernest S. Frerichs, and Richard Horsley. Philadelphia: Fortress, 1988.

Sanders, Jack T. "The Transition from Opening Epistolary Thanksgiving to Body in the Letters of the Pauline Corpus." *JBL* 81 (1962): 348–62.

Sauerwein, Daniel Ernest. "Inductive Bible Study: A Proposed Program of Study." DMin diss., Western Conservative Baptist Seminary, 1980.

Savage, Timothy B. *Power Through Weakness: Paul's Understanding of the Christian Ministry in 2 Corinthians.* SNTSMS 86. Cambridge: Cambridge University Press, 1996.

Schellenberg, Ryan S. *Rethinking Paul's Rhetorical Education: Comparative Rhetoric and 2 Corinthians 10–13.* ECL 10. Atlanta: Society of Biblical Literature, 2013.

Schlatter, Adolf von. *Paulus der Bote Jesu: Eine Deutung Seiner Briefe an die Korinther.* Stuttgart: Calwer, 1934.

Schubert, Paul. *Form and Function of the Pauline Thanksgivings.* Berlin: Töpelmann, 1939.

Scott, James M. *2 Corinthians.* NIBCNT. Peabody, MA: Hendrickson, 1998.

Segalla, Giuseppe. "Struttura Letteraria e Unità Della 2 Corinzi." *Teol* 13 (1988): 189–218.

Seifrid, Mark A. *The Second Letter to the Corinthians.* The Pillar New Testament Commentary. Grand Rapids: Eerdmans, 2014.

Semler, Johann S. *Paraphrasis II. Epistolae Ad Corinthios.* Halle: Hemmerde, 1776.

Smith, Craig Arnold. "Criteria for Identifying Chiasm of Design in New Testament Literature: Objective Means of Distinguishing Chiasm of Design from Accidental and False Chiasm." PhD diss., University of Bristol, 2009.

Soulen, Richard N. *Handbook of Biblical Criticism.* 2nd ed. Atlanta: John Knox, 1981.

Spicq, Ceslas. *Theological Lexicon of the New Testament*. Edited and translated by James D. Ernest. 3 vols. Peabody, MA: Hendrickson, 1994.
Sternberg, Meir. *The Poetics of Biblical Narrative: Ideological Literature and the Drama of Reading*. Bloomington: Indiana University Press, 1985.
Stirewalt, M. Luther. *Studies in Ancient Greek Epistolography*. RBS 27. Atlanta: Scholars Press, 1993.
Stowers, Stanley Kent. *The Diatribe and Paul's Letter to the Romans*. SBLDS 57. Chico, CA: Scholars Press, 1981.
Strachan, R. H. *The Second Epistle of Paul to the Corinthians*. MNTC. London: Hodder and Stoughton, 1935.
Stuart, Douglas K. "Exegesis." *ABD* 2:682–88.
Stuart, Douglas K. *Hosea–Jonah*. WBC 31. Dallas: Word, 1987.
Sundermann, Hans-Georg. *Der Schwache Apostel und die Kraft der Rede: Eine Rhetorische Analyse von 2 Kor 10-13*. Europäische Hochschulschriften XXIII 575. Frankfurt: Lang, 1996.
Talbert, Charles H. *Reading Luke: A Literary and Theological Commentary on the Third Gospel*. New York: Crossroad, 1982.
Tannehill, Robert C. *The Acts of the Apostles*. Vol. 2 of FF. Philadelphia: Fortress, 1989.
Tasker, R. V. G. *Second Epistle of Paul to the Corinthians: An Introduction and Commentary*. TNTC 8. Grand Rapids: Eerdmans, 1958.
Taylor, Mark Edward. *A Text-Linguistic Investigation into the Discourse Structure of James*. LNTS 311. London: T&T Clark, 2006.
Terry, Ralph Bruce. *A Discourse Analysis of First Corinthians*. Summer Institute of Linguistics and the University of Texas at Arlington Publications in Linguistics 120. Dallas: Summer Institute of Linguistics; University of Texas at Arlington, 1995.
Thompson, David L. *Bible Study That Works*. Rev. ed. Nappanee, IN: Evangel Publishing House, 1994.
Thrall, Margaret E. *A Critical and Exegetical Commentary on the Second Epistle of the Corinthians*. 2 vols. ICC. London: T&T Clark, 1994–2004.
Thrall, Margaret E. "A Second Thanksgiving Period in II Corinthians." *JSNT* 16 (1982): 101–24.
Traina, Robert A. "Inductive Bible Study Reexamined in Light of Contemporary Hermeneutics I: Interpreting the Text." Pages 53–83 in *Interpreting God's Word for Today: An Inquiry into Hermeneutics from a Biblical Theological Perspective*. Edited by Wayne McCown and James E. Massey. Wesleyan Theological Perspectives 2. Anderson, IN: Warner, 1982.
Traina, Robert A. "Inductive Bible Study Reexamined in Light of Contemporary Hermeneutics II: Applying the Text." Pages 85–109 in *Interpreting God's Word for Today: An Inquiry into Hermeneutics from a Biblical Theological Perspective*. Edited by Wayne McCown and James E. Massey. Wesleyan Theological Perspectives 2. Anderson, IN: Warner, 1982.
Traina, Robert A. *Methodical Bible Study: A New Approach to Hermeneutics*. New York: Ganis & Harris, 1952.
Turner, George Allen. *Exploring the Bible: Studies in Books of the Bible Using the "Inductive Method" of Approach*. Wilmore, KY: Turner, 1950.
Varner, William C. *The Book of James: A New Perspective: A Linguistic Commentary Applying Discourse Analysis*. Woodlands, TX: Kress Biblical Resources, 2010.
Vegge, Ivar. *2 Corinthians – A Letter About Reconciliation: A Psychagogical, Epistolographical, and Rhetorical Analysis*. WUNT 2/239. Tübingen: Mohr Siebeck, 2008.

Verbrugge, Verlyn D. *Paul's Style of Church Leadership Illustrated by His Instructions to the Corinthians on the Collection.* San Francisco: Mellen, 1992.
Wald, Oletta. *The New Joy of Discovery in Bible Study.* Rev. ed. Minneapolis: Augsburg Fortress, 2002.
Wallace, Daniel B. *Greek Grammar Beyond the Basics: An Exegetical Syntax of the New Testament.* Grand Rapids: Zondervan, 1996.
Wanamaker, Charles A. "'By the Power of God': Rhetoric and Ideology in 2 Corinthians 10–13." Pages 194–221 in *Fabrics of Discourse: Essays in Honor of Vernon K. Robbins.* Edited by David B. Gowler, L. Gregory Bloomquist, and Duane F. Watson. Harrisburg, PA: Trinity Press International, 2003.
Wanamaker, Charles A. *The Epistles to the Thessalonians.* NIGTC. Grand Rapids: Eerdmans, 1990.
Watson, Duane F. "Paul's Boasting in 2 Corinthians 10–13 as Defense of His Honor: A Socio-Rhetorical Analysis." Pages 260–75 in *Rhetorical Argumentation in Biblical Texts: Essays from the Lund 2000 Conference.* Edited by Anders Eriksson, Thomas H. Olbricht, and Walter G. Übelacker. Harrisburg, PA: Trinity Press International, 2002.
Watson, Duane F.. *The Rhetoric of the New Testament: A Bibliographic Survey.* Tools for Biblical Study 8. Blandford Forum, UK: Deo, 2006.
Watson, Duane F.. "Structuralism and Discourse Analysis." *DLNT*, 1129–34.
Weima, Jeffrey A. D. "Epistolary Theory." *DNTB*, 327–30.
Weima, Jeffrey A. D. *Paul the Ancient Letter Writer: An Introduction to Epistolary Analysis: Asbury Scholar.* Grand Rapids: Baker Academic, 2016.
Welch, John W. *Chiasmus in Antiquity: Structures, Analyses, Exegesis.* Hildesheim: Gerstenberg, 1981.
Westfall, Cynthia Long. *A Discourse Analysis of the Letter to the Hebrews: The Relationship Between Form and Meaning.* LNTS 297. London: T&T Clark, 2005.
White, Benjamin G. *Pain and Paradox in 2 Corinthians.* WUNT 2/555. Tübingen: Mohr Siebeck, 2021.
White, John L. "Introductory Formulae in the Body of the Pauline Letter." *JBL* 90 (1971): 91–97.
White, John L. *Light from Ancient Letters.* FF. Philadelphia: Fortress, 1986.
Wilson, R. McL. *Colossians and Philemon.* ICC. London: T&T Clark, 2005.
Windisch, Hans. *Der Zweite Korintherbrief.* KEK 6. Göttingen: Vandenhoeck & Ruprecht, 1924.
Witherington, Ben, III. *The Acts of the Apostles: A Socio-Rhetorical Commentary.* Grand Rapids: Eerdmans, 1998.
Witherington, Ben, III. *Conflict and Community in Corinth: A Socio-Rhetorical Commentary on 1 and 2 Corinthians.* Grand Rapids: Eerdmans, 1995.
Witherington, Ben, III. *New Testament Rhetoric: An Introductory Guide to the Art of Persuasion in and of the New Testament.* Eugene, OR: Cascade, 2009.
Witherington, Ben, III. *Paul's Narrative Thought World: The Tapestry of Tragedy and Triumph.* Louisville: Westminster John Knox, 1994.
Witherington, Ben, III. *The Paul Quest: The Renewed Search for the Jew of Tarsus.* Downers Grove, IL: InterVarsity Press, 1998.
Witherup, Ronald D. "Cornelius Over and Over and Over Again: 'Functional Redundancy' in the Acts of the Apostles." *JSNT* 15 (1993): 45–66.

Wright, N. T. *The New Testament and the People of God*. Vol. 1 of *Christian Origins and The Question of God*. London: SPCK, 1992.
Wright, N. T. *Paul: A Biography*. San Francisco: HarperOne, 2018.
Wright, N. T. *The Resurrection of the Son of God*. Vol. 3 of *Christian Origins and the Question of God*. London: SPCK, 2003.
Wünsch, Hans-Michael. *Der Paulinische Brief 2 Kor 1-9 Als Kommunikative Handlung: Eine Rhetorisch-Literaturwissenschaftliche Untersuchung*. Theologie 4. Munster: LIT, 1996.
Yamada, K. "Epistolary Theoretical and Rhetorical Analyses of 2 Cor. 1–9." *AJBI* 24 (1998): 83–116.
Yohn, Richard V. "Guide to Inductive Bible Study." DMin diss., Biola University, 1980.
Young, Frances M., and David F. Ford. *Meaning and Truth in 2 Corinthians*. Grand Rapids: Eerdmans, 1988.

Index of Biblical references

Note: The suffix 'f' following a page locator indicates a figure, 't' indicates a table. 'n' indicates a footnote, with the number following 'n' indicating the footnote number when there is more than 1 footnote on the page.

Old Testament
  Genesis
    1–11   10n. 30, 12n. 36
    3:4, 13   119
    3:13   119
    12–50   12n. 36
    38   13n. 42
  Exodus
    28:38   104
    31:18   127
    40:34–35   105
  Leviticus
    1:1   105
    1:3   105
    1:3–4 104
    1:5   105
    9:6   106
    9:23   106
  Joshua
    1–2   12n. 37
    3–24   12n. 37
    13:1–24:13   12n. 35
  Judges
    2:6–3:6   12n. 35
    21:25   11n. 31
  2 Samuel
    1–10   12n. 34
    1–20   12n. 34
    11–12   12n. 34
    13–20   12n. 34
  1 Kings   12n. 37
  2 Kings   12n. 37
    17:7–23   12n. 35
  Esther, 9:24–28   12n. 35
  2 Maccabees   62n. 39
  Job   12n. 37
    1–2   12n. 37
  Psalms
    8:1   13n. 40
    8:9   13n. 40
    15   12n. 36
    78:2–4   10n. 30
    114   141
    115 LXX   141
    115:1 LXX   141
  Proverbs, 1:7   10n. 30
  Wisdom
    4:10   104
    9:10   104
  Sirach, 26:29   118
  Isaiah
    1:22   118
    25:8   110
    49:8   142
  Jeremiah, 12:13   162
  Hosea
    8:7   162
    14:9   11n31
  Amos 11n. 32
  Jonah, 4:1–2   11n. 33
  Micah 13n. 39
  Haggai, 1:6   162

New Testament
  Matthew
    1:17   11n32
    1:23   14n46
    8:5   84n
    19:30   13n. 40
    20:16   13n. 40
    28:20   14n. 46
  Mark, 5:23   84n
  Luke, 8:41   84n
  John
    1:14   10n. 30

Index of Biblical References

1:19–12:50	10n. 30	1:3–7	23, 25, 26, 28, 32, 51, 65, 66–68, 73–82, 85, 88, 195, 202
20:31	13n. 38		
Acts of the Apostles	8n. 23		
1:8	11n. 31, 12n. 35	1:3–11	21, 29, 31, 32, 49, 84
2–7	11n. 31		
7:26	62n. 39	1:3–13:10	59, 64, 198, 208
7:58–28:31	12n. 34	1:6–7	65, 68, 75, 195
8–12	11n. 31	chs 1–7	23, 28, 49
13–28	11n. 31	1:7	66, 68, 84
15:23	58	chs 1–8	30
23:26	58	1:8	68, 100
Romans	163	1:8–2:11	65, 69–72, 73, 74, 195
1:1	57		
1:8	95	1:8–2:13	26, 73–82, 88, 89, 202, 211
1:10	95		
1:16–11:36	11n. 33	1:8–2:16	25, 26
1:18–11:36	11n. 33	1:8–7:16	43
6:19	151	1:8–9	30
7:25	149	1:8–10	65, 69, 195
1 Corinthians	21	1:8–11	17, 23, 28, 29, 32, 34, 65, 66, 67, 69, 75–77, 78, 195
1:1	57		
1:4–5	95		
1:8	95	1:8–16	26
14	191	chs 1–9	44, 184n. 56
14:16–17	191	1:10, 13	47
15:54	110	1:11	32, 65, 66, 69, 76, 86, 195
15:57	149		
16:1	151	1:12–2:11	45, 65, 69–72, 77–80, 195
2 Corinthians			
1:1	8, 56, 57	1:12–2:13	21, 69
1:1–2	21, 23, 25, 26, 28, 29, 31, 54–55, 56–59, 63, 194, 195, 198	1:12–2:17	28
		1:12–7:2	23
		1:12–9:15	23n. 10
		1:12–13:9	23
1:1–2:13	66, 73	1:12–13:10	31
1:1–2:17	24	1:12–14	29, 31, 32, 45, 46, 47, 65, 67, 70, 78, 79n, 195
1:1–7:16	135		
1:1–8	23		
1:1–11	23, 23n. 10, 31	1:15–2:2	65, 71, 79, 195
1:1–14	29	1:15–2:4	31
1:2	58	1:15–2:11	46, 47t, 79
1:3–2:11	80	1:15–7:16	31
1:3–2:13	36, 51, 65–88, 91, 143, 194, 195, 199, 202–203, 209, 210, 212	1:15–16	29, 30
		1:15–17	71
		1:17–22	29
		1:17–24	26, 27, 32
1:3–4	95	1:18/19–22	71
1:3–5	51, 65, 68, 74, 195	1:18–22	71

Index of Biblical References

1:23–2:2	71	3:1–6a	111, 116, 123, 196
1:23–2:11	29, 177	3:1–7:3	82, 85, 136, 139,
1:24	86		144, 145, 204
2:1–9:15	26, 32	3:1–7:16	24, 45, 86, 87, 99,
2:1–11	26		103, 104, 110, 111,
2:3	72		112, 123–146, 163,
2:3–4	72		164, 186, 194, 196,
2:3–11	65, 71, 72, 79, 196		200, 203–204, 210
2:4	106	3:1–9:15	82, 87, 112, 176,
2:5–11	31, 72, 79		183–187, 190, 201
2:12–13	26, 29, 30, 31, 65,	3:1–11	85, 110, 123,
	69, 72, 81–82, 94,		126–127, 133*t*,
	135, 196		139–144, 145, 196,
2:13	66		203
2:14	26, 92, 97, 98, 99,	3:1–13:4	25
	100, 103, 115	3:1–13:10	27, 32, 85, 88, 89,
2:14–3:18	26, 27		91, 93–97, 107, 120,
2:14–5:21	36		121, 124–125, 144,
2:14–7:3	82, 209		194, 200, 208, 209
2:14–7:4	21, 31, 39, 82, 135	3:1–18	8, 25
2:14–7:16	69	3:4–6	196
2:14–9:15	212	3:4–6a	123
2:14–13:10	73, 83–85, 88, 91,	3:6b	123, 196
	143, 194, 199, 208,	3:6b–11	123, 196
	209	3:7–11	110*n*, 123, 196
2:14–15	95	3:11	126
2:14–16	26, 49	3:12	123, 126, 129, 133*t*,
2:14–16a	92		196
2:14–17	26, 27, 29, 32, 81,	3:12–4:12	102, 108, 116, 123,
	82, 89, 91–121,		128–131, 140, 196
	124–125, 144, 187,	3:12–7:3	85, 123, 126,
	194, 196, 200, 208,		127–138, 139–144,
	209, 210, 211		145, 196, 203
2:14b–17	99	3:12–18	133*t*
2:15–16	111	3:13–18	123, 129, 196
2:15–16a	92	4:1	133*t*
2:16	110	4:1–2	130, 131
2:16a	91, 92	4:1–5:10	25, 26
2:16a/17	124	4:1–6	107
2:16b	92, 111	4:1–12	123, 196
2:17	25, 26, 32, 45, 92,	4:2	108, 112
	108, 109, 110*t*, 111,	4:3–6	130, 131
	118, 186	4:4–5	107
		4:5	99, 108
3:1	125	4:7	99, 131
3:1–3	37, 102, 123, 196	4:7–6:10	29
3:1–4:6	29	4:7–11	131
3:1–4:12	101	4:7–12	49, 112, 130
3:1–6:10	32	4:7–18	41
3:1–6:13	25, 28		

4:8–9	17, 112	6:11–7:4	29
4:10–12	99	6:11–13	142
4:12	129, 131, 132	6:14–7:1	21, 25, 28, 84, 105,
4:13	132, 133t		106, 142, 143, 144
4:13–5:10	104, 105, 110, 116,	6:16–18	143
	123, 131–134, 140,	7:1	106, 135
	196	7:2	135
4:13–14	133	7:2–4	142
4:13–15	134	7:2–16	25, 26, 28
4:13–16	123, 132, 133, 134,	7:3	110, 136
	141, 196	7:3–16	23, 24
4:15	133, 165	7:4	124, 135, 138, 196
4:16	133, 134	7:4/5	82
4:16–5:11a	37	7:4–16	82, 106, 110, 111,
4:17	100, 134		124, 136, 138–139,
4:17–5:5	124, 133, 134, 141,		144, 145, 196, 204
	196	7:5	29, 31, 138
4:17–5:10	133, 141	7:5–7	30, 124, 138, 139,
5:1–4	106		196
5:6	134	7:5–9:15	29
5:6–10	124, 133, 134, 141,	7:5–12	124, 138, 139, 196
	196	7:5–16	21, 31, 47, 73, 135
5:9	105, 134	7:6–16	29
5:10	131, 134	7:8–12	138, 139
5:11	47, 124, 134, 137,	7:10	111
	142, 196	7:12	106
5:11–6:2	25	7:13	84, 138, 139
5:11–7:1	26	7:13–16	124, 138, 196
5:11–7:3	105, 110, 124,	7:16	124, 138, 148
	134–138, 196	8:1	148
5:11–19	37, 111, 138	8:1–2	29, 30, 100, 147,
5:11b–21	37		150, 197
5:12–19	124, 137–138, 196	8:1–5	28
5:14–17	110, 136, 211	8:1–6	147, 149–150,
5:18–20	108, 109, 109t		160–161, 197, 205
5:20	137	8:1–9:15	21, 25, 26, 45, 63,
5:20–7:3	37, 105–106, 124,		86, 87, 100, 103,
	137–138, 143, 144,		106, 112, 144,
	196		147–166, 184, 194,
5:20–21	142		200, 204–206, 210
6:1	37, 165	8:1–9:16	197
6:1–10	49, 142	8:1–13:14	24
6:3–4a	112	8:2	29
6:3–10	17, 110	8:3–5	147, 197
6:3–13	25	8:3–6	147, 150, 197
6:4b–10	112	8:3–24	29
chs 6–7	36, 37	8:5	47
6:9	110	8:6	30, 147, 197
6:11–7:3	142	8:6–15	28

Index of Biblical References

8:7	147, 151, 197	9:10–11a	148, 156–157, 158, 197
8:7–9	147, 197	9:11–12	165
8:7–15	147, 150, 151–152, 158, 160–161, 161–162, 197, 205, 206	9:11b	158
		9:11b–12	148, 197
		9:11b–14	148, 155, 157, 158, 197
8:7b	151, 152, 160, 161, 162	9:13	148, 197
8:8	147, 197	9:14	148, 197
chs 8–9	28, 31, 36, 49, 84	9:15	148, 149, 168, 197
8:9	100, 116, 147, 197	10:1	149, 168
8:10–11	147, 197	10:1–11	31, 113, 167, 171, 172, 178, 198
8:10–15	147, 197		
8:11	160, 161	10:1–11:15	26
8:12	147, 197	10:1–12:13	167, 168–172, 181–183, 198, 207
8–13	24		
8:13–15	147, 197	10:1–13	190
8:16	152	10:1–13:4	25, 30
8:16–9:5	148, 153, 161, 197, 205	10:1–13:10	21, 23n. 10, 31, 36, 87, 100, 103, 109, 112, 113, 167–191, 195, 197, 201, 206–207, 212
8:16–9:15	152–155		
8:16–17	148, 197		
8:16–19	30		
8:16–24	28, 112, 148, 153, 154–155, 197	10:1–18	25, 28, 30, 167, 168, 171–172, 177–181, 198, 207
8:18–21	148, 197		
8:20	112	10:3–6	99
8:22	148, 197	10:5–6	177
8:23–24	148, 197	10:7–11	171
8:24	152	10:12–18	31, 113, 167, 171, 172, 198
ch. 9	31		
9:1	29, 30, 154	chs 10–13	28, 42, 44, 45, 47, 49, 184n. 56
9:1–2	148, 197		
9:1–4	154	11:1–11:21a	172–173
9:1–5	28, 148, 153, 154–155, 197	11:1–12:10	25, 169, 170, 181
		11:1–12:13	17, 28, 30, 87, 113, 167, 168, 169, 170, 171, 172–174, 177–181, 198, 207
9:2–24	29, 30		
9:3	30		
9:3–4	148, 154, 197		
9:5	30, 148, 153, 154, 197	11:1–12:18	28, 31
		11:1–21a	167, 173, 174, 180, 198
9:6–7	148, 156, 197		
9:6–11a	148, 155, 157, 158, 197	11:1–21b	113
		11:3–4	119
9:6–15	28, 148, 153, 155–158, 161–162, 197, 206	11:8–9	30
		chs 11–12	45
		11:16–12:10	26
9:8–9	148, 156, 197	11:21b	172, 173

11:21b–12:10	167, 173, 174, 180, 198	13:5–13	30, 31
11:21b–23a	180	13:6	47
11:23	113	13:9	41
11:23–12:10	49	13:10	30, 113, 168, 176–177, 198, 206
11:23–28	17	13:10–11	23, 24
11:23a	180	13:10–14	31
11:23b–11:29	174, 180	13:11	168, 198
11:23b–12:10	173, 180, 181	13:11–13	7, 21, 25, 26, 30, 54–55, 55t, 56n. 12, 59–63, 64, 168, 195, 198
11:30–33	174, 180		
12:1–5a	174, 180		
12:5b–10	174, 180		
12:7–10	84, 100, 116	13:11–13[14]	23n. 10
12:9	187n. 61, 188	13:11–14	31
12:9–10	100, 107, 174, 187–188, 201, 212	13:11b–13	60
		13:12–14	23
12:10	41, 169, 173, 174, 187n. 61, 208	13:13	7, 31, 198
		Galatians	163
12:11–13	167, 169, 181, 198	1:1	57
12:11–13:4	25	Ephesians, 1:1	57
12:11–13:10	26	Philippians	57n. 15, 163–164
12:13	169	1:1	57
12:14	28, 170, 174	1:3–4	95
12:14–13:4	30	1:11	95
12:14–13:10	113, 167, 170, 174–176, 181–183, 184, 198, 207	4:18	104, 105
		Colossians, 1:1	57
		1 Thessalonians	164
12:14–18	28, 175	1:1	57
12:14–21	167, 174, 175, 198	1:2	95
12:14a	167, 175, 198	2 Thessalonians, 1:1	57
12:14b–18	167, 198	1 Timothy	
12:18	30	1:1	57
12:19	45, 109, 110t, 174, 182	1:12	95
		2 Timothy, 1:1	57
12:19–13:13	28	Titus, 1:1	57
12:19–21	31, 167, 175, 198	Philemon	164
12:20	175	1:1	57
12:20–21	175	Hebrews	13n. 38, 13n. 39
13:1	168, 174, 175, 198	1:1–4	10n. 30
13:1–10	31, 168, 174, 175–176, 198	8:1	11n. 32
		13:22	11n. 31
13:2–9	168, 175, 198	James, 1:1	58
13:4	100	Revelation	11n. 33
13:5–9	30	2–3	11n. 33
13:5–10	25	4–22	11n. 33

Subject and Authors

Note: The suffix 'f' following a page locator indicates a figure, 't' indicates a table. 'n' indicates a footnote, with the number following 'n' indicating the footnote number when there is more than 1 footnote on the page.

agents 93n. 6
   of God 92–93, 96, 103–114, 120
   in ministry 85, 92, 93, 103–114, 194, 199
Amador, J. David Hester 29–31, 32, 46
ancient rhetoric 81
ancient writing and speech 94
antitheses 99
apology, of Paul 39–40, 44–45
apostleship, divine origin of 208
appeal formula 149
Arnold, Bill T. 12n. 34
Asbury Theological Seminary 4
Asia, Paul's experience of affliction in 40, 75–77, 85, 210, 212
asyndeton 125, 137
Attic Greek 128
Aus, Roger David 99
authority, of ministerial jurisdiction 172

Barnett, Paul W. 188
Bauer, David R. 4, 5, 6, 7, 9, 14, 16, 18
Baur, Ferdinand Christian 8n. 23
Belleville, Linda L. 23, 24, 42–43, 77, 135
berakah 66n. 2
Betz, Hans Dieter 20, 22, 42
The Biblical Seminary, New York 3, 4, 17
Black, David Alan 181n. 45, 183n. 53, 208
blaming 45–46
blessing 54, 66, 67, 67n. 10, 73–74, 95, 202, 210
boasting 69, 70, 87–88, 117, 144, 178–179, 188, 190, 200, 201
   causation 207
   foolish 169–170, 171, 173, 178, 182, 183, 189, 207
   mutuality of 77–80
   speech and 113
boldness 186

Booth, Wayne C. 8n. 22, 94
Bornkamm, Günther 39
Burton, Ernest D. 157

causation 11, 181–183
   comparative 163, 166, 200, 205
   with particularization 139–144, 168, 203
   with particularization and contrast 189, 207
   recurrence of 183–184, 201
chiastic structure 13, 34–35, 50
Christ 117, 129–130, 200
   agency of 116
   as the agent of divine encouragement 84n. 84
   centrality of 130
   eschatological vision of 116
   God as source of encouragement through 74
   God's knowledge as the gospel of 102
   grace of 100, 152, 160, 211
   as intermediate agent 92, 93f, 96, 114–118, 210–211
   Paul as a servant of 109, 180
   as the sender of the apostle 57
Christian, Timothy J. 185
Christ Jesus *see* Christ
Cicero 15
climax 10
   generalization with 187–188, 189, 201
closing 54, 55
Cohen, Ted 94
collection workers 112, 117, 153, 155, 161, 204
comparison 10
compositional study 6–7
Conceptual Integration Theory 16
concord (harmony) 41

conjunctive relations 76t
contrast 10
    causation with particularization and 177–181, 189, 190, 207
    particularization with 91, 93–97, 200
Corinthians
    Paul's plans to visit the 169, 174, 182, 189
    relationship between Paul and the 46
corruption, of God's word 119
counteragents
    of God 92–93, 97, 120
    of ministry 118–120
covenant(s)
    new 86, 102, 110, 127, 128, 140, 145, 203
    old 86, 102, 110, 116, 127, 128, 130, 136
credentials 142
cruciality 12, 14n. 49, 187n. 61

David, sin of adultery with Bathsheba and murder of Uriah 12n. 34
death
    and life 110–111, 115, 136
    suffering and 40
defense 168, 185
diatribe 12n. 36
discipline 177, 206
disclosure formula 68, 148–149
discourse analysis 16, 36–38, 50–51
discursive text 70
divine encouragement 74, 84
    Christ as the agent of 84n. 84
    and suffering 75, 85, 183n. 53, 187, 188, 212
        mutuality of 73–75
    vertical and horizontal dimensions of 80n. 69
divine paradox 131n. 38, 210
divine passives 100n. 33, 100n. 35, 102, 127
divine power, through weakness 212, 213
divine suffering, and encouragement 74, 75

edification, relationship between thanksgiving and 191, 210
encouragement 74, 84, 144
    and suffering 73, 75, 84, 85, 187, 188, 199, 212

Enos, Richard L. 15
epidiorthosis 170
epistolary criticism 22–24, 38, 42–44, 68, 135
Eusebius 62n. 39
exhortations 60–61, 64, 152, 206
    and the peace benediction 62n. 41
explanatory clause 157

false apostles 87, 97, 119–120
financial integrity 185, 186, 189, 201
Fitzgerald, John T. 42, 112
foolishness 170
forgiveness 79, 80, 200
Fuller, Daniel P. 17

generalization 11, 59n. 27, 181
    with climax 187–188, 189, 201
    structural relationship of 170n. 9, 171
gift of tongues 191
glory 105, 200
    to God 165
        manifestation through suffering 100
God
    agents of 92–93, 96, 103–114, 120
    as the cause of Paul's apostleship 57
    counteragents of 92–93, 97, 120
    glory to 165
    grace of 100, 150, 159, 160
    knowledge of 209
        as the gospel of Christ 102
        manifestation of 101–102, 103, 116
        servants proclaiming 140
    manifestation of
        glory through suffering 100
        life through death 99
        power through weakness 100
        wealth through poverty 100, 103
    servants of 97, 117, 130
    as source of encouragement through Christ 74
    triumphal procession 100, 115
    as ultimate agent of ministry 97–103
    word of 119, 145
    worship of 210
gospel
    defense of the 167–191, 201
    Paul's ministry to the 188

proclamation of the 87, 105, 123–146,
    164, 165, 183n. 53, 186, 191, 194,
    203, 204, 209
    with boldness 186
    by God's agents 107, 109
    response to the 57, 86, 147–166, 194
grace 88, 152, 161–162, 187, 200
    of Christ 100, 152, 160, 211
    of God 100, 150, 159, 160
grace benediction 59, 63, 64
Greco-Roman
    letters 43
    rhetorical handbooks 26
Greek
    Attic Greek 128
    conjunctions 38
    Koiné Greek 129
    New Testament Greek 128
Guthrie, George H. 39, 174

Hafemann, Scott J. 40, 108n
Harper, William Rainey 3
Harris, Leonard 115, 151, 184n. 56
Harvey, A. E. 40
Hays, Richard B. 33n. 51
Heiny, Stephen B. 94
Hellenistic rhetorical, psychagogical, and
    epistolary tradition 31
Hellerman, Joseph H. 57n. 15
hermeneutical model 193
holiness 106, 143, 144
holy kiss 62–63
Hubbard, Moyer V. 41

imagery, agricultural 156
implied author, of 2 Corinthians 8, 50
incense 103
inclusio 13, 159, 162, 168, 176, 205, 206
    preparation/realization with 56–59, 198
    structural relationship of 170
Inductive Bible Study (IBS) 1, 193
    origin and development of 3–6
    theoretical foundations of 6–18
Inductive Bible Study (Traina and Bauer) 5
insinuatio 44, 185
In Step with God's Word (Long) 5
instrumentation (statement of purpose)
    13, 176–177, 205, 206
intercalation 13

interchange 13, 180, 181
interjections 170
intermediate agency 115
interrogation 12
introduction 12

Jesus see Christ
Jesus Christ see Christ
joy 144
    and affliction 100n. 35
    mutuality of 79, 80

Keener, Craig S. 82
kiss, holy 62–63
Kistemaker, Simon J. 39
knowledge
    of God 209
    proclamation by servants 140
Koiné Greek 129
Kuist, Howard Tillman 15

Land, Christopher D. 36–37, 38, 50, 51
leadership 50
letter(s)
    of reconciliation 66n. 1, 73, 82n. 81
    types of 43
Levinsohn, Stephen H. 54n. 7, 68, 76, 92,
    126, 128, 133–134, 154, 157
life, death and 110–111, 115, 136
Lim, Kar Yong 48–49, 188
literary analysis 48–50
    based on chiastic structure 49
    narrative criticism 33–34, 48–49, 50
literary context 6
literary criticism 33–35, 38, 50
literary structure 19–38, 51–52, 193, 194, 208
Long, Fredrick J. 4, 5, 26–28, 32, 43, 44–45,
    97–98, 128, 135
Lord 200
    see also Christ
love 62, 88, 200
    mutuality of 79–80

McCant, Jerry W. 28, 45–46, 135
Macedonia
    God's grace given to churches in 100
    travel narrative to 72, 81
Macedonian churches 160–161
    as models for the Corinthians 205

Macedonians 87
major structural relationships 1, 9, 38, 53, 56–59, 91, 147, 176–188, 194, 198–202
  1:1–2 198
  1:3–2:13 72–88, 199, 202–203
  1:3–7 202
  1:3–13:10 198
  1:8–2:13 202
  2:14–13:10 199
  2:14–17 93–97, 200
  3:1–7:16 139–145, 163, 200, 203–204
  3:1–9:15 183–187, 201
  3:1–11 203
  3:1–13.10 200
  3:12–7:3 203
  8:1–6 205
  8:1–9:15 158–165, 166, 200, 204–206
  8:7–15 205, 206
  8:16–9:5 205
  9:6–15 206
  10:1–12:13 181–183, 207
  10:1–13:10 176–188, 201, 206–207
  10:1–18 177–181, 207
  11:1–12:13 177–181, 207
  12:9–10 187–188, 201
  12:14–13:10 181–183, 207
  13:10 176–177
  13:11, 13 198
  13:11–13 198
  analytical model of 17
  categories of 9–15, 193
  causation 11, 181–183, 189, 207
    comparative 200, 205
    with particularization 88, 168, 189, 199, 203
    with particularization and contrast 177–181, 190, 207
    recurrence of 183–184, 201
  chiasm 13
  climax 10, 187–188, 189, 201
  comparison 10
  contrast 10
  cruciality 12, 14n. 49
  generalization 11
    with climax 187–188, 189, 201
  inclusio 13
  instrumentation 13, 205, 206
  intercalation 13
  interchange 13
  interrogation 12
  particularization 10
    and causation with substantiation 88
    with contrast 200
    recurrence of 199
  preparation/realization 198
    /introduction 12
  rationale for 15–18
  recurrence 9, 14, 199–200, 205
    of causation 189
  rhetorical 14
  semantic 14
  substantiation 11, 204, 206
    particularization and causation with 73–82, 202–203
    with particularization and instrumentation 184–187, 189, 190, 201
  summarization 12, 198
metaphors, with rhetorical motivations 94
Methodical Bible Study (Traina) 4
middle voice 61n. 36
ministerial jurisdiction 172
ministry 92, 98–101, 115, 194
  agents in 85, 92, 93, 194, 199
  character of 61, 65–89
  content of 147–166
  cooperation of 69
  Corinthians' participation in 77
  counteragents of 118–120
  as a divine paradox 185, 209
  God as ultimate agent of 97–103
  God's agents in 103–114
  life and death in 99
  manifestation of God's knowledge 101–102
  mutuality
    of divine encouragement in 73–75
    of ministry through Paul's experience in Asia 75–77
  of the new covenant 110, 140, 145
  with partnership 143
  qualifications for 208
  sacrificial image of 104, 116
  to the saints 160, 164, 165, 166, 191, 200, 205
  theology of 194–195, 208–211
Moses 102, 129–130, 140

MSR *see* major structural relationships
mutuality 63, 65, 73, 79, 80, 83, 85, 199
　in 1:3–7 73–75, 88
　of boasting 77–80
　of divine encouragement in ministry
　　73–75
　of ministry 75–77
　and partnership 143
　of suffering and encouragement 69,
　　73, 75

narratio 30
narration 70
narrative criticism 33–34, 48–49, 50
new covenant 85, 86, 102, 110, 127, 203
　ministry of the 110, 140, 145
　proclamation of the 128
New Testament
　conjunctions in 68*n*. 14
　final form of 7–8
　narrative criticism 34
New Testament Greek 128
nonrestrictive relative clauses 157–158

oath formula 71*n*. 34
O'Brien, William E. 74, 95
Olbrechts-Tyteca, Lucie 29
old covenant 86, 102, 110, 116, 127, 128,
　　130, 136
Old Testament 143
　image of ritual purity in 106
　sacrificial images 104, 105, 116
　tent imagery of 107

participial clauses
　anaphoric and cataphoric prenuclear
　　133*t*
　anarthrous 126
particularization 10, 181, 199
　causation with 83–85, 139–144, 203
　and causation with substantiation
　　73–82, 88, 202
　with contrast 91, 93–97, 200
　ideological 73*n*. 43, 93*n*. 7
　recurrence of 85, 199
partition theories 20, 22
partnership 84, 143
Paul 8
　apology of 39–40, 44–45

beginning and closing of letters 58
change of travel plan 79
critical use of Paul in Acts 8*n*. 23
defense of status as a servant of Christ
　109, 190, 207
experience of affliction in Asia 40,
　75–77, 85, 210, 212
identification as an apostle 56–57
ministry to the gospel 188
offense against authority of 178
plans to visit the Corinthians 169, 174,
　182, 189
plan to visit the Corinthian church 71
relationship between the Corinthians
　and 46
as servant of Christ 109, 180
testimony to God's deliverance from
　his affliction in Asia 76
theology of ministry 194–195, 208–211
theology of weakness 211–213
peace 62
peace benediction 55*n*. 10, 62*n*. 41
Perelman, Chaïm 29
peristaseis catalogs 112, 180
peroratio 182
persuasion 137, 141–142
Pitts, Andrew W. 148*n*. 4
Porter, Stanley E. 148*n*. 4
Powell, Mark Allan 17
power 101
　through weakness 40–41
prenuclear participial clauses 126, 129,
　132, 133*t*
prenuclear participle 130
preparation/realization 12, 198
　/introduction 12
　with *inclusio* 63–64
problem-solution 83*n*. 82
prodiorthosis 173
Pseudo-Demetrius 42
Pseudo-Libanius 42

Ramsay, William Mitchell 8*n*. 23
reconciliation 41, 84, 117, 136
　to God 142
　to God's servants 62
　letter of 66*n*. 1, 73, 82*n*. 81
　between Paul and the Corinthians,
　　47–48

and peace 62n. 39
purpose of 143
recurrence 9, 14, 159, 162, 199–200, 205
   of causation 189
refutatio 168, 185
relative pronoun clauses 157
Resseguie, James L. 17
rhetoric 33
   ancient 81
   epideictic 28
   judicial 25, 28, 44, 46, 47
rhetorical criticism 24–33, 38, 44–48, 94, 149, 182
rhetorical speeches 15
rhetorical structures 14, 159
rhetorical techniques 173
Rillera, Andrew R. 76n. 55
Robbins, Vernon K. 16
Robertson, Archibald Thomas 128
Runge, Steven E. 70, 129, 153, 170
Ruskin, John 15, 17

sacrificial images 104, 105, 106, 116, 187
saints
   fiscal contribution to the 165
   ministry to the 160, 164, 165, 166, 191, 200, 205
salutation 54, 55, 208
   and closing 53–64
Satan 209
Saul, encounter with the Lord on the road to Damascus 12n. 34
Savage, Timothy B. 40–41, 177, 208
Schubert, Paul 95
Scott, James M. 41
Segalla, Giuseppe 34, 35, 49
Seifrid, Mark A. 23–24, 125
self-sacrifice 106, 160–161
semantic structures 14, 38, 159, 176
Semler, Johann S. 20
servants
   of God 97, 117, 130
      courage and integrity of 130
      proclamation God's knowledge 140
service 86, 199–200
Smith, Craig Arnold 35
socio-rhetorical interpretation 16
sorrow 111
   mutuality of 79, 80

sowing, and reaping 156
Spirit 141
structural relationships 8–18, 163
   see also major structural relationships
The Structure of Matthew's Gospel (Bauer) 4, 18
substantiation 11, 144–145, 161–162, 204, 206
   particularization and causation with 73–82, 202–203
   with particularization and instrumentation 184–187, 189, 190, 201
suffering 49, 67, 110, 140–141
   and death 40
   and divine encouragement 69, 73, 75, 212
   divine suffering and encouragement 74, 75
summarization 12, 59–63, 64, 198
Systemic Functional Linguistics (SFL) 36, 37

tent imagery 105, 106, 107
thanksgiving 67, 92, 95, 96, 149, 200
   difference between blessing and 67n. 10
   and edification 191, 210
   epistolary formula of 125
   introductory 66
theme, of 2 Corinthians 38–52, 193, 194
theology
   of ministry 194–195, 208–211
   of weakness 211–213
thesis statement 26, 27, 45, 47, 48, 82, 91–121, 187, 209, 210
Thrall, Margaret E. 20, 81, 95, 114
Timothy 8
Titus 81, 84, 87, 112, 139, 150, 153, 160
topical analysis 20–22, 38, 39–42
Torah 102
Traina, Robert A. 4, 5, 6, 7, 9, 14, 16, 17
Troas, travel narrative to 72, 81
truth 112, 128, 130, 140

unbelievers 84, 107, 130, 137, 143, 144

Vegge, Ivar 31–32, 47–48
vessels, of clay 99
vocative address 54, 68, 148, 168

Wallace, Daniel B. 115
weakness 101, 185, 186, 189, 201, 208
   divine power through 212, 213
   Paul's theology of 211–213
   power through 40–41
Weima, Jeffrey A.D. 54, 55, 63, 68, 149

White, Wilbert Webster 3, 15
Wilson, Jim 106*n*. 56
Windisch, Hans 43
Witherington III, Ben 25–26, 32, 44–45, 135
work 86, 199–200

www.ingramcontent.com/pod-product-compliance
Lightning Source LLC
Chambersburg PA
CBHW051520230426
43668CB00012B/1674